Critical Ethical and Societal Implications of the Metaverse

Esraa Hassan
Kafrelsheikh University, Egypt

Abeer Saber
https://orcid.org/0000-0002-9261-0927
Damietta University, Egypt

Deepak Gupta
https://orcid.org/0000-0002-3019-7161
Maharaja Agrasen Institute of Technology, India

Tamer Z. Emara
Damietta University, Egypt

IGI Global
Scientific Publishing
Publishing Tomorrow's Research Today

Vice President of Editorial Melissa Wagner
Director of Acquisitions Mikaela Felty
Director of Book Development Jocelynn Hessler
Production Manager Mike Brehm
Cover Design Jose Rosado

Published in the United States of America by
IGI Global Scientific Publishing
701 East Chocolate Avenue
Hershey, PA, 17033, USA
Tel: 717-533-8845 | Fax: 717-533-7115
Website: https://www.igi-global.com E-mail: cust@igi-global.com

Library of Congress Cataloging-in-Publication Data

Names: Hassan, Esraa, 1992- editor | Saber, Abeer, 1992- editor | Gupta, Deepak, 1983- editor | Emara, Tamer, 1983- editor
Title: Critical ethical and societal implications of the metaverse / Edited by Esraa Hassan, Abeer Saber, Deepak Gupta, Tamer Z. Emara.
Description: Hershey, PA : IGI Global Scientific Publishing, [2026] | Includes bibliographical references and index. | Summary: "This book delves into the complex questions surrounding privacy, security, equity, accessibility, digital identity, and the long-term psychological and sociological effects of prolonged engagement in virtual environments"-- Provided by publisher.
Identifiers: LCCN 2025026738 (print) | LCCN 2025026739 (ebook) | ISBN 9798337330433 hardcover | ISBN 9798337330440 paperback | ISBN 9798337330457 ebook
Subjects: LCSH: Metaverse--Social aspects | Metaverse--Moral and ethical aspects | Virtual reality--Social aspects | Artificial intelligence--Moral and ethical aspects
Classification: LCC TK5105.8864 .C75 2026 (print) | LCC TK5105.8864 (ebook)
LC record available at https://lccn.loc.gov/2025026738
LC ebook record available at https://lccn.loc.gov/2025026739
British Cataloguing in Publication Data
A Cataloguing in Publication record for this book is available from the British Library.

Table of Contents

Detailed Table of Contents

The metaverse—an interconnected network of immersive, persistent virtual worlds—is reshaping digital communication, work, commerce, and entertainment. While its cultural and economic implications have been widely explored, its environmental impact is a newer but increasingly urgent area of inquiry. This chapter investigates the metaverse's dual role about climate change as both a potential contributor to and mitigator of environmental harm. First, the chapter evaluates the metaverse's energy demands, particularly through the technologies that support it—cloud computing, blockchain infrastructure, and extended reality (XR) devices. It highlights concerns about the carbon footprint of data centers and the environmental cost of cryptocurrency mining, both of which undergird virtual economies. Second, it explores how the metaverse may help reduce emissions through the virtualization of traditionally high-carbon activities.

This chapter defines the Metaverse and traces its evolution from early virtual worlds to modern persistent ecosystems. It analyzes the fundamental architecture and technological enablers, including high-speed networking (5G/6G, edge computing), scalable cloud and distributed systems, and immersive hardware (VR/AR, haptics). The discussion also covers AI's role in graphics rendering and intelligent virtual agents. The economic and governance frameworks are explored, with a focus on blockchain for digital ownership and the importance of interoperability. The chapter

curricular goals, comprehensive teacher training, supportive policies, and inclusive, secure, and pedagogically sound design from developers. As XR becomes more affordable and accessible, it paves the way for hybrid learning environments, global virtual classrooms, and immersive problem-solving experiences. Technological advancements such as 5G, AI, haptics, IoT, and blockchain will further enrich XR's educational impact by enabling personalized learning, real-time analytics, and secure credentialing.

This chapter explores how the Metaverse can fundamentally reshape education to create more inclusive and equitable learning opportunities for all. It examines how persistent 3D worlds, real-time interaction, and digital embodiment can democratize access to high-quality, engaging educational content. By providing virtual classrooms, immersive simulations, and skill-building platforms, the Metaverse offers a powerful new approach to lifelong learning for diverse populations, from K–12 students to professionals. The chapter critically addresses key challenges and ethical considerations, including ensuring digital equity, protecting learner identity, and establishing frameworks for responsible governance. Through case studies, theoretical frameworks, and current trends, this chapter provides a forward-looking analysis of how education can evolve within the Metaverse to meet the urgent needs of learners in the 21st century.

The research is limited to news and comments about female metaverse athletes Kim "Geguri" Se-Yon and Sasha "Scarlett" Hostyn, who stand out with their recent global success. Accordingly, more than half of the 221 news and comments about female players were discriminatory and negative statements (n=128). Cybersexism (n=61) is prominent in these statements. There are 43 expressions on the theme of humiliation, othering, exclusion and 24 negative attitudes towards the player personality. As a result of the research, it was observed that female athletes are exposed to inequalities in the metaverse in parallel with real life. Sexist statements have come to the fore in discriminatory comments, it seems that the external opinions of female athletes are mercilessly criticized and their voices cannot be tolerated. On the other hand, the performances of female metaverse athletes are not believed and are considered inadequate because they are women.

This chapter explores the proliferation of digital identity systems across Africa, highlighting both their potential to enhance social inclusion and administrative efficiency and their risks to privacy and human rights. It investigates the tension between national security imperatives and the protection of fundamental legal rights, employing a qualitative, descriptive methodology informed by policy documents, academic literature, and case studies from Nigeria, Kenya, and South Africa. The analysis demonstrates that while legal frameworks for data protection are increasingly present, their effectiveness is frequently compromised by national security priorities, infrastructural limitations, and digital literacy gaps. The chapter contends that technocratic or purely legalistic approaches are inadequate and proposes a human-rights-by-design framework emphasizing public trust, ethical AI governance, and gender-inclusive considerations as essential foundations for sustainable policy.

Preface

INTRODUCTION

The metaverse, once a speculative concept relegated to science fiction, is now rapidly unfolding as a tangible extension of our digital and social lives. As immersive virtual environments grow in complexity and adoption, they introduce not only new possibilities for human interaction and innovation but also significant ethical and societal challenges that demand urgent and rigorous examination.

Critical Ethical and Societal Implications of the Metaverse was conceived as a response to this critical juncture. Recognizing the transformative potential of metaverse technologies—and the risks they may pose—we set out to assemble a multidisciplinary collection of perspectives that could inform, challenge, and guide ongoing conversations around their development and deployment.

This edited volume brings together leading thinkers and researchers from diverse disciplines—technology ethics, sociology, law, policy, psychology, and more—to address the pressing questions surrounding the metaverse. Our contributors move beyond technical descriptions to critically analyze the social impact of these immersive platforms, with particular attention to issues of privacy, security, equity, accessibility, digital identity, and the psychological and sociological consequences of prolonged virtual engagement.

Our goals in curating this collection are fivefold:

- To provide a comprehensive and multidisciplinary analysis of the ethical and societal implications of the metaverse.
- To identify and examine the key challenges and opportunities related to privacy, security, equity, accessibility, and identity in virtual environments.
- To foster critical dialogue and promote informed decision-making among stakeholders.

- To contribute to the development of ethical frameworks, policy recommendations, and best practices for responsible design and governance.
- To create a resource that helps shape a more equitable and ethical future for the metaverse.

This book is intended for a wide audience. We hope it will serve as a valuable resource for researchers and academics seeking to deepen scholarly inquiry, for policymakers and regulators working to balance innovation with societal safeguards, and for industry professionals committed to developing ethically responsible platforms. We also envision it as an accessible tool for educators, students, technology ethicists, and members of the general public who wish to better understand the far-reaching implications of virtual worlds.

Ultimately, this volume is not just about identifying problems; it is about imagining and contributing to solutions. The metaverse presents us with a pivotal opportunity: to shape a digital future that reflects our highest ethical standards and deepest societal values. It is our hope that this book will play a meaningful role in that endeavor.

ORGANIZATION OF THE BOOK

This volume opens with **Chapter 1: The Metaverse and Climate Change: Virtual Innovation for a Sustainable Future**, which introduces a timely and underexplored topic—how the metaverse intersects with environmental sustainability. The chapter critically examines the dual role of the metaverse as both a potential environmental liability, due to its high energy consumption and reliance on blockchain infrastructure, and as a sustainability tool through the virtualization of high-emission activities. It sets the stage for broader discussions on technological trade-offs and responsible innovation.

In **Chapter 2: Technological Foundations of the Metaverse**, readers are guided through the evolution and architecture of the metaverse. This foundational chapter explores enabling technologies such as cloud computing, immersive hardware, and blockchain, as well as the sociotechnical systems that support virtual platforms. It emphasizes the interplay between infrastructure, ethical development, and sustainable innovation, framing the metaverse as a complex system with global implications for equity and access.

Chapter 3: The Role of Speech Processing in the Metaverse focuses on how natural language technologies—automatic speech recognition, natural language processing, and text-to-speech—are transforming communication in immersive digital spaces. The chapter highlights ethical challenges related to privacy, surveillance, and algorithmic bias, particularly as voice becomes a primary interface for interaction. It also considers accessibility and inclusion, emphasizing the need for diverse voices in the design of voice-enabled systems.

Turning to education, **Chapter 4: Exploring the Future of Education** examines the transformative potential of VR, AR, and XR technologies in classrooms and learning environments. The chapter provides a balanced assessment of XR's ability to enhance engagement and accessibility while addressing barriers to adoption, including cost, policy gaps, and teacher readiness. It advocates for thoughtful integration aligned with pedagogy and inclusive design principles.

Building on this, **Chapter 5: Learning in the Metaverse** envisions a more holistic transformation of education through persistent virtual worlds. This chapter explores how the metaverse could democratize access to high-quality learning experiences across age groups and geographies. It critically examines challenges in digital equity, identity protection, and governance, providing forward-looking insights for educational institutions, technologists, and policymakers.

Chapter 6: Cognitive Intelligence in Human-Centered Education presents an applied case in biomedical engineering education. Through AI-powered XR gamification, it illustrates how immersive and adaptive technologies can bridge theoretical learning with practical, occupational training. This chapter foregrounds the Technological Pedagogical Content Knowledge (TPCK) framework, offering a unique perspective on how the metaverse can enhance STEM and healthcare education.

Shifting to digital culture, **Chapter 7: Impact of Generational Culture of Gen Z and Millennials** investigates how these two tech-native generations are shaping social interaction and community-building in virtual environments. By leveraging theories of social presence and digital capital, this chapter provides a nuanced, generationally informed analysis of identity, belonging, and sociality in the metaverse. It offers valuable insight into the evolving nature of human connection in digitally mediated spaces.

Chapter 8: Being a Female Athlete in the Metaverse brings to light persistent gender-based discrimination and cybersexism within virtual sports and gaming. Drawing from media analysis of prominent female metaverse athletes, this chapter reveals how sexism continues to manifest in digital environments, reflecting broader societal biases. It calls for deeper reflection on equity, representation, and the ethical responsibilities of platform developers and communities.

In **Chapter 9: Digital Identity Policy-Making in Africa**, the focus shifts to regional governance and the intersection of digital identity, human rights, and national security. Through case studies from Nigeria, Kenya, and South Africa, this chapter critically examines the tension between state control and individual freedoms in emerging identity systems. It proposes a "human-rights-by-design" approach, advocating for ethical AI, public trust, and gender inclusion as pillars of sustainable digital policy.

Chapter 10: Ethical AI in Virtual Worlds delves into the design and deployment of AI-driven avatars and agents in virtual environments. The chapter interrogates how these systems shape user behavior, influence moral reasoning, and raise questions about autonomy, manipulation, and consent. Drawing from gaming and educational platforms, it proposes frameworks for ethical AI development that prioritize fairness, accountability, and human dignity in virtual interactions.

Concluding the volume, **Chapter 11: Metaverse Governance** and **Chapter 12: The Metaverse in Action** offer pragmatic frameworks for policy and practice. Chapter 11 outlines seven governance domains—from digital identity and access to labor rights and algorithmic fairness—and provides people-centered policy recommendations to address emerging inequities and risks. Chapter 12 complements this with real-world use cases in work, education, and industry, illustrating how the metaverse is already transforming daily life. Yet, it also raises critical questions around mental health, privacy, and digital citizenship, urging a balance between innovation and ethics.

Together, these chapters form a multidisciplinary mosaic of the ethical, societal, and practical dimensions of the metaverse. They reflect the collaborative spirit of this volume: to interrogate, inform, and ultimately shape the responsible development of immersive digital worlds.

CONCLUSION

As we stand at the threshold of an era defined by immersive digital experiences, the metaverse offers both an unprecedented frontier of possibility and a profound ethical challenge. This volume—*Critical Ethical and Societal Implications of the Metaverse*—aims not merely to document technological developments, but to interrogate them through the lenses of ethics, equity, human rights, and societal well-being.

Across the chapters, a consistent message emerges: the metaverse is not a neutral space. It is shaped by the values embedded in its design, the structures of access and exclusion it reinforces or disrupts, and the policies—or lack thereof—that govern its development. From environmental sustainability and educational equity to identity politics and algorithmic bias, the metaverse is already impacting the fabric of our lives in subtle and significant ways.

Our hope is that this volume serves as a foundational resource for researchers, practitioners, educators, policymakers, and the wider public. But more than that, we hope it inspires critical reflection, collaborative dialogue, and bold action. The future of the metaverse is not predetermined—it is still being written. It is our collective responsibility to ensure that this future is inclusive, ethical, and beneficial to all.

Chapter 1
The Metaverse and Climate Change:
Virtual Innovation for a Sustainable Future

Wael A. Awad
Independent Researcher, Egypt

Amena Mahmoud
https://orcid.org/0009-0006-9909-0430
Independent Researcher, Egypt

ABSTRACT

The metaverse—an interconnected network of immersive, persistent virtual worlds—is reshaping digital communication, work, commerce, and entertainment. While its cultural and economic implications have been widely explored, its environmental impact is a newer but increasingly urgent area of inquiry. This chapter investigates the metaverse's dual role about climate change as both a potential contributor to and mitigator of environmental harm. First, the chapter evaluates the metaverse's energy demands, particularly through the technologies that support it—cloud computing, blockchain infrastructure, and extended reality (XR) devices. It highlights concerns about the carbon footprint of data centers and the environmental cost of cryptocurrency mining, both of which undergird virtual economies. Second, it explores how the metaverse may help reduce emissions through the virtualization of traditionally high-carbon activities.

DOI: 10.4018/979-8-3373-3043-3.ch001

INTRODUCTION: THE METAVERSE IN THE AGE OF CLIMATE CRISIS

Background

Over the past decade, the metaverse has rapidly evolved from a speculative concept into a dynamic, increasingly accessible technological reality. Often described as a persistent, immersive, and interoperable virtual ecosystem, the metaverse combines a range of advanced digital technologies—including virtual reality (VR) (Sharma et al., 2024), augmented reality (AR), mixed reality (MR), and 3D internet environments—to enable users to interact, socialize, work, and create within shared digital spaces. Early iterations of the metaverse can be seen in platforms such as Meta's Horizon Worlds, Decentraland, Roblox, and Fortnite Creative, which have laid the groundwork for more expansive, interconnected virtual experiences. These platforms demonstrate the shifting paradigm from conventional two-dimensional internet interfaces to spatial, embodied interactions that mimic and, in some cases, surpass physical world capabilities (Cappa, 2023).

This technological shift is unfolding amid a backdrop of unprecedented environmental challenges. The Earth is facing a worsening climate emergency, marked by rising global temperatures, frequent extreme weather events, melting polar ice, and accelerating biodiversity loss. Climate scientists warn that without immediate and sustained action to reduce greenhouse gas emissions; the planet will reach irreversible tipping points. In response, governments, businesses, and civil society are mobilizing to transition toward more sustainable practices, invest in renewable energy, and innovate in green technologies (Mahmoud et al., 2025).

Paradoxically, the digital revolution—of which the metaverse is a prominent frontier—has itself become both a contributor to and a potential solution for the climate crisis (Nair et al., 2024). Data centers, high-performance computing, blockchain technologies, and the proliferation of connected devices all demand significant energy resources, often powered by carbon-intensive grids (Nafus at el., 2021). The metaverse, by integrating these technologies at scale, may further strain energy systems and exacerbate digital carbon footprints. Yet, it also offers novel opportunities to reimagine how humans live, work, and interact in ways that can reduce environmental impact.

Understanding the role of the metaverse in the context of climate change thus requires a dual lens: one that examines its ecological cost, and another that explores its capacity for sustainable transformation. As the boundaries between the physical and digital continue to blur, it becomes increasingly critical to assess the metaverse not merely as a technological innovation, but as a socio-environmental force that could shape the future trajectory of our planet (Allam et al., 2022).

Motivation

As the climate crisis intensifies, the need for systemic transformation across all sectors becomes more urgent. Digital technologies, while often positioned as enablers of sustainability, also pose serious environmental challenges. Currently, the information and communication technology (ICT) sector accounts for approximately 2% to 4% of global greenhouse gas emissions—a footprint on par with the aviation industry (Houston & Reay, 2011).

The metaverse, as an ecosystem that integrates several of these technologies, presents a complex environmental paradox. On one hand, its infrastructure—reliant on energy-hungry data centers, cloud computing, edge networks, and advanced display hardware—could significantly increase electricity consumption and associated emissions. High-end VR headsets, GPU-intensive rendering, and decentralized platforms (especially those using blockchain) further contribute to this load. Without careful design and regulation, the growth of the metaverse could become a climate liability (Allam et al., 2022).

On the other hand, the metaverse holds transformative potential for climate mitigation and adaptation. By enabling remote work, virtual conferences, and immersive education, it can dramatically reduce the need for physical travel—one of the largest contributors to carbon emissions globally. Additionally, digital twins—virtual replicas of real-world systems—can be used to simulate and optimize energy usage in urban planning, building design, and industrial processes. Immersive environmental simulations can also enhance public awareness, policymaking, and education around climate change by providing experiential understanding of abstract or distant phenomena (Allam et al., 2022).

Furthermore, the metaverse can foster new forms of environmental activism and collaboration. Virtual spaces can host global climate summits, citizen science projects, and decentralized sustainability communities, removing geographical and socio-economic barriers to participation. Through gamification and interactive storytelling, environmental issues can be made more engaging and personally relevant, especially to younger generations (Allam et al., 2022).

The motivation for examining the metaverse in the context of climate change is thus twofold: first, to critically evaluate the environmental costs of its rapid expansion, and second, to explore how it can be harnessed as a strategic tool for climate action. This dual perspective is essential for ensuring that the digital future we are building aligns with the ecological imperatives of our time. Rather than viewing the metaverse as an isolated technological development, it must be situated within the broader sustainability discourse—subject to the same scrutiny, expectations, and aspirations that define our response to the climate crisis.

Purpose and Scope

This paper aims to analyze the complex relationship between the metaverse and climate change. We examine the environmental costs of its underlying technologies, potential for emission reduction, role in promoting sustainability awareness, challenges like digital inequality and rebound effects, and policy directions for a climate-resilient metaverse.

CARBON FOOTPRINT OF THE METAVERSE: INFRASTRUCTURE AND ENERGY CONSUMPTION

Data Centers and Cloud Infrastructure

The metaverse is underpinned by a vast and complex digital infrastructure, with data centers and cloud computing forming its technological backbone (Gamal et al., 2025; Saber et al., 2018). These facilities support core functionalities such as real-time rendering, cloud-based VR streaming, artificial intelligence-driven personalization, and persistent storage of vast amounts of user data. As metaverse platforms scale in size and interactivity, the computing demands placed on data centers will grow exponentially, leading to significant increases in energy consumption.

Data centers are among the most energy-intensive components of the digital ecosystem. They require not only massive electricity input to operate servers but also extensive cooling systems to maintain optimal performance temperatures. Some hyperscale providers such as Google, Amazon Web Services (AWS), and Microsoft Azure have announced commitments to carbon neutrality or 100% renewable energy sourcing, the global picture is less optimistic. Many data centers, especially those located in regions with fossil fuel-dependent energy grids, still operate with high carbon intensity (Korada, 2024).

Moreover, rendering immersive metaverse environments in real time is substantially more energy-intensive than conventional internet use. A high-resolution VR session with cloud rendering, for example, can consume up to ten times the bandwidth and power of streaming a standard video (Khan, 2023). When multiplied across millions of users engaging in simultaneous sessions—often in virtual offices, events, or gaming worlds—the energy impact becomes substantial. Edge computing solutions, aimed at reducing latency and offloading computational workloads to localized mini-data centers, may mitigate network congestion but do not fully address overall power consumption.

As metaverse platforms grow in complexity—integrating photorealistic graphics, AI-driven avatars, and persistent digital economies—the energy footprint of cloud infrastructure will remain a central concern. Therefore, aligning data center operations with global climate targets requires not only continued investment in renewable energy but also innovations in cooling technologies, intelligent load balancing, and carbon-aware workload scheduling (Lifelo et al., 2024).

Blockchain and Virtual Economies

A defining feature of the metaverse is its embrace of decentralized digital ownership and virtual economies, often underpinned by blockchain technology. Non-fungible tokens (NFTs), smart contracts, and digital currencies enable users to own, trade, and monetize assets in ways previously unimaginable. However, these innovations carry significant environmental costs, particularly when built on energy-intensive blockchain networks (Alshahrani et al., 2023).

Proof-of-work (PoW) blockchains like Bitcoin and, until recently, Ethereum, consume vast amounts of energy due to their consensus mechanisms, which require miners to solve complex mathematical problems (Lasla et al., 2022). Bitcoin alone has an annual energy consumption comparable to that of entire nations such as Argentina or Norway. In the context of the metaverse—where NFTs, virtual land, and decentralized finance (DeFi) systems are increasingly prevalent—these energy demands are amplified.

The transition of Ethereum to a proof-of-stake (PoS) mechanism, which has reportedly reduced its energy use by over 99%, marks a significant step toward sustainable blockchain practices. PoS protocols eliminate the need for computationally intensive mining, instead relying on validators who are selected based on their stake in the network. However, not all metaverse projects have adopted PoS or similarly efficient mechanisms. Many platforms still use legacy chains or operate on Layer 1 infrastructures with high environmental footprints (Asif & Hassan, 2023).

Promising alternatives include Layer 2 solutions (e.g., Polygon, Arbitrum) that handle transactions off-chain before settling them on a main chain, thereby drastically reducing energy use. Additionally, "green" NFTs—created and traded on low-energy blockchains—are gaining traction as environmentally conscious options for creators and consumers alike. Yet, widespread adoption of these innovations remains uneven (Pennino et al., 2022).

To ensure that the growth of the metaverse does not come at the expense of planetary health, developers, investors, and users must prioritize eco-conscious design principles. Regulatory frameworks may also need to evolve to incentivize the use of sustainable consensus mechanisms and to discourage environmentally harmful practices within the Web3 ecosystem.

Hardware and Electronic Waste

While much of the metaverse experience is software-driven, its realization depends heavily on specialized hardware. Extended reality (XR) devices—including virtual reality headsets, augmented reality glasses, haptic feedback suits, and motion-tracking equipment—are the primary interfaces that connect users to immersive digital environments. However, the environmental implications of producing, consuming, and discarding these devices are profound (Venkatakrishnan, 2023).

The manufacturing of XR hardware is resource- and energy-intensive. Devices often contain rare earth elements, such as neodymium and dysprosium, which are mined through processes that cause significant ecological damage and toxic waste. The extraction of these materials not only contributes to habitat destruction and water contamination but also involves substantial carbon emissions across the supply chain. Furthermore, the global demand for these components exerts pressure on geopolitical resource dependencies, raising ethical and sustainability concerns (Ikeh, 2025).

Once manufactured, XR devices typically have short life cycles due to rapid technological advancements and limited repairability. Consumers are often encouraged to upgrade every few years, contributing to the mounting problem of electronic waste (e-waste) (Cairns, 2025).

The disposal of these devices poses its own set of challenges. Improper recycling can release hazardous materials, while informal e-waste processing in developing countries endangers both ecosystems and human health. Addressing this issue requires a systemic shift in how XR hardware is designed and managed. Modular, repairable, and upgradable designs can extend device lifespans, while improved recycling infrastructure and take-back programs can reduce waste.

In addition, manufacturers must embrace circular economy principles—using recycled materials, minimizing packaging waste, and designing for disassembly. Policy interventions, such as extended producer responsibility (EPR) regulations and right-to-repair laws, can also help shift the industry toward more sustainable practices (Nashid, 2024).

As the metaverse ecosystem expands, the environmental footprint of its hardware must not be overlooked. Mitigating e-waste and improving resource efficiency are essential components of a broader strategy to ensure that immersive technologies contribute positively to a sustainable digital future.

THE METAVERSE AS A CLIMATE SOLUTION: DEMATERIALIZATION AND VIRTUAL EFFICIENCY

Virtual Work and Reduced Travel

The COVID-19 pandemic catalyzed a global shift toward remote work and virtual collaboration, demonstrating that many activities traditionally requiring physical presence could be effectively conducted online. This shift had significant environmental implications, notably in the form of reduced travel, lower office energy consumption, and decreased use of physical resources. The metaverse, with its immersive and interactive capabilities, builds on this trend by offering a more engaging and spatially rich alternative to conventional video conferencing tools (Mitchell, 2023).

Metaverse platforms can replicate the experience of physical offices, classrooms, and meeting venues through 3D environments where users interact as avatars. Virtual meeting spaces such as Spatial, Meta's Horizon Workrooms, and Virbela enable teams to collaborate in real time with a heightened sense of presence and engagement. These platforms go beyond flat screen communication by incorporating spatial audio, gesture recognition, and shared virtual objects, making remote interaction more natural and productive.

From a sustainability standpoint, this digital transformation can lead to substantial reductions in greenhouse gas emissions. Business travel—especially long-haul flights for conferences, client meetings, and trade shows—represents a major contributor to corporate carbon footprints. According to the International Energy Agency (IEA), aviation accounts for approximately 2.5% of global CO_2 emissions, a figure that rises significantly when non-CO_2 effects at high altitudes are considered. Transitioning to metaverse-based conferencing and virtual expos offers a low-carbon alternative that preserves the collaborative benefits of in-person engagement (Dsouza, 2025; Batra et al., 2024).

Education and training also stand to benefit. Virtual campuses allow universities and corporate training programs to offer immersive, location-independent learning experiences. Students and professionals can attend virtual labs, simulations, and seminars without commuting, thereby reducing emissions linked to transportation and physical campus operations. The scalability of such solutions also increases access to high-quality education while minimizing ecological footprints.

However, realizing these benefits requires ensuring that metaverse platforms themselves are energy-efficient and operate on low-carbon infrastructures. Sustainable data center management, green cloud services, and optimization of XR hardware will be crucial to maintaining a net-positive climate impact.

Digital Twins and Smart Cities

Among the most promising applications of the metaverse for environmental sustainability is the deployment of digital twins—real-time, dynamic virtual replicas of physical entities such as buildings, transportation networks, or entire cities. Digital twins leverage the metaverse's immersive capabilities to visualize, analyze, and optimize complex systems before making costly real-world changes. This enables more efficient resource use, smarter design decisions, and proactive environmental management.

Urban environments, which account for over 70% of global CO_2 emissions, stand to gain immensely from this technology. Municipalities and planners can use metaverse-powered digital twins to simulate traffic flow, test green infrastructure, evaluate the impact of climate adaptation measures, and monitor energy usage across districts. For instance, virtual simulations can model how a new transit system might reduce congestion or how building retrofits can improve energy efficiency (Lifelo et al., 2024).

In the private sector, corporations use digital twins to optimize supply chains, reduce emissions, and monitor the environmental performance of buildings and manufacturing plants. By preemptively identifying inefficiencies and predicting system failures, organizations can lower energy consumption, minimize waste, and extend the life cycles of assets.

The integration of artificial intelligence (AI) and Internet of Things (IoT) sensors further enhances the capabilities of digital twins, allowing for real-time data collection and adaptive optimization. When hosted in a metaverse environment, these tools offer collaborative, multi-user experiences that enable cross-sectoral engagement—from policymakers and engineers to citizens and stakeholders (Emara et al., 2025).

Thus, digital twins exemplify how the metaverse can serve as a powerful climate tool—not only by reducing the need for resource-intensive trial and error, but by enabling data-driven environmental governance at scale.

Sustainable Consumer Behavior and Virtual Commerce

As digital experiences become increasingly immersive and desirable, the metaverse presents new opportunities for rethinking consumerism in ways that support environmental sustainability. A central concept in this transition is dematerialization—the replacement of physical goods and services with virtual equivalents that require fewer natural resources and generate less waste.

Virtual fashion shows, digital clothing, online concerts, and virtual real estate are becoming mainstream components of metaverse economies. These experiences often replicate or enhance their physical counterparts without the associated carbon emissions from manufacturing, shipping, venue operations, or travel. For instance, a digital fashion item used to dress an avatar may substitute a fast-fashion purchase, eliminating the environmental costs of textile production, packaging, and transportation. Major brands such as Gucci and Nike have already launched virtual collections within platforms like Roblox and Decentraland, signalling a shift toward low-carbon consumer engagement (Innocent, 2024).

Virtual concerts offer similar sustainability benefits. Events hosted in platforms like Fortnite or Wave attract millions of participants without requiring travel, lighting, or physical infrastructure. While digital platforms do consume energy, their environmental impact can be orders of magnitude lower if powered by renewable energy and optimized for efficiency.

Importantly, the metaverse also has the potential to reshape consumer values. Gamified experiences and immersive storytelling can encourage more sustainable mindsets by visualizing climate data, simulating future scenarios, or rewarding eco-conscious behaviours within virtual ecosystems. Platforms can integrate carbon footprint tracking or sustainability badges into user profiles, nudging individuals toward greener decisions both online and offline.

Nevertheless, the environmental promise of virtual commerce is not automatic. It requires intentional design choices, transparency in energy use, and a cultural shift toward valuing digital experiences as sufficient substitutes for material consumption. Without these safeguards, virtual consumerism risks becoming an additional layer of ecological strain rather than a solution.

EMPOWERING ENVIRONMENTAL ACTION THROUGH IMMERSIVE ENGAGEMENT

Virtual Environmental Education

Traditional climate education—largely reliant on textbooks, lectures, and abstract data—often struggles to convey the urgency and scale of the environmental crisis. The metaverse offers a transformative alternative by enabling deeply immersive educational experiences that bring climate science to life. Within virtual environments, students and the public can move beyond passive learning to explore ecological systems and climate dynamics firsthand.

In these metaverse spaces, learners can "walk" through melting glaciers, witness the deforestation of the Amazon, or explore coral bleaching events under the ocean—experiences that would be logistically or physically impossible in the real world. These vivid, emotionally resonant interactions create lasting impressions and promote a deeper cognitive and emotional connection to the material. Research in educational psychology has shown that immersive simulations enhance knowledge retention, engagement, and empathy—critical elements for motivating action on complex global issues like climate change.

Virtual reality (VR) experiences are already being deployed by environmental NGOs, academic institutions, and tech companies to promote awareness and education. For example, the Stanford Ocean Acidification Experience places users inside a virtual coral reef, showing how rising CO_2 levels threaten marine biodiversity. Similarly, Greenpeace has developed VR documentaries that immerse users in endangered ecosystems, aiming to mobilize support for conservation efforts.

The metaverse also supports active, constructivist learning approaches, where students participate in environmental problem-solving tasks or collaborate on virtual sustainability projects. Gamified simulations can teach users about energy budgeting, waste management, and ecological restoration in engaging, interactive ways. Furthermore, educators can use metaverse tools to build interdisciplinary curricula that merge environmental science with geography, ethics, economics, and policy.

As XR hardware becomes more accessible and education platforms more scalable, immersive environmental education has the potential to reach global audiences, particularly in underserved regions where field trips, labs, or climate workshops are not feasible. However, ensuring equitable access and culturally relevant content remains a critical challenge that must be addressed in parallel.

Simulations for Climate Policy and Modelling

One of the most powerful yet underutilized applications of the metaverse lies in its capacity to simulate large-scale environmental systems for policy design and decision-making. Climate change is a multifaceted challenge that spans disciplines and sectors—agriculture, energy, transportation, urban planning, and public health. The ability to visualize the interconnected impacts of different policy pathways in a shared, interactive environment could revolutionize how governments and institutions approach climate action.

Metaverse platforms equipped with AI and big data analytics can support dynamic simulations that model the outcomes of various climate policies over time. Policymakers and stakeholders can observe, in real-time, how a carbon tax might affect energy consumption, how rising sea levels could displace populations in coastal cities, or how shifts in rainfall patterns might influence food security. These simulations allow users to experiment with mitigation and adaptation strategies in a risk-free setting—enhancing strategic foresight and collaborative planning.

For example, climate models integrated into a digital twin of a city could help test green infrastructure upgrades, assess flood mitigation plans, or evaluate the carbon savings of different public transit options. By bringing together representatives from urban development, environmental agencies, and civil society in shared virtual spaces, the metaverse can facilitate more inclusive, transparent, and coordinated decision-making processes.

Beyond governments, international organizations such as the UN and World Bank can leverage metaverse-based simulations to communicate climate scenarios to diverse global audiences. These platforms can also serve as training environments for emergency response teams, humanitarian workers, and local authorities tasked with implementing climate resilience programs.

Importantly, the immersive nature of these simulations can bridge the "information-action gap" often seen in policy development, where the abstract nature of scientific projections hinders urgency and consensus. By making data visually and emotionally compelling, the metaverse can transform climate modeling from a niche expert activity into a shared public dialogue.

Green Advocacy and Digital Activism

Activism has always been a critical driver of environmental change, and the metaverse offers a new frontier for amplifying advocacy in inclusive, creative, and low-carbon ways. Virtual spaces enable activists to organize protests, awareness campaigns, art installations, and global summits—without the environmental costs typically associated with mass gatherings such as travel, physical infrastructure, and material consumption.

Virtual protests and environmental events have already begun to reshape the nature of digital advocacy. For instance, Earth Day celebrations within games like *Minecraft*, *Roblox*, and *Fortnite* have reached millions of users across the globe, especially younger demographics. These in-game events often include interactive learning modules, virtual clean-ups, and immersive storytelling that highlight urgent environmental challenges. They not only raise awareness but also engage participants in meaningful dialogue through gamified, community-driven experiences.

The metaverse also serves as a powerful tool for democratizing activism. Individuals and communities that face barriers to participation in physical protests—due to geography, political repression, disability, or economic constraints—can voice their concerns and contribute to global conversations from within accessible digital platforms. This inclusivity can help elevate marginalized perspectives, particularly from climate-vulnerable regions that are often underrepresented in mainstream environmental discourse.

Virtual spaces can host eco-art galleries, sustainability expos, hackathons, and policy town halls that foster creative expression and civic engagement. Artists, designers, and technologists can collaborate on immersive installations that visualize climate impacts, explore indigenous knowledge systems, or imagine regenerative futures. These cultural interventions often reach audiences beyond traditional scientific or policy circles, cultivating broader societal engagement with environmental issues.

Moreover, blockchain-based tools such as decentralized autonomous organizations (DAOs) can enable new forms of digital environmental governance. Activist communities can fundraise, vote on campaigns, and coordinate action in transparent, decentralized ways that reflect the values of collective ownership and accountability.

Nevertheless, to ensure that digital activism in the metaverse contributes meaningfully to climate goals, platforms must uphold principles of ethical design, privacy, and inclusivity. They must also be powered by sustainable infrastructure to avoid undermining the very causes they support.

CHALLENGES, RISKS, AND POLICY RECOMMENDATIONS

Rebound Effects and Consumption Paradox

While the metaverse holds promise for reducing the environmental impact of physical infrastructure and travel through virtualization, it simultaneously risks triggering rebound effects—situations were gains in efficiency lead to increased overall consumption. This paradox threatens to undermine many of the sustainability benefits associated with immersive digital technologies, (Raad & Rashid, 2023; Tiwari et al., 2025; Al-Kfairy et al., 2025; Bhati et al., 2024).

As virtual experiences become more immersive, convenient, and entertaining, users may spend significantly more time in energy-intensive environments. For example, prolonged use of high-resolution VR platforms, especially those reliant on cloud rendering or real-time processing, can generate substantial energy demands. Additionally, as XR (extended reality) devices evolve rapidly, users are incentivized to frequently upgrade to newer, more powerful hardware. This accelerates the production cycle, intensifies the consumption of raw materials, and increases electronic waste—adding to the ecological footprint the metaverse was meant to reduce, (Raad & Rashid, 2023; Tiwari et al., 2025; Al-Kfairy et al., 2025; Bhati et al., 2024).

This phenomenon is not unique to the metaverse. Historically, advancements in energy-efficient technologies (from LED lighting to fuel-efficient cars) have often been offset by behavioural or systemic changes that lead to greater overall consumption—a dynamic well-documented in environmental economics as the Jevons Paradox or rebound effect, (Raad & Rashid, 2023; Tiwari et al., 2025; Al-Kfairy et al., 2025; Bhati et al., 2024).

In the context of the metaverse, mitigating rebound effects requires both technological and behavioural interventions. On the technical side, platforms must prioritize low-energy rendering, efficient server management, and optimization of virtual environments to reduce unnecessary computing loads. On the behavioural side, awareness campaigns and nudging strategies can promote conscious digital consumption—encouraging users to limit unnecessary usage, avoid excessive hardware turnover, and engage with more sustainable virtual products, (Raad & Rashid, 2023; Tiwari et al., 2025; Al-Kfairy et al., 2025; Bhati et al., 2024).

Ultimately, designing for sufficiency—rather than unbounded expansion—must become a guiding principle in metaverse development. Balancing innovation with restraint will be key to realizing a truly sustainable digital future, (Raad & Rashid, 2023; Tiwari et al., 2025; Al-Kfairy et al., 2025; Bhati et al., 2024).

Equity and Access

The environmental and economic benefits of the metaverse are not distributed evenly across the globe. While affluent, tech-enabled regions may reduce emissions through virtualization and digital dematerialization, under-resourced communities often face disproportionate burdens—from the environmental costs of mining rare earth elements to the social exclusion stemming from limited connectivity and digital literacy.

The manufacture of XR hardware relies on minerals like cobalt, lithium, and rare earth metals, much of which are extracted from the Global South under exploitative or environmentally damaging conditions. Communities near mining operations often experience toxic pollution, deforestation, and water scarcity, while workers may endure unsafe labor practices. Meanwhile, electronic waste—especially from short-lived devices—frequently ends up in developing countries, where informal recycling practices can release harmful chemicals and endanger human health.

Furthermore, the promise of virtual inclusion is meaningless if large populations lack the infrastructure to participate. Many regions still suffer from unreliable internet access, unstable electricity, and unaffordable device costs—rendering metaverse platforms inaccessible. Without deliberate interventions, these disparities could deepen global digital divides and further entrench climate injustice.

To address these challenges, climate equity must become a foundational principle of metaverse development. Governments and industry leaders must invest in global digital infrastructure, support fair trade practices in mineral sourcing, and fund safe e-waste management systems. At the design level, developers should build platforms that are bandwidth-efficient and compatible with a wide range of devices.

International institutions can play a key role by establishing climate justice frameworks that guide responsible technology deployment. Public-private partnerships should aim to extend affordable access to marginalized populations while ensuring that those who bear the environmental costs also receive the economic and social benefits of digital inclusion.

Regulatory and Design Interventions

Unlocking the metaverse's sustainability potential requires proactive governance and responsible design, grounded in interdisciplinary collaboration. Unlike traditional internet ecosystems, the metaverse spans multiple domains—energy use, device manufacturing, data privacy, digital ownership, and spatial design—making holistic regulation both challenging and essential.

Effective governance should include sustainability-specific policies and standards, such as:

- **Sustainable design requirements** for XR hardware: emphasizing modularity, repairability, and energy efficiency.
- **Carbon transparency labelling** on digital goods, platforms, and services, enabling users to make informed environmental choices.
- **Green certifications** for virtual real estate, NFTs, and blockchain-based assets, similar to LEED or ENERGY STAR in the physical world.
- **Incentives for renewable-powered platforms**, including tax breaks or priority in app stores and marketplaces.
- **Digital circular economy policies**, supporting the reuse, recycling, and ethical disposal of XR devices and components.

Governments should also play a direct role in shaping a greener metaverse through funding and innovation initiatives. This includes supporting R&D in sustainable computing, offering grants for climate-positive virtual projects, and establishing incubators for green metaverse startups. Public procurement policies can set demand-side signals by prioritizing virtual engagement solutions that meet verified sustainability criteria.

Most importantly, cross-sectoral governance models are needed. Environmental scientists, technologists, ethicists, economists, and policymakers must collaborate to establish regulatory frameworks that are both future-ready and ethically grounded. This could include multi-stakeholder initiatives like a Metaverse Sustainability Standards Forum, akin to existing bodies that govern internet or AI safety standards.

In the absence of clear policy, market-driven expansion may prioritize profit over sustainability. A coordinated, foresight-driven approach is essential to ensure that the metaverse not only avoids worsening the climate crisis but actively contributes to its solution.

CONCLUSION

The metaverse is not intrinsically sustainable or unsustainable—it is a neutral framework, a digital frontier whose environmental footprint will be determined by the values, decisions, and design principles embedded within it. As with many transformative technologies, its long-term implications hinge on the intentions and actions of a diverse ecosystem of stakeholders, including developers, policy-makers, corporate leaders, and end-users. If left unchecked, the expansion of the metaverse could significantly increase energy consumption, accelerate e-waste production, deepen global digital divides, and contribute to ecological degradation. The convergence of high-performance computing, blockchain-based economies, and hardware manufacturing poses serious environmental risks—especially when growth is prioritized over responsibility. The rebound effects of convenience-driven virtualization and the rapid obsolescence of XR devices are just two examples of how even well-meaning innovations can produce unintended consequences.

However, the metaverse also holds unprecedented potential to support climate solutions at scale. When powered by renewable energy, governed by inclusive policy, and informed by circular design principles, it can become a strategic tool in the global fight against climate change. Immersive education platforms can cultivate climate literacy and empathy. Digital twins and virtual modelling can drive efficiency in urban planning, infrastructure development, and disaster preparedness. Virtual workspaces and events can reduce emissions from commuting and global travel, while digital economies may offer lower-carbon alternatives to material consumption—provided they are built on energy-efficient infrastructure. The next decade represents a pivotal convergence of two parallel trajectories: the race to mitigate the climate crisis, and the accelerated development of immersive digital ecosystems. Aligning these pathways will require interdisciplinary collaboration across technology, environmental science, design, ethics, and policy. It will also necessitate bold regulatory frameworks, investments in sustainable infrastructure, and grassroots innovation that prioritizes equity and accessibility.

In short, the metaverse must not be treated as a separate or secondary domain to sustainability efforts, but as a critical arena for climate action. By intentionally steering its evolution toward ecological responsibility and social inclusion, we can ensure that this emerging digital universe contributes meaningfully to a low-carbon, resilient, and just future. The challenge is immense—but so is the opportunity. The question is not whether the metaverse will be part of our climate future, but how we will shape it to serve people and planet alike.

REFERENCES

Al-Kfairy, M., Alrabaee, S., Alfandi, O., Mohamed, A. T., & Khaddaj, S. (2025). Navigating ethical dimensions in the metaverse: Challenges, frameworks, and solutions. *IEEE Access : Practical Innovations, Open Solutions, 13*, 79996–80018. DOI: 10.1109/ACCESS.2025.3564498

Allam, Z., Sharifi, A., Bibri, S. E., Jones, D. S., & Krogstie, J. (2022). The metaverse as a virtual form of smart cities: Opportunities and challenges for environmental, economic, and social sustainability in urban futures. *Smart Cities, 5*(3), 771–801. DOI: 10.3390/smartcities5030040

Alshahrani, A., Mahmoud, A., El-Sappagh, S., & Ali Elbelkasy, M. S. (2023). An Internet of Things Based Air Pollution Detection Device for Mitigating Climate Changes. *Information Science Letters, 12*(4), 1891–1900. DOI: 10.18576/isl/120413

Asif, R., & Hassan, S. R. (2023). Shaping the future of Ethereum: Exploring energy consumption in Proof-of-Work and Proof-of-Stake consensus. *Frontiers in Blockchain, 6*, 1151724. DOI: 10.3389/fbloc.2023.1151724

Batra, R., Arora, S., Sharma, M. M., Rana, S., Raheja, K., Saber, A., & Shah, M. A. (2024). Integration of LSTM networks with gradient boosting machines (GBM) for assessing heating and cooling load requirements in building energy efficiency. *Energy Exploration & Exploitation, 42*(6), 2191–2217. DOI: 10.1177/01445987241268075

Bhati, N., Duggar, R., & Saber, A. (2024). Empowering Safety by Embracing IoT for Leak Detection Excellence. In *Innovations in Machine Learning and IoT for Water Management* (pp. 231–251). IGI Global Scientific Publishing.

Cairns, C. N. (2005, May). E-waste and the consumer: improving options to reduce, reuse and recycle. In *Proceedings of the 2005 IEEE International Symposium on Electronics and the Environment,* 2005. (pp. 237-242). IEEE. DOI: 10.1109/ISEE.2005.1437033

Cappa, M. L. (2023). From Web 2.0 to the Metaverse: analyzing the evolution of platform-based business models and the creator economy. Academic Press.

Dsouza, L. F. (2025). Hydrogen Aircraft and Sustainable Development: Efficiency, Innovation, and Environmental Impact. *Innovation, and Environmental Impact.*

Emara, T. Z., Hassan, E., Elbedwehy, S., & Saber, A. (2025). A Historical Perspective on Artificial Intelligence in Applied Life Sciences. In *The Role of Artificial Intelligence in Advancing Applied Life Sciences* (pp. 49–86). IGI Global Scientific Publishing. DOI: 10.4018/979-8-3693-9208-9.ch002

Gamal, A., Elsayed, N. E., & Saber, A. (2025). Interoperable electronic medical record Framework based on Microservice architecture. *Egyptian Journal of Artificial Intelligence.*

Houston, K., & Reay, D. S. (2011). The impact of information and communication technology on GHG emissions: How green are virtual worlds? *Carbon Management, 2*(6), 629–643. DOI: 10.4155/cmt.11.62

Ikeh, O. (2025). Advancing Technology and Addressing Toxicity: The Dual Impacts of Rare Earth Elements on Materials and the Environment. *NIPES-Journal of Science and Technology Research, 7*(2), 275–286. DOI: 10.37933/nipes/7.2.2025.19

Innocent, S. (2024). Eco-Friendly Fashion: The Role of Instagram and Virtual Fashion in Sustainability Development Efforts. Academic Press.

Khan, K. (2023). Advancements and Challenges in 360 Virtual Reality Video Streaming: A Comprehensive Review of Cloud-Based Solutions. *International Journal of Advanced Networking and Applications, 15*(04), 6053–6062.

Korada, L. (2024). Digital Transformation Balanced with Sustainability Goals. *Journal of Engineering and Applied Sciences Technology. J Eng App Sci Technol, 6*(5), 2-7.

Lasla, N., Al-Sahan, L., Abdallah, M., & Younis, M. (2022). Green-PoW: An energy-efficient blockchain Proof-of-Work consensus algorithm. *Computer Networks, 214*, 109118. DOI: 10.1016/j.comnet.2022.109118

Lifelo, Z., Ding, J., Ning, H., & Dhelim, S. (2024). Artificial intelligence-enabled metaverse for sustainable smart cities: Technologies, applications, challenges, and future directions. *Electronics (Basel), 13*(24), 4874. DOI: 10.3390/electronics13244874

Lifelo, Z., Ding, J., Ning, H., & Dhelim, S. (2024). Artificial intelligence-enabled metaverse for sustainable smart cities: Technologies, applications, challenges, and future directions. *Electronics (Basel), 13*(24), 4874. DOI: 10.3390/electronics13244874

Mahmoud, A., Aurangzeb, K., Alhussein, M., & Manal, S. A. E. (2025). Harnessing deep learning to analyze climate change impacts on crop production. *Alexandria Engineering Journal, 125*, 67–82. DOI: 10.1016/j.aej.2025.04.008

Mitchell, A. (2023). Collaboration technology affordances from virtual collaboration in the time of COVID-19 and post-pandemic strategies. *Information Technology & People, 36*(5), 1982–2008. DOI: 10.1108/ITP-01-2021-0003

Nafus, D., Schooler, E. M., & Burch, K. A. (2021). Carbon-responsive computing: Changing the nexus between energy and computing. *Energies*, *14*(21), 6917. DOI: 10.3390/en14216917

Nair, A. J., Manohar, S., Mittal, A., & Chaudhry, R. (2024). Unleashing digital frontiers: Bridging realities of augmented reality, virtual reality, and the metaverse. In *The metaverse dilemma: Challenges and opportunities for business and society* (pp. 85–112). Emerald Publishing Limited. DOI: 10.1108/978-1-83797-524-220241006

Nashid, S. M. (2024). Circular economy in IT device lifecycle: analysing European Union market practices and policy alignment. Academic Press.

Pennino, D., Pizzonia, M., Vitaletti, A., & Zecchini, M. (2022). Blockchain as IoT Economy enabler: A review of architectural aspects. *Journal of Sensor and Actuator Networks*, *11*(2), 20. DOI: 10.3390/jsan11020020

Raad, H., & Rashid, F. K. M. (2023). The metaverse: Applications, concerns, technical challenges, future directions and recommendations. *IEEE Access : Practical Innovations, Open Solutions*, *11*, 110850–110861. DOI: 10.1109/ACCESS.2023.3321650

Saber, A., Al-Zoghby, A. M., & Elmougy, S. (2018, January). Big-data aggregating, linking, integrating and representing using semantic web technologies. In *International Conference on Advanced Machine Learning Technologies and Applications* (pp. 331-342). Cham: Springer International Publishing. DOI: 10.1007/978-3-319-74690-6_33

Sharma, M., Mahajan, Y., & Saber, A. (2024). Using Augmented Reality (AR) and the Internet of Things (IoT) to improve water management maintenance and training. In *Innovations in Machine Learning and IoT for Water Management* (pp. 252-270). IGI Global Scientific Publishing.

Tiwari, M., Zhou, Y., Childs, A., Chang, L. Y., & Ferrill, J. (2025). Metaverse policing: A systematic literature review of challenges and recommendations. *Computers in Human Behavior*, *166*, 108591. DOI: 10.1016/j.chb.2025.108591

Venkatakrishnan, R. (2023). *All Hands on Deck: Choosing Virtual End Effector Representations to Improve Near Field Object Manipulation Interactions in Extended Reality* (Doctoral dissertation, Clemson University).

Chapter 2
Technological Foundations of the Metaverse

Abeer Saber
https://orcid.org/0000-0002-9261-0927
Faculty of Computers and Artificial intelligence, Damietta University, Egypt

Aya Gamal
Faculty of Computers and Artificial intelligence, Damietta University, Egypt

Esraa Hassan
Faculty of Artificial Intelligence, Kafrelsheikh University, Egypt

Tamer Z. Emara
https://orcid.org/0000-0001-6730-9449
Faculty of Computers and Artificial Intelligence, Damietta University, Egypt

ABSTRACT

This chapter defines the Metaverse and traces its evolution from early virtual worlds to modern persistent ecosystems. It analyzes the fundamental architecture and technological enablers, including high-speed networking (5G/6G, edge computing), scalable cloud and distributed systems, and immersive hardware (VR/AR, haptics). The discussion also covers AI's role in graphics rendering and intelligent virtual agents. The economic and governance frameworks are explored, with a focus on blockchain for digital ownership and the importance of interoperability. The chapter highlights the link between these technologies and global sustainability goals, specifically in industry, innovation, and infrastructure; decent work and economic growth; and reduced inequalities. Finally, the text addresses key challenges, such as

DOI: 10.4018/979-8-3373-3043-3.ch002

technical limitations, societal risks, and ethical issues. It underscores the need for interdisciplinary research and cross-sector collaboration to ensure the Metaverse's future is inclusive, secure, and sustainable.

INTRODUCTION

The Metaverse is an evolving concept that describes a vast, interconnected network of immersive virtual environments where users can interact with each other and digital content in real-time. Enabled by a combination of emerging technologies—including virtual reality (VR), augmented reality (AR) (Sharma et al., 2024), artificial intelligence (AI) (Emara et al., 2025a), blockchain, and high-speed networking—the Metaverse offers an experience that is not only interactive and visually rich but also persistent and continuous. In this space, users are represented by customizable avatars and can engage in a wide array of activities, from socializing and entertainment to education, commerce, and remote collaboration (Davis et al., 2009).

Unlike traditional digital platforms that are often fragmented and limited in scope, the Metaverse aspires to create a unified, immersive digital universe that mirrors—and in some ways, surpasses—the physical world (Sadeghi-Niaraki et al., 2025). It emphasizes presence, allowing users to feel as though they truly "exist" within these digital spaces, and continuity, ensuring that virtual experiences and identities persist across sessions and platforms. The Metaverse blurs the boundaries between physical and digital realities, offering new paradigms for human interaction, economic exchange, and content creation (Mourtzis et al., 2022).

While the Metaverse remains under active development and lacks a single, universally accepted definition, it is broadly understood as the convergence of multiple digital technologies and platforms into a shared, persistent 3D environment. It integrates the graphical and social elements of 3D virtual worlds with real-time communication, decentralized asset ownership through blockchain, and intelligent automation via AI. This fusion enables users to move seamlessly between different virtual domains—such as immersive games, virtual workplaces, online education environments, and digital marketplaces—creating a cohesive and interoperable digital ecosystem. As the Metaverse continues to mature, it holds the potential to reshape how individuals experience the internet, transforming it from a place we visit into a space we inhabit (Rawat & Hagos, 2024).

Historical Evolution: From Virtual Worlds to the Metaverse

The roots of the Metaverse can be traced back to early virtual worlds in the late 20th century. One of the first notable platforms was *MUD* (Multi-User Dungeon), a text-based multiplayer environment developed in the late 1970s. These early platforms allowed users to explore virtual spaces and interact with one another, albeit in very limited and primitive forms compared to modern standards (Downey, 2014).

In the 1990s and early 2000s, graphical virtual worlds like *Active Worlds*, *there*, and *Second Life* introduced more complex and visually immersive environments (Salt et al., 2008). These platforms enabled users to create avatars, build structures, and engage in virtual economies. *Second Life*, launched in 2003, was particularly influential, offering a user-generated digital world that mirrored many features now associated with the Metaverse, such as digital commerce, virtual land ownership, and social interaction (Hemachandran & Rodriguez, 2023).

With the advent of more sophisticated hardware and networking technologies, the concept of the Metaverse began to evolve beyond simple virtual worlds. The rise of massively multiplayer online games (MMOs) like *World of Warcraft* and *EVE Online* further demonstrated the potential of persistent, large-scale virtual environments. However, these were still siloed experiences limited to specific purposes, such as gaming, without true interoperability or cross-platform continuity (Keatinge, 2010).

The modern vision of the Metaverse gained momentum in the 2010s and 2020s, as companies like Meta (formerly Facebook), Microsoft, and Epic Games began investing heavily in immersive digital platforms. The introduction of VR headsets, advancements in cloud computing, and the integration of blockchain technologies laid the groundwork for a more decentralized and expansive Metaverse. Today, the Metaverse continues to evolve as a dynamic concept that promises to reshape how people interact with digital content, communicate, and live in an increasingly virtual world (Ball, 2024).

Chapter Roadmap

This chapter provides a comprehensive overview of the Metaverse by examining its key components, historical context, and future implications. It begins with an introduction to the Metaverse and its evolution from early virtual worlds, establishing the foundation for understanding its technological and societal significance. The chapter then explores the core technical layers that enable Metaverse, including high-speed networking, scalable cloud and distributed systems, and immersive interaction technologies such as VR/AR and haptics. It further delves into real-time graphics, AI-driven interactions, and the use of blockchain for digital ownership and decentralized identity. Governance and interoperability challenges are also addressed, highlighting the tension between open standards and proprietary ecosystems. Finally, the chapter outlines major open challenges—ranging from technical limitations to ethical and societal risks—while identifying promising interdisciplinary research opportunities that will shape the future development of the Metaverse.

INFRASTRUCTURE LAYER

High-Speed Networking (5G/6G, Edge Computing)

The success of the Metaverse relies on ultra-fast, low-latency internet connections, building upon foundational research in network efficiency and power-saving mechanisms for wireless systems, making 5G and the emerging 6G technologies critical enablers (Zawish et al., 2024; Emara et al., 2014; Emara, 2016; Emara, 2018). These advanced communication networks offer significantly higher data transfer speeds, reduced latency, and the ability to connect a vast number of devices simultaneously. For immersive Metaverse experiences—such as real-time virtual meetings, multiplayer VR gaming, and 3D social interactions—these capabilities are essential to maintain fluidity and synchronicity between users.

6G, which is still under research and development, is expected to push the boundaries even further with data rates up to 100 times faster than 5G, and latency potentially reduced to under one millisecond. This advancement will support richer, more detailed virtual environments, instantaneous interactions, and seamless streaming of high-resolution content. Additionally, 6G will likely enable more intelligent network services through integrated AI, enhancing real-time optimization and personalization within the Metaverse (Mahmoud et al., 2021; Shen et al., 2023).

Edge computing complements these high-speed networks by processing data closer to the user, at the "edge" of the network rather than in distant centralized servers. This minimizes the time required to send and receive data, further reducing latency. In the Metaverse, where milliseconds matter in delivering lifelike responsiveness, edge computing ensures a more stable and consistent experience. It also allows for localized content generation and contextual awareness, improving performance for users in diverse geographic locations (Pan & McElhannon, 2017).

Cloud & Distributed Systems (Scalable Persistence)

Beyond fast networking, the Metaverse depends on powerful backend systems capable of scalable persistence—the ability to maintain continuous, synchronized digital environments regardless of user scale or geographic distribution. Cloud computing provides the necessary infrastructure by offering vast, flexible computing resources that can dynamically scale based on demand. Platforms like AWS, Microsoft Azure, and Google Cloud play a central role in hosting Metaverse services and storing vast amounts of user-generated content (Ball, 2024).

To support billions of concurrent users and complex 3D simulations, the Metaverse requires not just scale, but distribution. Distributed systems break workloads across many servers and regions, ensuring high availability and fault tolerance. If a single node fails, others can take over seamlessly critical for an environment where downtime or data loss would severely impact user trust and immersion. Foundational research in distributed data management systems is essential for achieving this unprecedented scale (Emara et al., 2025c; Emara & Huang, 2019a; Emara & Huang, 2019b). The development of new models to process large-scale data efficiently on smaller clusters is a key area of research to achieve this scalability (Trinh et al., 2022). Distributed ledger technologies, such as blockchain, are also being explored to manage identity, ownership, and transactions within the Metaverse (Shaikh & Jammal, 2024).

Persistent virtual worlds also demand robust data synchronization to ensure that every user's view of the digital world is consistent and up to date. For example, if one user modifies a virtual object or environment, others must see that change instantly. This requires a sophisticated coordination of real-time data streaming, storage replication, and state management—all enabled by modern cloud architectures. Effectively managing geographically distributed data is a core component of this challenge (Emara et al., 2023). Together, high-speed networking and cloud-based distributed systems form the technological backbone of the Metaverse, allowing it to scale and evolve as a seamless, global, and persistent digital reality.

INTERACTION LAYER

The Interaction Layer serves as the critical interface between the user and the Metaverse, acting as the gateway through which individuals perceive, navigate, and influence immersive digital environments. It is responsible for translating human input—whether through gestures, speech, eye movement, or physical motion—into meaningful interactions within virtual worlds. At its core, this layer bridges the gap between physical reality and virtual experience, enabling users to feel present, responsive, and engaged within 3D digital spaces (Park & Kim, 2022).

This layer comprises a sophisticated integration of hardware and software technologies that work together to provide high levels of immersion, realism, and responsiveness. On the hardware side, devices such as Virtual Reality (VR) headsets, Augmented Reality (AR) glasses, motion trackers, and haptic feedback gear allow users to sense and manipulate the digital environment in ways that closely mimic real-world interactions. These devices provide input (e.g., head movement, hand gestures) and output (e.g., stereoscopic visuals, tactile sensations), creating a multisensory experience that enhances the illusion of "being there" in the Metaverse (Rubio-Tamayo et al., 2017).

On the software side, real-time graphics engines (like Unity or Unreal Engine) render visually rich and interactive 3D environments, while artificial intelligence (AI) powers dynamic elements such as responsive avatars, non-player characters (NPCs), and voice recognition systems. AI algorithms are also crucial for enabling contextual awareness—allowing the environment to respond intelligently to user behavior. For example, AI-driven NPCs can engage in natural conversations, adapt to user preferences, and simulate human-like emotions, making virtual interactions feel authentic and personalized.

Furthermore, the Interaction Layer incorporates natural user interface (NUI) design principles, which emphasize intuitive engagement mechanisms such as gaze control, voice commands, and touch-based manipulation. These interfaces reduce the learning curve and cognitive load, making digital environments more accessible to non-technical users and allowing for deeper, more meaningful experiences. As interaction becomes more fluid and lifelike, the boundary between user intention and system response continues to dissolve (Hsiao et al., 2017).

Importantly, this layer is not only about enabling interaction but also about orchestrating user experience—ensuring that what users see, hear, and feel is synchronized, believable, and emotionally engaging. Achieving this requires careful coordination between sensory inputs (like visuals and audio), system performance (latency, frame rate), and psychological cues (presence, agency, and immersion). As such, the Interaction Layer plays a central role in shaping how users perceive reality in the Metaverse.

As technologies evolve, the Interaction Layer is expected to become more adaptive, intelligent, and personalized, incorporating biometric feedback (like heart rate or stress levels) to tailor virtual experiences in real time. In future iterations, users may even interface with the Metaverse through brain-computer interfaces (BCIs), enabling direct neural control over digital actions, thus pushing the boundaries of human-computer interaction further than ever before (Paniagua-Gómez & Fernandez-Carmona, 2025).

In summary, the Interaction Layer is fundamental to delivering the immersive, interactive, and intelligent experiences that define the Metaverse. By integrating advanced hardware, real-time rendering, and AI-driven interaction design, it allows users to engage with digital environments in ways that feel natural, intuitive, and increasingly indistinguishable from physical reality.

Immersive Hardware (VR/AR, Haptics)

Immersive hardware is foundational to user interaction in the Metaverse. Virtual Reality (VR) devices, such as the Meta Quest or HTC Vive, fully immerse users in a computer-generated 3D environment by blocking out the physical world. Users experience a sense of "presence" in the virtual space, moving and interacting through head and hand tracking. Augmented Reality (AR), on the other hand, overlays digital elements onto the physical world using smart glasses or mobile devices, blending real and virtual experiences (Dionisio et al., 2013).

Haptic technologies enhance immersion by simulating the sense of touch. Devices like haptic gloves, vests, or even full-body suits provide physical feedback, allowing users to feel pressure, vibration, texture, or resistance when interacting with virtual objects. For example, when picking up a virtual item or shaking hands with an avatar, users receive tactile responses that increase the realism of the interaction. These technologies are essential for developing highly engaging applications in fields like training, healthcare, gaming, and remote collaboration.

Real-Time Graphics & AI Rendering

To maintain a believable and seamless environment, the Metaverse requires real-time graphics rendering. This involves the rapid generation of 3D images that respond to user movements and inputs without perceptible delay. Modern rendering engines like Unreal Engine 5 and Unity use advanced techniques such as ray tracing, dynamic lighting, and global illumination to create photorealistic visuals that adapt in real time (Ismail & Buyya, 2023).

AI-based rendering is increasingly playing a critical role. Through techniques like neural rendering, machine learning models can predict and fill in visual details, reduce rendering times, and enhance frame rates, even on limited hardware. This is especially important for delivering rich experiences on wireless devices such as AR glasses or mobile VR headsets. AI can also assist in auto-generating textures, character animations, and environmental details, reducing the burden on human designers and making content production more scalable. AI's integration into the Metaverse extends to practical applications, such as using advanced vision transformer architectures to classify and analyze visual data within these virtual spaces (Hassan et al., 2025a; Emara et al., 2025b).

AI for Interaction (NPCs, Content Moderation)

Artificial Intelligence (AI) drives intelligent and responsive interactions within the Metaverse. Non-Player Characters (NPCs)—virtual agents that populate virtual environments—are becoming more lifelike and dynamic through AI. Modern NPCs can respond to user input with natural language processing (NLP), simulate human emotions, and adapt behaviors based on past interactions. This makes them useful not only in games but also in training simulations, customer service, and virtual companionship (Wang et al., 2025). AI models can also be used to enhance the social aspect of the Metaverse by providing location-based recommendations for events and social connections (Trinh et al., 2019).

Another crucial function of AI in the interaction layer is content moderation. With the open nature of the Metaverse and user-generated content, maintaining safe, respectful, and inclusive environments is a significant challenge. AI moderation tools automatically detect and flag inappropriate behavior, hate speech, or harmful content in real-time voice and text interactions. Some systems use computer vision to monitor visual content as well. These intelligent systems often rely on efficient feature selection to accurately analyze data and make real-time decisions (VuThi et al., 2024). These tools help enforce community standards and reduce reliance on manual moderation, which is often slow and inconsistent (Al-Kfairy et al., 2025).

In summary, the Interaction Layer combines immersive devices, advanced graphics, and intelligent systems to enable seamless and engaging user experiences in the Metaverse. As these technologies continue to advance, interactions will become more natural, social, and meaningful bringing us closer to truly inhabiting digital worlds.

ECONOMY & GOVERNANCE LAYER

The Economy & Governance Layer is a foundational pillar of the Metaverse that determines how digital value is generated, exchanged, and maintained in a virtual ecosystem (Huawei et al., 2023). As the Metaverse evolves into a vast, interconnected network of platforms, the mechanisms governing economic activity and social coordination are becoming increasingly critical. This layer encompasses a wide range of components, including digital ownership, identity management, virtual currencies, smart contracts, and interoperability protocols that facilitate seamless integration across multiple virtual environments.

One of the most transformative aspects of this layer is digital ownership, made possible through blockchain technology and non-fungible tokens (NFTs). NFTs enable users to own unique digital assets such as virtual land, wearable avatars, 3D objects, artwork, and other in-world items. This ownership is cryptographically secured and verifiable on a decentralized ledger, allowing for transparent transactions and reducing the risk of duplication or fraud. With NFTs, digital goods acquire real economic value, and users can trade, sell, or monetize their virtual assets across different platforms (Singh et al., 2025).

Closely tied to ownership is the concept of decentralized identity (DID). In contrast to traditional login systems managed by centralized authorities, DID systems allow users to control their digital identities independently. This self-sovereign model ensures privacy, enhances security, and allows users to carry their identity across platforms, maintaining consistency and reputation in a variety of virtual spaces. This continuity is essential for creating a persistent digital persona, which can be used for social interaction, employment, education, and commerce within the Metaverse (Zwitter et al., 2020).

The Economy & Governance Layer also relies heavily on virtual currencies and economic incentives. Many platforms utilize their own cryptocurrencies or tokens, which serve as mediums of exchange, reward systems, or governance tools. These digital currencies can be earned through user participation, creation of digital content, or performance in virtual services, and in some cases can be converted into real-world currency. This opens up new economic opportunities such as play-to-earn games, virtual entrepreneurship, and digital freelancing, fostering a creator-driven economy (Evans, 2014).

Smart contracts further automate transactions and agreements in the Metaverse. These are self-executing code structures embedded in blockchain that enforce terms without intermediaries. Smart contracts can be used to manage property rights, facilitate decentralized commerce, automate royalties, or execute voting mechanisms in decentralized autonomous organizations (DAOs). Their programmable nature enhances transparency, reduces disputes, and promotes trust in digital exchanges (Wright, 2020).

Beyond individual transactions, the governance aspect of this layer plays a crucial role in maintaining order, fairness, and cooperation across the Metaverse. This includes moderation policies, community standards, and platform-level regulations. As user-generated content proliferates and diverse communities converge, governance structures must address issues such as harassment, misinformation, digital rights, and ethical behavior. Both centralized (platform-controlled) and decentralized (community-led) governance models are being explored to strike a balance between safety and freedom.

A central challenge in the Economy & Governance Layer is interoperability. Currently, many Metaverse platforms function as closed ecosystems, limiting the portability of assets and identities. To realize a unified Metaverse, open standards and protocols must be adopted to allow for the transfer of assets, currencies, and identities between platforms. Efforts by groups like the Metaverse Standards Forum and the Web3 Foundation aim to promote these standards, fostering collaboration and cross-platform compatibility (Yang et al., 2025).

Ultimately, the Economy & Governance Layer defines not only how users interact with virtual goods and services but also how they participate in shaping the rules and values of the digital worlds they inhabit. As the Metaverse continues to mature, this layer will determine whether it evolves into an inclusive, user-driven society or remains fragmented and controlled by a few dominant players. Its design and implementation will have long-term implications for digital sovereignty, economic fairness, and the democratization of virtual space.

Blockchain (Digital Ownership, Decentralized Identity)

Blockchain technology plays a pivotal role in enabling secure, transparent, and decentralized economic activity within the Metaverse. Through blockchain, users can prove digital ownership of assets like virtual land, clothing, avatars, artwork, and in-game items using non-fungible tokens (NFTs). Each NFT represents a unique digital asset recorded on a blockchain, ensuring that ownership is verifiable, traceable, and cannot be duplicated or tampered with (Sestino et al., 2022).

In addition to asset ownership, blockchain enables decentralized identity systems. Rather than relying on centralized platforms to manage user accounts, users can have self-sovereign identities (SSI)—digital identities controlled solely by the individual, stored securely on a blockchain. These identities can be used to log into multiple Metaverse platforms, manage reputation, and protect privacy, without relying on a single provider like Meta or Google. This decentralization promotes user empowerment and prevents monopolistic control over digital lives (Mühle et al., 2018).

Blockchain also supports smart contracts, which are self-executing programs that manage transactions and rules automatically. For example, creators can set rules for how royalties are paid when digital art or assets are resold. This not only creates new revenue streams but also ensures fair and transparent economic practices across the Metaverse (Khan et al., 2021).

Interoperability Standards (Open vs. Proprietary Ecosystems)

A truly open Metaverse depends on interoperability—the ability for users, assets, and identities to move freely across different virtual worlds and platforms. Open standards are essential to achieving this vision. These include common file formats (like USD for 3D assets), identity protocols (such as W3C's DID), and networking standards that allow cross-platform compatibility. Organizations like the Metaverse Standards Forum are actively working to define such protocols to ensure different systems can work together seamlessly (Genise & David, 2021).

However, the current landscape is still highly fragmented, with many companies developing proprietary ecosystems (Gawer & Cusumano, 2014). For instance, Meta's Horizon Worlds, Roblox, and Fortnite each have closed platforms where avatars, currencies, and virtual items cannot be transferred outside their own environment.

These "walled gardens" limit user freedom and reduce the overall utility of virtual assets. While they may offer more centralized control and user safety, they restrict the broader vision of an open, user-driven Metaverse.

The challenge moving forward is to find a balance between open innovation and platform security. If key players can agree on shared standards while allowing room for proprietary innovation, the Metaverse could evolve into a truly interconnected space where creators, users, and businesses benefit from broader access, ownership portability, and cross-platform collaboration (Ali et al., 2023).

In conclusion, the Economy & Governance Layer underpins the trust, freedom, and value exchange in the Metaverse. With blockchain ensuring ownership and decentralized identity, and interoperability defining how platforms cooperate, this layer will determine how democratic, inclusive, and economically viable the Metaverse becomes in the future.

OPEN CHALLENGES AND FUTURE DIRECTIONS

As the Metaverse moves from vision to reality, it faces a complex set of technical, social, and ethical challenges that must be addressed for it to achieve widespread acceptance and sustainability. While significant progress has been made in immersive technologies, networking, and digital economies, many fundamental issues remain unresolved. Understanding these open challenges is essential for guiding future innovation and responsible development (Ali et al., 2023).

Technical Limitations: Scalability and Latency

The ambition of the Metaverse hinges critically on overcoming one of its most formidable technical barriers: scalability. The vision of a truly seamless, interconnected virtual world implies the ability to support not just millions, but potentially billions of concurrent users, all interacting in real-time within persistent 3D environments. This scale of operation demands an immense, unprecedented leap in both computing and networking infrastructure beyond what currently exists or is widely deployed (Hatami et al., 2024).

The complexity of this challenge is multifaceted. Firstly, achieving low latency across widely distributed systems is paramount. In a traditional online game, a few hundred players might interact on a single server, with latency measured in tens of milliseconds. The Metaverse, however, envisions massive, shared spaces where users from across the globe, with varying internet connections, need to feel present and interact instantly with their environment and with each other. Every action, from moving an avatar to picking up a virtual object or having a conversation, must be processed and reflected in near real-time, regardless of physical distance between users or servers. This requires innovative networking protocols and intelligent data routing that minimize lag and ensure a fluid, responsive experience.

Simultaneously, maintaining synchronization across these vast, distributed systems is an engineering feat of epic proportions. If one user sees an object in one location while another user sees it elsewhere, the illusion of a shared reality crumbles. Every object's state, every avatar's position, and every environmental change must be consistent for all participants. This involves complex state management, consensus mechanisms, and data replication strategies to ensure that the "truth" of the virtual world is universally agreed upon and updated in real-time for everyone involved, even as billions of individual interactions occur concurrently.

Furthermore, this must all be delivered while upholding high graphical fidelity and responsiveness. Users expect rich, detailed, and visually stunning environments, along with smooth animations and immediate reactions to their inputs. Delivering this quality to potentially low-power devices, across vast distances, without overwhelming local hardware or network bandwidth, is a significant rendering and streaming challenge. It involves highly optimized 3D asset streaming, dynamic level-of-detail management, and efficient rendering pipelines.

While promising technologies are emerging, they are not yet universally mature or fully optimized for the Metaverse's demanding requirements. 5G offers significant improvements in bandwidth and lower latency compared to previous generations, making it a crucial enabler. However, its widespread global availability is still progressing, and even 5G may struggle to provide the sustained, ultra-low latency connections needed for truly photorealistic, highly interactive, and concurrent experiences across billions of users. The sheer volume of data transferred for such an immersive experience could still strain even 5G networks.

Edge computing, which brings computation and data storage closer to the source of data generation (i.e., the user's device or local network), is another vital component. By processing data closer to the user, edge computing can dramatically reduce latency, making interactions feel more immediate. However, the deployment of a truly pervasive and robust edge computing infrastructure, capable of handling the diverse computational needs of the Metaverse on a global scale, is still in its nascent stages. It requires massive investment in new hardware, distributed server networks, and sophisticated orchestration software.

Similarly, cloud rendering holds immense promise by offloading the intensive graphical processing from local devices to powerful remote servers in the cloud, then streaming the rendered visuals back to the user. This allows users to experience high-fidelity graphics on less powerful hardware, like standalone VR headsets or smartphones. Yet, cloud rendering introduces its own set of challenges, primarily related to the latency inherent in streaming video over the internet, and the consistent quality of that stream. Any significant lag or visual artifacts due to network fluctuations can break immersion. Moreover, the economic models and infrastructure scaling for truly global, real-time cloud rendering for billions of users are still being developed.

In essence, while these technologies represent crucial steps forward, they currently face limitations in terms of ubiquitous availability, cost-effectiveness, and full optimization for the unprecedented demands of a fully realized, seamless Metaverse. Bridging this gap requires continuous innovation in network architecture, distributed systems design, rendering pipelines, and the strategic deployment of next-generation infrastructure on a global scale.

Hardware Constraints and Accessibility

Indeed, beyond the formidable infrastructure demands, a fundamental limitation hindering the widespread adoption of the Metaverse lies squarely in the realm of hardware. Current Virtual Reality (VR) and Augmented Reality (AR) devices, which serve as the primary portals into these immersive digital realms, are still plagued by several critical shortcomings that collectively limit their accessibility, comfort, and ultimately, their mainstream appeal (Abendschein et al., 2023).

Firstly, bulkiness and ergonomics remain significant barriers. Many contemporary VR headsets resemble clunky goggles strapped to the face, often front-heavy and requiring external wires or powerful tethered PCs. This physical imposition quickly leads to discomfort, neck strain, and a general feeling of being encumbered, making extended use challenging and off-putting for casual users. While standalone headsets have emerged, reducing the need for external connections, they still often retain a substantial form factor to accommodate onboard processors and batteries. For the Metaverse to become as ubiquitous as smartphones, hardware must evolve into sleek, lightweight designs that can be worn for hours without conscious effort, perhaps resembling regular glasses or even contact lenses.

Secondly, the high cost of these devices creates a steep barrier to entry for many consumers. Premium VR headsets can run into hundreds or even thousands of dollars, placing them out of reach for a significant portion of the global population. This price point not only limits individual adoption but also restricts the ability of developers to build for a truly mass market, creating a chicken-and-egg problem where limited user base can deter content creation, and vice versa. Reducing manufacturing costs through economies of scale, advancements in component technology, and more efficient production processes will be crucial for democratizing access to the Metaverse.

Moreover, the user experience is frequently hampered by persistent technical issues. Motion sickness, often referred to as "VR sickness," remains a significant problem for a subset of users. This discomfort arises primarily from the sensory mismatch between what the eyes perceive (motion within the virtual environment) and what the inner ear (vestibular system) senses (a lack of physical movement). Even minute delays (latency) between head movements and the corresponding visual update in the headset can trigger this disorientation, leading to nausea, headaches, and general malaise. Overcoming this requires near-zero latency, higher refresh rates on displays, and potentially new haptic feedback systems or sophisticated "comfort modes" in content design.

Limited battery life is another practical constraint. The powerful processors, high-resolution displays, and intricate tracking systems within VR/AR devices are incredibly power-hungry. This often results in short usage times, necessitating frequent recharging and interrupting the immersive experience. For the Metaverse to be truly persistent and always-on, like a mobile phone, devices need to offer significantly extended battery longevity without adding prohibitive weight or heat. Innovations in battery chemistry, energy-efficient display technologies, and optimized power management are vital (Ritsos, 2006).

Finally, restricted fields of view (FOV) limit immersion. Many current headsets provide a relatively narrow window into the virtual world, making it feel like looking through binoculars. This "tunnel vision" effect breaks the sense of presence and reduces the feeling of truly being in the Metaverse. Achieving wider FOVs without introducing optical distortions, increasing bulk, or reducing pixel density per degree will be a major area of optical engineering advancement.

To transcend these limitations and truly make the Metaverse an inclusive and widely adopted platform, future hardware development must prioritize several key aspects. Devices need to become significantly lighter, moving towards the form factor of everyday eyewear. They must be more affordable, bringing the technology within reach of the average consumer. Critically, they must be ergonomically suitable for extended use, ensuring comfort, minimizing heat generation, and mitigating motion sickness for prolonged immersion. This holistic approach to hardware design, prioritizing comfort and accessibility alongside performance, will be essential for transforming the Metaverse from a niche technology into a pervasive and seamless part of daily life.

Interoperability and Standardization Gaps

Despite efforts to promote open standards, the Metaverse remains fragmented. Most current platforms are siloed, with proprietary ecosystems that restrict asset portability and user mobility. Without industry-wide agreement on file formats, identity protocols, and content compatibility, the vision of a unified, interconnected Metaverse will remain elusive. Promoting standardization while balancing innovation and intellectual property rights is a key technical and governance challenge (Rawat & Hagos, 2024).

Societal Risks: Privacy and Surveillance

The Metaverse raises significant concerns about privacy and surveillance. With technologies that track eye movements, gestures, speech, and biometric data, users are more exposed than ever before. Companies operating Metaverse platforms could potentially gather detailed behavioral data, creating new avenues for exploitation, targeted advertising, and manipulation. Without strong privacy regulations, users risk losing control over their digital identities and personal information (Huang et al., 2023).

Digital Inequality and Inclusion

Access to the Metaverse may exacerbate existing digital divides. Those without access to high-speed internet, advanced hardware, or technical literacy may be excluded from participating in this emerging digital economy. There is also a risk that the Metaverse could become dominated by wealthier users and corporations, further marginalizing underserved populations. Ensuring equity in access and representation must be a priority in both design and policy (Lanteri et al., 2025).

Psychological and Social Impact

Extended use of immersive technologies may have psychological effects, especially on children and vulnerable populations. Concerns include addiction, social isolation, and altered perceptions of reality. The blurring of digital and physical identities may also affect mental health and self-esteem. Designing responsible user experiences, setting usage limits, and providing psychological support are essential to mitigate these risks.

Content Moderation and Governance

Maintaining safe and inclusive environments in the Metaverse presents major governance challenges. As users create and share vast amounts of content, platforms must implement effective moderation systems to combat harassment, hate speech, and harmful behavior. AI can assist, but human oversight remains essential. Furthermore, the decentralized nature of some Metaverse projects complicates the enforcement of community standards and legal accountability.

Ethical Design and Algorithmic Bias

The use of AI in avatars, NPCs, moderation, and personalization introduces the risk of algorithmic bias. AI systems trained on biased data can reinforce stereotypes or exclude certain user groups. Ethical design practices must prioritize fairness, transparency, and inclusivity. Developers and researchers need to audit algorithms and ensure that AI systems enhance, rather than hinder, the user experience for diverse populations.

Research Opportunities in Human-Computer Interaction

The advent of the Metaverse, characterized by its deeply immersive and interactive virtual environments, represents a fertile ground for extensive research, particularly in fields dedicated to understanding human behavior and interaction with technology. This digital frontier opens vast research opportunities in Human-Computer Interaction (HCI), cognitive science, and behavioral psychology, offering unprecedented conditions to study human phenomena that are difficult or impossible to replicate in the physical world (Al-Kfairy et al., 2024).

In Human-Computer Interaction (HCI), the Metaverse presents a paradigm shift in how users engage with digital systems. Researchers can delve into novel interaction modalities that go far beyond traditional screens and keyboards. This includes exploring the efficacy and intuitiveness of natural user interfaces like hand tracking, full-body tracking, eye-tracking, and voice commands within 3D spatial environments. How do users learn new gestural languages? What are the most intuitive ways to navigate complex virtual spaces? How can haptic feedback, spatial audio, and even olfactory or gustatory cues be integrated to enhance immersion and interaction fidelity? Furthermore, designing for accessibility in the Metaverse is crucial. Research is needed to develop interfaces and tools that accommodate users with diverse abilities, ensuring that the immersive experience is inclusive and usable for everyone, regardless of physical or cognitive limitations. This involves studying how assistive technologies can integrate seamlessly into virtual environments and how avatar customization can empower diverse self-representation.

Within cognitive science, the Metaverse serves as an unparalleled laboratory for understanding fundamental cognitive processes. Researchers can study how the brain processes information in highly immersive, multi-sensory environments, and how this differs from real-world perception. For instance, studies can investigate spatial cognition in virtual worlds – how users build mental maps, navigate, and remember locations in vast digital landscapes. The impact of virtual presence – the psychological feeling of "being there" in a virtual environment – on cognitive functions like memory, attention, and problem-solving is a rich area of inquiry. Researchers can precisely control virtual stimuli and environments to conduct experiments on perception, decision-making, and learning that would be impractical or unethical in reality. This includes understanding phenomena like the "Proteus effect," where an avatar's appearance influences a user's behavior and self-perception, even outside the virtual environment.

Behavioral psychology finds immense new avenues in the Metaverse. The ability to create controlled social scenarios within virtual environments allows researchers to study complex social dynamics in ways previously unimaginable. How do avatars affect identity and social dynamics? Users can embody avatars that are vastly different from their physical selves, raising questions about self-representation, identity exploration, and the fluidity of identity in digital spaces. Research can explore how avatar appearance influences social interactions, perception by others, and the formation of virtual communities. The dynamics of group behavior, cooperation, and conflict in immersive, persistent virtual worlds can be observed and analyzed. Furthermore, the Metaverse offers unique opportunities to study how virtual presence influences communication. Non-verbal cues, such as gaze, body language (captured through full-body tracking), and proxemics (personal space) take on new significance in 3D environments. Researchers can investigate how these elements contribute to the richness and effectiveness of virtual communication, and how they might differ from face-to-face interactions.

The knowledge gleaned from these research endeavors can profoundly inform better design practices for Metaverse platforms, making them more intuitive, engaging, and comfortable for users. It can guide the development of innovative accessibility tools, ensuring the Metaverse is a truly inclusive space. Beyond core design, these insights have immense potential for educational applications, enabling highly immersive and interactive learning experiences, from virtual field trips to simulated surgical training. In therapeutic applications, the Metaverse can offer controlled environments for exposure therapy for phobias, social skills training for individuals with autism spectrum disorder, or even remote psychological counseling, allowing therapists to observe and interact with patients in simulated real-world scenarios. The convergence of these fields offers a holistic understanding of the human element in the Metaverse, paving the way for its responsible and beneficial evolution.

Innovation in Decentralized Infrastructure

On the infrastructure side, the Metaverse encourages research in decentralized systems, including blockchain scalability, distributed storage, and decentralized autonomous organizations (DAOs). These technologies promise to empower users with ownership and governance rights, but they also require further research to ensure they are secure, scalable, and user-friendly. Legal frameworks and technical solutions must evolve in parallel to enable trustless systems at global scale.

In conclusion, the Metaverse is not just a technical endeavor—it is a socio-technical transformation that intersects with law, ethics, psychology, economics, and design. Its future hinges on solving foundational challenges while promoting responsible, inclusive innovation. Collaboration between academia, industry, policymakers, and civil society will be essential to guide the Metaverse in a direction that benefits all. As we look ahead, it is clear that the Metaverse is still in its formative stage, offering a fertile ground for research, experimentation, and thoughtful evolution.

CONCLUSION

The Metaverse represents a bold reimagining of how people interact, work, and live in digital spaces. Its realization is made possible by a constellation of foundational technologies—including high-speed networking (5G/6G and edge computing), cloud and distributed systems for scalable persistence, immersive hardware like VR/AR and haptics, real-time graphics rendering, and artificial intelligence for interaction and moderation. Additionally, blockchain provides the backbone for digital ownership and decentralized identity, while interoperability standards are vital for connecting otherwise fragmented ecosystems.

Despite rapid advancements, the Metaverse remains an emerging frontier filled with complex challenges and unanswered questions. Overcoming these obstacles requires more than just technical innovation—it demands a coordinated, ethical, and inclusive approach to development. Issues such as data privacy, equitable access, digital governance, content moderation, and the psychological effects of immersive environments highlight the need for deeper understanding and responsible implementation.

To ensure the Metaverse evolves into a safe, inclusive, and sustainable digital ecosystem, there must be a call for interdisciplinary collaboration. Engineers, designers, ethicists, psychologists, policymakers, and educators must work together to shape not only the technical infrastructure but also the societal frameworks that will govern these virtual spaces. By integrating diverse perspectives and expertise, we can build a Metaverse that reflects human values, fosters creativity, and supports a globally connected society.

REFERENCES

Abendschein, R., Desai, S., & Astell, A. J. (2023). Towards accessibility guidelines for the metaverse. In *Proceedings of the CHI* (Vol. 23). ACM.

Al-Kfairy, M., Alomari, A., Al-Bashayreh, M. G., & Tubishat, M. (2024). *Unveiling the metaverse: A survey of user experience, social dynamics, and technological interoperability*. Preprint.

Al-Kfairy, M., Alrabaee, S., Alfandi, O., Mohamed, A. T., & Khaddaj, S. (2025). Navigating ethical dimensions in the metaverse: Challenges, frameworks, and solutions. *IEEE Access : Practical Innovations, Open Solutions*, *13*, 79996–80018. Advance online publication. DOI: 10.1109/ACCESS.2025.3564498

Ali, M., Naeem, F., Kaddoum, G., & Hossain, E. (2023). Metaverse communications, networking, security, and applications: Research issues, state-of-the-art, and future directions. *IEEE Communications Surveys and Tutorials*, *26*(2), 1238–1278. DOI: 10.1109/COMST.2023.3347172

Ball, M. (2024). *The metaverse: Fully revised and updated edition: Building the spatial internet*. Liveright Publishing.

Davis, A., Murphy, J., Owens, D., Khazanchi, D., & Zigurs, I. (2009). Avatars, people, and virtual worlds: Foundations for research in metaverses. *Journal of the Association for Information Systems*, *10*(2), 1. DOI: 10.17705/1jais.00183

Dionisio, J. D. N., Burns, W. G.III, & Gilbert, R. (2013). 3D virtual worlds and the metaverse: Current status and future possibilities. *ACM Computing Surveys*, *45*(3), 1–38. DOI: 10.1145/2480741.2480751

Downey, S. (2014). History of the (virtual) worlds. *The Journal of Technology Studies*, *40*(2), 54–66. DOI: 10.21061/jots.v40i2.a.1

Emara, T. (2018). Adaptive Power-Saving Mechanism for VoIP Over WiMAX Based on Artificial Neural Network. In Waluyo, A. B. (Ed.), *Algorithms, Methods, and Applications in Mobile Computing and Communications* (pp. 158–177). IGI Global. DOI: 10.4018/978-1-5225-5693-0.ch007

Emara, T., Hassan, E., Trinh, T., Li, G., & Saber, A. (Eds.). (2025b). *The Role of Artificial Intelligence in Advancing Applied Life Sciences*. IGI Global Scientific Publishing. DOI: 10.4018/979-8-3693-9208-9

Emara, T. Z. (2016). Maximizing Power Saving for VoIP over WiMAX Systems. *International Journal of Mobile Computing and Multimedia Communications, 7*(1), 32–40. DOI: 10.4018/IJMCMC.2016010103

Emara, T. Z., Ashraf, R., Saber, A., Trinh, T., & Awad, W. (2025c). A Data Processing Algorithm to Approximate Big Stream Data Analysis. *2nd IEEE International Conference on Machine Intelligence and Smart Innovation (ICMISI 2025)*. DOI: 10.1109/ICMISI65108.2025.11115782

Emara, T. Z., Hassan, E., Elbedwehy, S., & Saber, A. (2025a). A historical perspective on artificial intelligence in applied life sciences. In *The Role of Artificial Intelligence in Advancing Applied Life Sciences* (pp. 49–86). IGI Global Scientific Publishing. DOI: 10.4018/979-8-3693-9208-9.ch002

Emara, T. Z., & Huang, J. Z. (2019a). A distributed data management system to support large-scale data analysis. *Journal of Systems and Software, 148*, 105–115. DOI: 10.1016/j.jss.2018.11.007

Emara, T. Z., & Huang, J. Z. (2019b). RRPlib: A spark library for representing HDFS blocks as a set of random sample data blocks. *Science of Computer Programming, 184*, 102301. DOI: 10.1016/j.scico.2019.102301

Emara, T. Z., Saleh, A. I., & Arafat, H. (2014). Power saving mechanism for VoIP services over WiMAX systems. *Wireless Networks, 20*(5), 975–985. DOI: 10.1007/s11276-013-0650-5

Emara, T. Z., Trinh, T., & Huang, J. Z. (2023). Geographically distributed data management to support large-scale data analysis. *Scientific Reports, 13*(1), 17783. Advance online publication. DOI: 10.1038/s41598-023-44789-x PMID: 37853092

Evans, D. S. (2014). Economic Aspects of Bitcoin and Other Decentralized Public-Ledger Currency Platforms. University of Chicago Coase-Sandor Institute for Law & Economics Research Paper No. 685. DOI: 10.2139/ssrn.2424516

Gawer, A., & Cusumano, M. A. (2014). Industry platforms and ecosystem innovation. *Journal of Product Innovation Management, 31*(3), 417–433. DOI: 10.1111/jpim.12105

Genise, N., & David, B. (2021). Cryptography review of W3C verifiable credentials data model (VCDM) and decentralized identifiers (DIDs) standards and cryptography implementation recommendations. Academic Press.

Hassan, E., Saber, A., Emara, T., & Elbedwehy, S. (2025a). Enhanced Monkeypox Skin Lesion Classification Using Pooling-based Vision Transformer Architecture. In *The Role of Artificial Intelligence in Advancing Applied Life Sciences*. IGI-Global. DOI: 10.4018/979-8-3693-9208-9.ch010

Hatami, M., Qu, Q., Chen, Y., Kholidy, H., Blasch, E., & Ardiles-Cruz, E. (2024). A survey of the real-time metaverse: Challenges and opportunities. *Future Internet*, *16*(10), 379. DOI: 10.3390/fi16100379

Hemachandran, K., & Rodriguez, R. V. (Eds.). (2023). *The business of the metaverse: How to maintain the human element within this new business reality*. CRC Press.

Hsiao, S.-W., Lee, C.-H., Yang, M.-H., & Chen, R.-Q. (2017). User interface based on natural interaction design for seniors. *Computers in Human Behavior*, *75*, 147–159. DOI: 10.1016/j.chb.2017.05.011

Huang, Y., Li, Y. J., & Cai, Z. (2023). Security and privacy in metaverse: A comprehensive survey. *Big Data Mining and Analytics*, *6*(2), 234–247. DOI: 10.26599/BDMA.2022.9020047

Huawei, H., Qinnan, Z., Taotao, L., Qinglin, Y., Zhaokang, Y., Junhao, W., Xiong, Z., Jianming, Z., Wu, J., & Zheng, Z. (2023). Economic systems in the metaverse: Basics, state of the art, and challenges. *ACM Computing Surveys*, *56*(4), 1–33. DOI: 10.1145/3626315

Ismail, L., & Buyya, R. (2023). Metaverse: A vision, architectural elements, and future directions for scalable and realtime virtual worlds. *arXiv preprint arXiv:2308.10559.*

Keatinge, M. (2010). *The expression and constraint of human agency within the massively multiplayer online games of World of Warcraft and Eve-Online: A comparative case study* (Doctoral dissertation, National University of Ireland Maynooth).

Khan, S. N., Loukil, F., Ghedira-Guegan, C., Benkhelifa, E., & Bani-Hani, A. (2021). Blockchain smart contracts: Applications, challenges, and future trends. *Peer-to-Peer Networking and Applications*, *14*(5), 2901–2925. DOI: 10.1007/s12083-021-01127-0 PMID: 33897937

Lanteri, A., Esposito, M., & Cappuccio, M. (2025). Maximizing the economic, environmental, and social impact of the metaverse. *Environmental, and Social Impact of the Metaverse. SSRN.*

Mahmoud, H. H. H., Amer, A. A., & Ismail, T. (2021). 6G: A comprehensive survey on technologies, applications, challenges, and research problems. *Transactions on Emerging Telecommunications Technologies*, *32*(4), e4233. DOI: 10.1002/ett.4233

Mourtzis, D., Panopoulos, N., Angelopoulos, J., Wang, B., & Wang, L. (2022). Human centric platforms for personalized value creation in metaverse. *Journal of Manufacturing Systems*, *65*, 653–659. DOI: 10.1016/j.jmsy.2022.11.004

Mühle, A., Grüner, A., Gayvoronskaya, T., & Meinel, C. (2018). A survey on essential components of a self-sovereign identity. *Computer Science Review*, *30*, 80–86. DOI: 10.1016/j.cosrev.2018.10.002

Pan, J., & McElhannon, J. (2017). Future edge cloud and edge computing for internet of things applications. *IEEE Internet of Things Journal*, *5*(1), 439–449. DOI: 10.1109/JIOT.2017.2767608

Paniagua-Gómez, M., & Fernandez-Carmona, M. (2025). Trends and challenges in real-time stress detection and modulation: The role of the IoT and artificial intelligence. *Electronics (Basel)*, *14*(13), 2581. DOI: 10.3390/electronics14132581

Park, S.-M., & Kim, Y.-G. (2022). A metaverse: Taxonomy, components, applications, and open challenges. *IEEE Access : Practical Innovations, Open Solutions*, *10*, 4209–4251. DOI: 10.1109/ACCESS.2021.3140175

Rawat, D. B., & Hagos, D. H. (2024). Metaverse survey & tutorial: Exploring key requirements, technologies, standards, applications, challenges, and perspectives. *arXiv preprint arXiv:2405.04718.*

Ritsos, P. D. (2006). *Architectures for untethered augmented reality using wearable computers* (Doctoral dissertation, University of Essex). University of Essex Repository.

Rubio-Tamayo, J. L., Gertrudix Barrio, M., & García García, F. (2017). Immersive environments and virtual reality: Systematic review and advances in communication, interaction and simulation. *Multimodal Technologies and Interaction*, *1*(4), 21. DOI: 10.3390/mti1040021

Sadeghi-Niaraki, A., Rahimi, F., Azlan, N. A. E. B., Song, H., Ali, F., & Choi, S.-M. (2025). Groundbreaking taxonomy of metaverse characteristics. *Artificial Intelligence Review*, *58*(8), 244. DOI: 10.1007/s10462-025-11243-5

Salt, B., Atkins, C., & Blackall, L. (2008). Engaging with Second Life: Real education in a virtual world. Academic Press.

Sestino, A., Guido, G., & Peluso, A. M. (2022). *Non-fungible tokens (NFTs). Examining the Impact on Consumers and Marketing Strategies, 1–15.* IGI Global. DOI: 10.1007/978-3-031-07203-1

Shaikh, S., & Jammal, M. (2024). Survey of fault management techniques for edge-enabled distributed metaverse applications. *Computer Networks, 254*, 110803. DOI: 10.1016/j.comnet.2024.110803

Sharma, M., Mahajan, Y., & Saber, A. (2024). Using augmented reality (AR) and the Internet of Things (IoT) to improve water management maintenance and training. In *Innovations in Machine Learning and IoT for Water Management* (pp. 252–270). IGI Global Scientific Publishing.

Shen, L.-H., Feng, K.-T., & Hanzo, L. (2023). Five facets of 6G: Research challenges and opportunities. *ACM Computing Surveys, 55*(11), 1–39. DOI: 10.1145/3571072

Singh, B., Wongmahesak, K., & Chandra, S. (2025). Transforming digital ownership and assessing role of blockchain technology and NFTs in future economy. In *Practical Strategies and Case Studies for Online Marketing 6.0* (pp. 343–368). IGI Global Scientific Publishing. DOI: 10.4018/979-8-3373-2058-8.ch015

Trinh, T., Duc, L. P., Tran, C. T., Duy, T. T., & Emara, T. Z. (2022). A New Stratified Block Model to Process Large-Scale Data for a Small Cluster. In *Lecture Notes on Data Engineering and Communications Technologies* (Vol. 124, pp. 253–263). Springer Science and Business Media Deutschland GmbH. DOI: 10.1007/978-3-030-97610-1_21

Trinh, T., Nguyen, N., Wu, D., Huang, J. Z., & Emara, T. Z. (2019). A New Location-Based Topic Model for Event Attendees Recommendation. In *2019 IEEE-RIVF International Conference on Computing and Communication Technologies (RIVF)* (pp. 106–111). DOI: 10.1109/RIVF.2019.8713716

VuThi, K., VuongThi, N., NguyenXuan, H., Emara, T. Z., & Trinh, T. (2024). Feature Selection Based on Top Frequency. In M. and N. L. A. and L. K. Y. Nguyen Thi Dieu Linh and Dawson (Eds.), Proceedings of the International Conference on Intelligent Systems and Networks (pp. 58–65). Springer Nature Singapore. DOI: 10.1007/978-981-97-5504-2_7

Wang, Y., Wang, L., & Siau, K. L. (2025). Human-centered interaction in virtual worlds: A new era of generative artificial intelligence and metaverse. *International Journal of Human-Computer Interaction, 41*(2), 1459–1501. DOI: 10.1080/10447318.2024.2316376

Wright, A. (2020). The rise of decentralized autonomous organizations: Opportunities and challenges. *Stanford Journal of Blockchain Law & Policy, 4*, 1.

Yang, L., Ni, S.-T., Wang, Y., Yu, A., Lee, J.-A., & Hui, P. (2025). Interoperability of the metaverse: A digital ecosystem perspective review. *IEEE Engineering Management Review*, *53*(3), 29–54. Advance online publication. DOI: 10.1109/EMR.2025.3564923

Zawish, M., Dharejo, F. A., Khowaja, S. A., Raza, S., Davy, S., Dev, K., & Bellavista, P. (2024). AI and 6G into the metaverse: Fundamentals, challenges and future research trends. *IEEE Open Journal of the Communications Society*, *5*, 730–778. DOI: 10.1109/OJCOMS.2024.3349465

Zwitter, A. J., Gstrein, O. J., & Yap, E. (2020). Digital identity and the blockchain: Universal identity management and the concept of the "self-sovereign" individual. *Frontiers in Blockchain*, *3*, 26. DOI: 10.3389/fbloc.2020.00026

Chapter 3
The Role of Speech Processing in the Metaverse:
Bridging Human Communication and Virtual Worlds

Daniel Raj K.
https://orcid.org/0009-0001-9863-5682
Dr. G.U. Pope College of Engineering, India

G. Ponseka
https://orcid.org/0009-0007-5521-3715
Dr. G.U. Pope College of Engineering, India

Robinson Joel M.
https://orcid.org/0000-0002-3030-8431
KCG College of Technology, India

A. Ananthakumari
https://orcid.org/0009-0004-7255-945X
Dr. G.U. Pope College of Engineering, India

Benitlin Subha K.
https://orcid.org/0009-0001-4153-7790
Kings Enginerring College, India

S. Sumathi
https://orcid.org/0000-0003-0518-7591
University VOC College of Engineering, India

L. Jenefas
https://orcid.org/0009-0006-6997-9255
Dr. G.U. Pope College of Engineering, India

ABSTRACT

The metaverse, blending AR, VR, and persistent digital spaces, is reshaping how people interact and communicate. Speech processing covering ASR, NLP, and TTS is vital in enabling intuitive, voice-driven experiences like real-time translation, smart agents, and personalized avatars. This chapter explores these technologies'

DOI: 10.4018/979-8-3373-3043-3.ch003

impact on user experience while addressing critical ethical concerns such as voice data privacy, surveillance, bias, and synthetic voice misuse. It highlights challenges in digital identity and accessibility, especially for marginalized users. With real-world case studies, it advocates for transparent, inclusive, and ethical voice tech governance in virtual spaces.

INTRODUCTION

The metaverse is becoming a big deal, a new digital world that blends our physical and virtual lives. It's built on technologies like virtual reality (VR), augmented reality (AR), artificial intelligence (AI), and blockchain (Saarinen (2025; Kumar et al., 2024) and it's set to change how we connect, work, and play online. As more people spend time in these virtual spaces, we need to find natural, easy ways to communicate. That's where speech processing comes in—it's a key technology for making the metaverse feel more human.

Speech processing technologies—like recognizing what people say (automatic speech recognition), understanding the meaning behind their words (natural language understanding) (Saarinen, 2025; Kumar et al., 2024) and creating lifelike voices (text-to-speech) —allow us to talk to virtual characters, move through virtual worlds, and interact with AI in ways that feel like real conversations. Voice is fast, accessible, and full of emotion, which makes it perfect for creating a sense of realism and presence in immersive environments. As these virtual worlds aim to be more authentic and responsive, voice technology is becoming a fundamental part of the metaverse.

However, relying so much on speech in virtual spaces brings up some serious ethical questions. Our voice data is incredibly personal. It can reveal our identity, emotions, health, and where we're from. When this data is collected in the metaverse—often without us even realizing it—it raises major concerns about privacy, surveillance, and the commercial use of our personal information. Plus, since our voice can be a unique identifier, there's a risk of it being misused. Voice cloning, impersonation, and AI-generated deepfakes could threaten trust and security in these digital worlds, (Zhao et al., 2022; Yang et al., 2022).

Another big problem is the bias in speech recognition systems. These systems can struggle to understand people with different accents, dialects, or speech impediments, as well as those who speak less common languages. When the technology fails to work, users can feel excluded and frustrated, undermining the promise of an inclusive metaverse. This digital exclusion highlights larger inequalities in how AI is designed and used.

This guide will explore the role of speech processing in the metaverse, looking at the technology itself, how it's being used, and the major ethical and social issues that come with it. By examining case studies and analyzing these topics, we'll shed light on both the great potential and the real dangers of voice-based interaction in the metaverse. Our goal is to show how speech technologies can make the metaverse a more natural and engaging place while also advocating for ethical guidelines, inclusive design, and responsible innovation that protect users and ensure everyone can participate equally.

Figure 1. Speech processing in metaverse

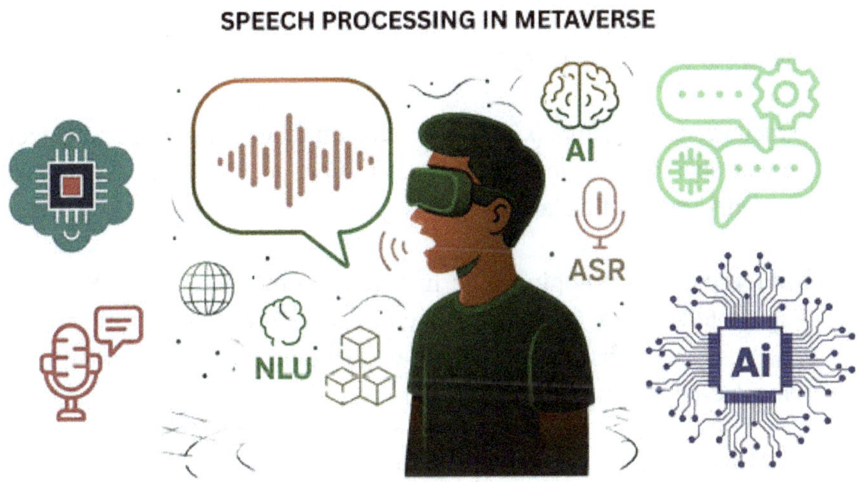

THE EVOLUTION OF VOICE TECHNOLOGY

The journey of speech processing shows how we've moved from basic, command-driven systems to sophisticated, AI-powered conversational interfaces. This progress is crucial for creating the seamless, voice-based interactions we see in today's virtual environments.

From Rules to Data

Early voice systems were simple. They relied on hand-coded rules and could only understand a small number of words. The big change came with machine learning, especially with Hidden Markov Models (HMMs), (Hsu, 2012). This allowed systems to learn from data, making them much more accurate.

The Deep Learning Revolution

The real breakthrough happened in the 2010s with deep learning, (Mehrish et al., 2023; Bak et al., 2024). Technologies like deep neural networks (DNNs) and recurrent models made voice recognition incredibly precise. These are the same technologies that power today's virtual assistants, allowing for real-time speech recognition, voice synthesis, and natural language understanding (Kumar et al., 2024; Mehta & Gupta, 2025) in virtual reality and metaverse platforms.

The Metaverse Landscape

The metaverse is a complex digital ecosystem that blends immersive technologies to create shared, persistent virtual worlds. For speech to play a central role, it's essential to understand this landscape.

- **Immersive Technologies:** The metaverse combines Virtual Reality (VR), Augmented Reality (AR), and Mixed Reality (MR). These technologies create experiences that either simulate or enhance the real world. Voice is a critical component for interacting within these immersive spaces, making conversations feel more natural, (Zagalo et al., 2012; Saarinen, 2025).
- **Decentralization and Interoperability:** Powered by technologies like blockchain, the metaverse allows users to own their digital assets and identities. This means you can take your virtual items and identity from one platform to another. Your voice can become a key part of this cross-platform identity.
- **Social and Experiential Platforms:** Platforms like Meta Horizon Worlds, Decentraland, and Roblox show how the metaverse is a place for socializing, gaming, and commerce. In these environments, voice is vital for real-time interaction and building social connections with people from all over the world, (Kumar et al., 2024).

ETHICAL AND SOCIETAL CONCERNS

As voice technology becomes a core part of the metaverse, it brings significant ethical challenges. Addressing these issues—from privacy to fairness—is crucial for building a responsible and inclusive digital future.

- **Privacy and Surveillance:** The continuous collection of voice data in virtual spaces raises serious concerns about privacy. Without your informed consent, this data can be used for profiling or other intrusive purposes.
- **Bias and Exclusion:** Many voice systems struggle to recognize diverse accents, dialects, or speech impairments. This can lead to an unequal experience and exclude some users from participating fully.
- **The Threat of Voice Cloning:** The rise of advanced voice synthesis and cloning technologies creates a risk of identity theft and fraud. This can make it hard to know who you're really talking to and can undermine trust in virtual interactions.

THE POWER OF VOICE AS A HUMAN-CENTERED INTERFACE

Speech is our most natural form of communication, making it an ideal interface for the metaverse. It goes beyond simple commands to enable authentic, emotional, and personalized interactions.

- **A Natural Experience:** Voice interfaces reduce the need for complex physical inputs, allowing you to interact with virtual worlds in a more intuitive and fluid way. It's like talking to a person rather than typing on a keyboard.
- **Emotional Connection:** Your voice carries emotion and nuance. In the metaverse, this helps create more realistic avatars and deepens social bonds within virtual spaces.
- **Personalization:** Your voice data can be used to tailor your experience in real time, adapting responses, environments, or avatars based on your unique preferences and behavior.

SUPPORTING THEORIES FOR SPEECH IN THE METAVERSE

Several theories help us understand the profound role of speech in virtual environments, from how we use it to how it shapes our experiences.

- **Human-Computer Interaction (HCI):** This field focuses on how people engage with technology. In the metaverse, it helps us understand the usability of voice interfaces and how they can be combined with other actions like hand gestures.
- **Embodied Cognition:** This theory suggests that our understanding is tied to our body and environment. In a virtual world, this means your experience

is enhanced when your voice, avatar movements, and surroundings are all in sync.

- **Socio-Technical Systems Theory:** This framework looks at the interplay between technology and society. It helps us analyze the wider social impact of voice technology within virtual communities.

MAKING THE METAVERSE ACCESSIBLE AND INCLUSIVE

Voice processing has the potential to make the metaverse more accessible, but only if its design prioritizes the needs of all users.

- **Assistive Communication:** Voice interfaces can empower people with disabilities, particularly those with limited motor skills, to navigate and interact independently.
- **Language Diversity:** Supporting multiple languages and dialects is key to ensuring global participation and inclusion.
- **The Equity Challenge:** A significant hurdle is overcoming the bias in datasets. If voice models aren't trained on diverse speech patterns, they can lead to an inconsistent or exclusionary experience for some users.

VOICE AS A DIGITAL IDENTITY

In the metaverse, your voice is not just a tool; it's a part of your digital identity. It can be used to represent individuality, authenticity, and security.

- **Biometric Security:** Your unique voice pattern can serve as a form of biometric identification, offering a convenient and secure way to log in or personalize your avatar's behavior.
- **Authentic Expression:** You can use voice avatars and modulation to project an identity that aligns with your personal preferences, offering a new level of self-expression.
- **The Risk of Manipulation:** The same technology that allows for unique self-expression also enables voice cloning and deepfakes, which can erode trust and make it difficult to verify who you're talking to.

SPEECH PROCESSING APPLICATIONS IN THE METAVERSE

Speech processing technologies play a pivotal role in shaping how users interact, navigate, and communicate within the metaverse, (Bae, 2022; Wang et al., 2023). From enabling voice-controlled environments to powering intelligent virtual assistants, these applications enhance user immersion, accessibility, and personalization. As metaverse platforms evolve, speech becomes a core interface that supports real-time engagement, emotional expression, and seamless collaboration across virtual spaces.

Figure 2. Speech processing applications in the metaverse

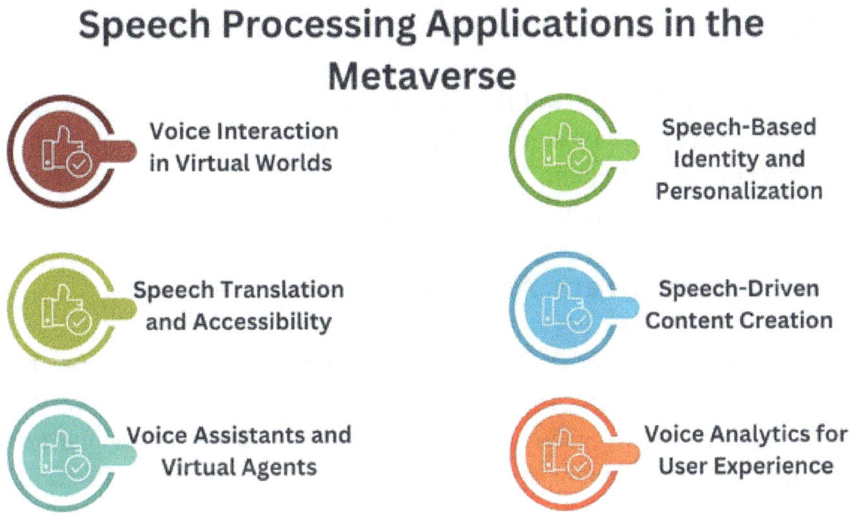

Voice Interaction in Virtual Worlds

Voice interaction is transforming the way users engage within virtual worlds, offering a more natural and immersive alternative to text or gesture-based inputs. By enabling real-time, spoken communication, it enhances the sense of presence, fosters social connection, and allows for more intuitive control in complex virtual environments.

- **Real-Time Communication:** Enables seamless conversations between users and avatars in shared virtual spaces.
- **Hands-Free Navigation:** Allows users to control environments or perform tasks using voice commands.

- **Enhanced Social Presence:** Adds tone, emotion, and nuance to interactions, making virtual experiences feel more human and connected.

Speech-Based Identity and Personalization

In the metaverse, speech is more than a communication tool—it becomes a unique identifier and a medium for tailoring experiences. Voice-based technologies can recognize individual users, adapt virtual environments to their preferences, and enable expressive digital identities, making interactions more secure, personalized, and immersive.

- **Voice Biometrics:** Uses unique vocal traits to verify identity and enable secure access.
- **Personalized Avatars and Responses:** Adapts tone, content, or interactions based on user speech patterns and preferences.
- **Self-Expression through Voice Modulation:** Allows users to modify or enhance their voice to reflect chosen digital identities.

Speech Translation and Accessibility

Speech translation plays a crucial role in bridging language barriers within the metaverse, enabling users from diverse linguistic backgrounds to interact seamlessly. Coupled with accessibility features, these technologies ensure a more inclusive digital environment, where communication remains fluid and accessible to all, regardless of language or disability.

- **Real-Time Multilingual Communication:** Speech translation enables users to converse across languages instantly, enhancing global interaction.
- **Assistive Speech Recognition:** Provides alternative communication for individuals with speech impairments, enabling participation in virtual spaces.
- **Closed Captioning and Voice-to-Text:** Ensures accessibility by converting speech into text for users with hearing impairments, (Lee et al., 2021).

Voice Assistants and Virtual Agents

Voice assistants are integral to the user experience in the metaverse, providing on-demand assistance and controlling virtual environments. These AI-driven agents can understand natural language, respond contextually, and guide users through complex virtual spaces, improving usability and engagement.

- **Natural Language Interaction:** Enables users to communicate with virtual agents using everyday language, enhancing ease of use.
- **Contextual Awareness:** Voice assistants adapt their responses based on the virtual environment and user behavior.
- **Task Automation:** Helps users perform tasks efficiently, from navigating virtual spaces to managing digital assets.

Speech-Driven Content Creation

In the metaverse, speech-driven content creation allows users to create, modify, and manipulate virtual environments using their voices. This enables a more dynamic and creative process, offering an intuitive alternative to traditional, text or gesture-based inputs.

- **Voice-Controlled Design Tools:** Users can modify digital environments, objects, or avatars by speaking commands.
- **AI-Generated Voice Content:** Speech processing technologies generate voiceovers or audio content for immersive experiences.
- **Interactive Storytelling:** Voice enables users to influence or co-create narrative elements, enhancing engagement in virtual worlds.

Voice Analytics for User Experience

Voice analytics in the metaverse can extract valuable insights from spoken interactions, including sentiment, emotion, and intent, (Zhao et al., 2022). These insights help personalize experiences, refine virtual environments, and enhance user satisfaction by responding to emotional and behavioral cues.

- **Emotion Recognition:** Analyzes tone, pitch, and cadence to detect user emotions, adjusting interactions accordingly.
- **Sentiment Analysis:** Gauges the user's attitude or mood, allowing virtual agents to respond empathetically.
- **Behavioural Insights:** Identifies patterns in speech to predict user preferences and optimize virtual interactions.

Speech for Collaborative Workspaces

In the metaverse, speech processing supports collaboration in virtual workspaces, making it easier for teams to interact and work together in real-time, regardless of geographic location. Voice facilitates hands-free communication, efficient decision-making, and seamless collaboration across complex virtual environments, (Kumar et al., 2024).

- **Voice-Controlled Collaboration Tools:** Facilitates hands-free collaboration, allowing users to manage tasks, share content, and interact without interrupting workflow.
- **Real-Time Communication:** Ensures smooth, synchronous communication between team members in virtual environments.
- **Task Delegation and Workflow Management:** Voice commands help automate task assignments and manage projects in real-time, improving productivity.

CASE STUDIES AND INDUSTRY IMPLEMENTATIONS

As the metaverse continues to expand, several industries are adopting speech processing technologies to enhance user interaction, accessibility, and engagement. Real-world implementations—from virtual collaboration platforms to gaming and education—demonstrate how voice interfaces can create more intuitive, inclusive, and immersive digital experiences. These case studies not only showcase the practical benefits of voice integration but also reveal ethical, technical, and design challenges that developers must navigate. This section explores notable examples where speech processing has been effectively applied within metaverse ecosystems.

Gaming Industry: Voice Interaction in Virtual Worlds

In the gaming industry, speech processing has transformed how players interact with characters, environments, and other users. Voice-driven gameplay has not only enhanced immersion but also enabled players to experience deeper, more personalized interactions within digital worlds.

- **Voice-Controlled Gameplay:** Games like Star Trek: Bridge Crew use voice commands to control actions, offering a hands-free and immersive experience.
- **Speech-Driven NPC Interactions:** Games like Red Dead Redemption 2 incorporate voice recognition to enhance non-player character (NPC) interactions, making the world feel more dynamic.
- **Multiplayer Voice Communication:** Platforms like Discord integrate voice chat for real-time player communication, facilitating seamless collaboration and social interaction in multiplayer environments.

Virtual Education: Enhancing Learning through Voice Technology

Voice technologies have made significant strides in virtual education, enabling interactive, adaptive, and personalized learning experiences. Educational institutions and platforms are adopting speech processing tools to enhance engagement and accessibility for students in virtual classrooms.

- **Speech-Activated Learning Tools:** Virtual classrooms utilize voice assistants to help students navigate through materials and ask questions during lessons.
- **Language Learning Platforms:** Applications like Duolingo use speech recognition to evaluate pronunciation, helping learners improve their speaking skills interactively.
- **Inclusive Education:** Tools such as Microsoft's Immersive Reader use speech-to-text and voice synthesis to assist students with learning disabilities, promoting accessibility in virtual learning environments.

Virtual Healthcare: Speech Processing in Telemedicine

In the healthcare sector, speech processing enhances patient care through virtual consultations, voice-powered health tracking, and improved accessibility for patients with disabilities. Voice interfaces allow doctors and patients to interact naturally, improving the overall telehealth experience.

- **Voice-Enabled Patient Interactions:** Virtual healthcare platforms, like Babylon Health, use voice assistants to streamline patient consultations, providing quicker responses and diagnoses.
- **Speech for Disability Assistance:** Tools such as Nuance's Dragon Medical One assist medical professionals with voice commands for dictation and hands-free note-taking, improving workflow efficiency.
- **Remote Health Monitoring:** Speech-driven health apps enable patients to report symptoms and receive feedback from virtual health assistants, reducing the need for in-person visits.

Corporate and Enterprise Solutions: Voice for Collaboration and Productivity

In the business world, speech processing is being integrated into virtual workspaces, enhancing productivity, communication, and decision-making. Enterprises are adopting voice technology to improve team collaboration and create more efficient, immersive work environments.

- **Voice-Activated Productivity Tools:** Platforms like Microsoft Teams use voice commands to manage schedules, meetings, and collaboration tasks, enhancing workflow efficiency.
- **Real-Time Translation and Transcription:** Tools such as Zoom incorporate speech-to-text and translation features, enabling smooth communication in multilingual, global teams.
- **Voice-Driven Data Analytics:** Virtual assistants integrated with enterprise systems help executives access data insights and generate reports using natural language queries.

Social Platforms: Enhancing Interaction with Speech

In social metaverse platforms, voice processing facilitates communication, emotional connection, and social presence. Platforms are increasingly relying on voice interfaces to create more immersive and engaging social spaces where users interact in real-time, (Chakraborty & Dadhich, 2023).

- **Voice Avatars and Identity Expression:** Social platforms like VRChat and Rec Room use voice customization to help users express identity through personalized voice avatars.
- **Voice Interaction for Socializing:** Virtual worlds such as Second Life integrate voice chat to enable spontaneous and real-time conversations among users in shared spaces.
- **Emotional and Social Context:** Platforms incorporate emotion detection and sentiment analysis, enabling avatars to adjust behavior based on the user's tone and mood.

Speech Processing in Virtual Commerce

In virtual commerce, voice technology is enhancing how users interact with digital marketplaces, improving product discovery, transactions, and customer service. Voice-driven shopping experiences and conversational agents are reshaping the e-commerce landscape in the metaverse.

- **Voice-Activated Shopping Assistants:** Virtual shopping assistants guide users through product selections and make purchasing recommendations, offering hands-free interactions.

- **Speech for Payment and Transactions:** Platforms like Amazon Alexa and Google Assistant allow voice commands for seamless purchasing and payment in virtual environments.
- **Customer Support via Voice:** Virtual agents powered by speech recognition handle customer queries, troubleshooting, and support in real-time.

Speech Technology in Virtual Tourism and Travel

Speech processing is revolutionizing virtual tourism by enabling users to explore and interact with virtual destinations through voice commands, (Zagalo et al., 2012). This enhances the experience by offering personalized tours, local language interactions, and navigation assistance.

- **Voice-Guided Virtual Tours:** Speech-based navigation helps users explore virtual tourist sites, museums, and cities with an interactive, hands-free experience.
- **Multilingual Support for Travelers:** Voice translation tools provide real-time multilingual communication, assisting tourists in understanding local languages and cultures.
- **Voice for Customization:** Virtual travel platforms use speech to personalize experiences based on users' preferences, from itinerary planning to destination recommendations.

Speech for Security and Authentication in the Metaverse

Speech processing plays a crucial role in securing virtual environments, providing biometric authentication and voice-based security measures. Voice biometrics offers a secure and convenient alternative to traditional password-based systems, ensuring privacy and safety in the metaverse.

- **Voice Biometrics for Authentication:** Voice recognition is used for secure login processes, ensuring that only authorized users can access certain virtual spaces.
- **Fraud Prevention:** Voiceprints are used to detect potential fraud or unauthorized access, making virtual transactions and interactions more secure.
- **Seamless User Identification:** Integrating voice authentication enhances user experience by simplifying access without compromising security.

Speech-Driven Gaming and Interactive Entertainment

In the entertainment sector, speech processing has revolutionized how users interact with games and virtual experiences, offering more immersive, hands-free control over gameplay. From voice commands in virtual environments to voice-based NPC interactions, speech enhances both the player's experience and the overall entertainment value.

- **Voice-Controlled Game Mechanics:** Speech technology in games like Madden NFL allows players to control in-game actions through voice commands, creating a more dynamic and immersive experience.
- **Interactive Storytelling in Games:** Speech recognition enables players to influence narratives and character interactions in real time, as seen in games like Mass Effect and Detroit: Become Human.
- **Social Interaction in Virtual Gaming Worlds:** Games such as Fortnite and Minecraft integrate voice chat features to enable more natural and real-time communication players, enhancing social engagement.

Virtual Reality (VR) and Augmented Reality (AR) Integration With Speech

In VR and AR, speech processing enhances immersion by allowing users to interact with virtual environments naturally. Speech serves as a primary tool for navigation, task completion, and communication in these highly immersive spaces.

- **Hands-Free Navigation in VR/AR:** Users can navigate and interact with virtual objects using voice commands, improving accessibility and user experience.
- **Voice-Activated Object Manipulation:** Speech technology allows users to manipulate virtual objects or environments, such as resizing or moving items in a VR space using only voice.
- **Immersive Virtual Interactions:** In AR and VR environments like Microsoft HoloLens, voice interaction provides a more fluid and intuitive user experience, enabling users to control the environment through natural language.

Speech-Based Feedback and Virtual Coaching

In training and simulation environments, speech-based feedback is used to guide users, providing real-time coaching and performance evaluation. Whether in professional training or personal development, speech recognition systems help users refine skills and improve outcomes.

- **Voice-Activated Training Programs:** In virtual simulations, users receive speech-driven feedback on their actions, guiding them through step-by-step instructions.
- **Performance Evaluation:** Virtual coaches analyze user responses and provide constructive feedback to enhance learning in environments like virtual fitness coaching or skill-building platforms.
- **Real-Time Assistance for Skill Development:** Speech-based systems help users learn new skills by providing hands-free guidance in real-time, from virtual cooking lessons to language practice.

ETHICAL IMPLICATIONS OF SPEECH IN THE METAVERSE

The integration of speech processing technologies in the metaverse brings about significant ethical challenges that must be addressed to ensure a fair, secure, and respectful virtual environment. As speech becomes a primary mode of interaction, concerns around data privacy, user consent, and surveillance arise. The ability to capture and analyze voice data can lead to unintended consequences, such as unauthorized use of personal information, biased recognition algorithms, and issues with voice cloning. Furthermore, the accessibility of voice-based interactions in the metaverse must consider equity, ensuring that individuals with disabilities or those speaking non-standard dialects are not marginalized. This section delves into these ethical concerns and explores frameworks that can help guide the responsible development and deployment of speech technologies in immersive virtual spaces.

Privacy Concerns in Voice Data Collection

The collection of voice data in the metaverse raises significant privacy concerns. Voice data is inherently personal, and its collection, storage, and use need to be handled with the utmost care to avoid misuse and ensure user consent.

- **Data Ownership and Control:** Users should have control over their voice data, determining how it's used, stored, and shared.
- **Unauthorized Access:** Voice data can be accessed and misused by third parties, leading to privacy violations.
- **Long-Term Storage Risks:** The prolonged storage of voice data increases the risk of it being compromised in the future.

Bias and Discrimination in Speech Recognition Systems

Speech recognition systems often exhibit biases based on accent, gender, or race, which can marginalize users who do not fit the "norm" of these systems. This presents an ethical challenge of fairness and inclusivity.

- **Accent and Dialect Issues:** Systems may struggle with non-native accents or regional dialects, leading to inaccurate responses.
- **Gender and Age Bias:** Systems may underperform when recognizing voices that don't conform to typical gender or age norms.
- **Cultural Sensitivity:** Lack of cultural context can result in the misinterpretation of speech, particularly in diverse virtual environments.

Figure 3. Ethical implications of speech in the metaverse

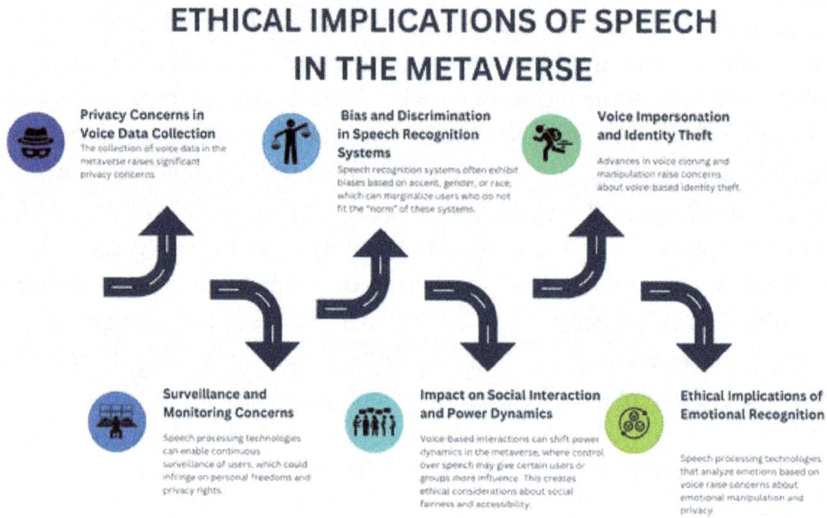

Voice Impersonation and Identity Theft

Advances in voice cloning and manipulation raise concerns about voice-based identity theft. Impersonating someone's voice can have serious ethical implications in terms of fraud, misrepresentation, and unauthorized access to secure environments.

- **Voice Cloning Technology:** Technology that mimics someone's voice can be used maliciously, leading to fraud or identity theft.
- **Privacy Violations:** Unauthorised use of someone's voice for personal gain is an invasion of privacy.
- **Authenticity and Trust Issues:** The ability to fake a voice undermines trust and authenticity, especially in security-sensitive areas.

Consent and Transparency in Voice Data Usage

Ensuring users are fully informed about how their voice data is being used is vital. Consent should be clear, and transparency should guide the collection, processing, and sharing of this data.

- **Clear Consent Mechanisms:** Users must understand how their data will be used and explicitly agree to it.
- **Opt-Out Options:** There should be a mechanism for users to opt out of voice data collection if they choose.
- **Transparent Data Usage Policies:** Platforms should disclose how voice data is processed, analyzed, and shared, ensuring transparency.

Surveillance and Monitoring Concerns

Speech processing technologies can enable continuous surveillance of users, which could infringe on personal freedoms and privacy rights. The ethical question arises as to where the line should be drawn between security and individual liberty, (Chakraborty & Dadhich, 2023).

- **Surveillance without Consent:** Continuous voice monitoring can happen without users' knowledge, leading to unwarranted surveillance.
- **Emotional Profiling:** Voice analysis can be used to track users' emotional states, potentially profiling individuals without their consent.
- **Balancing Safety and Privacy:** While surveillance can increase security, it may also compromise users' privacy, raising ethical concerns.

Impact on Social Interaction and Power Dynamics

Voice-based interactions can shift power dynamics in the metaverse, where control over speech may give certain users or groups more influence. This creates ethical considerations about social fairness and accessibility.

- **Voice as a Social Identifier:** Users with specific vocal traits may be unfairly judged or discriminated against based on their voice.
- **Power Imbalances:** Those with clear, 'standardized' voices may dominate conversations or interactions, marginalizing others.
- **Manipulation of Voice for Influence:** Some users may use voice manipulation to exert undue influence over others, raising ethical concerns around consent.

Accessibility Challenges in Speech-Based Interactions

Speech-based systems can inadvertently exclude individuals with disabilities or speech impairments. This raises concerns about inclusivity and fairness in voice-driven interactions within the metaverse.

- **Speech Disabilities:** Users with speech impairments may struggle to interact effectively with speech-driven platforms, leading to exclusion.
- **Language Barriers:** Non-native speakers or those with speech impediments may face challenges in voice recognition systems, creating accessibility issues.
- **Alternative Interaction Methods:** The metaverse must ensure that voice isn't the only mode of interaction, offering alternatives for those who need them.

Ethical Implications of Emotional Recognition

Speech processing technologies that analyze emotions based on voice raise concerns about emotional manipulation and privacy. The ability to detect and respond to emotions could be misused for marketing or social control.

- **Emotional Manipulation:** Understanding emotions through voice could be used to influence decisions or behaviors in an unethical manner.
- **Privacy Concerns in Emotional Data:** Users may not consent to the collection or analysis of their emotional responses, which could be invasive.
- **Ethical Use of Emotional Data:** Ethical guidelines are needed to ensure that emotional data is used responsibly and not exploited for commercial or manipulative purposes.

SOCIETAL IMPACTS AND FUTURE CHALLENGES

The integration of speech processing in the metaverse is poised to significantly transform societal interactions, communication, and digital participation. As voice becomes a dominant form of interaction in virtual spaces, it can enhance accessibility, inclusivity, and personalization. However, it also presents new challenges, such as potential social inequalities, privacy concerns, and the erosion of social norms in digital environments. This section explores the broader societal impacts of speech technologies, focusing on both the benefits and the challenges that lie ahead in the evolution of speech-driven virtual worlds.

Impact of Speech Processing on Communication and Social Interaction

Speech processing is reshaping the way people connect in the metaverse. Unlike text-based chat, which can sometimes feel mechanical or slow, voice brings spontaneity, warmth, and presence into digital spaces. When you hear someone's tone, pause, or laughter, the conversation feels more human, even if you are thousands of miles apart. At the same time, this shift also raises questions about how our social lives may change as digital voices become central to our relationships.

Enhancing Real-Time Communication

Voice technology makes conversations in virtual spaces flow more like those in the physical world.

- **Natural Flow**: Speaking is faster and more intuitive than typing. It allows people to express themselves fully—capturing hesitations, excitement, or humor in ways that text alone cannot.
- **Rich with Emotion**: Tone, pitch, and rhythm add layers of meaning. A simple "I'm fine" can sound happy, tired, or sad depending on the voicc. This depth helps people understand each other better and fosters empathy.
- **Instant Feedback**: Real-time voice exchange strengthens engagement. Instead of waiting for typed replies, users can respond immediately, creating a stronger sense of presence in the metaverse.

Building Social Connections and Virtual Relationships

Beyond efficiency, speech processing plays a powerful role in shaping communities and relationships in digital spaces.

- **Global Bridges**: Voice communication allows people from different parts of the world to connect naturally, breaking down cultural and geographic barriers. A student in India can collaborate with a designer in France as if they were in the same room.
- **Community Bonds**: Shared conversations create deeper connections than avatars or visuals alone. Virtual communities built around voice can feel more authentic because interactions are based on lived experiences and emotions rather than appearances.
- **Challenges of Over-Reliance**: While voice strengthens digital bonds, it also risks reducing face-to-face interactions in real life. Too much dependence on virtual conversations might contribute to feelings of social isolation, especially if online interactions begin replacing in-person ones.

Voice as a Tool for Personalization and Identity

Your voice becomes a unique signature in the metaverse, just as distinct as your avatar's appearance.

- **Shaping Your Space:** Systems can learn your tone and style to create personalized virtual environments. For example, if you speak with a calm and measured tone, your virtual space might adapt with softer colors and ambient sounds. This personalization boosts user engagement and satisfaction.
- **Custom Avatars and Assistants:** Your voice profile can be used to generate custom avatars and personal AI assistants that reflect your personality. This level of customization allows for a more authentic and immersive experience.
- **Expressing Identity:** Users can modify their voice to express a unique digital identity, exploring different genders, ages, or even fantastical personas. However, this raises important ethical questions, as **voice cloning and deepfakes** present serious risks to trust and privacy, making it difficult to distinguish between a real person and a synthetic voice.

Accessibility With Speech Technology

Voice technology is a powerful tool for making the metaverse accessible to everyone, especially those with disabilities.

- **Hands-Free Navigation:** For individuals with mobility or vision challenges, voice commands offer a simple, hands-free way to navigate virtual spaces. This integration with screen readers and other assistive technologies makes the metaverse more usable and inclusive.

- **Breaking Down Language Barriers:** Real-time speech-to-text and translation services are essential for global communication. They allow people from different linguistic backgrounds to communicate effortlessly. Additionally, real-time subtitling ensures that users who are hearing-impaired can participate fully in conversations.

Ethics of Voice Data

The widespread collection of voice data in the metaverse comes with significant ethical responsibilities.

- **Privacy and Surveillance Risks:** Constant voice monitoring could compromise personal privacy. Platforms must find a balance between providing a secure environment and respecting a user's right to digital freedom.
- **Data Security:** Voiceprints are highly sensitive and vulnerable to data breaches. Companies have a major responsibility to securely store this data and use it ethically, ensuring that it is not misused or sold without user consent.

Social Inequalities

Despite its promise, speech technology can perpetuate existing social inequalities.

- **Economic and Geographic Gaps:** Not everyone has access to the high-quality devices and fast internet connections needed for seamless speech-driven experiences.
- **Bias in Systems:** Many current systems struggle with diverse accents, dialects, and speech patterns, leading to misrecognition and frustration. Designing inclusive systems that are fair to all users is essential to avoid creating a new digital divide.

Human-AI Interaction

Voice brings AI closer to a human-like level of interaction, but this comes with both benefits and risks.

- **Emotion-Aware AI:** While AI that can detect emotion in your voice can seem empathetic, there's a risk of manipulation. We must ensure these systems are designed to support, not exploit, human emotions.

- **Balancing Connections:** Over-reliance on AI companions could weaken our need for genuine human connections. The goal should be to use AI to enhance, not replace, real social interaction.

Education and Learning

Voice technology is transforming how we learn and work in virtual environments.

- **Personalized Learning:** In educational metaverse spaces, students can get real-time voice feedback on their work, enabling personalized lessons and adaptive tutoring. However, challenges with cost and infrastructure remain.
- **Enhanced Productivity:** In virtual workplaces, voice-activated tools allow for hands-free multitasking and streamlined collaboration. While this may automate some jobs, it also creates a demand for new skills. A key challenge is managing the blurring line between work and personal life, which can lead to increased stress.

Work and Productivity

- **Tools for Efficiency:** Voice-activated tools enable hands-free work, multitasking, and streamlined collaboration, enhancing productivity in virtual offices.
- **Job Displacement vs. Reskilling:** While automation may displace some jobs, it also creates new roles and demands for reskilling.
- **Blurred Boundaries:** The integration of voice tools into both work and personal life can blur boundaries, raising concerns about increased stress and burnout.

FUTURE DIRECTIONS AND RESEARCH OPPORTUNITIES

The metaverse is not just about building bigger digital worlds—it is about making them feel alive, human, and meaningful. Voice is one of the most natural ways we connect with others, so it is no surprise that speech processing is becoming the backbone of interaction in these spaces. In the future, voice will not simply be a tool to issue commands; it will carry our emotions, languages, identities, and even our ethical values into digital life.

This next stage of research is about more than technical innovation. It is about asking: *How do we create systems that are fair, accessible, and culturally sensitive? How do we protect voices while also empowering them? And how do we make sure these technologies respect the environment while enriching our lives?* Answering these questions will require collaboration across technology, psychology, law, and society.

Emotionally Aware Voice

We do not just speak in words—we speak in feelings. A happy laugh, a frustrated sigh, or a trembling voice often says more than sentences ever could.

- **Understanding Sentiment**: Future voice systems will be able to sense emotions hidden in tone, pitch, or rhythm. Imagine calling technical support in the metaverse and the AI instantly recognizes your frustration, then softens its voice and offers step-by-step guidance in a calm and supportive way.
- **Responsive Avatars**: Avatars will evolve from being simple digital characters to empathetic companions. They will smile, pause, or change their voice to match your mood. This could be life-changing in spaces like virtual therapy or online classrooms, where empathy can make all the difference.
- **Ethical Balance**: Of course, there is a fine line between support and manipulation. Using someone's emotions without consent can be dangerous. That's why future research must put ethical guardrails in place—ensuring transparency, fairness, and user choice.

Breaking Language Barriers

One of the promises of the metaverse is a world where people from different corners of the globe can meet, share, and collaborate instantly. But language often stands in the way.

- **Real-Time Translation**: Picture attending a global business meeting or a cultural festival in the metaverse. You speak in Tamil, and someone else hears you instantly in Spanish—without delay. That's the dream of real time translation.
- **Cultural Accuracy**: Yet translation is not just about words. It is about meaning. For example, a friendly phrase in English might sound disrespectful in Japanese if translated too literally. Future systems will need to respect cultural context, tone, and politeness.
- **Equity for All Languages**: A bigger challenge is supporting smaller, low-resource languages. Many communities risk being left behind if only global languages dominate. The future must include building speech datasets for

underrepresented languages, preserving diversity and ensuring everyone has a voice online.

Protecting Voice and Privacy

Our voices are deeply personal. They reveal not just identity, but also emotions, age, and even health conditions. That makes protecting them in the metaverse an urgent priority.

- **Data Ownership**: Users must have the right to decide how their voice is stored, shared, or deleted. Consent frameworks, much like GDPR, should become the global standard.
- **Guarding Against Cloning**: With deepfake technology, voices can now be cloned with frightening accuracy. Imagine someone using your voice to commit fraud or spread misinformation. Future systems must be able to detect and block such impersonation.
- **Global Standards**: Because the metaverse is global, one country's rules will not be enough. Policymakers across borders must work together to create shared guidelines for protecting voices.

Making Systems Inclusive

Not everyone speaks the same way, and technology must adapt to people—not the other way around.

- **Accessibility for All**: For individuals with disabilities, voice-based systems can be empowering. A person with motor impairments could use voice to move around virtual spaces. Someone with speech challenges could use tailored recognition tools to express themselves more freely.
- **Accents and Dialects**: Many current systems fail when faced with strong accents or regional dialects. The future must move past this bias and embrace the full spectrum of human speech.
- **Personalization**: Imagine setting up your virtual assistant to sound like your favorite teacher, or adjusting its speaking style to be fast and professional for work, but slow and friendly at home. Personalization will make digital agents feel less robotic and more like trusted companions.

Towards Sustainable Voice Tech

Behind every AI voice system lies massive computing power—and energy consumption. Sustainability must be part of the future.

- **Smarter Models**: Instead of relying on giant, resource-hungry algorithms, researchers are working on lightweight models that run on smaller devices like smart glasses or wearables.
- **Local Processing**: By processing speech directly on your device (edge computing) instead of sending it to the cloud, we can cut down on both energy use and privacy risks.
- **Green Training**: Training AI often consumes as much energy as powering a small town. Using renewable-powered data centers and reusing pre-trained models will help reduce the environmental footprint.

Voice in Collaboration and Learning

In the metaverse, voice will not just be for chatting—it will power creativity, education, and teamwork.

- **Creative Tools**: Imagine sketching a 3D model or writing a script with nothing but your voice. This opens doors for artists, designers, and even those who cannot use traditional tools.
- **Virtual Classrooms**: Voice-based tutors could guide students in real time, adjusting their tone and pace to match each learner's style. For instance, slowing down for beginners or offering challenging problems to advanced learners.
- **Workspaces of the Future**: In virtual offices, AI voice assistants could schedule tasks, summarize discussions, or coordinate projects, making teamwork smoother and more productive.

Looking at Long-Term Impacts

The future is not just about building technology but also about understanding how it changes us as people.

- **Cognitive and Social Shifts**: How will daily interaction with voice AI affect the way we think, learn, or socialize? Will children grow up speaking differently if their main conversational partner is a digital assistant?

- **Measuring Inclusivity**: New ways of measuring user satisfaction and fairness are needed. Success cannot only be about accuracy—it must also include accessibility, cultural sensitivity, and emotional well-being.
- **Ethical Responsibility**: Long-term studies must continue to explore risks like addiction, over-reliance, or misuse of voice systems. By keeping ethics at the center, we can ensure the metaverse remains a space that serves humanity rather than exploits it.

SPEECH PROCESSING AND USER ENGAGEMENT IN VIRTUAL ECONOMIES

As virtual economies continue to grow within the metaverse, speech processing technology is becoming a critical component in shaping user engagement. By integrating voice interactions into digital environments, it eliminates the need for traditional input devices like keyboards or touchscreens, making user experiences more intuitive and seamless. Speech enables a more immersive, hands-free, and natural way for users to interact with virtual marketplaces, social spaces, and gaming environments. In virtual economies, speech processing not only facilitates easier transactions but also enriches social interactions, gamified elements, and the personalization of experiences, driving higher participation, retention, and commerce. This integration fosters a user-friendly ecosystem where both social and economic dynamics can evolve fluidly and efficiently, ensuring that voice remains a pivotal driver of engagement in virtual worlds.

Voice-Driven Transactions and E-Commerce

Voice-enabled transactions offer users a seamless and intuitive way to interact with virtual marketplaces and complete purchases.

- **Voice-Activated Product Discovery:** Users can effortlessly search for products through speech, making virtual shopping faster and more engaging.
- **Efficient Voice Payments:** Speech processing simplifies payment methods, allowing users to complete transactions just by speaking, ensuring speed and convenience.
- **Voice-Activated Negotiation and Bargaining:** Users can negotiate prices and terms in virtual marketplaces using voice, enabling real-time interactions and dynamic pricing based on speech cues.

Gamification and Speech-Enhanced User Experience

Voice processing will add a new dimension to gaming, making the interaction more immersive and responsive.

- **Voice-Controlled Gameplay:** Players can execute in-game actions through voice commands, enhancing the gaming experience and making it feel more natural.
- **Dynamic and Personalized Storylines:** Voice inputs influence the progression of narratives, allowing for customized story arcs and interactive dialogue with NPCs.
- **Enhanced Multiplayer Coordination:** Real-time voice communication fosters better collaboration and strategy in multiplayer games, enhancing teamwork and player interaction.

Speech in Social Interaction and Virtual Communities

Voice technology improves the social dynamics within the metaverse, enabling more authentic and meaningful communication.

- **Seamless Socializing:** Users can communicate and socialize in virtual environments using only their voice, creating more spontaneous and natural interactions.
- **Speech-Driven Event Participation:** Users can host, manage, and engage in virtual events through voice commands, making event coordination easier and more interactive.
- **Voice as a Cultural and Personal Identity Marker:** Voice characteristics such as tone, accent, and style can express personal or cultural identities, fostering a sense of belonging and individuality in virtual communities.

Accessibility and Inclusion through Voice Interaction

Voice-driven interactions provide critical accessibility benefits for users with disabilities, ensuring that the virtual economy is inclusive.

- **Speech-Based Navigation for Disabled Users:** Speech processing systems provide hands-free navigation, making virtual spaces more accessible for people with mobility or vision impairments.

- **Real-Time Speech-to-Text for Hearing-Impaired Users:** Instant voice-to-text translations allow hearing-impaired users to participate fully in conversations and activities within virtual environments.

Emotional and Social Engagement through Voice

Speech processing enhances the emotional depth and social bonding within virtual worlds.

- **Emotion Recognition in Speech:** AI systems can detect emotions from voice tone, creating more empathetic interactions and responses from avatars or virtual assistants.
- **Voice-Enhanced Social Presence:** Voice adds layers of emotional context to communication, fostering deeper social connections and enhancing the realism of virtual interactions.

Security, Privacy, and Trust in Voice-Driven Economies

With the increasing use of voice for transactions and interactions, ensuring the security and privacy of users becomes crucial.

- **Voice Authentication for Secure Transactions:** Voice biometrics offer a secure method for confirming user identity during transactions, enhancing the overall security of virtual economies.
- **Protecting Voice Data Privacy:** Addressing concerns about data privacy and ensuring that voice data is handled ethically and securely will be critical to maintaining user trust.

CONCLUSION

Speech processing is completely changing the game in the metaverse. It's making our interactions feel more human, more natural, and much more real. Think about it: our voices aren't just for talking anymore. They're becoming the key to how we explore and connect in these virtual worlds. Voice technology is now at the center of everything, from making the metaverse easier for everyone to use, to creating personalized experiences that feel like they were made just for us. Our voices are even helping to shape our digital identities and keep our virtual transactions safe. Of course, with all this incredible potential comes some big responsibilities. We have to be smart about things like privacy, making sure everyone feels included, and using this technology ethically. But as voice becomes our main way of interacting in the metaverse, it's clear that it's going to keep transforming how we talk, connect, and live in these digital spaces. That's why it's such an exciting area for future a lot of research and innovation.

REFERENCES

Bae, S.-G. (2022). A Study on Metaverse Spatial Acoustic Adaptation to Minimize Environmental Adaptation Using Spatial Sounds Around Accessors. *International Journal of Engineering Trends and Technology*, *70*(1), 206. DOI: 10.14445/22315381/IJETT-V70I1P206

Chakraborty, S., & Dadhich, A. (2023). Dialogue and Metaverse: A Scenario. In *Dynamics of Dialogue, Cultural Development, and Peace in the Metaverse* (pp. 11). IGI Global. https://www.igi-global.com/chapter/dialogue-and-metaverse/314987

Hsu, H.-P. (2012). Interactive and Cognitive Models in the Social Network Environment for Designing. In Cheok, M. T. L., Gay, R. K. L., & Liu, J. W. S. (Eds.), *Speech, Image, and Language Processing for Human Computer Interaction: Multi-Modal Advancements* (pp. 22–43). IGI Global., DOI: 10.4018/978-1-4666-0954-9.ch003

Kumar, J., Arora, M., & Bayram, G. E. (Eds.). (2024). *Research, Innovation, and Industry Impacts of the Metaverse*. IGI Global. DOI: 10.4018/979-8-3693-2607-7

Kumar, S., Madikeri, S., Zuluaga-Gomez, J., Thorbecke, I., Villatoro-Tello, E., Burdisso, S., Motlicek, P., Pandia, K., & Ganapathiraju, A. (2024). TokenVerse: Towards Unifying Speech and NLP Tasks via Transducer-based ASR. *arXiv*. https://web3.arxiv.org/abs/2407.04444

Lee, S.-H., Lee, Y.-E., & Lee, S.-W. (2021). Toward Imagined Speech Based Smart Communication System: Potential Applications on Metaverse Conditions. *arXiv*. https://arxiv.org/abs/2112.08569

Mehrish, A., Majumder, N., Bhardwaj, R., Mihalcea, R., & Poria, S. (2023). A Review of Deep Learning Techniques for Speech Processing. *arXiv*. https://arxiv.org/abs/2305.00359

Mehta, S., & Gupta, S. K. (Eds.). (2025). *Impact and Potential of Machine Learning in the Metaverse*. IGI Global., https://www.igi-global.com/book/impact-potential-machine-learning-metaverse/341592

Saarinen, S. (2025). Technology Convergence and the Metaverse. In Martins, L. B., & Moutinho, L. A. M. (Eds.), *Impacts of Sensetech on Society* (pp. 1–20). IGI Global., DOI: 10.4018/979-8-3693-7147-3.ch001

Wang, Y., Ravanelli, M., & Yacoubi, A. (2023). Metaverse Virtual Interview Platform Leveraging Generative AI and Speech Recognition. *ResearchGate*. https://www.researchgate.net/publication/382070538_Metaverse_Virtual_Interview_Platform_Leveraging_Generative_AI_and_Speech_Recognition

Yang, K., Markovic, D., Krenn, S., Agrawal, V., & Richard, A. (2022). Audio-Visual Speech Codecs: Rethinking Audio-Visual Speech Enhancement by Re-Synthesis. *arXiv*. DOI: 10.1109/CVPR52688.2022.00805

Zagalo, N., Morgado, L., & Boa-Ventura, A. (Eds.). (2012). *Virtual Worlds and Metaverse Platforms: New Communication and Identity Paradigms*. IGI Global. DOI: 10.4018/978-1-60960-854-5

Zhao, Y., Jiang, J., Chen, Y., Liu, R., Yang, Y., Xue, X., & Chen, S. (2022). AI-based Visual Speech Recognition Towards Realistic Avatars and Lip-Reading Applications in the Metaverse. *Applied Soft Computing*. https://dl.acm.org/doi/10.1016/j.asoc.2024.111906

Chapter 4
Exploring the Future of Education:
A Review of VR, AR, and XR Applications

Zokir Mamadiyarov
Mamun University, Uzbekistan

Anorgul Atajanova
https://orcid.org/0009-0000-5468-8187
Urgench State Pedagogical Institute, Uzbekistan

Erkin Iskandarov
Urgench State University, Uzbekistan

Munir Ahmad
https://orcid.org/0000-0003-4836-6151
Survey of Pakistan, Pakistan

ABSTRACT

This chapter explores the transformative potential of Virtual Reality (VR), Augmented Reality (AR), and Extended Reality (XR) in reshaping educational experiences. Immersive technologies offer unique opportunities for experiential learning that enhance engagement, understanding, and retention across various educational levels. While VR field trips and simulations offer powerful pedagogical value, the chapter also highlights significant challenges, technical, financial, ethical, and institutional, that hinder widespread adoption. Effective integration of XR requires alignment with curricular goals, comprehensive teacher training, supportive policies, and inclusive, secure, and pedagogically sound design from developers. As

DOI: 10.4018/979-8-3373-3043-3.ch004

XR becomes more affordable and accessible, it paves the way for hybrid learning environments, global virtual classrooms, and immersive problem-solving experiences. Technological advancements such as 5G, AI, haptics, IoT, and blockchain will further enrich XR's educational impact by enabling personalized learning, real-time analytics, and secure credentialing.

INTRODUCTION

Virtual reality, augmented reality, and extended reality are immersive technologies that are changing the boundaries between the physical and digital worlds. With further development of these technologies, they are also entering more and more domains, such as education, healthcare, manufacturing, urbanism, and cultural preservation, essentially reshaping the way people perceive, interact with, and process digital data in the context of physical space (Kawal et al., 2024; Nair et al., 2024; Vasarainen et al., 2021).

Virtual Reality (VR) can be defined as a situation where the users are fully immersed in a simulated computerized environment, usually, with the help of head-mounted displays (HMDs) and other sensory devices used to redefine real-life inputs with a manmade solution (Calisto & Sarkar, 2024; Lampropoulos & Kinshuk, 2024). Augmented Reality (AR), on the other hand, is about providing real-time information based on digital information like text, images, or animations, and layering it on top of what the user perceives to be real, but in no way does it replace reality (Barta et al., 2025; Koumpouros, 2024). The term Extended Reality (XR) is used as an umbrella term that describes both VR and AR, along with Mixed Reality (MR), which covers the whole spectrum of immersive technologies spreading between the digital world and the real world (Akbar et al., 2024; Alhakamy, 2024).

The history behind these technologies comprises a reciprocating interaction of the invention in computer graphics, sensor systems, and human-computer interaction. The origins of VR theories can be traced back when the great works like Sensorama by Morton Heilig and Sword of Damocles by Ivan Sutherland preconditioned the idea of immersive display systems (Abes et al., 2025). AR started to appear in the early 1990s (Garg et al., 2024) and was first utilized in industry and medical scenarios, but with the advent of mobile devices and location-aware technologies, consumer use became possible.

The recent decade has seen the overlap of capacity in VR and AR, which, with the development of processing power, real-time rendering, spatial computing, artificial intelligence, and 5G connectivity, has resulted in the emergence of XR as a complete system of immersive interaction. This intersection has not only created better accessibility, as well as usability, to immersive technologies, but it has also led to larger-scale adoption, including use in large systems and platforms, including the digital twin, smart cities, and the newly emerging metaverse. This chapter gives a background introduction to the technology of VR, AR, and XR as well as its conceptual development, technical development, and increasing uses. Placing these tools in a wider context of technology and society, the discussion creates the preconditions to reflect on the fact that immersive environments are transforming the experiences of users, the choices, and the future of digital interaction.

CURRENT APPLICATIONS IN EDUCATION

Virtual Reality (VR) and Its Applications in Education

VR is the computer-generated, three-dimensional world within which users take part in a simulated environment/experience, which recreates the real or imagined space. Usually, VR is experienced with HMDs and other motion-tracking devices, which allow the wearer to actually engage digital objects and move within a virtual space in real-time. VR does not simply aim to mimic the real; it aims to facilitate the experience of a highly detailed and sensory-laden environment that considers user interaction and into which users can become immersed and have a sense of both presence and a sense of agency in the virtual space. Originally, VR was applied in such industries where it was necessary to train, simulate, and entertain, e.g., aviation, military, and entertainment. VR has also gradually become a universal platform with disruptive capabilities in various industries, one of which is education (Kamińska et al., 2019; Smutny et al., 2019).

Within the circle of education, VR has also become a potent educational tool that can transform the traditional understanding of teaching and learning conditions. VR connects theory and practice because it helps to achieve immersive learning experiences. Physical interaction with scientific concepts, historic sites, and abstract systems enables students to learn and remember better through mutual interaction. VR's capacity to immerse has the benefit of promoting experiential learning, accommodating various learning styles, and accessing some learning possibilities that are inhibited by conditions of time, cost, or location (Crogman et al., 2025; Dubiel et al., 2025; Sümer & Vaněček, 2025).

Medical and nursing education is one of the most influential types of VR use, especially for practical experience, due to the unavoidably high cost, danger, or ethical considerations that may limit practice. Apps can provide a high-fidelity clinical scenario within which learners may undertake procedures, react to emergencies, and their responses may be monitored in real time in a safe, low-stakes learner environment. Such simulations increase cognitive and psychomotor development, decrease clinical decision-making, and it is a repeatable basis-thereby a crucial addition to conventional medical training programs (Huai et al., 2024; Neher et al., 2025).

VR is also playing a tremendous role in primary and secondary education, especially in virtual field trips. Such apps as Google Expeditions allow students to explore historical landmarks, natural ecosystems, or even other planets, such as Mars, without visiting them at all. The experiences not only enhance the subject knowledge but also build curiosity, international consciousness, and intercultural understanding. VR can present the equivalent learning opportunities to students in under-resourced or rural regions, thus enhancing equal access to education (Cao et al., 2024; Jin et al., 2024).

Moreover, VR simulations are becoming particularly useful in the fields that demand visual spatial thinking or systems thinking. Courses in engineering, physics, and others may present students with complex systems, like in the case of working with a Labster platform or zSpace, which offer the possibility to experiment with scientific phenomena and perform virtual laboratory experiments. Such simulations eliminate the dangers of physical labs, allow cost-effective instruction, and provide reusable scenarios that can be used to teach over and over again- that is why they can contribute to a scalable and efficient solution in STEM education.

Augmented Reality (AR) and Its Applications in Education

Augmented Reality (AR) refers to a technology that involves overlaying real-world situations with digital data, which can be in the form of images, animations, text, or sound, and can be done in real time so that the user can be able to have improved perception and interaction in his/her immediate surroundings. contrary to Virtual Reality, in which the user is put in an entirely digital environment, AR augments the actual location by overlaying contextual data that can be viewed via smartphones or tablets or through wearables composed of AR-ready glasses. This is a perfect fusion of the digital and physical that allows creating interactive and space-conscious experiences, those that react to what the user does and where he is (Crogman et al., 2025; Sümer & Vaněček, 2025).

Over the last ten years, AR has become an augmented reality, and its development was stimulated by computer vision, mobile processing power, and cloud computing. Although AR has only recently been applicable in education sectors, it has been gaining a lot of momentum in such domains, and this has been attributed to its increased applications in increasing the levels of student engagement and learning. Subtly rendering abstract or otherwise complicated subjects more concrete, interactive, and visually appealing, AR can be used to serve a broad scope of teaching goals, including developing goal-oriented understanding, down to learning skills (Mirza et al., 2025; Zhang & Yao, 2025).

During formal learning, AR modifies interaction between students and textbooks and other materials. The use of interactive AR textbooks has become popular, especially in subjects dealing with science, technology, engineering, and mathematics (STEM), whose abstract scientific and mathematical concepts gain advantage through visualization (Jiang et al., 2025; Zhang et al., 2024). An example is the Elements 4D, which enables students to play with wooden blocks that represent various chemical elements, and when viewed using a set of AR app, the blocks blister with animations of chemical reactions, enabling students to visualize chemical reactions. In the same way, educational tools (such as the Merge Cube) can enable students to navigate 3D models of anatomical objects (or planets, or historical relics), using the palms of their hands, encouraging spatial thinking and interest in learning curricular material.

In addition to the classroom, AR is already found in vocational and technical education (Boel et al., 2023, 2024; Ortega-Gras et al., 2023). Apps like Scope AR and Wikitude Studio superpose the step-by-step digital instruction over real-world equipment so that a learner can learn procedures like engine repair or electrical circuit assembly by getting the real-time instructions. It is an easy way to do experiential and practical learning without attending to instructors all the time and is more useful in those training situations where there is little or expensive physical equipment to come to grips with.

AR is also, potentially, relevant to inclusive education, providing devices that support the multiple learning needs and differences. As an example, coloring books like Quiver transform children's coloring pages to three-dimensional animation so that young students, especially those with developmental disorders or learning disabilities, find it easier to manipulate the content using the multisensory interactive feature. AR flashcards and object recognition tools offer real-time visual and aural feedback as concepts are recognized, vocabulary or phrases, and are useful to aid memory retention, especially supporting pronunciation in cases of repetitive, interactive learning.

Extended Reality (XR) and Its Applications in Education

Extended Reality (XR) is an umbrella terminology that covers the entire range of immersive technologies that include VR, AR, and MR. XR is the intermediate between the utterly physical and the entirely virtual that allows customers to have access to worlds with dynamic connections between digital and physical things. Alongside breakneck innovations in spatial computing, real-time rendering, cloud infrastructure, artificial intelligence, and sensor integration, these technologies are becoming more intertwined. In addition, XR goes beyond enhancing the way users interact with digital content, but transforms both the character of interaction, collaboration, and learning in a variety of settings (Ortega-Gras et al., 2023).

XR is also advancing new teacher-focused pedagogical models in education, especially in the concept of blended and hybrid learning. Out of the ability to co-exist and supplement each other, XR facilitates the development of multimodal and flexible learning spaces. Such environments rather support both synchronous and asynchronous learning, promote a student-centered manner, and facilitate the idea of differentiated instruction using adaptive content delivery and immersivity (Huang & Tseng, 2025; Khlaif et al., 2024; Liarokapis et al., 2024).

A notable example of this involvement of XR in the education industry is the creation of blended learning solutions in which LMS is coupled with face-to-face learning sessions. Due to consumer and researcher demand, universities are moving more towards the engagement of XR platforms like Engage and AltspaceVR to complement Learning Management Systems (LMS). They provide virtual classrooms, where the students join lectures, group discussions, and complete their assignments through interaction in shared, virtual, and interactive environments with the help of the avatars. Such a method not only opens doors to remote learners, but also covers the shortcomings of conventional online learning, developing a stronger sense of presence, community, and engagement. Figure 1 shows the XR implementation funnel.

Figure 1. XR implementation funnel

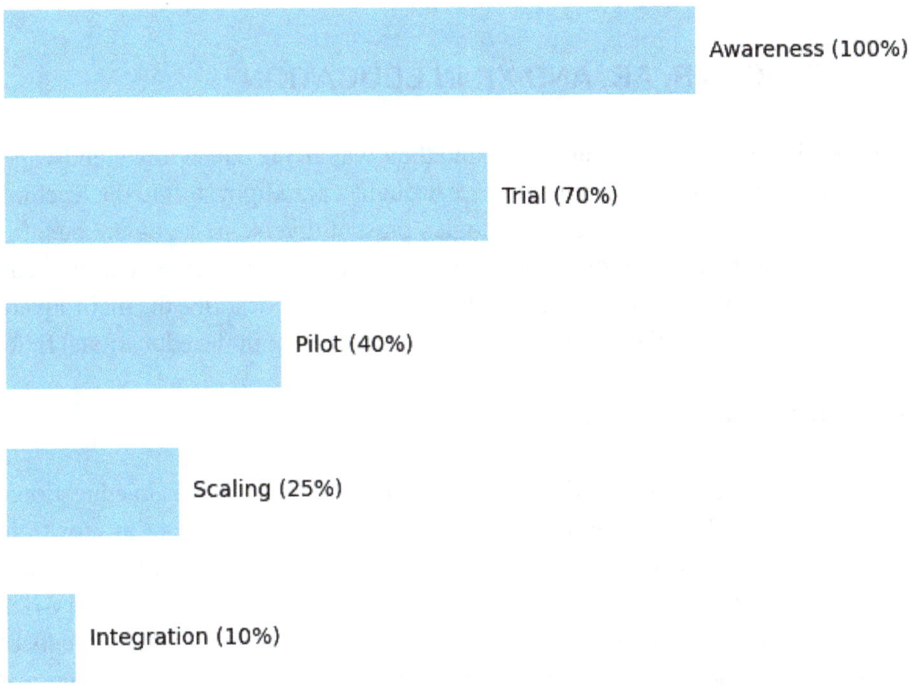

XR can also be used to create collaborative virtual spaces where team-based learning, critical thinking, and creative problem-solving are possible (Assaf et al., 2024; Wu et al., 2024a). In architectural, engineering, and design fields, learners may also enter collaborative XR spaces to collaborate on composing 3D models, brainstorming structural concepts, and performing designs in real-time. Other companies can enable geographically distributed teams to collaborate on digital objects as though they are in the same physical studio, and as such, the systems eliminate logistical issues and facilitate international cooperation.

The increased adaptation of adaptive learning systems, where the learning process is customized to suit an individual through the use of real-time data, is another key development in XR-enhanced education. XR platforms that incorporate machine learning algorithms, behavioral analytics, and biometric sensors support user performance and engagement measurement to change content complexity or style of presentation. As an example, the ClassVR platform is capable of following eye movement and interaction patterns and subsequently comes up with heatmaps that can give educators an idea of how students were focused and engaged. These analytics allow more specific feedback, early detection of learning problems, and constant improvement of teaching methods.

BENEFITS OF VR, AR, AND XR IN EDUCATION

Immersive technologies that have found their way in the educational landscape, often in the form of VR, AR, and XR, have brought a paradigm shift to the teaching and learning environment. The technologies present diverse pedagogical benefits compared with the conventional and extend beyond effective delivery of content, but rather, the overall learning process. The sections below describe the main advantages that are related to the application of VR, AR, and XR in the educational field.

Enhanced Engagement

Among the most common advantages of immersive technologies in educational practice, it is possible to note that they may contribute to a substantial growth in the involvement of the students. VR, AR, and XR attract more attention than traditional lectures and textbooks because, in their presence, interactive, sensory-rich environments are created. The students no longer have to be passive recipients of information, but rather become active in the immersive scenarios, simulations, and experiences. The non-linear AR-based learning experience, the virtual field trips, the gamified learning environment, and the interactive AR applications create curiosity and provide continuous engagement and encourage students to learn more about the materials. Such an elevated stage of interaction may result in higher participation, better attendance, and more enthusiasm in learning at any stage of education.

Improved Understanding and Knowledge Retention

The 3D technologies of VR, AR, and XR contribute to enhanced conceptualization of knowledge because it is easy to visualize the concept of a complex, abstract topic, which is hard to understand via text or an itemized image (Partarakis & Zabulis, 2024). As an example, students could have the opportunity to view the human circulatory system in 3D, play with molecular structures, or see the time-based transformation of food webs in the ecosystem. The prospect of manipulating content spatially and temporally favors experiential learning, which has been found to increase retention levels and application of the learned to real-life situations. Moreover, the immersive environments may be adjusted to personal learning styles: visual, auditory, or kinesthetic, and provide us with more effective and personal learning paths.

Increased Accessibility and Inclusivity

Virtual realities also increase the availability of education through the elimination of geographical, physical, and socioeconomic boundaries (Balakrishnan & Kumar, 2024; Poggianti et al., 2025). Distanced learners also no longer have to be in a physical classroom to have a fully immersive experience, and students in underserved or rural areas will have access to high-end educational experiences and materials they would not otherwise have access to. AR can be used to assist learners with disabilities, providing a text-to-speech signal to translate immediately, the interface is adjustable, and multisensory feedback. Moreover, safe and guided simulations can be used on learners with anxiety or those with cognitive issues so that they learn at their natural pace and not fear that they cannot learn.

Support for Skills Development and Practice

More than content delivery, VR, AR, and XR can be used, especially in the context of acquiring practical and professional skills. These technologies offer realistic simulations in such areas as medicine, engineering, aviation, and vocational training that allow the learners to safely practice protocols, use equipment, or constrained decision-making processes. The approach is a combination of theory and practicality and takes into consideration the actual world problem solving by way of inculcating the skill of repeated, risk-free practice into the students. Particular XR platforms also demonstrate the use of a haptic response and gesture recognition, which increases the presence and efficacy of the skills training.

Fostering Collaboration and Communication

XR technologies make possible new types of collaborative learning not limited by the concerns of physical space (Wu et al., 2024b). Learners have an opportunity to communicate with each other and with tutors in common virtual spaces, they co-create knowledge, collaborate on solving assignments, and experience cross-cultural interactions. These joint XR environments encourage teamwork, negotiation, and communication, which are the competencies that are becoming more and more crucial in the contemporary working environment. In addition, avatars and spatial audio in virtual classrooms have the potential to facilitate a feeling of presence and community that is not present in traditional online study.

Real-Time Feedback and Adaptive Learning

The other notable benefit of an immersive learning environment is the capability to present real-time feedback dependent on the performance and interaction of the learner. XR systems integrated analytics may measure the degree of engagement, progress, and skill development. This information can be further applied to control the content difficulty, give personal feedback, or suggest other learning resources. The dynamic response of adaptive learning systems to the demands of the learner maximizes the effectiveness of instructions and offers the possibility of continuous development of the quality of learning.

CHALLENGES AND LIMITATIONS OF VR, AR, AND XR IN EDUCATION

Although the use of VR, AR, and XR in education may be quite a game-changer, their implementation is hampered by a variety of issues. These constraints are in the technical, financial, pedagogical, administrative, and ethical planes (Bhaskaran & Mahbub, 2024a; Khlaif et al., 2024; Liu et al., 2024). Comprehension of such categories and the concrete barriers in each is quite necessary to develop the feasible plans for implementation and the long-term adoption system.

Technical Challenges

There are many technical issues regarding the introduction of VR, AR, and XR into the learning context. These problems are based on the requirements of the infrastructure, interoperability of devices, and the reliability of immersive technologies. To implement them successfully and use them further in the future, these problems have to be deeply comprehended and resolved (Bhaskaran & Mahbub, 2024b; Khan et al., 2024). The main technical issues are the requirement of hardware and software, compatibility with the systems, the ease of use, and other upcoming issues like network dependency, scalability, and environmental restrictions, as documented in Table 1.

Hardware and Software Requirements

Among the most eminent technical obstacles concerning the adoption of immersive technologies in education is that it is a costly, hardware and software-intensive process. Immersive learning environments generally demand head-mounted displays (HMDs) like Meta Quest, HTC Vive, or Microsoft HoloLens, which cost a few hundred dollars and up to thousands of dollars apiece. Such devices may be required to be attached to high-performance computers with superior graphics processing units (GPUs), conferring additional cost and difficulty. This degree of infrastructure is not accessible in numerous low-resource learning environments, especially in developing countries or villages in rural locations.

Besides, VR and AR software require enormous storage, recurrent upgrades, and excellent computational capability to execute complicated 3D simulations or on-the-fly overlay. As an example, scientific simulations in Labster (science laboratories) or Anatomage Table (gross anatomy display) necessarily call for up-to-date computing equipment in addition to very fast internet connectivity to deliver and streaming material properly. These applications could be turned unusable in regions with interruptions in electricity or low bandwidth on the internet, which is the worst-case scenario in terms of usage and reachability.

System Compatibility and Maintenance

The manufacturers and software companies developing immersive technologies can be very diverse, so the created ecosystem tends to be fragmented. Hardware devices can run off alternate operating systems (i.e., Windows Mixed Reality, Android, proprietary XR platforms), and educational software is not always compatible with all equipment. As an example, an AR app that was built in an iOS environment might fail to run on Android-based tablets used in schools. Its failure to interoperate hinders deployment, raises the support costs, and reduces the portability of the content between platforms.

There is a constant problem of maintenance. Extended reality devices also have to be regularly recalibrated, to have regular firmware updates and software patching, and even debugging of sensory input or tracking technologies. As an example, a HoloLens device deployed in STEM may be less tracking-accurate after some time or need a recalibration in other lighting conditions. Lacking a specific IT-composed staff or a technician, teachers will be unprepared to carry out the maintenance of such systems, resulting in lapses and lowered instructional time.

Usability and Technical Glitches

Even in the case where the needed hardware and software exist, usability is a continual issue. Most of the XR systems come with high learning curves for both the educators and the students. Elaborate user interfaces, unreliable controls, or counter-intuitive navigation may be discouraging. Take, for instance, a teacher who does not know much about XR will not be able to collaboratively launch a multi-user VR session, start simulations, or fix minor problems in the classroom. The other common problem that can disrupt the lessons and make the technology less reliable is technical glitches. Typical issues are crashes, display rendering latency, incompatibility between different software or overheating of the devices, or object tracking mistakes.

An example such as opening an XR-equipped chemistry laboratory would be that in case the system stalls during an experiment or the model of a molecule vanishes in rendering error, the entire experience of immersion breaks down as well as frustration, and the learning process is derailed. Negative experience will cause both students and teachers to resist, which is likely to discourage the uptake of immersive technologies in the long run.

Network Dependency and Bandwidth Constraints

Most XR platforms are based on cloud-based architecture and streamed in real-time to present the interactive content. When using apps like Google Expeditions, Engage, or ClassVR, they may need a continuous fast internet connection to display a setting, download multimedia elements, or assist real-time collaboration among users. In bandwidth-limited environments, such features can be slow, not load, or perform terribly.

In addition, network congestion may temperately or even fully freeze an immersive session, especially in multiplayer-based or cloud-rendered XR experiences. Computers with undeveloped digital infrastructure or weak connectivity are an issue when it comes to the use of XR tools that require an internet connection. One disadvantage is that offline modes are insufficiently present or worse, limited in features, and thus cannot be used in low connectivity settings. Scalability and management of devices

Scalability and Device Management

Large-scale adoption is technically demanding in immersive technologies, particularly in institutions that have a large number of students. XR devices have a tendency toward being unique and cannot just be spun up (on identical machines) throughout the use of centralized systems, the way software can in more traditional computer labs today. As an example, putting dozens of VR headsets out, charging and storing them before and after a large class will be a burden logistically and technically.

Also, most XR systems are not designed to scale up in classes. Multi-user settings can become unstable through synchronization errors, audio interferences, or can run slowly as additional users join a system. In the absence of effective device management solutions, organizations encounter problems trying to ensure uniform user assessment and avoid malpractices involving the utilization of loss of equipment.

Environmental and Spatial Constraints

Another condition of successful immersive technologies application is physical space. Some VR solutions even need special open spaces to allow freedom of movement/tracking, and AR systems can be based on bright environments and clearly defined surfaces in order to get proper rendering. They cannot be met easily in overcrowded classrooms, in small laboratories, or in areas with bad lighting. To give one example, the process of establishing a VR lab in one of the older school buildings, partially lacking floor space and with outdated electrical systems, might present a serious impediment to implementation.

Table 1. Technical challenges

Challenge	Description	Example	Implications
Hardware & Software Requirements	Need for high-end devices and computing power	VR headsets, spatial sensors, and compatible PCs	Limits adoption in under-resourced schools; high barrier to entry
System Compatibility & Maintenance	Lack of interoperability and need for frequent updates	Content not working across platforms; outdated firmware	Increased IT workload; reduced usability and reliability
Usability & Technical Glitches	Bugs, crashes, or rendering issues that hinder smooth experiences	Lag in 3D simulations; calibration errors	Frustration among users reduces confidence in XR tools
Connectivity Limitations	Dependence on strong internet and network infrastructure	Cloud-based XR platforms fail in low-bandwidth areas	Excludes rural or poorly connected institutions
Technical Support Deficiencies	Absence of on-site XR technicians or IT personnel	Teachers doubling as troubleshooters	Disrupts classroom flow; discourages long-term use

Financial Challenges

The second challenge is finance, as one of the most remarkable obstacles to the proliferation of VR, AR, and XR. Even though these technologies present the possibility of revolutionizing, they can be costly and need a consistent investment to be integrated. This section highlights the different aspects of financial issues, such as high start-up expenses, continuing costs of running operations, inequity of resources, and absence of a sustainable funding model. Table 2 shows a brief overview of these challenges.

High Initial Investment

A significant upfront cost to integrate immersive technologies into the corporate environment is one of the greatest financial issues. Acquiring the XR-ready devices (head-mounted displays, e.g., Oculus Quest 3, HTC Vive Pro, Microsoft HoloLens) and compatible high-performance computers, motion sensors, and other peripherals might make a significant impact on the finances of an institution. Moreover, educational XR software tends to be proprietary, and special permission must be obtained to access it, which is also an additional burden on the payment of the initial price.

As an example, a simple VR lab with 10-15 high-quality headsets, specific workstations, and spatial tracking systems can be created with a basic cost reaching USD 30.000-50.000. When it comes to a given yearly fee in the case of Engage or Labster, the cost of licensing immersive content can be from several hundred dollars to several thousand, depending on the number of users. These costs are a prohibitive number to a public facility, especially in developing nations or in less-funded school districts.

Ongoing Costs and Sustainability

The cost of implementing XR is not concluded after the initial purchase. Schools should also take into consideration various recurrent expenses, which entail:

- Headsets and controllers are subject to wear and tear, especially in high-use environments. Replacing parts or servicing hardware adds to the long-term cost.
- Many XR platforms operate on subscription models, requiring annual or monthly payments. These costs may escalate as institutions scale up or adopt more advanced features.
- When off-the-shelf content does not align with local curricula, institutions may need to commission or develop their own XR modules, which requires hiring instructional designers, 3D artists, and developers.
- Staff must be regularly trained to keep pace with changing technology. Workshops, certifications, and in-house training programs represent a recurring expenditure.

Hardware obsolescence is also caused by the swift speed and rate of hardware development in XR. The gadgets that are deemed cutting-edge today might go obsolete in two to three years. Such a limited life cycle leads to higher overall ownership costs and deters long-term financial planning without a vision of how institutions can upgrade or plan on leasing their equipment.

Resource Disparities and the Digital Divide

Inequality is further worsened by financial constraints, as they become inequalities within and between educational systems. Well-funded institutions in cities with a high level of resources can access the money of donors, foreign education grants, or national innovation projects, which enable them to explore new technologies. In sharp contrast, local schools, state colleges, as well as local education centers often do not have the funds or administrative backing with regard to undertaking such projects.

An example may be the case of a university in a metropolitan area where an AR-powered biology course delivered using tablet computers with custom applications may be a reality, whereas in a rural state school, it may have a problem even with bare-bones computer laboratories. Not only does this divide led to increased inequality in education, but it also restricts the availability of underprivileged learners to the digitally focused skills of the future.

Moreover, when funding of immersive technologies is allocated to specific departments (e.g., engineering or medical sciences) and not all of them (such as humanities or arts faculties), intra-institutional inequalities can take place because such departments are perceived as less important or applicable. These imbalances make interdisciplinary access to XR difficult and impede institutional success in digital innovation strategies.

Lack of Dedicated Funding Streams

The lack of long-term earmarked funding mechanisms toward immersive education technologies is also another fatal financial issue. Short-term grants, pilot projects, or donor-funded innovation labs usually initiate a large number of XR adoption undertakings. Although they may be valuable drivers, they cannot provide continuity long term or scale.

An example is when a school is given a single grant by a country-wide digital transformation project to experiment with AR in the science classes. Nevertheless, at the termination of the grant, institutional funds are sometimes unavailable to renew software licenses, protect equipment, and extend the project to other topics. Consequently, such technology ends up underutilized or is abandoned, hence the wastage of investment and stakeholder frustrations.

Further, XR financial planning is also in competition with other urgent institutional requirements like faculty hiring, building repair, or conventional ICT investment. Without the concrete requirements of the policy or national plans, developments of immersive technologies are often placed at the bottom of any available budgets.

Currency Fluctuations and Import Dependencies (Context-Specific)

XR devices and software have an added exposure to fluctuations in foreign currency, import tariffs, and international supply chain shocks that is especially high in most developing countries where they are imported. Environmental factors such as a fall in the exchange rate of the local currency or tightening of trade policies can further reduce access due to the increased effectiveness of XR adoption. It is especially important in such countries as Pakistan, Nigeria, or Argentina, where the ultimate cost of imported educational technology is directly affected by the level of macroeconomic volatility.

Table 2. Financial challenges

Challenge	Description	Example	Implications
High Initial Investment	Cost of XR hardware, licenses, and infrastructure	VR lab setup costing $30,000+	Prohibitive for public or low-budget institutions
Ongoing Costs & Sustainability	Recurring expenses for upgrades, repairs, and training	Annual license renewals, hardware obsolescence	Difficult to maintain long-term implementation
Resource Disparities	Uneven distribution of resources between schools or regions	Urban private schools have XR; rural public schools do not	Deepens the digital divide; increases educational inequality
Funding Gaps & Short-Term Grants	Lack of dedicated, long-term funding streams	Pilot XR project ends after grant expires	Limits the scalability and continuity of XR initiatives
Currency & Import Issues	XR tech dependency on foreign markets and volatile currencies	Headset prices rise due to currency devaluation	Increases cost unpredictability in developing countries

Pedagogical Challenges

Although VR, AR, and XR can be very effective in advancing teaching activities, many obstacles regarding their effective pedagogical implementation should be considered. These are more than technical issues and issues involving finances, but they reach into the aspects of teaching and learning itself. Areas of main pedagogical concern entail the problems with the curriculum alignment and absence of instructional paradigm, difficulties in assessment and evaluation, differences in the learner readiness as well as interdisciplinary content development. Table 3 summarized the key pedagogical challenges.

Curriculum Integration

The first difficulty is how to align the XR content with recognized curricula and the formal learning objectives. A lot of immersive applications are designed and built commercially or more generally enriching education, not in line with nationally or institutionally set standards. Consequently, the instructors might experience that although the XR content in question is interesting in itself, it does not appeal directly to the specified areas of competence or standards that they must teach.

So, an application developed to educate about planetary systems might focus on interactivity or on 3D visualizations, without talking about the specific learning objectives in the astronomy unit in a school, e.g., orbital mechanics or comparing planetary data. The educators are then left with the choice to add more materials to go with the technology or not use it at all because of the incompatibility. In those areas characterized by strict curriculum and stakeholder-based exams (e.g., South Asia or certain corners of Africa), the teacher might fear taking up the XR technologies that are not directly compatible with the test-driven mindset. This causes a disparity between novel pedagogy and performance-based educational systems.

Lack of Instructional Models and Pedagogical Frameworks

The second significant limitation is the lack of well-developed instructional models tailored to XR-based learning. As much as immersive technologies indicate new horizons in the practice of experiential pedagogy, student-centered pedagogy, and constructivism, the majority of teaching professionals do not have clear directions on how to design, conduct, and assess XR-enhanced lessons.

Subsequently, XR can be entered into the classrooms more as an experiment or a technological demonstration object as opposed to an organized way of learning. In a specific case like this, an educator may choose to implement a VR simulation of an archaeological site; however, he or she does not integrate it into a larger inquiry-related activity or address it with regard to historical thinking skills. Such a pedagogical system of disconnection may be a source of empty involvement and shallow learning.

What is more, XR requires refashioning the plans of lessons, management, and time distribution across the classroom. A change in instructions demands a paradigm shift in instructional approaches, where instructors are meant to become facilitators and designers of immersive experiences, and the process of designing involves a combination of both conceptual and skill training.

Assessment and Evaluation

Standardized tests like multiple-choice, essay, or oral tests are not adequate tests to gauge learning when using immersive environments. XR is commonly applied during the encouragement of experiential, procedural, or collaborative learning areas that could not be efficiently measured based on the specifications of standardized assessment.

As an example, in a virtual chemistry lab in which students perform simulated experiments, procedural fluency, safety awareness, and critical thinking could be listed as essential learning outcomes, whose assessment is hard to achieve with paper-based testing. Likewise, the soft skills of collaboration and teamwork, spatial thinking, and digital literacy can become a focus of an XR collaboration project, but they do not require traditional grading rubrics.

There is a demand for innovative assessment frameworks capable of employing performance-based, portfolio, or real-time assessment-based evaluation practices. Other XR platforms, such as ClassVR or VictoryXR, have implemented their analytics and tracking progress tools, but these are currently non-standard and not totally aligned with how institutions evaluate their subjects.

Learner Readiness and Cognitive Load

Pedagogical concern is another problem because not all learners are ready to use immersive technologies. There are differences among students in their comfort using technology or their spatial thinking abilities and cognitive endurance with virtual experiences. Depending on the case, XR environments may prove to be overwhelming for younger students or students with learning disabilities.

Moreover, the experience may be flawed by ensuring that the poorly-designed XR experiences may bring about cognitive overload, wherein the learner is preoccupied with navigating the interface or responding to sensory stimuli that when it comes to the actual educational material, they find it difficult to digest. To take the example of a VR game, which shirt the students in an earthquake event, can look great, but amidst all of that visual stimulus, the objectives and activities are unclear, and as a result, the learners might remember all the details of the simulation rather than the details of the nature of geological science. In response to this, the XR content will have to work on scaffolded experiences, simplistic interfaces, and instructional clarity, where the cognitive load is controlled and pedagogical objectives are not sidelined.

Interdisciplinary Content Gaps

Amazingly, the current applications of XR are mostly programmed with a high emphasis on STEM subjects, including biology, engineering, and computer science utilities, leaving content gaps in the humanities, arts, and social sciences. This poses a difficulty to the development of comprehensive learning in which a comprehensive curriculum is manifested.

An example is that a student can use VR to visit a human cell or simulate a physics experiment, but there are many fewer XR applications allowing one to critically engage with literature, philosophy, or civil education. This bias inhibits the ability to consider XR having pedagogical value and use it in interdisciplinary or liberal arts.

The complexity of XR-related content design, mixing educationally relevant content, high-quality content, and contextually grounded, in an extremely broad pool of subjects, means that such work needs to be done by groups of educators, designers, and subject-matter experts, an interdisciplinary effort that is not only time-consuming but also resource-intensive.

Table 3. Pedagogical challenges

Challenge	Description	Example	Implications
Curriculum Integration	Misalignment between XR content and existing syllabi	VR content not covering exam-relevant topics	Limits adoption in formal instruction
Lack of Instructional Models	No clear frameworks for XR-based teaching	No lesson plans or guides for using XR meaningfully	Inconsistent use; novelty over pedagogical depth
Assessment & Evaluation	Difficulty assessing experiential or collaborative learning	Traditional tests don't capture soft skills or procedural knowledge	Misrepresents student learning outcomes
Learner Readiness & Cognitive Load	Students may be overstimulated or disoriented in XR environments	Discomfort during immersive field trips	Affects comprehension and motivation
Disciplinary Imbalance	Lack of XR content for arts, humanities, or civic education	Focus mainly on STEM topics	Limits curriculum-wide adoption

Administrative and Institutional Challenges

To successfully incorporate immersive technologies (including, but not limited to, VR, AR, and XR in education, the availability of devices or software is not enough, but it is much closer to institutional structures, policies, and leadership supporting said integration. Most times hidden barrier is administrative, which can hinder large-scale adoption even in highly resourced settings. The section discusses some of the main institutional matters, such as preparedness of teachers, infrastructure preparedness, procurement policies, vision, and culture of the organization where whereas Table 4 reviews the key administrative challenges.

Teacher Preparedness and Professional Development

Teachers are critical to the embrace and effectiveness of XR technologies, but most educators are not ready to use the gadgets in their classrooms. XR environments may require the familiarity of new kinds of hardware, new kinds of practice (new ways of teaching), and transformation of content delivery to the facilitation of experiences, all of which are not typically part of teacher education.

The problem is also complicated by the lack of specific professional development programs. In most countries, educational XR still lacks workshops, certifications, or practical training tailored specifically to educational XR. To illustrate, a pilot program in Pakistan could have supplied a local school with XR headsets, yet, teachers have no such training modules to get them to work effectively, be localized, and language-friendly.

Also, teachers tend to view immersive technologies as supplements to what is already a heavy school workload and not as something that enables better pedagogy. Even the willing teachers are likely to fall back on traditional methodology without constant mentorship, time allowances, and institutional incentives. Another type of resistance to change is demonstrated by the old faculty who are not very comfortable with new technologies.

Infrastructure Readiness

There should also be a readiness of physical and digital infrastructures in the administration. XR also demands specific spaces in which they can be used: spacious rooms that allow navigation and have reasonable conditions of ventilation, electric power, and safety. Indicatively, VR labs need a minimum of 2m x 2m of space per user to use so-called room-scale tracking, which is impractical in a busy classroom. Logistics of device management are also important: institutions should have safe storage infrastructure and charging infrastructure as well as asset tracking systems that prevent the possibility of damage, theft, or dislocation of XR equipment. There is also an inability to make full use of devices due to loss. The need to keep devices in a safe place is at times not always practiced.

Another deciding factor is connectivity. Most immersive learning environments work on the cloud or necessitate high-speed internet connectivity in order to stream content and engage multiple users or deliver real-time renders. Those schools that have unstable Wi-Fi access, low bandwidth, or low IT personnel might have difficulty presenting XR content in a smooth manner. In locations where at least basic infrastructure might be available, it might be difficult to be compatible with the rest of the systems (e.g., LMS, authentication protocols).

Policy and Procurement Processes

Another institutional bottleneck occurs in the form of slow or unclear procurements. Most learning institutions have bureaucratic structures that are not best suited to take advantage of the rapidly changing acquisition of technology. The XR hardware and software can either fail to appear in the approved categories to be procured, or current tendering practices can be used that slow down the delivery and implementation process.

Also, regulatory uncertainty regarding the use of immersive technology in the classroom can generate top-down reluctance to dive into things, particularly in matters of privacy of data collected, time spent on screens, or digital well-being. There is a possibility that administrators would evade the implementation of the XR because of perceived legal liability or due to non-compliance with government requirements. As an example, an XR investment in a university department in a South Asian nation might be funded by an international grant, but the processes of finance in the institution may hold back acquisition by months because of necessary authorizations, supplier limits, or audit provisions that do not even contemplate technology-specific spending, such as app subscriptions or content licenses. Leadership Vision and Institutional Strategy

Top-down vision and 360-degree coordination are often needed to introduce immersive technology into education, and it is often lacking. In most of the institutions, single and independent faculty members or IT departments do the innovation, and curriculum developers or the senior leadership do not have much to do with it. Attachment to leadership is also essential to implementing strategies in goal setting, resource allocation, and institutional missions. As an example, when the rector or principal of a university puts emphasis on XR as an element of a general e-learning strategy, investment could come faster, interdisciplinary projects may get promoted, and it will be easier to provoke modifications in policy. By contrast, executive support is usually lacking and typically leads to poorly integrated programs that are under-resourced and prematurely terminated.

Organizational Culture and Change Management

Organizational culture also determines resistance to technological innovation. Rigid hierarchies, conservative pedagogies, or a lack of internal communications may be a factor that deters experimentation with XR in institutional settings. Faculty can be afraid that the immersive tools will destroy the traditional lecturing process or will force researchers to start the redesign of the course materials anew.

There is usually a lack of change management strategies. Effective implementation of XR needs collaborative, iterative processes where implementation is guided by feedback loops among the teachers, the students, and the administrators. The absence of mechanisms to facilitate the mentioned dialogue and reflection can lead to the indifference or even cynicism of such attempts to introduce XR.

Lack of Technical and Instructional Support Staff

Where the devices have been bought and infrastructure exists, there always remains the problem of dedicated support staff. Institutions tend to overlook the importance of XR technicians, instructional designers, or integration specialists who can assist educators in integrating immersive lessons into their classroom practice. In a common occurrence, a school may get XR kits in a donor-driven program, but without the provision of the human resources to work with the equipment day-to-day, troubleshoot connectivity, or perform maintenance functions. The pressure, in turn, is shifted onto teachers, who are already stretched thin, to act as instructors of the content, as well as tech support, lowering success and use.

Table 4. Administrative and institutional challenges

Challenge	Description	Example	Implications
Teacher Preparedness	Teachers lack training, confidence, or time to use XR	Overwhelmed by XR interfaces, fear of tech replacing teaching	Low uptake; underutilized investments
Infrastructure Readiness	Physical space, storage, power, and network needs	No charging stations or VR-compatible rooms	Delays implementation; limits scalability
Policy & Procurement Barriers	Slow or unclear processes for purchasing and integrating XR	XR is not listed in approved procurement categories	Administrative bottlenecks; missed opportunities
Leadership & Strategic Vision	Lack of top-down support or planning	No institutional roadmap for XR	Fragmented, short-lived initiatives
Lack of Support Personnel	No dedicated XR technicians or learning designers	Teachers managing the setup and troubleshooting alone	Reduces classroom effectiveness; increases burnout

Ethical and Legal Challenges

With increasing application in an educational setting, obviously, immersive technologies such as VR, AR, and XR bring about several ethical and legal issues. These issues are not confined to technical implementation alone; rather, they touch on privacy, inclusion, sensitivity to culture, and responsible content design. The problem is that, unlike digital tools, XR technologies engage learners in multisensory, highly data-saturated environments, and that increases the opportunities of positive influences and the risks of data misuse or control failures. Table 5 outlines the key ethical and legal challenges.

Privacy and Data Security

When using XR systems in many cases, it is necessary to constantly monitor and track extremely sensitive personal data, such as biometric indicators (eye tracking, facial expressions, pupil dilation, hand gestures), location data, movement patterns, emotional reactions, and voice recordings. Such fine data collection may support adaptive learning and real-time feedback, as well as bring considerable data privacy and surveillance threats.

The protection of the data is even more crucial in an educational setting, especially when it involves underage students. As an illustration, ClassVR and other XR platforms deployed in K-12 classrooms can capture user activity in terms of gaze and body movement data. Such data may be misused, used in commercial interests, or may fall into the hands of unauthorized users when mishandled or kept in an insecure environment.

Legal regulations like the General Data Protection Regulation (GDPR) in Europe and the Family Educational Rights and Privacy Act (FERPA) in the U.S. demand severe constraints on the use of data, including the need for informed consent, data minimization, and transparency. Nevertheless, not all institutions have internal regulations governing the use of XR data, and commercial vendors might not be adhering fully to educational data protection guidelines. Consider, as an example, a school that implements a VR biology lab without telling the parents what kind of biometric information the system collects or how it can allow third-party providers to access such data, which is a severe red flag in terms of legality and ethics.

Equity and Inclusion

Although XR technologies provide an opportunity for inclusive and differentiated learning, they can become a reproduction of the current inequalities unless they are well planned. Students with disabilities, in particular, visual or auditory impairments, will find most of the XR applications hard to use because of the absence of screen readers, haptic feedback, or other forms of interaction. In the same way, students with neurodiverse conditions can be overwhelmed with immersive experiences that can be misaligned.

In addition, the digital divide might be ongoing due to inequality in the allocation of devices and connectivity. Rural/underserved schools and their students may not be in a position to invest in XR, which puts them at a disadvantage with students in well-funded urban schools. To give an example, a school that lacks enough Wi-Fi bandwidth or device inventory cannot institute collaborative XR field trips and simulations, shutting its students out of the opportunities of immersive learning. Designing XR experiences using the principles of the Universal Design of Learning (UDL), providing multimodal interfaces, and enabling them to work offline is essential in making these technologies equitable. Institutions should also have inclusive procurement and deployment policies that will prevent further marginalization of vulnerable learner populations.

Content Ethics and Bias

Immersive worlds make more than a content delivery system; immersive experiences can influence perceptions, emotions, and even beliefs of learners. As such, the XR content should be subjected to high ethics. The most common challenges surrounding representation, cultural bias, stereotyping, and historical inaccuracy may possess enhanced influence in the immersive environment because of better representation and subjective perception. As an example, a VR history simulation of the encounter between colonialists or of ancient civilizations can be biased, giving a Eurocentric perspective or not including indigenous perspectives, and strengthening biased worldviews. In the same way, characters and avatars with non-diversity in terms of race, gender, or physical ability can also make the students feel excluded and propagate exclusivity.

A bias can also be known to exist in AI-assisted adaptive learning implemented in XR systems. When algorithms differentiate learning experiences and are developed based on how a user behaves, there is a possibility of cultural/socioeconomic premise within the algorithm, explicitly or implicitly, that can perpetuate a discriminatory result. The content creators should also liaise with various stakeholders and embrace ethics review mechanisms as well as use culture-responsive design to alleviate such risks. Teachers are also advised to critically regard XR content before deployment and inculcate reflection discussions to assist students in handling complicated issues responsibly.

Psychological and Cognitive Impact

Long-term effects of long-term exposure to immersive environments can present psychological and cognitive impacts, particularly to younger learners. Depending on the degree of realism of XR experiences, users can develop motion sickness (cybersickness), disorientation, fatigue, or stronger emotional responses.

As an instance, a VR module, which reproduces the environment of a natural disaster or war zone as a means to build empathy, may create trauma or anxiety in a given group of students. Such experiences can even be counterproductive unless one is properly debriefed after the experience and provided with emotional support. Ethical use of XR in education thus needs age-appropriate design, specific learning goals, and facilitation by the instructor so that emotional well-being is enshrined. The schools are expected to set up the rules of time length, mental health, and psychological safety during the XR-based classes.

Intellectual Property and Copyright

XR has an immersive nature, which should include input of third-party content, 3D resources like models, audio files, virtual tours, and brand logos, and this may come into conflict with intellectual property (IP) rights. Teachers will be unaware of infringing XR experiences by using copyrighted materials without permission in the classrooms, or learners will misuse XR artifacts through remixing and sharing experiences of others and violating their rights. Higher education presents a different ownership/licensing situation when student-generated XR projects could be commercialized or published, and rights should be specific in the application domain. Open licensing rules, fair use, and the attribution of content provided in immersive settings should be advised by institutions.

Informed Consent and Ethical Use Policies

Lastly, the use of XR technologies requires taking an age-appropriate and transparent informed consent process. Students and their guardians need to know which data is being collected, to what use it is going to be put, and what risks are associated with the participation in XR activities. Consent is especially relevant in research-based or experimental XR in education opportunities because this type of use case can pose the risk of such boundaries dissolving. Ethical policies should also be clear to specify the acceptable use in certain cases where deemed acceptable, such as remote collaboration, interaction via avatars, and simulated violence.

Table 5. Ethical and legal challenges

Challenge	Description	Example	Implications
Privacy & Data Security	Sensitive data collected without clear safeguards	Eye-tracking, voice data in VR are used without consent	Legal non-compliance (e.g., GDPR, FERPA); loss of trust
Equity & Inclusion	Marginalization of students with disabilities or poor digital access	No support for blind students; low-income schools lack devices	Deepens educational inequities
Content Ethics & Bias	Immersive content can perpetuate stereotypes or inaccuracies	Colonial narratives in VR history simulations	Reinforces bias; impacts perception
Psychological Impact	Intense or traumatic experiences affecting mental well-being	Earthquake simulation triggers anxiety	Emotional distress; needs psychological safeguards
IP and Copyright	Unclear ownership or misuse of third-party content	Unlicensed 3D models used in student projects	Legal liability; confusion over content reuse
Informed Consent	Students are unaware of data usage or risks	No parental consent forms for XR classroom use	Ethical violations; legal exposure

CONCLUSION

The chapter has discussed how VR, AR, and XR could be transformative in the setting of education. Such immersive technologies are transforming how knowledge is delivered, assimilated, and remembered since they provide learners with an experience that cannot be achieved by traditional pedagogical tools. In elementary classrooms, virtual field trips have been used to increase engagement, develop a profound grasp of abstract ideas, and give inclusive learning experiences across disciplines and levels. Nevertheless, although the instrumental advantages are obvious, various technical, financial, pedagogical, institutional, and ethical difficulties in implementing it on a large scale were also described in the chapter.

It is also advised that educators should not consider XR as something new, but a valuable educational tool. In order to be as effective as possible, it should be incorporated into properly developed instructional systems and coordinated with the curricular outcomes. To efficiently allow teachers to implement XR in their classrooms, training and professional development programs are required to empower them with their competence and courage to implement XR in their classrooms. Meanwhile, policymakers should also be among the most decisive factors to offer the education facilities the required infrastructural support, investments, and regulatory atmosphere that can enable the education providers to imbibe and maintain these technologies. On their side, technology developers have to focus on inclusive design, data security, and harmony with educational needs, and to make sure that XR tools become innovative, but not only that, but also commonplace, ethical territories, and sound pedagogical.

With the future in mind, XR has a chance to become the pillar of the digital learning settings. And as the technology is becoming less expensive, larger, and easier to use, we expect to see an easier transition to the hybrid educational environment where virtual and real environments are seamlessly intertwined. The potential of immersive learning is being broadened quickly due to technological advances. Virtual experience will be enhanced by haptic feedback, spatial computing, and volumetric video improvements to perfectly align the virtual world with the real one in terms of realism and emotional appeal. The emergence of 5G and edge computing will minimize latency, and real-time collaboration in an XR environment will be possible even in locations that have limited infrastructure. Hardware is getting easier to carry around and use, eliminating certain obstacles concerning expenses and availability. Such innovations are going to improve not only the quality of the XR but also make the experience more relevant and practical not only among educators but also among learners.

Moreover, other emerging technologies will define the future of XR in education since this technology will evolve alongside them. Personalized learning experiences. Individualized pathways in XR can allow for real-time modifications in content to meet user needs and performance inside the XR environment. Artificial intelligence will make this possible. Big data analytics will enable educators to learn more about the outcomes of the learning process, and they will be able to adjust their instruction more clearly. Units will be connected to the Internet of Things (IoT), which will enable the establishment of an immersive simulation that communicates with physical environments and gadgets. Even blockchain technologies might be involved in the safe storage + validation of the learning gains inside the XR platforms, providing fresh opportunities in the assessment and credentialing of experiential learning.

There is a growing body of research and development work on the pedagogical use of XR. Research is underway to review the cognitive and neuro effects of immersive learning and how experiences impact memory, emotional involvement, and problem-solving skills. At the same time, cross-disciplinary partnerships make the XR more inclusive and culturally responsive, addressing the issues of representation, accessibility, and bias. New formative assessment models are also under discussion, the focus being on learning outcomes that are more related to the experience and interaction of XR.

To sum up, immersive technologies have almost unlimited potential for revolutionizing education, yet the successful implementation of such technologies demands an agency-wide collaboration. Technological innovation alone should not be the subject of interest; learning must be at the center of attention; with the way individuals are involved and the way of gauging. Onward, we will be faced with the question of how to design and develop XR experiences that are not merely technically spectacular, to deliver experiences that are not only pedagogically meaningful, ethically sound, and accessible to all. Education of the future depends on how we incorporate imagination with insight, innovation with inclusion, and XR technologies are one of the best weapons we can harness that can help us achieve that beloved vision.

REFERENCES

Abes, Z., Fairchild, N., Lin, S., Wahba, M., Xiao, K., & Fisher, S. S. (2025). The Immersive Archive: Archival Strategies for the Sensorama & Sutherland HMD. *Proceedings - 2025 IEEE International Conference on Artificial Intelligence and EXtended and Virtual Reality, AIxVR 2025*, 307–312. DOI: 10.1109/AIxVR63409.2025.00059

Akbar, K., Passaro, A., Di Gioia, M., Martini, E., Dragone, M., Zullo, A., & Stasolla, F. (2024). Reviewing the Horizon: The Future of Extended Reality and Artificial Intelligence in Neurorehabilitation for Brain Injury Recovery. *Information, 15*(8), 501. DOI: 10.3390/info15080501

Alhakamy, A. (2024). Extended Reality (XR) Toward Building Immersive Solutions: The Key to Unlocking Industry 4.0. *ACM Computing Surveys*, *56*(9), 1–38. Advance online publication. DOI: 10.1145/3652595

Assaf, R., Mendes, D., & Rodrigues, R. (2024). Cues to fast-forward collaboration: A Survey of Workspace Awareness and Visual Cues in XR Collaborative Systems. *Computer Graphics Forum*, *43*(2), e15066. DOI: 10.1111/cgf.15066

Balakrishnan, N., & Kumar, T. (2024). Transforming lives of Sensory Impaired Individuals through Extended Reality (XR). *Procedia CIRP*, *128*, 846–851. DOI: 10.1016/j.procir.2024.07.067

Barta, S., Gurrea, R., & Flavián, C. (2025). Augmented reality experiences: Consumer-centered augmented reality framework and research agenda. *Psychology and Marketing*, *42*(2), 634–650. DOI: 10.1002/mar.22143

Bhaskaran, V., & Mahbub, U. (2024). Immersive User Experiences: Trends and Challenges of Using XR Technologies. *Computer Vision: Challenges, Trends, and Opportunities*, 260–278. DOI: 10.1201/9781003328957-12/IMMERSIVE-USER-EXPERIENCES-TRENDS-CHALLENGES-USING-XR-TECHNOLOGIES-VASUDEV-BHASKARAN-UPAL-MAHBUB

Boel, C., Dekeyser, K., Lemal, M., Rotsaert, T., Valcke, M., Schellens, T., & Struyf, D. (2024). Towards a Framework for a Nation-Wide Implementation of Augmented, Virtual and Mixed Reality in K-12 Technical and Vocational Education. *TechTrends*, *68*(2), 295–306. Advance online publication. DOI: 10.1007/s11528-023-00925-y

Boel, C., Rotsaert, T., Valcke, M., Vanhulsel, A., & Schellens, T. (2023). Applying educational design research to develop a low-cost, mobile immersive virtual reality serious game teaching safety in secondary vocational education. *Education and Information Technologies, 29*(7), 8609–8646. DOI: 10.1007/s10639-023-12126-4

Calisto, M. de L., & Sarkar, S. (2024). A systematic review of virtual reality in tourism and hospitality: The known and the paths to follow. *International Journal of Hospitality Management, 116*, 103623. DOI: 10.1016/j.ijhm.2023.103623

Cao, S., Chu, J., Zhang, Z. C., & Liu, L. (2024). The effectiveness of VR environment on primary and secondary school students' learning performance in science courses. *Interactive Learning Environments, 32*(10), 7321–7337. DOI: 10.1080/10494820.2024.2312921

Crogman, H. T., Cano, V. D., Pacheco, E., Sonawane, R. B., & Boroon, R. (2025). Virtual Reality, Augmented Reality, and Mixed Reality in Experiential Learning: Transforming Educational Paradigms. *Education Sciences, 15*(3), 303. DOI: 10.3390/educsci15030303

Dubiel, A., Kamińska, D., Zwoliński, G., Ramić-Brkić, B., Agostini, D., & Zancanaro, M. (2025). Virtual reality for the training of soft skills for professional education: Trends and opportunities. *Interactive Learning Environments, 33*(5), 3261–3281. Advance online publication. DOI: 10.1080/10494820.2025.2450634

Garg, D. , Dubey, N., Goel, P., Ramoliya, D., Ganatra, A., Kotecha, K., Selvam, R., Hiremath, P., Cs, S. K., Ramakrishna Bhat, R., Garg, D., Dubey, N., Goel, P., Ramoliya, D., Ganatra, A., & Kotecha, K. (2024). Improvisation in Spinal Surgery Using AR (Augmented Reality), MR (Mixed Reality), and VR (Virtual Reality). *Engineering Proceedings, 59*(1), 186. DOI: 10.3390/engproc2023059186

Huai, P., Li, Y., Wang, X., Zhang, L., Liu, N., & Yang, H. (2024). The effectiveness of virtual reality technology in student nurse education: A systematic review and meta-analysis. *Nurse Education Today, 138*, 106189. DOI: 10.1016/j.nedt.2024.106189 PMID: 38603830

Huang, T. C., & Tseng, H. P. (2025). Extended Reality in Applied Sciences Education: A Systematic Review. *Applied Sciences, 15*(7), 4038. DOI: 10.3390/app15074038

Jiang, H., Zhu, D., Chugh, R., Turnbull, D., & Jin, W. (2025). Virtual reality and augmented reality-supported K-12 STEM learning: trends, advantages and challenges. *Education and Information Technologies, 30*(9), 12827–12863. DOI: 10.1007/s10639-024-13210-z

Jin, S., Huang, J., & Zhong, Z. (2024). Application of Immersive Technologies in Primary and Secondary Education. *Frontiers of Digital Education, 1*(2), 142–152. DOI: 10.1007/s44366-024-0001-3

Kamińska, D., Sapiński, T., Wiak, S., Tikk, T., Haamer, R. E., Avots, E., Helmi, A., Ozcinar, C., & Anbarjafari, G. (2019). Virtual Reality and Its Applications in Education: Survey. *Information, 10*(10), 318. DOI: 10.3390/info10100318

Kawal, P., Dhillon, S., & Tinmaz, H. (2024). Immersive realities: A comprehensive guide from virtual reality to metaverse. *Journal for the Education of Gifted Young Scientists, 12*(1), 29–45. DOI: 10.17478/jegys.1406024

Khan, H. U., Ali, Y., Khan, F., & Al-antari, M. A. (2024). A comprehensive study on unraveling the advances of immersive technologies (VR/AR/MR/XR) in the healthcare sector during the COVID-19: Challenges and solutions. *Heliyon, 10*(15), e35037. Advance online publication. DOI: 10.1016/j.heliyon.2024.e35037 PMID: 39157361

Khlaif, Z. N., Mousa, A., & Sanmugam, M. (2024). Immersive Extended Reality (XR) Technology in Engineering Education: Opportunities and Challenges. *Technology. Knowledge and Learning, 29*(2), 803–826. DOI: 10.1007/s10758-023-09719-w

Koumpouros, Y. (2024). Revealing the true potential and prospects of augmented reality in education. *Smart Learning Environments, 11*(1), 1–62. DOI: 10.1186/s40561-023-00288-0

Lampropoulos, G., & Kinshuk. (2024). Virtual reality and gamification in education: a systematic review. *Educational Technology Research and Development, 72*(3), 1691–1785. DOI: 10.1007/s11423-024-10351-3

Liarokapis, F., Milata, V., & Skola, F. (2024). Extended Reality Educational System with Virtual Teacher Interaction for Enhanced Learning. *Multimodal Technologies and Interaction, 8*(9), 83. DOI: 10.3390/mti8090083

Liu, W., Auernhammer, J., Ohashi, T., Portales, C., & Kourtesis, P. (2024). A Comprehensive Review of Multimodal XR Applications, Risks, and Ethical Challenges in the Metaverse. *Multimodal Technologies and Interaction, 8*(11), 98. DOI: 10.3390/mti8110098

Mirza, T., Dutta, R., Tuli, N., & Mantri, A. (2025). Leveraging augmented reality in education involving new pedagogies with emerging societal relevance. *Discover Sustainability, 6*(1), 1–15. DOI: 10.1007/s43621-025-00877-8

Nair, A. J., Manohar, S., Mittal, A., & Chaudhry, R. (2024). Unleashing Digital Frontiers: Bridging Realities of Augmented Reality, Virtual Reality, and the Metaverse. *The Metaverse Dilemma: Challenges and Opportunities for Business and Society*, 85–112. DOI: 10.1108/978-1-83797-524-220241006

Neher, A. N., Bühlmann, F., Müller, M., Berendonk, C., Sauter, T. C., & Birrenbach, T. (2025). Virtual reality for assessment in undergraduate nursing and medical education – a systematic review. *BMC Medical Education, 25*(1), 1–11. DOI: 10.1186/s12909-025-06867-8 PMID: 39743510

Ortega-Gras, J. J., Gómez-Gómez, M. V., Bueno-Delgado, M. V., Garrido-Lova, J., & Cañavate-Cruzado, G. (2023). Designing a Technological Pathway to Empower Vocational Education and Training in the Circular Wood and Furniture Sector through Extended Reality. *Electronics (Basel), 12*(10), 2328. Advance online publication. DOI: 10.3390/electronics12102328

Partarakis, N., & Zabulis, X. (2024). A Review of Immersive Technologies, Knowledge Representation, and AI for Human-Centered Digital Experiences. *Electronics, 13*(2), 269. DOI: 10.3390/electronics13020269

Poggianti, C., Chessa, S., Pelagatti, S., & Kocian, A. (2025). Immersive technologies for inclusive digital education: A systematic survey. *Human Behavior and Emerging Technologies, 2025*(1), 8888303. DOI: 10.1155/hbe2/8888303

Smutny, P., Babiuch, M., & Foltynek, P. (2019). A review of the virtual reality applications in education and training. *Proceedings of the 2019 20th International Carpathian Control Conference, ICCC 2019*. DOI: 10.1109/CarpathianCC.2019.8765930

Sümer, M., & Vaněček, D. (2025). A systematic review of virtual and augmented realities in higher education: Trends and issues. *Innovations in Education and Teaching International, 62*(3), 811–822. DOI: 10.1080/14703297.2024.2382854

Vasarainen, M., Paavola, S., & Vetoshkina, L. (2021). A Systematic Literature Review on Extended Reality: Virtual, Augmented and Mixed Reality in Working Life. *Internationa Journal of Virtual Reality, 21*(2), 1–28. DOI: 10.20870/IJVR.2021.21.2.4620

Wu, S., Stendal, K., & Thapa, D. (2024a). *Emerging Trends in XR-mediated Virtual Team Collaboration in Digital Workspaces: A Systematic Literature Review*. DOI: 10.1007/978-3-031-57189-3_5

Wu, S., Stendal, K., & Thapa, D. (2024b). Emerging trends in XR-mediated virtual team collaboration in digital workspaces: A systematic literature review. *Advances in Information Systems Development: Information Systems Development, Organizational Aspects, and Societal Trends*, 85–108.

Zhang, S., & Yao, Z. (2025). The challenge of the application of augmented reality in science education in China: A systematic review. *Disciplinary and Interdisciplinary Science Education Research, 7*(1), 1–13. DOI: 10.1186/s43031-025-00123-1

Zhang, Y., Feijoo-Garcia, M. A., Gu, Y., Popescu, V., Benes, B., & Magana, A. J. (2024). Virtual and Augmented Reality in Science, Technology, Engineering, and Mathematics (STEM) Education: An Umbrella Review. *Information, 15*(9), 515. DOI: 10.3390/info15090515

Chapter 5
Learning in the Metaverse:
Virtual Classrooms, Immersive Experiences, and Beyond

Abeer Saber
https://orcid.org/0000-0002-9261-0927
Faculty of Computers and Artificial intelligence, Damietta University, Egypt

Esraa Hassan
Faculty of Artificial Intelligence, Kafrelsheikh University, Egypt

Samar Elbcdwchy
Faculty of Artificial Intelligence, Kafrelsheikh University, Egypt

Tamer Z. Emara
https://orcid.org/0000-0001-6730-9449
Faculty of Computers and Artificial intelligence, Damietta University, Egypt & Faculty of Computers, Information, and Artificial Intelligence, Damietta National University, Egypt

ABSTRACT

This chapter explores how the Metaverse can fundamentally reshape education to create more inclusive and equitable learning opportunities for all. It examines how persistent 3D worlds, real-time interaction, and digital embodiment can democratize access to high-quality, engaging educational content. By providing virtual classrooms, immersive simulations, and skill-building platforms, the Metaverse offers a powerful new approach to lifelong learning for diverse populations, from K–12 students to professionals. The chapter critically addresses key challenges and ethical considerations, including ensuring digital equity, protecting learner identity,

DOI: 10.4018/979-8-3373-3043-3.ch005

and establishing frameworks for responsible governance. Through case studies, theoretical frameworks, and current trends, this chapter provides a forward-looking analysis of how education can evolve within the Metaverse to meet the urgent needs of learners in the 21st century.

INTRODUCTION

The metaverse is a rapidly evolving concept that refers to a collective, virtual space composed of persistent 3D digital worlds, often connected through the internet. These environments are designed to be persistent, meaning they continue to exist and change even when users are not actively interacting with them (Dionisio et al., 2013). Unlike traditional websites or games, which reset or close when exited, metaverse spaces are ongoing and shared among multiple users. This continuity allows for long-term social interaction, content creation, and economic activity within virtual worlds that mirror or extend reality (Ball, 2024).

A defining feature of the metaverse is interoperability—the seamless interaction between different platforms, applications, and virtual spaces. In an interoperable metaverse, users can carry their digital identities, assets, and experiences across multiple environments without interruption. This creates a unified digital ecosystem where tools, currencies, and avatars are not locked into a single application. As the metaverse grows, this interoperability will be key in enabling large-scale collaboration, learning, and content exchange across institutions and user communities (Abilkaiyrkyzy et al., 2023).

Immersion is another core element of the metaverse. Through advanced technologies such as virtual reality (VR), augmented reality (AR), spatial audio, and haptic feedback, users can experience a deep sense of presence in a digital environment (Dudley et al., 2023). Unlike passive media such as videos or slideshows, immersive platforms encourage users to engage with content and others in lifelike, 3D settings. This can evoke emotions, attention, and behaviors similar to those in real-world scenarios, making the metaverse particularly powerful for interactive applications like gaming, social networking, and—importantly—education (Hadi et al., 2024).

In the field of education, the metaverse introduces new levels of engagement that go beyond traditional learning methods. By participating in interactive, game-like simulations or exploring dynamic virtual classrooms, students become active contributors to their learning journey (Damaševičius & Sidekerskienė, 2024). For example, a history student could walk through a digital reconstruction of ancient Egypt, interacting with artifacts and historical figures, while a science student might perform chemistry experiments in a safe, virtual lab. These interactive experiences foster curiosity, improve retention, and make learning more enjoyable (Johnston et al., 2025).

Another significant benefit is accessibility. The metaverse can democratize education by enabling learners from different regions, backgrounds, or physical abilities to access high-quality resources and experiences. Students who are geographically isolated or have limited access to educational facilities can attend virtual lectures, collaborate with peers worldwide, or explore educational content without leaving their homes. In addition, virtual environments can be tailored to accommodate various learning needs, including those of students with disabilities, ensuring a more inclusive educational experience (Yeganeh et al., 2025).

Finally, the metaverse supports experiential learning, a pedagogy where knowledge is acquired through real-world practice and reflection. In metaverse-based education, learners are not just passive recipients of information, they become participants in realistic, scenario-based activities. This is especially beneficial for disciplines that require practical training, such as medicine, engineering, or business. By simulating real-life situations, students can experiment, make decisions, and learn from outcomes in a risk-free setting. This approach enhances critical thinking, collaboration, and problem-solving skills, preparing students for complex challenges in their future careers.

Motivation

Traditional e-learning, while effective in many ways, often falls short in delivering deeply engaging, interactive, and realistic learning experiences. Most online education relies heavily on static content like video lectures, PDFs, slide presentations, and text-based discussion boards. While convenient and scalable, these formats can feel passive and disconnected, especially for learners who thrive in hands-on, social, or immersive environments. The lack of real-time interaction, limited opportunities for experiential learning, and minimal personalization often result in reduced motivation, low retention rates, and limited practical skill development (Rao et al., 2024).

Another limitation of traditional e-learning is its struggle to replicate the social dynamics and collaborative aspects of in-person education. Classroom discussions, group work, and spontaneous peer interactions are hard to recreate in flat, two-dimensional interfaces. Students may feel isolated or disengaged without the visual and emotional cues that come from face-to-face interaction. Moreover, certain fields like engineering, healthcare, and the arts require spatial understanding and practice-based learning that is difficult to achieve through standard online platforms (Garner, 2017).

The metaverse bridges these gaps by offering fully immersive, 3D environments where learners can interact with content, instructors, and each other in real time.

Instead of watching a lecture, students can *experience* a concept—walking through a digital twin of a historical site, conducting a science experiment in a virtual lab, or practicing a language in a simulated cultural environment. These immersive experiences stimulate multiple senses, promoting deeper engagement, better retention, and more effective learning (Yeganeh et al., 2025).

Furthermore, the metaverse enables rich social interaction through avatars and real-time voice or gesture-based communication. Students can collaborate on projects, attend live lectures, or participate in simulations alongside peers from around the world, fostering a strong sense of presence and community. This social dimension reintroduces many of the human elements missing from traditional e-learning and supports the development of soft skills such as teamwork, empathy, and communication.

Personalization is another area where the metaverse improves upon traditional models. AI-driven avatars and adaptive environments can tailor learning paths to each student's pace, preferences, and needs. Learners can choose how they navigate content, revisit experiences, or engage with supplementary materials in a way that suits their unique learning style. This flexibility is especially valuable for diverse learners and those with special educational requirements (Noomene & Abed, 2025).

In essence, while traditional e-learning laid the foundation for digital education, the metaverse represents the next leap forward. By combining immersion, interactivity, and personalization, it addresses many of the shortcomings of current platforms and opens up new possibilities for making education more inclusive, engaging, and effective.

Transforming Learning Across Levels: The Metaverse in K-12, Higher Education, and Professional Training

The metaverse presents exciting possibilities for K-12 education, offering young learners immersive and interactive experiences that align with their natural curiosity and play-based learning tendencies. Through virtual field trips, 3D storytelling, and gamified lessons, educators can bring abstract concepts to life and make subjects like math, science, and history more engaging. For instance, instead of reading about planets in a textbook, students can explore the solar system firsthand in a virtual space. Additionally, the metaverse can cater to different learning styles and needs, offering accessible and adaptive experiences for students with learning disabilities or language barriers, thereby supporting more inclusive classrooms (Guan et al., 2024).

In higher education, the metaverse enhances academic depth and collaboration by creating opportunities for experiential learning and global engagement. Universities can build virtual campuses where students attend lectures, conduct lab work, and collaborate on group projects regardless of physical location. Complex fields like architecture, medicine, or environmental science can be taught using realistic simulations and models, allowing students to apply theory in lifelike contexts. For example, medical students can perform virtual surgeries, while engineering students can construct and test digital prototypes. This hands-on experience reinforces knowledge and prepares students for real-world challenges (Hosseini et al., 2025).

Professional training also benefits significantly from metaverse technologies, especially in industries where practical experience and quick decision-making are critical. In fields such as aviation, healthcare, manufacturing, and emergency response, immersive simulations can be used to train professionals in safe, controlled environments. These simulations allow trainees to practice high-risk tasks without real-world consequences, receive instant feedback, and repeat scenarios until mastery is achieved. Additionally, soft skills such as leadership, communication, and negotiation can be honed through role-playing exercises in virtual meeting rooms or simulated business settings.

Beyond technical skills, the metaverse fosters continuous learning and professional development. Corporations and training institutions can create customized virtual environments where employees access resources, attend workshops, and participate in mentorship programs. Because these environments are persistent and available globally, they support flexible, on-demand learning that fits into busy professional schedules. This model aligns well with the needs of modern workers who require lifelong learning and reskilling to keep up with rapidly changing industries and technologies.

Overall, the metaverse provides unique value across all educational levels—*sparking imagination in K-12 students, deepening understanding in higher education, and strengthening skills in the workforce*. By offering immersive, accessible, and scalable learning environments, it bridges gaps that traditional methods often leave behind. As adoption increases, educators and institutions must ensure thoughtful integration that aligns with educational goals, supports equity, and prepares learners for the digital age (Chen et al., 2023).

The chapter begins by defining the Metaverse and contextualizing its relevance to education, particularly in contrast to the limitations of conventional e-learning platforms. It then explores the core components of virtual learning environments, such as digital avatars, immersive classrooms, and real-time collaboration tools. Following this, the discussion shifts to key applications in K–12 education, higher education, and corporate or professional training. Specific use cases and emerging technologies—including VR/AR platforms, AI tutors, and blockchain-based credentialing—are analyzed. The chapter concludes by outlining future directions, including technological trends, research gaps, and policy implications, offering a comprehensive vision of how the Metaverse may continue to reshape education in the years to come.

TECHNOLOGICAL FOUNDATIONS

Core Technologies

Exploring the Power of Immersive Technologies: VR, AR, and MR

Virtual Reality (VR) is one of the most well-known immersive technologies and has made significant strides in education, entertainment, and training. Devices like the *Oculus Rift* and *Meta Quest* create fully immersive 3D environments where users are visually and audibly transported into virtual worlds. In education, VR can simulate real-world environments and scenarios, allowing learners to explore historical events, conduct virtual science experiments, or walk through architectural designs. This full immersion blocks out the physical world, encouraging focus and presence, which can enhance learning outcomes and engagement (Wohlgenannt et al., 2020).

Augmented Reality (AR) overlays digital content onto the real world, allowing users to see and interact with virtual objects in their physical surroundings. This is commonly experienced through smartphones, tablets, or specialized devices like *Microsoft HoloLens*. In classrooms, AR can bring static content to life—for example, textbooks that project 3D models of the human body or planets. Unlike VR, AR does not require users to disconnect from their physical environment, making it ideal for blending digital enhancements with real-world contexts, especially in K-12 and field-based learning (Sharma et al., 2024).

Mixed Reality (MR) takes both VR and AR a step further by merging physical and digital environments in real time. Using MR headsets like *HoloLens 2*, users can interact with digital objects as if they were part of the physical world, using natural gestures and spatial awareness. This creates opportunities for collaborative learning, remote instruction, and detailed simulations. For instance, in medical training, MR can project holographic organs that students can examine and manipulate while receiving real-time feedback from instructors, even if they are in different locations.

These technologies are increasingly being used in professional and technical training, where realism and safety are critical. In aviation, pilots train in VR flight simulators that replicate cockpit experiences. In manufacturing, workers use AR headsets to follow real-time assembly instructions or perform quality checks. MR is especially powerful for remote collaboration—engineers can meet in shared holographic workspaces to co-design machinery or diagnose technical issues. The ability to visualize and interact with complex data or systems makes these tools invaluable for enhancing precision, reducing errors, and speeding up learning curves (Saber et al., 2018; Emara et al., 2025c).

As immersive technologies like VR, AR, and MR become more accessible and affordable, their integration into education and industry is accelerating. They support new modes of learning that are interactive, experiential, and personalized. While each technology has distinct advantages, their convergence within the metaverse and related platforms creates opportunities for a richer, more connected digital future. Educators, developers, and institutions must collaborate to ensure these tools are used thoughtfully to enhance—not replace—traditional teaching and training methods.

AI and Avatars: Redefining Instruction With Intelligent Agents in the Metaverse

Artificial Intelligence (AI) plays a foundational role in the metaverse, particularly through the use of avatars—digital representations of users and non-player characters (NPCs) that can act as instructors, guides, or learning companions. AI-powered NPCs can serve as virtual teachers or tutors, delivering content, answering questions, and adapting their behavior based on student interactions. Unlike static course materials or pre-recorded videos, these NPC instructors can respond in real-time, simulate emotions, and create dynamic conversations, making the learning process more engaging and human-like (Emara et al., 2025b).

One of the most powerful applications of AI in education is the development of personalized learning agents. These intelligent avatars can track a student's progress, learning style, preferences, and performance to tailor the educational experience to individual needs. For example, a personalized AI tutor might slow down to explain a complex math problem or suggest alternative learning resources if a student is struggling. This level of customization is difficult to achieve in traditional classrooms or even with standard e-learning platforms, but AI makes it scalable and responsive.

In virtual classrooms or training simulations, AI avatars can also function as role-players or scenario facilitators. In healthcare training, for instance, an AI avatar could simulate a patient with changing symptoms, allowing medical students to practice diagnostic skills in a controlled yet realistic environment. In business or leadership courses, avatars can represent team members, clients, or competitors, providing learners with opportunities to develop interpersonal, negotiation, and decision-making skills. These simulations enable repeated practice and instant feedback without real-world risks (Zechner et al., 2024).

AI also enhances accessibility and inclusivity in learning environments. Language translation, speech recognition, and adaptive communication styles allow AI agents to support learners from diverse linguistic and cultural backgrounds, as well as those with disabilities. For example, an AI avatar could use sign language for a hearing-impaired student or simplify language for younger or non-native learners. This ensures that educational content is not only engaging but also equitable and accessible to a wider range of students.

As the metaverse evolves, the integration of AI and avatars holds immense potential to redefine the role of educators and learners. Rather than replacing human teachers, AI can support them by handling repetitive tasks, providing data-driven insights, and enabling deeper personalization. At the same time, learners benefit from more responsive, interactive, and immersive experiences. The key lies in thoughtful design—balancing automation with human connection, and ensuring that AI-driven avatars enhance, rather than detract from, the educational journey (Kumar et al., 2023).

Blockchain in Education: Securing Credentials and Empowering Learners in the Metaverse

Blockchain technology is emerging as a critical infrastructure for the metaverse, offering new levels of security, transparency, and autonomy in digital interactions. In the context of education, one of its most impactful applications is secure credentialing. Traditional academic records and certifications are often stored in centralized databases, making them vulnerable to tampering, fraud, or loss. Blockchain enables institutions to issue tamper-proof digital diplomas, certificates, and transcripts that can be easily verified by employers or other institutions without relying on intermediaries. These credentials are permanently recorded on a decentralized ledger, ensuring authenticity and long-term accessibility (Gadekallu et al., 2022).

Beyond credentials, blockchain facilitates decentralized ownership of educational assets. In the metaverse, learners engage with digital content—such as textbooks, simulations, projects, or achievements—that can be tokenized as unique, transferable assets using non-fungible tokens (NFTs). This allows students to truly own their educational journey, collecting verifiable records of skills, accomplishments, and participation across platforms. For example, a student might earn an NFT for completing a coding course, which can then be added to their personal digital portfolio and recognized across different virtual campuses or professional networks (Enache, 2023).

Blockchain also supports interoperability between educational platforms, a key aspect of the metaverse's vision. With decentralized identity systems, learners can use a single digital wallet or profile to access courses, materials, and credentials across various institutions and platforms without losing control of their data. This makes lifelong learning more seamless, as individuals can accumulate knowledge and certifications across multiple providers without being locked into proprietary systems (Williams, 2025).

In addition, blockchain can enable new economic models for education. Students and educators can participate in decentralized learning ecosystems where content creators are rewarded directly through smart contracts. For instance, a teacher who designs a popular virtual physics lab could earn micro-payments each time it is used by a student or institution. This encourages innovation, rewards contribution, and fosters a more participatory educational economy where value is fairly distributed among stakeholders.

Ultimately, blockchain empowers learners by giving them control over their credentials, educational records, and digital assets. As education increasingly moves into the metaverse, blockchain ensures that these components are secure, portable, and verifiable. By decentralizing ownership and reducing reliance on centralized institutions, it promotes transparency, trust, and equity—essential values in shaping the future of global education.

IoT and Haptics: Bringing Physical Sensation into Digital Learning

The integration of the Internet of Things (IoT) and haptic technology into the metaverse is transforming how learners interact with digital environments, especially in fields requiring hands-on training. IoT refers to a network of interconnected physical devices—such as sensors, wearables, and smart tools—that collect and share data in real time. When combined with haptic devices, which simulate touch and physical feedback, these technologies create realistic, tactile experiences that bridge the gap between virtual and physical learning. This is especially valuable in technical education, medical training, and vocational fields where physical interaction is essential (Jagatheesaperumal et al., 2024).

Haptic feedback allows users to feel texture, resistance, pressure, or vibration while interacting with virtual objects. For instance, students using haptic gloves or controllers can "feel" the tension of a muscle during a virtual surgery or sense the vibration of machinery in an engineering simulation. These physical cues enhance immersion and realism, helping learners build muscle memory and refine fine motor skills. Unlike passive video or static simulations, haptic-enabled environments promote active learning through realistic engagement with tools, materials, and scenarios (Biswas & Visell, 2021).

Meanwhile, IoT devices provide a constant stream of contextual data that can be used to monitor performance, track progress, and personalize training experiences. In smart learning labs or virtual workshops, IoT sensors can detect how a student holds a tool, the pressure applied during a task, or environmental conditions like temperature or noise. This data can be analyzed in real time to provide feedback or adaptive challenges, making learning more responsive and effective. For example, a welding simulator could adjust resistance or visual cues based on the user's technique and performance (Emara et al., 2025c; Trinh et al., 2022).

In professional and industrial training, the combination of IoT and haptics has far-reaching implications. For instance, trainees in hazardous fields such as firefighting, construction, or chemical handling can practice dangerous procedures in a risk-free virtual environment, while still receiving realistic sensory feedback. This not only improves safety but also allows for repeated practice without the cost or risk associated with real materials or equipment. In medical education, haptic tools allow students to perform delicate procedures like suturing or catheter insertion with a level of tactile precision previously possible only in real clinical settings (Redford, 2021).

As these technologies become more refined and affordable, their educational applications will continue to expand. Together, IoT and haptics are redefining experiential learning, allowing students to engage with the digital world in a physical, intuitive way. By enabling touch, motion, and real-time feedback within virtual environments, they close the sensory gap in remote education and make immersive, skill-based training more accessible and effective across disciplines.

Infrastructure Requirements for Implementing the Metaverse in Education

Successfully integrating the metaverse into education requires a robust hardware infrastructure that balances performance with accessibility. On one end of the spectrum are affordable VR headsets like the Meta Quest series, which offer wireless, standalone functionality and are increasingly used in schools due to their cost-effectiveness and ease of use. On the other end are high-end immersive environments, such as CAVEs (Cave Automatic Virtual Environments), which are room-sized setups that use multiple projectors and motion tracking to create shared, walk-in 3D experiences. While CAVEs provide unmatched immersion, they are expensive and complex, making them more suitable for universities and specialized training centers. The challenge lies in making immersive hardware scalable and equitable for broader adoption in K-12 and underfunded institutions (Manjrekar et al., 2014).

Network infrastructure is another critical factor, as immersive metaverse applications require high-speed, low-latency connectivity to function effectively—especially in real-time collaborative or data-heavy environments. Technologies like 5G and edge computing are essential to support these demands. 5G offers faster data speeds and lower latency, enabling smoother interactions in multi-user VR or AR experiences. Meanwhile, edge computing reduces the delay caused by data transmission to centralized servers by processing information closer to the user's device. Together, these technologies ensure that immersive learning experiences are seamless, responsive, and not hindered by buffering or lag (Koppolu, 2025). This is especially true for data-intensive applications, where the performance of the system relies on efficient data management to support large-scale data analysis (Emara et al., 2023; Emara & Huang, 2019a; Emara & Huang, 2019b).

Equally important are the platforms that host educational content in the metaverse. Several platforms are leading the way by providing accessible, collaborative, and content-rich environments. Roblox Education enables young learners to design games and interactive experiences while learning coding and logic. ENGAGE offers a professional virtual learning and collaboration environment used by universities, enterprises, and training organizations to host lectures, workshops, and immersive simulations (Bell & Morris, 2009). Mozilla Hubs, an open-source platform, allows users to create and enter shared 3D spaces via a browser, making it more accessible for schools with limited resources or hardware capabilities (Brown et al., 2021). Each platform varies in technical requirements, content offerings, and customization flexibility, so institutions must choose based on their pedagogical goals and student needs.

To support all these components, technical support and digital literacy are also vital. Educators and IT teams must be trained not only to use these technologies but also to troubleshoot common issues and integrate them effectively into the curriculum. Schools and institutions may also need to upgrade internal systems, including Wi-Fi networks, cloud storage, and device compatibility, to meet the demands of high-bandwidth applications and large-scale deployment.

In summary, implementing the metaverse in education is not just about acquiring headsets or downloading software—it requires a comprehensive infrastructure that spans hardware, networking, platforms, and human support. Institutions must evaluate their current capabilities and make strategic investments that ensure long-term sustainability, scalability, and equity in access. With the right infrastructure, the metaverse can become a powerful, immersive extension of today's digital classrooms.

Balancing Accessibility and Immersion in Educational Metaverse Experiences

One of the key challenges in adopting the metaverse for education lies in balancing accessibility and immersion. Immersive technologies like VR, AR, and haptics promise highly engaging, hands-on learning experiences—but they often come with significant costs and infrastructure demands. On the other hand, more accessible solutions, such as smartphone-based VR or web-based 3D platforms, are easier to deploy but offer more limited interactivity and sensory depth. Educators and institutions must navigate these trade-offs to deliver effective and equitable learning experiences (Khan & Alamäki, 2023).

Smartphone-based VR solutions, such as Google Cardboard or web-enabled AR experiences, are among the most accessible forms of immersive technology. They are low-cost, easy to distribute, and compatible with widely available devices. These solutions can introduce students to basic 3D environments and virtual simulations without requiring expensive hardware. However, their immersive quality is limited, they lack precise motion tracking, high-resolution graphics, and haptic feedback. This can reduce the sense of presence and limit their effectiveness for complex, skill-based training.

At the other extreme, high-end immersive setups—like full-body haptic suits, advanced VR headsets, or motion-tracking rooms—deliver deeply engaging and realistic experiences. These systems can simulate touch, resistance, and spatial awareness, making them ideal for fields such as medicine, engineering, or technical trades where physical precision is crucial. However, the high cost, specialized hardware, and need for large physical spaces often restrict their use to well-funded universities, labs, or corporate training programs, limiting their scalability across mainstream education.

The ideal solution often lies in hybrid approaches that combine accessibility with meaningful immersion. For example, using mid-range standalone VR headsets like Meta Quest allows for decent immersion (hand tracking, 3D sound, spatial navigation) without requiring a PC or external sensors. Platforms like Mozilla Hubs or ENGAGE can also be accessed across devices, from desktops to headsets, ensuring that students with different levels of access can still participate. This tiered approach supports inclusion while maximizing engagement for those with the necessary tools (Poolsawas & Chotikakamthorn, 2023).

Ultimately, the trade-off between accessibility and immersion is not just technical, it is also pedagogical. The level of immersion needed should align with the learning objectives. A virtual museum tour for a history class may not require full haptics, whereas surgical training might. By matching technology to context, and planning scalable strategies, educators can ensure that the metaverse enhances learning without creating new barriers or inequities. As hardware becomes more affordable and infrastructure improves, the gap between accessibility and full immersion is expected to narrow over time.

IMMERSIVE LEARNING EXPERIENCES

Gamification and Engagement

Gamification—the use of game design elements in non-game contexts—is a powerful tool for enhancing engagement, motivation, and learning outcomes in the metaverse. By integrating game mechanics such as points, challenges, rewards, and progression into educational experiences, gamification transforms passive learning into active exploration. In immersive environments, these elements become even more compelling, as students are not just playing—they are living the experience, which boosts focus, collaboration, and emotional connection to the content (Christopoulos & Mystakidis, 2023).

A widely recognized example is Minecraft Education Edition, which uses a sandbox-style 3D world to promote collaborative problem-solving and creativity. In educational settings, students work together to build structures, solve challenges, and simulate real-world scenarios—from designing sustainable cities to reenacting historical events. This open-ended, goal-oriented gameplay fosters critical thinking, teamwork, and digital literacy. Because students are active participants shaping their environment, they develop a sense of ownership and agency in their learning process—key drivers of intrinsic motivation (Meusa, 2025).

Unlike traditional learning environments, gamified metaverse platforms often support intrinsic motivation—learning driven by internal curiosity and personal satisfaction rather than external rewards. For example, a student exploring a virtual biology lab might pursue additional experiments simply out of interest, not because it's graded. The autonomy to choose paths, the joy of discovering new knowledge, and the satisfaction of solving in-world problems make learning feel purposeful and fun. This stands in stark contrast to rigid curricula or passive video-based instruction, which may fail to hold students' attention or adapt to individual interests (Yang et al., 2024).

In conclusion, gamification in the metaverse bridges motivation and mastery, combining the cognitive benefits of immersive technology with the emotional and psychological rewards of game-based learning. Platforms like Minecraft Education demonstrate how play and learning can coexist productively, while psychological theories such as flow offer a framework for designing educational experiences that sustain attention and drive growth. By tapping into these principles, educators can build virtual environments that don't just teach—they captivate.

Virtual Labs and Field Trips: Expanding Experiential Learning in the Metaverse

Virtual labs and field trips are revolutionizing experiential learning by offering safe, scalable, and immersive alternatives to traditional hands-on activities. These digital experiences allow students to engage with complex processes, distant environments, or expensive equipment without the constraints of physical space or logistical limitations. As part of the broader metaverse ecosystem, virtual labs and field trips enhance accessibility while maintaining the interactivity and realism essential for deep understanding (Fitrianto & Saif, 2024).

One standout example is Labster, a platform that provides fully immersive VR biology and chemistry labs. Students can conduct experiments such as DNA sequencing, cell analysis, or chemical reactions in a controlled, virtual environment—complete with realistic instruments, guided tutorials, and instant feedback. These labs reduce the cost and safety concerns associated with real-life science facilities, especially in underfunded schools. Similarly, Google Expeditions enables students to take guided virtual tours of historic landmarks, natural wonders, and cultural sites from around the world using affordable VR headsets or mobile devices, offering a sense of presence and discovery that textbooks cannot replicate (Theatre & Wright, 2023).

In a virtual lab, a student can repeat an experiment multiple times without fear of wasting resources or making irreversible mistakes. In virtual field trips, learners can navigate environments freely, pausing to explore areas that interest them most. This level of autonomy enhances critical thinking and curiosity, two key components of deeper learning. It also helps bridge equity gaps, ensuring that students in remote or low-resource settings gain access to the same high-quality educational opportunities as their peers.

In essence, virtual labs and field trips empower educators to bring the world into the classroom—and the classroom into the world. By leveraging platforms like Labster and Google Expeditions, schools can offer engaging, high-impact learning experiences regardless of physical limitations. Backed by data and growing accessibility, these immersive tools represent a pivotal step toward more inclusive, interactive, and effective education in the age of the metaverse.

Adaptive Learning Environments in the Metaverse: Personalization and Ethical Challenges

One of the most promising applications of the metaverse in education is the development of adaptive learning environments powered by artificial intelligence (AI) (Sakr et al., 2020; Ahmed et al., 2022; Saber et al., 2023; Saber et al., 2021; Hassan et al., 2024; Bhatnagar et al., 2024; Saber et al., 2025; Emara et al., 2025a). These systems analyze a learner's behavior, performance, and preferences to customize the pace, difficulty, and presentation of educational content, a process that relies on advanced feature selection and data modeling (NguyenDuc et al., 2025; VuThi et al., 2024; TrinhHuy et al., 2025). In the metaverse, this customization becomes even more dynamic, as students can interact with AI-powered avatars and intelligent agents in real-time, receiving immediate, tailored feedback. Platforms like Carnegie Learning have begun exploring this potential with AI-driven math tutors embedded in virtual environments, where students solve problems, get step-by-step guidance, and learn at their own pace within immersive, gamified contexts.

These systems analyze a learner's behavior, performance, and preferences to customize the pace, difficulty, and presentation of educational content, a process that relies on advanced feature selection and data modeling (NguyenDuc et al., 2025; VuThi et al., 2024; TrinhHuy et al., 2025).

The benefit of such adaptive systems is clear: they help address the diverse learning needs of students more effectively than traditional one-size-fits-all approaches. For instance, a student struggling with algebra can receive additional explanations and simpler examples, while an advanced learner can be challenged with complex applications and exploratory tasks. The metaverse enhances this experience by embedding learners in 3D environments where they can visualize abstract concepts, interact with manipulatives, and collaborate with peers or AI tutors in real time. This makes learning more responsive, personalized, and engaging (Yang et al., 2019).

However, the use of AI in education raises important ethical concerns, particularly regarding bias in algorithmic personalization. AI systems are only as unbiased as the data they are trained on, and if the underlying datasets reflect historical inequalities or incomplete representations of learners, the system may unintentionally favor certain groups while disadvantaging others (Mergen et al., 2025). For example, students from underrepresented communities might receive overly simplified content, be wrongly categorized as low-performing, or be denied opportunities to advance. These biases can reinforce systemic disparities rather than mitigate them.

Transparency and accountability are crucial in designing adaptive systems within the metaverse. Developers and educators must ensure that AI models are trained on diverse datasets, regularly audited for bias, and explainable in their decision-making processes. Students and teachers should also have visibility and control over how personalization occurs, including the ability to override or adjust system-generated paths. Ethical frameworks and oversight mechanisms must be in place to protect privacy, promote fairness, and ensure that these tools serve the educational interests of all learners (Kumar et al., 2023).

In conclusion, AI-driven adaptive learning in the metaverse holds immense potential to transform education, making it more inclusive, personalized, and effective. But this potential can only be fully realized if ethical challenges are addressed head-on. Balancing technological innovation with fairness, transparency, and human oversight is essential to creating learning environments that not only adapt to students but also empower them.

VIRTUAL CLASSROOMS IN THE METAVERSE

Design Principles for Immersive Learning

The effectiveness of virtual classrooms in the metaverse depends heavily on thoughtful design principles that prioritize realism, interaction, and inclusivity. Unlike traditional video conferencing platforms, metaverse-based classrooms use immersive technologies to simulate real-world learning environments. Key features such as spatial audio and non-verbal cues dramatically enhance communication and presence. With spatial audio, students hear voices based on avatar positioning—just as they would in a physical room—making discussions feel more natural and reducing confusion in group settings. Innovations like Meta's Codec Avatars push this further by capturing facial expressions and subtle gestures in real-time, creating lifelike avatars that convey emotion, engagement, and attention (Pervez et al., 2024).

In virtual learning spaces, non-verbal communication plays a crucial role in replicating the social dynamics of a physical classroom. Hand gestures, eye contact, posture, and proximity allow teachers to gauge student participation and foster peer-to-peer interaction. These cues help create a sense of co-presence and social connection, which are often missing in flat video-based learning. This emotional realism is especially important in K-12 and higher education settings, where interpersonal development and collaboration are integral to the learning process (Anderson & Rainie, 2022).

To support active learning, metaverse classrooms incorporate interactive tools such as virtual whiteboards, 3D models, and real-time annotation features. Digital whiteboards function like their physical counterparts but can be enhanced with multimedia elements, live drawing, and collaborative input from students. These tools encourage participation and visual thinking, making abstract concepts easier to grasp. Teachers can annotate content, organize ideas spatially, and enable students to contribute visually during lessons—an essential component for both STEM and humanities education.

Breakout rooms in virtual environments offer additional opportunities for collaboration and focused discussion. Students can seamlessly move into smaller, customizable spaces where they can work on group projects, engage in peer reviews, or receive individualized instruction. Unlike traditional platforms, metaverse breakout rooms can be designed with thematic elements, spatial privacy, and interactive tools that match the activity's goals. This flexibility supports a variety of pedagogical strategies, from project-based learning to flipped classrooms.

Global Collaboration in the Metaverse: Connecting Classrooms Across Borders

One of the most transformative potentials of the metaverse in education is its ability to foster global collaboration. Through immersive, real-time interaction, students and educators from different countries can engage in shared learning experiences that promote cross-cultural understanding, global citizenship, and digital fluency.

Platforms like IVECA use virtual classrooms and avatars to simulate international learning spaces, allowing students to communicate through voice, gestures, and shared content (Nasir et al., 2024). These programs go beyond text-based communication by leveraging interactive environments and cultural simulations.

However, implementing global collaboration in the metaverse does not come without challenges. One significant obstacle is time zone differences. Coordinating live sessions between students on opposite sides of the globe can be logistically complex, often requiring early or late meetings that may not be sustainable for long-term projects. Some programs address this by combining synchronous and asynchronous interactions—allowing students to leave video or voice messages or contribute to persistent digital workspaces when live communication isn't possible.

Another major hurdle is language barriers, which can hinder fluid interaction and full participation in collaborative tasks. While the metaverse offers innovative solutions—such as real-time translation tools and multilingual AI avatars—these technologies are still evolving and may not always capture nuance or cultural context accurately. Educators must design activities that are inclusive and provide scaffolding to help students navigate language differences, such as using visual aids, simplified instructions, or multilingual content where possible.

Teacher Roles and Pedagogy in the Metaverse: Evolving from Lecturers to Learning Facilitators

The rise of the metaverse in education is reshaping the traditional role of teachers, shifting them from lecturers delivering content to facilitators guiding interactive, student-centered learning. In immersive environments, where learners can explore, experiment, and collaborate independently, the teacher becomes a "guide on the side" rather than a "sage on the stage." This pedagogical shift encourages inquiry-based, experiential, and problem-solving approaches, where students construct knowledge through real-time interaction with digital content, peers, and AI-driven tools (Kempton, 2017).

In the metaverse, educators are tasked with designing and orchestrating learning experiences that foster autonomy, creativity, and critical thinking. For example, instead of simply explaining a historical event, a teacher might guide students through a virtual reenactment, prompting them to analyze decisions, engage in role-play, or reflect on multiple perspectives. This approach aligns with constructivist and connectivity learning theories, where the teacher's role is to support exploration, provide context, and facilitate meaningful dialogue.

Professional development for teaching in the metaverse should also include training in avatar-based communication, spatial classroom design, and management of interactive tools like digital whiteboards, breakout zones, and virtual labs. Teachers must learn how to read digital body language, foster engagement in 3D spaces, and manage student participation across varied levels of immersion (e.g., headset users vs. desktop users). Additionally, understanding the ethical implications of AI tutors, data privacy, and digital equity is essential for responsible metaverse instruction.

CHALLENGES AND ETHICAL CONSIDERATIONS

Privacy & Security in Educational Metaverses

As educational institutions integrate immersive technologies into classrooms, privacy and data security emerge as pressing concerns. VR platforms collect a vast array of sensitive information—from biometric data like eye movement and voice patterns to behavioral analytics, location data, and user interactions. Ensuring compliance with data protection regulations such as the General Data Protection Regulation (GDPR) is essential, especially when minors are involved. Schools and platform developers must establish transparent policies regarding data ownership, consent, and retention (McCullagh, 2016; Emara & Huang, 2019a). Students and educators need to know who controls their data, how it's stored, and how it may be used or shared. Without strong safeguards, educational metaverses risk becoming spaces of surveillance rather than empowerment. Data management and topic modeling of user interactions within these platforms also pose significant challenges, requiring careful consideration of privacy and security (Trinh et al., 2019).

Another ethical concern is the growing risk of deepfakes and identity manipulation within virtual environments. In education, where trust and authenticity are vital, the misuse of AI-generated avatars or voices poses significant dangers (Swenson, 2023). Malicious actors could impersonate instructors, peers, or public figures using deepfake technology to spread misinformation or manipulate classroom discourse. This could erode trust, disrupt learning, and cause psychological harm. To address this, institutions must implement verification tools, avatar authentication protocols, and digital literacy programs to help students recognize and respond to manipulated content. As the boundaries between real and virtual continue to blur, safeguarding authenticity, consent, and personal agency must be a central ethical priority in the design and governance of educational metaverse platforms.

Digital Equity in the Metaverse: Bridging Access Gaps in Global Education

While the metaverse holds immense potential to transform education, it also brings to light critical issues of digital equity. High-quality immersive experiences often require expensive hardware such as VR headsets, powerful computers, and reliable broadband internet—resources that many students and schools, especially in low-income communities, cannot afford. These cost barriers risk deepening the digital divide, where well-resourced institutions gain access to cutting-edge tools while underfunded ones fall further behind. Without intentional policies to subsidize devices, upgrade infrastructure, and support inclusive design, the metaverse could reinforce existing inequalities rather than reduce them (Allam et al., 2022).

The global digital divide, particularly between the Global North and South, further complicates equitable access. Many regions in the Global South struggle with inconsistent internet coverage, limited access to electricity, and a lack of educational technology training. In such contexts, immersive platforms that depend on real-time connectivity and high-bandwidth usage are not feasible. To address this, developers and policymakers must prioritize low-bandwidth alternatives, mobile-compatible experiences, and localized content that meets the needs of diverse learners. Closing this divide will require international collaboration, investment in infrastructure, and a commitment to making the metaverse an inclusive educational space—not just for those with advanced tools, but for learners everywhere, by addressing the underlying network challenges of power saving and connectivity (Emara, 2018; Emara, 2016; Emara et al., 2014).

Psychological Effects of Metaverse-Based Learning: Risks and Considerations

As immersive technologies become more prevalent in education, understanding their psychological effects is critical—particularly for young and developing learners. One common issue is cybersickness, a form of motion sickness triggered by a disconnect between visual input and physical movement in virtual environments. Symptoms can include dizziness, nausea, and disorientation, which may disrupt learning and discourage prolonged use. While newer headsets and optimized software are improving user comfort, not all students respond the same way, and long-term exposure has yet to be fully studied. Educators must monitor student reactions closely, offer breaks, and ensure that participation in VR activities is flexible and optional where needed.

Another concern is identity dissociation, especially when learners use avatars that significantly differ from their real-world selves. For younger students still developing a sense of self, prolonged immersion in avatar-based interactions can blur the line between real and virtual identities, potentially affecting self-esteem, body image, or social behavior. Combined with reduced face-to-face interaction, this raises questions about how virtual environments impact communication skills, empathy, and emotional development. While the metaverse can foster creativity and collaboration, it must be designed with safeguards that support healthy socialization, reinforce real-world identity, and provide opportunities for guided reflection. Striking a balance between digital immersion and psychological well-being is essential for responsible metaverse-based education.

CASE STUDIES IN METAVERSE EDUCATION: INSIGHTS FROM K-12, HIGHER ED, AND CORPORATE TRAINING

Metaverse technologies are already being applied across different educational contexts with promising results. In K-12 education, Finland has pioneered the use of VR-based history lessons, where students virtually explore reconstructed historical sites such as ancient Rome or medieval Europe. These experiences make abstract content tangible and emotionally resonant, fostering engagement and retention. Teachers report higher student motivation and deeper historical understanding, particularly among visual and kinesthetic learners. However, implementing these programs requires investment in hardware and training, posing challenges for broad adoption in less-resourced schools.

In higher education, Stanford University has embraced immersive learning through its virtual campus built on the ENGAGE platform. Students can attend lectures, interact with professors and peers as avatars, and participate in simulations or global collaborations. The virtual campus was notably used to support remote learning during the COVID-19 pandemic and continues to enhance access to guest speakers and interactive labs. While the setup offers clear pedagogical benefits—such as increased flexibility and student engagement—the high-end technical infrastructure needed for full immersion raises questions about long-term costs and equitable access for all students.

In the corporate sector, Boeing has adopted augmented reality (AR) to revolutionize aircraft assembly training. Using AR headsets, technicians receive real-time instructions and visual overlays that guide them through complex tasks, reducing errors and accelerating onboarding time. The results have been substantial: Boeing reported a 25% reduction in production time and a 40% improvement in productivity. While the return on investment is clear for large-scale manufacturers, the upfront costs and technical complexity may limit scalability for smaller companies or industries with fewer resources.

Applying a learning outcome vs. cost analysis reveals a consistent trend: immersive technologies significantly enhance comprehension, engagement, and skill acquisition, but they require substantial financial, technical, and human resource investments. For K-12, impact must be weighed against limited budgets; in higher ed, the focus is on broadening access while maintaining quality; and in corporate settings, the ROI often justifies the cost when training is complex and high-stakes.

FUTURE DIRECTIONS AND CONCLUSION

Emerging Trends

As the educational metaverse continues to evolve, several emerging technologies are set to further transform how we teach and learn. One major development is the rise of AI-generated virtual worlds, powered by platforms like OpenAI's text-to-3D generation tools. These systems allow educators to create rich, interactive environments simply by describing them in natural language, dramatically reducing the time and expertise needed for immersive content creation. This could democratize metaverse development in schools, enabling teachers to tailor lessons to specific learning goals or student interests. Another frontier is brain-computer interfaces (BCIs), which aim to link neural activity directly with digital systems. While still experimental, BCIs could one day enable more intuitive interaction with virtual environments, potentially allowing students to manipulate virtual objects or navigate simulations through thought alone, creating unparalleled levels of immersion and accessibility.

Open Research Questions

Despite rapid innovation, several critical research questions remain unanswered. A key concern is the long-term cognitive impact of sustained use of immersive technologies—particularly on attention span, memory, and mental health. While short-term studies show positive effects on engagement and retention, more longitudinal research is needed to ensure these tools support healthy development, especially in younger learners. Another pressing issue is the need for interoperability standards. As the metaverse expands, seamless integration across platforms is essential to avoid fragmented learning experiences. Organizations like the Metaverse Standards Forum are working to develop universal protocols that ensure virtual assets, identities, and experiences can move smoothly between ecosystems, but much work remains in this space.

Conclusion

In summary, the metaverse represents a paradigm shift in education, offering immersive, personalized, and collaborative learning experiences that go beyond the limits of physical classrooms. From VR history lessons in Finland to Boeing's AR training in aviation, early case studies show significant gains in engagement, comprehension, and real-world application. However, realizing this potential at scale requires more than just technology—it demands visionary policy, sustained investment, and comprehensive educator training. Policymakers must prioritize digital equity, infrastructure development, and privacy safeguards. Institutions should invest in tools and training that empower teachers as designers of immersive pedagogy. As we stand on the cusp of a new era in learning, the call to action is clear: to ensure the metaverse becomes a transformative force not just for some, but for all learners around the world.

REFERENCES

Abilkaiyrkyzy, A., Elhagry, A., Laamarti, F., & El Saddik, A. (2023). Metaverse key requirements and platforms survey. *IEEE Access : Practical Innovations, Open Solutions*, *11*, 117765–117787. DOI: 10.1109/ACCESS.2023.3325844

Ahmed, A. S., Keshk, A. E., Abo-Seida, O. M., & Sakr, M. (2022). Tumor detection and classification in breast mammography based on fine-tuned convolutional neural networks. *International Journal of Computers and Information*, *9*(1), 74–84.

Allam, Z., Sharifi, A., Bibri, S. E., Jones, D. S., & Krogstie, J. (2022). The metaverse as a virtual form of smart cities: Opportunities and challenges for environmental, economic, and social sustainability in urban futures. *Smart Cities*, *5*(3), 771–801. DOI: 10.3390/smartcities5030040

Anderson, J., & Rainie, L. (2022). The metaverse in 2040. *Pew Research Center*, *30*(4), 1–203. https://www.pewresearch.org/internet/2022/06/30/the-metaverse-in-2040

Ball, M. (2024). *The metaverse: Fully revised and updated edition: Building the spatial internet*. Liveright Publishing.

Bell, A., & Morris, G. (2009). Engaging professional learning in online environments. *Australasian Journal of Educational Technology*, *25*(5), 799–813. DOI: 10.14742/ajet.1116

Bhatnagar, R., Hassan, E., Saber, A., Shams, M. Y., & Elbedwehy, S. (2024, November). Enhanced Vision Transformer with Lion Optimizer for accurate classification of monkeypox skin images. In *2024 4th International Conference on Technological Advancements in Computational Sciences (ICTACS)* (pp. 1897–1902). IEEE. DOI: 10.1109/ICTACS62700.2024.10840567

Biswas, S., & Visell, Y. (2021). Haptic perception, mechanics, and material technologies for virtual reality. *Advanced Functional Materials*, *31*(39), 2008186. DOI: 10.1002/adfm.202008186

Brown, R., Habibi-Luevano, S., Robern, G., Wood, K., Perera, S., Uribe-Quevedo, A., & Brown, C. (2021). Employing Mozilla Hubs as an alternative tool for student outreach: A design challenge use case. In *Interactive mobile communication, technologies and learning* (pp. 213–222). Springer International Publishing.

Chen, X., Zou, D., Xie, H., & Wang, F. L. (2023). Metaverse in education: Contributors, cooperations, and research themes. *IEEE Transactions on Learning Technologies*, *16*(6), 1111–1129. DOI: 10.1109/TLT.2023.3277952

Christopoulos, A., & Mystakidis, S. (2023). Gamification in education. *Encyclopedia, 3*(3), 1223–1243. DOI: 10.3390/encyclopedia3040089

Damaševičius, R., & Sidekerskienė, T. (2024). Virtual worlds for learning in metaverse: A narrative review. *Sustainability (Basel), 16*(5), 2032. DOI: 10.3390/su16052032

Dionisio, J. D. N., Burns, W. G.III, & Gilbert, R. (2013). 3D virtual worlds and the metaverse: Current status and future possibilities. *ACM Computing Surveys, 45*(3), 1–38. DOI: 10.1145/2480741.2480751

Dudley, J., Yin, L., Garaj, V., & Kristensson, P. O. (2023). Inclusive immersion: A review of efforts to improve accessibility in virtual reality, augmented reality and the metaverse. *Virtual Reality (Waltham Cross), 27*(4), 2989–3020. DOI: 10.1007/s10055-023-00850-8

Emara, T. (2018). Adaptive Power-Saving Mechanism for VoIP Over WiMAX Based on Artificial Neural Network. In Waluyo, A. B. (Ed.), *Algorithms, Methods, and Applications in Mobile Computing and Communications* (pp. 158–177). IGI Global. DOI: 10.4018/978-1-5225-5693-0.ch007

Emara, T., Hassan, E., Trinh, T., Li, G., & Saber, A. (Eds.). (2025b). *The Role of Artificial Intelligence in Advancing Applied Life Sciences*. IGI Global Scientific Publishing. DOI: 10.4018/979-8-3693-9208-9

Emara, T. Z. (2016). Maximizing Power Saving for VoIP over WiMAX Systems. *International Journal of Mobile Computing and Multimedia Communications, 7*(1), 32–40. DOI: 10.4018/IJMCMC.2016010103

Emara, T. Z., Ashraf, R., Saber, A., Trinh, T., & Awad, W. (2025c). A Data Processing Algorithm to Approximate Big Stream Data Analysis. *2nd IEEE International Conference on Machine Intelligence and Smart Innovation (ICMISI 2025)*. DOI: 10.1109/ICMISI65108.2025.11115782

Emara, T. Z., Hassan, E., Elbedwehy, S., & Saber, A. (2025a). A historical perspective on artificial intelligence in applied life sciences. In *The role of artificial intelligence in advancing applied life sciences* (pp. 49–86). IGI Global Scientific Publishing. DOI: 10.4018/979-8-3693-9208-9.ch002

Emara, T. Z., & Huang, J. Z. (2019a). A distributed data management system to support large-scale data analysis. *Journal of Systems and Software, 148*, 105–115. DOI: 10.1016/j.jss.2018.11.007

Emara, T. Z., & Huang, J. Z. (2019b). RRPlib: A spark library for representing HDFS blocks as a set of random sample data blocks. *Science of Computer Programming, 184*, 102301. DOI: 10.1016/j.scico.2019.102301

Emara, T. Z., Saleh, A. I., & Arafat, H. (2014). Power saving mechanism for VoIP services over WiMAX systems. *Wireless Networks*, *20*(5), 975–985. DOI: 10.1007/s11276-013-0650-5

Emara, T. Z., Trinh, T., & Huang, J. Z. (2023). Geographically distributed data management to support large-scale data analysis. *Scientific Reports*, *13*(1), 17783. Advance online publication. DOI: 10.1038/s41598-023-44789-x PMID: 37853092

Enache, M. C. (2023). NFTs in education. *Economics and Applied Informatics*, *3*, 188–193.

Fitrianto, I., & Saif, A. (2024). The role of virtual reality in enhancing experiential learning: A comparative study of traditional and immersive learning environments. *International Journal of Post Axial: Futuristic Teaching and Learning*, 97–110.

Gadekallu, T. R., Huynh-The, T., Wang, W., Yenduri, G., Ranaweera, P., Pham, Q.-V., da Costa, D. B., & Liyanage, M. (2022). Blockchain for the metaverse: A review. *arXiv preprint arXiv:2203.09738.*

Garner, T. A. (2017). Applications of virtual reality. In *Echoes of other worlds: Sound in virtual reality: Past, present and future* (pp. 299–362). Springer International Publishing.

Guan, J.-Q., Wang, W.-Z., Wang, X.-F., Zhu, J., & Hwang, G.-J. (2024). Effects of a VR-based collaborative painting approach on primary students' creativity and collaborative quality in art courses. *Educational Technology Research and Development*, *72*(4), 2187–2211. DOI: 10.1007/s11423-024-10371-z

Hadi, R., Melumad, S., & Park, E. S. (2024). The metaverse: A new digital frontier for consumer behavior. *Journal of Consumer Psychology*, *34*(1), 142–166. DOI: 10.1002/jcpy.1356

Hassan, E., Saber, A., El-kenawy, E. S. M., Bhatnagar, R., & Shams, M. Y. (2024, August). Early detection of black fungus using deep learning models for efficient medical diagnosis. In *2024 International Conference on Emerging Techniques in Computational Intelligence (ICETCI)* (pp. 426–431). IEEE. DOI: 10.1109/ICETCI62771.2024.10704103

Hosseini, S. T. M., Qayumi, K., Pourabbasi, A., Haghighi, E., Sabet, B., Koohpaei, A., Shafiei, Z., Hosseini, M. M., & Nemati, P. (2025). Are we ready to integrate modern technologies into the medical curriculum for students? A systematic review. *Discover Education*, *4*(1), 114. DOI: 10.1007/s44217-025-00521-7

Jagatheesaperumal, S. K., Ahmad, K., Al-Fuqaha, A., & Qadir, J. (2024). Advancing education through extended reality and internet of everything enabled metaverses: Applications, challenges, and open issues. *IEEE Transactions on Learning Technologies, 17*, 1120–1139. DOI: 10.1109/TLT.2024.3358859

Johnston, C. L., Wheeler, A., Nunn, A., & Escobar, E. (2025). Teaching the ancient world with reproductions: Using 3D printed objects in authentic active history learning. In *Ancient pasts for modern audiences* (pp. 166–200). Routledge.

Kempton, G. A. (2017). Creativity in education: Exploring teacher experiences of creativity through an immersion studies learning framework [Doctoral dissertation, Queensland University of Technology]. *QUT ePrints.*

Khan, U. A., & Alamäki, A. (2023). Designing an ethical and secure pain estimation system using AI sandbox for contactless healthcare. *SSRN.* DOI: 10.3991/ijoe.v19i15.43663

Koppolu, H. K. R. (2025). *Engineering the digital backbone of the future: Data infrastructure, 5G connectivity, cloud networks, and AI solutions across media, telecom, and healthcare industries*. Deep Science Publishing.

Kumar, D., Haque, A., Mishra, K., Islam, F., Mishra, B. K., & Ahmad, S. (2023). Exploring the transformative role of artificial intelligence and metaverse in education: A comprehensive review. *Metaverse Basic and Applied Research, 2*, 21. DOI: 10.56294/mr202355

Kumar, D., Haque, A., Mishra, K., Islam, F., Mishra, B. K., & Ahmad, S. (2023). Exploring the transformative role of artificial intelligence and metaverse in education: A comprehensive review. *Metaverse Basic and Applied Research, 2*, 21. DOI: 10.56294/mr202355

Manjrekar, S., Sandilya, S., Bhosale, D., Kanchi, S., Pitkar, A., & Gondhalekar, M. (2014). CAVE: An emerging immersive technology—A review. In *2014 UKSim-AMSS 16th International Conference on Computer Modelling and Simulation* (pp. 131–136). IEEE.

McCullagh, K. (2016). *The general data protection regulation: A partial success for children on social network sites?* Forum Iuris.

Mergen, A., Çetin-Kılıç, N., & Özbilgin, M. F. (2025). Artificial intelligence and bias towards marginalised groups: Theoretical roots and challenges. In *AI and diversity in a datafied world of work: Will the future of work be inclusive?* (Vol. 12, pp. 17–38). Emerald Publishing Limited. DOI: 10.1108/S2051-233320250000012004

Meusa, H. (2025). Beyond entertainment—An analysis of Minecraft: Education Edition as an inclusive educational platform for diverse learners. *SSRN.*

Nasir, S. M., Hashim, M. E. A. H., Chee, K. N., Kamaruddin, N. H., Wibawanto, W., & Hanapiah, M. M. (2024). Enhancing student engagement in learning management systems through exploration of avatars in virtual classrooms: A systematic review. *Journal of Advanced Research in Applied Sciences and Engineering Technology,* 187–200.

NguyenDuc, H., VuThi, K., NguyenDinhVi, D., Emara, T. Z., & Trinh, T. (2025). A Hybrid Feature Selection Paradigm for High-Dimensional Data. In H. A. Le Thi, H. M. Le, & Q. T. Nguyen (Eds.), Advances in Data Science and Optimization of Complex Systems (pp. 239–250). Springer Nature Switzerland. DOI: 10.1007/978-3-032-00267-9_22

Noomene, W., & Abed, M. (2025). Adaptive educational avatars: A systematic review of generative AI and metaverse integration for personalized learning. *SSRN.* DOI: 10.2139/ssrn.5276474

Pervez, F., Shoukat, M., Usama, M., Sandhu, M., Latif, S., & Qadir, J. (2024). Affective computing and the road to an emotionally intelligent metaverse. *IEEE Open Journal of the Computer Society*, *5*, 195–214. DOI: 10.1109/OJCS.2024.3389462

Poolsawas, B., & Chotikakamthorn, N. (2023). Using Mozilla Hubs for online teaching: A case study of an innovation design method course. In *Proceedings of the 17th International Multi-Conference on Society, Cybernetics and Informatics (IMSCI 2023)* (pp. 7–12). DOI: 10.54808/IMSCI2023.01.7

Rao, S. P., Sekhar, S. C., Yadav, T. C., Kumar, V. P., & Haran, B. H. (2024). Implementing experiential learning strategies for enhanced business education in India: Challenges and opportunities. *Journal of Informatics Education and Research*, *4*(3), 20–33.

Redford, A. C. (2021). Perceptions of the use of augmented and virtual reality supporting emergency response education and training [Doctoral dissertation, Capella University]. *ProQuest Dissertations Publishing.*

Saber, A., Al-Zoghby, A. M., & Elmougy, S. (2018). Big-data aggregating, linking, integrating and representing using semantic web technologies. In *International conference on advanced machine learning technologies and applications* (pp. 331–342). Springer International Publishing. DOI: 10.1007/978-3-319-74690-6_33

Saber, A., Hassan, E., Elbedwehy, S., Awad, W. A., & Emara, T. Z. (2025). Leveraging ensemble convolutional neural networks and metaheuristic strategies for advanced kidney disease screening and classification. *Scientific Reports, 15*(1), 12487. DOI: 10.1038/s41598-025-93950-1 PMID: 40216822

Saber, A., Hussien, A. G., Awad, W. A., Mahmoud, A., & Allakany, A. (2023). Adapting the pre-trained convolutional neural networks to improve the anomaly detection and classification in mammographic images. *Scientific Reports, 13*(1), 14877. DOI: 10.1038/s41598-023-41633-0 PMID: 37689757

Saber, A., Sakr, M., Abo-Seida, O. M., & Keshk, A. (2021, May). Automated breast cancer detection and classification techniques–a survey. In *2021 International Mobile, Intelligent, and Ubiquitous Computing Conference (MIUCC)* (pp. 200–207). IEEE. DOI: 10.1109/MIUCC52538.2021.9447655

Sakr, M., Saber, A., Abo-Seida, O. M., & Keshk, A. (2020). Machine learning for breast cancer classification using K-star algorithm. *Applied Mathematics & Information Sciences, 14*(5), 855–863. DOI: 10.18576/amis/140513

Sharma, M., Mahajan, Y., & Saber, A. (2024). Using augmented reality (AR) and the Internet of Things (IoT) to improve water management maintenance and training. In *Innovations in machine learning and IoT for water management* (pp. 252–270). IGI Global Scientific Publishing.

Swenson, A. (2023). Teaching digital identity: Opportunities, challenges, and ethical considerations for avatar creation in educational settings. *Brazilian Creative Industries Journal, 3*(2), 41–58. DOI: 10.25112/bcij.v3i2.3538

Theatre, W. L., & Wright, J. (2023). Labs and learning technologies. In *Variety in Chemistry Education/Physics Higher Education Conference (ViCE/PHEC) 2023.*

Trinh, T., Duc, L. P., Tran, C. T., Duy, T. T., & Emara, T. Z. (2022). A New Stratified Block Model to Process Large-Scale Data for a Small Cluster. In *Lecture Notes on Data Engineering and Communications Technologies* (Vol. 124, pp. 253–263). Springer Science and Business Media Deutschland GmbH. DOI: 10.1007/978-3-030-97610-1_21

Trinh, T., Nguyen, N., Wu, D., Huang, J. Z., & Emara, T. Z. (2019). A New Location-Based Topic Model for Event Attendees Recommendation. In *2019 IEEE-RIVF International Conference on Computing and Communication Technologies (RIVF)* (pp. 106–111). DOI: 10.1109/RIVF.2019.8713716

TrinhHuy, T., Trinh, T., NguyenViet, H., Emara, T. Z., & VuongThi, N. (2025). Event scale prediction in event-based social networks. 11th EAI International Conference on Industrial Networks and Intelligent Systems, Da Nang, Vietnam. https://doi.org/10.1007/978-3-032-02362-9_3

VuThi, K., VuongThi, N., NguyenXuan, H., Emara, T. Z., & Trinh, T. (2024). Feature Selection Based on Top Frequency. In M. and N. L. A. and L. K. Y. Nguyen Thi Dieu Linh and Dawson (Eds.), Proceedings of the International Conference on Intelligent Systems and Networks (pp. 58–65). Springer Nature Singapore. DOI: 10.1007/978-981-97-5504-2_7

Williams, S. (2025). Decentralized identity management for academic credentials using blockchain technology. *SSRN.*

Wohlgenannt, I., Simons, A., & Stieglitz, S. (2020). Virtual reality. *Business & Information Systems Engineering*, *62*(5), 455–461. DOI: 10.1007/s12599-020-00658-9

Yang, S., Tian, H., Sun, L., & Yu, X. (2019). From one-size-fits-all teaching to adaptive learning: The crisis and solution of education in the era of AI. *Journal of Physics: Conference Series*, *1237*(4), 042039. DOI: 10.1088/1742-6596/1237/4/042039

Yang, W., Fang, M., Xu, J., Zhang, X., & Pan, Y. (2024). Exploring the mediating role of different aspects of learning motivation between metaverse learning experiences and gamification. *Electronics (Basel)*, *13*(7), 1297. DOI: 10.3390/electronics13071297

Yeganeh, L. N., Fenty, N. S., Chen, Y., Simpson, A., & Hatami, M. (2025). The future of education: A multi-layered metaverse classroom model for immersive and inclusive learning. *Future Internet*, *17*(2), 63. DOI: 10.3390/fi17020063

Zechner, O., Schrom-Feiertag, H., Wespi, R., Pretolesi, D., Nguyen, Q., & Tscheligi, M. (2024). Enhancing mixed reality simulation training technology with real-time performance visualization: Mixed methods study with medical first responders. *JMIR XR and Spatial Computing*, *1*(1), e57655. DOI: 10.2196/57655

Chapter 6

Cognitive Intelligence in Human-Centered Education:

An AI Extended Reality Gamification

Ugochukwu Okwudili Matthew
https://orcid.org/0000-0003-0828-9710
Federal University of Lavras, Brazil

David Oyekunle
https://orcid.org/0009-0007-3994-1712
University of Salford, UK

Jazuli Sanusi Kazaure
https://orcid.org/0000-0001-7681-2177
Hussaini Adamu Federal Polytechnic, Nigeria

Mgbike Francisca Chinenye
https://orcid.org/0009-0008-3244-2598
Federal College of Education (Technical), Umunze, Nigeria

Blessing Adeni Amakuro
https://orcid.org/0009-0009-8648-8062
Niger Delta University, Nigeria

ABSTRACT

The field of biomedical engineering (BME) combines engineering principles with key science, technology, engineering, and mathematics (STEM) to affect scientific

DOI: 10.4018/979-8-3373-3043-3.ch006

inquiries in biology, medicine, and health systems and applied technology to enhance public health for diagnosis and therapeutics. The health education for the emerging topics involves transforming every lesson into an artificial intelligence interactive virtual reality (VR), augmented reality (AR), and mixed reality (MR) experimental gamification. The primary goal of this study is to improve occupational efficiency in biomedical engineering education through the use of Technological Pedagogical Content Knowledge (TPCK) framework to better prepare students for the demands of real-world medical professional practice. In the chapter, the authors developed an adaptive federated cloud computing learning system that examined how AR and VR technologies are used in biomedical engineering education to promote occupational efficiency in healthcare sector.

INTRODUCTION

Biomedical engineering (BME) education is confronted with significant pedagogical challenges, leading to enduring skill gaps between theoretical understanding and practical application, due to institutions reliance on outdated instructional methods that do not resonate with digitally native students, and restricted access to modern laboratory facilities due to financial and infrastructural limitations (Fuchs, Vasudevan, & Butcher, 2025). These issues hinder students' ability to develop hands-on competencies, interdisciplinary thinking, and real-world problem-solving skills. This study addresses these gaps by integrating immersive simulations, adaptive learning pathways, and gamified experiences. This fusion empowers students to explore complex biomedical systems interactively, receive personalized feedback, and collaborate in virtual lab environments regardless of geographic or economic situations. It transforms education into a dynamic, participatory experience where learners engage deeply through immersive technologies, fostering equitable access, personalized growth, and the development of skills aligned with tomorrow's BME challenges. The education industry is always looking for new and creative ways to enhance instructional methodology in a manner to engage students, in other to yield fruitful results. Immersive technologies, like augmented reality (AR), virtual reality (VR) and mixed reality (MR) solutions, are opening up new facets of learning experiences through cognition, providing access to methodologically diverse and highly engaging educational pedagogy (Asoodar, Janesarvatan, Yu, & de Jong, 2024). Examining the amazing realm of immersive technologies and their potential to transform educational experiences, this study explored the future of education. For biomedical engineering students, the use of AR, VR, and MR technologies in the classroom offers a game-changing chance to improve learning outcomes and redefine the educational business (Saudagar, Kumar, & Khan, 2024). These immersive solutions enable students to actively construct knowledge, close the gap between theory and practice, and develop critical problem-solving, teamwork, and communication skills necessary for success in the workforce of the twenty-first century by offering creative and captivating learning environments. The use of AR, VR, and MR solutions in education can assist match learning experiences with the requirements and demands of the twenty-first century, as technology continues to transform the workplace (Kandemir, Ulusoy, & Kandemir, 2024). In order to improve healthcare standards and modernize medical equipment manufacture, BME education studies the basic application of engineering concepts to biological and medical problems (Prestigiacomo, Chan, & Kark, 2024). By offering innovative solutions to biological and medical issues, BME significantly improves people's lives through its emphasis on new technologies for medical imaging, immersive technology, rehabilitation, and illness diagnoses (Montesinos, Santos-Diaz, Salinas-Navarro, & Cendejas-Zaragoza, 2022).

BME education combines biology, medicine, and engineering to train students in developing innovative healthcare technologies, emphasizing both theoretical foundations and practical skills for designing medical devices, diagnostics, and therapeutic systems that improve patient care and clinical outcomes (AKHTAR, 2024). An essential force for individual development, public health, world peace, and environmental sustainability, education is a universal human right that propels advancement for people, communities, and ecosystems (Supriya et al., 2024; Ugochukwu O Matthew & Kazaure, 2020). As a result, education fosters collaboration, introduces fresh perspectives, fortifies institutions, and contributes to long-term economic growth and scientific advancement. As a branch of BME, clinical engineering focuses on enhancing healthcare delivery through efficient use of medical technology. Using cutting-edge technical solutions, it entails the administration, creation, and use of medical systems and technologies to improve patient care, guarantee safety, and assist clinical procedures in healthcare settings. In addition to working with government regulators on hospital audits and inspections, clinical engineers also teach and oversee biomedical equipment technicians and provide technical advice to other hospital employees, such as physicians, administrators, and information technology (IT) practitioners within the healthcare sector (Akhtar, 2024). Clinical engineers support upgrading of the design of medical equipment in addition to closing the communication gap between end users and product developers by providing training in the development of products and point-of-use experience. The field of BME integrates engineering concepts with essential science, technology, engineering, and mathematics (STEM) to advance scientific discoveries in biology, medicine, and health systems, using technology to improve public health, specifically in the areas of disease diagnosis and treatment (Montesinos et al., 2022). With a predicted 5% rise in jobs from 2022 to 2032 involving the study and development of solutions to biological and medical problems, BME is one of the fastest growing engineering specializations in the world, with 117,935 biomedical engineers working in 129 countries (Fermin & Tan, 2020). BME experts are employed in great numbers by the health technology and healthcare industries, hospitals and other public service sectors, academic institutions, governmental organizations, and national regulatory authorities. Indeed, biomedical engineers are essential to precision medicine and the advancement of healthcare systems in general, as the World Health Organization (WHO) has formally recognized (Thacharodi et al., 2024). The American College of Clinical Engineering (ACCE) described a BME as a professional who applies engineering and managerial skills to healthcare technology in order to support and advance patient care (Koch, Romani, Oliveira, & Tanaka, 2022).

In this study, our idea is based on the novel definition of the experiential learning space that had already been proposed in (Taghian, Abo-Zahhad, Sayed, & Abd El-Malek, 2023), (D. Oyekunle, Claude, Waliu, Adekunle, & Matthew, 2024) making way for cloud-based collaborative platforms to enhance BME real–time interactive education. Interestingly, we use wearable technology to collect physiological and behavioral information in real-world situations, enabling immersive learning activities. By doing this, we hope to raise students' motivation and perception of the course material and learning objectives in order to enhance their academic achievement and competency growth providing training scenarios that safely resemble reality. In order to educate students on the occupational demands of the twenty-first century, immersive education 5.0 pedagogy has emerged as a new paradigm for educational technology that is based on sustainability, human-centeredness, innovation, and collaboration (D. O. Oyekunle, Nwaiku, et al., 2025). Teaching students about sustainability, assisting them in acquiring sustainable skills, and motivating them to take action that aligned with the demands of education 5.0 which contribute significantly to the achievement of sustainability. The idea of education 5.0 human centeredness is to create a sustainable global education system where each lesson is an interactive experimentation and practical gamification involving VR, AR and MR experiences (Supriya et al., 2024),(Radianti, Majchrzak, Fromm, & Wohlgenannt, 2020). The extended reality (XR) technology is revolutionizing several industries, including education, by creating immersive and captivating pedagogical experiences that were unimaginable in the past (Murala & Panda, 2023). AR which involves superimposing digital data such as photos, videos, and 3D models onto the physical environment, enhances users' perceptions and interactions with their surroundings. With a smartphone, tablet, or specialist AR glasses, the digital content is usually shown in real time. Users can observe and interact with virtual things using AR technology while remaining cognizant of their immediate surroundings. With VR technology, a user can be fully immersed in a simulated digital environment that may not even be close to the real world (Putawa & Sugianto, 2024; Hamilton, McKechnie, Edgerton, & Wilson, 2021). Wearing a VR headset allows users to enter an interactive, movement-responsive virtual world through the creation of the illusion that users are truly inside a virtual environment, the technology seeks to provide users with a sensation of presence and immersion. There are interesting educational prospects for the technology due to the unique features of both AR and VR.

Virtual reality environment (VRE) settings allow users to interact with a computer-simulated digital ecosystem, creating an automated experiences that makes users feel as though they are performing tasks in the actual world (Yadav, 2025). The user can respond to a simulation or abstract concept in this interactive digital scenario to gain comprehension and learn how to do specific activities. Interesting, these immersive mixed reality technologies are integrating with 3D artificial intelligence (AI), machine learning (ML), cloud computing services, and Internet of Things (IoT) to power training, robotics interactions and automation for healthcare industry services, particularly in compelling extreme digital healthcare automation. With the use of deep learning-based 3D AI, users can accurately detect 3D objects in a variety of orientations and with any shape or size in its existential nomenclature. When creating complicated 3D models and digital twins with their real-world counterparts, this method may be applied to enterprise use cases and is scalable to any arbitrary shape. This method of 3D object tracking will enable end users to genuinely merge the real and virtual worlds in biomedical engineering applications, opening up a wide range of health applications such as precisely contextual work instructions for training, the detection of defects and errors in human anatomy rendered in 3D imagery and data visualization design (Lungu et al., 2021). With XR technology, users of VR and AR can undergo immersive experiences that transport them to other digital locations for context engagement. The development of soft skills for a variety of educational applications and human-centric design are key components of a new phase of civilizational and intellectual growth. The combination of contemporary technologies and human professional specialization defines it. These cutting-edge technologies are used by Industry 5.0 to encourage cooperation amongst important stakeholders in the education sector, preserving the efficacy and efficiency of the teaching and learning process, which encourages a balance between technical and soft skills. Advances in cognitive and learning science theories offer transformative potential for biomedical engineering and biomedical informatics education (Tripathi, Hajra, Mulukutla, Shreshtha, & Maity, 2025). These insights contribute to more personalized, adaptive, and interactive learning experiences that align with modern pedagogical strategies. Through methods like immersive simulation, metacognitive feedback, and AI-enhanced instruction, students gain deeper conceptual understanding and better retention of complex biomedical concepts. Incorporating these innovations into instructional design improves curriculum relevance, fosters interdisciplinary thinking, and bridges the gap between theory and clinical practice. As a matter of fact, evolving methodologies reshape biomedical education into a dynamic, learner-centered ecosystem equipped to meet twenty-first-century healthcare challenges. This research work is structured into introduction, background of the study, study hypothesis, research objectives, theoretical framework, research question, study methodology, system model design, implementation of the design and conclusion.

BACKGROUND OF STUDY

BME education integrates engineering principles with biological sciences to equip learners with the skills needed to address complex medical challenges. As healthcare evolves, traditional teaching methods often fall short in bridging theory and practice. Immersive technologies such as AI-enhanced VR, AR, and MR are transforming BME training by offering interactive, gamified environments that simulate clinical scenarios, enhance spatial understanding, and personalize learning (Kini, Ganeshrao, & Siddalingaswamy, 2024). These innovations foster deeper engagement, accelerate skill acquisition, and prepare students for the demands of modern medical practice. Education 5.0 empowers this process through immersive, AI-powered, personalized learning focused on creativity and collaboration. Industry 5.0 complements it by integrating intelligent automation with human-centric innovation, preparing students with both technical and soft skills for healthcare advancement. Society 5.0 expands the educational vision by promoting inclusive, sustainable growth, where digital transformation serves public well-being. Together, these paradigms foster a responsive, interdisciplinary, and ethically grounded learning ecosystem capable of preparing future biomedical professionals for global healthcare needs and emerging societal challenges. Integrating Education 5.0, Industry 5.0, and Society 5.0 into BME education fosters a forward-thinking, sustainable learning paradigm that emphasizes human-centered innovation. Education 5.0 prioritizes personalized, immersive, and empathetic learning environments powered by AI, AR, VR, and XR technologies, allowing students to engage deeply with complex biomedical concepts. In parallel, Industry 5.0 brings in technological sophistication and extreme automation while maintaining a balance with soft skills, creativity, adaptability, and collaboration, which are vital in healthcare innovation (Islam, Sepanloo, Woo, Woo, & Son, 2025). Society 5.0 broadens this vision by promoting inclusivity and sustainability, ensuring that digital transformation meets social needs equitably. The fusion of these paradigms results in a dynamic educational ecosystem where simulation-based learning prepares students to address real-world clinical challenges, encourages cross-disciplinary collaboration, and nurtures future biomedical professionals who are technically adept and socially conscious. This holistic approach transforms biomedical educationist into a resilient and innovative force for global health progress.

Despite the increasing availability of immersive technologies, BME education still relies heavily on traditional instructional strategies that fall short in cultivating experiential learning, adaptive pedagogy, and real-world readiness. Current teaching methods often lack personalization, interactivity, and technological integration needed to engage students in complex clinical simulations and interdisciplinary skill development. As medical education evolves to meet the demands of Industry 5.0 and Society 5.0, there's an urgent need to adopt Education 5.0 principles, human-centeredness, sustainability, creativity, and collaboration (Tyagi & Nair, 2024). However, educators face significant challenges in effectively implementing AI-powered XR tools due to a lack of structured frameworks, ethical integration of cognitive data, and scalable delivery systems. This study addresses the gap by proposing an adaptive federated learning system supported by the Technological Pedagogical Content Knowledge (TPCK) framework to transform BME education into an immersive, intelligent, and inclusive learning ecosystem. The rapid advancements in technical computing have transformed the many BME fields, including medical engineering, health informatics, and engineering, especially in the areas of human health and medical science (Z. AKHTAR, 2024). BME develop, redesign, and test devices that improve the tracking, diagnosis, and treatment of major human health concerns using a methodical educational approach. The intending sustainable future of health education entails gamifying every lesson through experimental AR, MR, and VR with AI (Hassan, Rahim, Hoong, & Mostafa, 2024). With the development of three dimensional (3D) models, XR technology is transforming a number of industries, most notably medical education, by offering previously unthinkable immersive and fascinating experiences. Through immersive experiences enabled by XR technology, users of AR, VR, and MR can explore new regions inside the model design via simulation-based learning, where one can display digital content over real-world settings, explore virtual worlds, and interact with virtual objects, all of which encourage generative imagination (D. Oyekunle, Claude, et al., 2024).

By defining the technological foundations, guiding principles, fundamental values, and vital components of Education 5.0 for BME education, the authors of this study pushed the adoption of high-tech in the development of interactive educational pedagogy in Society 5.0. This marked a major shift in the field of instructional technology, fostering critical thinking and multidisciplinary problem-solving skills in Industry 5.0, which significantly improved the use of generative AI in the creation of conversational education pedagogy. Human-centeredness, sustainability, creativity, and teamwork are the cornerstones of a new educational paradigm that seeks to prepare students for the challenges of the twenty-first century. Educational gamification involving AR and VR transforms passive learning into dynamic, immersive experiences (Lampropoulos, Keramopoulos, Diamantaras, & Evangelidis, 2022). AR overlays digital content onto real-world environments, allowing students to interact with 3D models, quizzes, and storytelling in real time. VR immerses learners in fully simulated scenarios, enabling exploration of complex subjects like biomedical engineering or anatomy. Game elements such as challenges, rewards, and feedback, boost motivation, engagement, and retention. Together, AR and VR gamification promote experiential learning, collaboration, and adaptability while supporting personalized instruction aligned with cognitive and emotional needs, preparing learners for high-stakes, interdisciplinary contexts like health and technology. In the evolving landscape of higher education and technological innovation, the fusion of cognitive intelligence, AI, XR, and gamification marks a paradigm shift toward human-centered learning. Cognitive intelligence anchored in adaptive learning processes and real-time response systems, facilitates personalized and context-aware educational experiences that mirror human cognition (Peterson, 2024). This approach empowers learners to engage dynamically with content, aligning with individual strengths and promoting metacognitive awareness.

As an interdisciplinary field combining engineering principles with core STEM foundations, BME actively integrates scientific inquiry across biology, medicine, and health systems. The complexity of BME topics, from biomechanics and tissue engineering to bioinstrumentation and medical imaging demands educational tools that are both flexible and immersive (Linsenmeier & Saterbak, 2020). AI-driven XR environments offer rich simulations, enabling learners to visualize anatomical structures in 3D, manipulate virtual devices, and perform virtual procedures with haptic feedback. When combined with gamified elements such as challenges, progress trackers, and reward systems, these environments foster motivation, collaboration, and skill acquisition in authentic biomedical contexts (Cascella, Cascella, Monaco, & Shariff, 2023). In alignment with Industry 5.0's emphasis on human-centered innovation, the convergence of these technologies supports BME education by encouraging creativity, adaptability, and problem-solving. Learners are not passive recipients but active agents navigating complex virtual ecosystems modeled on real-world biomedical applications. Data analytics play a central role in refining these systems, constantly tailoring instructional pathways to optimize student performance and engagement. This study explores how such cognitive-intelligent platforms can revolutionize BME education, building future-ready learners equipped to solve interdisciplinary challenges and contribute meaningfully to sustainable healthcare innovation. Through this lens, education becomes not only more intelligent but more equitable and empowering.

RESEARCH OBJECTIVE

The primary objective of this study is to explore how cognitive intelligence powered by AI, XR, AR gamification can revolutionize human-centered education within BME education. It aims to investigate the pedagogical impact of immersive technologies such as VR, AR, and MR, in fostering adaptive and personalized learning environments that respond to individual student needs. Central to this study is evaluating how AI algorithms contribute to real-time feedback, student-specific content delivery, and interdisciplinary problem-solving. It also seeks to measure the role of gamified XR platforms in enhancing student motivation, skill acquisition, and procedural learning, particularly in clinical decision-making contexts. Another core aim is to identify the ethical design principles essential for integrating cognitive data into XR-enhanced education systems safely and responsibly. The study aligns with Industry 5.0 values, human-centeredness, sustainability, creativity, and inclusive growth to position education as a dynamic ecosystem that equips learners for biomedical challenges of the future. Ultimately, the study intends to develop theoretical frameworks and practical models to guide educators, developers, and institutions in creating next-generation immersive learning experiences that are intelligent, engaging, and empathetically human-focused.

STUDY HYPOTHESIS

This study formulated five clear hypotheses that align with study objectives. It is predicted that research based on this taxonomy would produce more significant findings, particularly in the area of digitally mediated health education. In a world where education technology is becoming more interconnected, this framework seeks to improve comparative knowledge and overcome methodological fragmentation. This paper formulated the following Alternative Hypothesis (H_1):

H1: AI-powered VR simulations in biomedical engineering education significantly enhance students' conceptual understanding compared to conventional methods.

H2: Integrating cognitive intelligence into immersive learning environments will enhance learner adaptability and problem-solving in biomedical simulations.

H3: XR-based gamified instruction will increase student motivation and engagement compared to non-interactive digital modules.

H4: AI-personalized feedback within biomedical XR platforms will improve student performance and procedural accuracy.

H5: Students learning through human-centered AI gamification will exhibit greater interdisciplinary collaboration and retention of biomedical concepts over time.

THEORETICAL FRAMEWORK

Educational technology driven by Education 5.0, Industry 5.0, and Society 5.0 embraces human-centered, technologically advanced, and socially inclusive learning approaches (Carayannis & Morawska, 2023). This approach nurtures critical thinking, adaptability, and social responsibility, creating a responsive educational ecosystem that equips learners to innovate and thrive in a rapidly evolving world. It emphasizes personalized instruction through AI, VR, AR, and XR to foster creativity, responsiveness, and critical thinking. Industry 5.0 contributes intelligent automation while preserving essential soft skills, and Society 5.0 ensures sustainable development and equitable access (Oyekunle, Matthew, Bakare, Fatai, & Asnui, 2024). These elements combine to create adaptable curricula, support lifelong learning, and align classroom experiences with evolving global needs. The result is an educational ecosystem capable of driving innovation and societal resilience. With the goal of fusing the real world with a digital twin world that can be interacted with, XR is a catch-all term that unifies VR, MR, and AR, allowing users to immerse themselves in a virtual or augmented reality environment (Mendoza-Ramírez, Tudon-Martinez, Félix-Herrán, Lozoya-Santos, & Vargas-Martínez, 2023). One of AR and VR technologies' primary features is their unique immersive experience that require the use of VR goggles to magnify organs to view details and further dissect them to view internal structures and processes. Students can observe and interact with genuine organs and the various sections of the human body through MR, AR, and VR in medical education. With AR and VR technology, medical education for students is enhanced and made much more realistic by HoloAnatomy and other VR-based applications that zoom into the human anatomy (Herrington, Rea, & Poyade, 2022). According to (Aland et al., 2023), students' access to augmented reality medical education with 3D Organon can help them become less reliant on the availability of medical labs, instructors, and lab specialists. It is possible for medical students to become extremely self-sufficient without sacrificing the standard of their education. Medical education and nursing training have demonstrated the value of VR, AR, MR, XR as an instructional aids in the fast evolving modern digital environment characterized by extreme automation. VR is a versatile tool that can be used to replicate arthroscopy surgeries and enhance ophthalmologic tests (Ong, Tan, Lam, & Koh, 2021). Medical professionals and nurse educators can benefit from immersive technology-based training that emphasizes skill transferability into the clinical field and offers a rich, dynamic, engaging, and safe learning environment (Tang, Chau, Kwok, Zhu, & Ma, 2022). It promotes experiential learning, bridges the gap between theory and practice, and improves the transfer and acquisition of skills.

The XR leverages locally available or shareable visual data gathering to create individualized experiences through real-time responses to a virtual stimulus. This data is sent to the human senses via a cascaded 5G network infrastructure, cloud computing technology that works in tandem with the source of data to contribute to increased user capacity. These applications will most likely help advance extended reality in the future. AR allows professionals to be prepared for a wide range of events by simulating a wide range of scenarios, from normal operations to emergency situations. Under AR's close supervision, people can practice the responses they give, hone their skills, and gain proficiency with machinery, ensuring that they are not just trained but also knowledgeable (Bryant & Hemsley, 2024). While AR is a disruptive technology in itself, it is far more effective when combined with other cutting-edge technologies like cloud infrastructure, IoT, and AI, which enable real-time data capturing and analysis (Rane, Choudhary, & Rane, 2023). Employees doing machine inspections while using AR glasses may have IoT sensors built into the goggles, enabling them to display data like temperature, pressure, and other operating parameters in real time. This gives the user a complete view of the machine's condition and its digital environment. By merging AR technology with AI algorithms, operators can not only monitor data in real time but also predict potential issues, give maintenance recommendations, and even recommend operational changes for increased efficiency (Savaglio et al., 2020). According to (Tang et al., 2022), medical and clinical workers can benefit from rich, dynamic, safe, and engaging learning experiences through immersive technology-based training that emphasizes the transferability of skills into the clinical setting. It enhances the transfer and development of skills, closes the theory-practice gap, and promotes learning-by-doing (van As & Cooke, 2024). Scholars now frequently use VR, AR, and MR technologies as teaching tools to augment, enhance, or even replace conventional teaching techniques in medical education and training which prompted medical students' anatomy education to use of technology (Yang, 2023). On the other hand, medical and healthcare practices typically require a wide range of practical abilities which had induced technology such as VR, AR, and MR to be used to improve procedural and practical teaching (Navarro-Parra & Chiappe, 2024). In order to foster technological agility in medical and nursing education, the impacts of simulated training interventions are currently being extensively explored. Studies using randomized controlled trials show that training based on immersive technology may enhance students' acquisition of knowledge. Immersive technology is thought to give students a fresh approach to learning and make it easier for them to pick up crucial medical concepts and procedures. VR in particular can be used to produce an accurate and highly interactive operative simulation with opportunities for recording and analyzing findings, especially with the growing usage of virtual training for practitioners and students in the healthcare or medical areas (Barteit, Lanfermann, Bärnighausen, Neuhann, & Beiersmann, 2021).

The precision and workflow of clinical abilities including surgery, diagnosis, image reconstruction, and intra-operative viewing could be completely transformed by AR and MR technology (Mulukuntla, 2025). The VR and AR have grown in importance as surgical technology becomes more integrated. This technology has a lot of potential for orthopaedics since it allows users to superimpose digital images on their vision of the real world. The current study looked into how immersive technology might be used in biomedical engineering and medical education. According to (Lungu et al., 2021), who evaluated the efficacy of AR in surgical oncology training and procedures, noting that AR can enhance surgical outcomes as well as all other clinical visits. Examining the psychological consequences of simulation training, it was shown that AR can create training scenarios that are both realistically achievable and emotionally authentic (Kaplan et al., 2021). According to (Liu et al., 2024), immersive technology is promoting empathy in medical education by showcasing how VR may effectively reduce the emotional and cognitive divide between patients and healthcare practitioners. VR's capacity to enhance retention of complicated anatomical knowledge, complements the empathic approach, examining how these technologies might greatly improve instructional results and learner performance/engagement while synthesizing their many contributions. While AR superimposes digital information on the real world, VR immerses the user in a fully virtual environment and MR allows the user to see the real world and place virtual objects within it, allowing for interaction between the two worlds to provide a variety of clinical scenarios and opportunities for repetitive practice (Barteit et al., 2021). This aspect of the educational revolution that VR and AR are driving is crucial because these technologies help people communicate and comprehend medical concepts more deeply. Furthermore, the creation of virtual reality training programs tailored to medical procedures and anatomy instruction highlighted how effective these programs are at enhancing procedural competencies and learning objectives (Gupta et al., 2023). Enhancing the visibility of anatomical features through the practical applications of AR is a crucial aspect for surgical planning and educational objectives. While AR training will not, at least not anytime soon, replace traditional medical schools, it will augment classroom instruction with location-independent access to standardize digital content (Jiang et al., 2022). By using AR platforms, information can be gathered, progressed, monitored, and updates can be done easily as new materials become available. Healthcare applications of augmented reality include complete anatomy, which offers an inside-the-body experience, shoulder arthroscopy, which educates users about arthroscopy procedures (Zuñiga-Aviles & Cruz-Martinez, 2024).

The use of immersive AR, XR, and VR simulation environments is necessary for the cloud IoT framework to achieve long-term e-learning in healthcare higher education (Akpan, 2024). In order to create the desired immersive learning environment, it will connect with interactivity as well as collaborative resources. Both instructors and learners will be able to participate in virtual conference rooms for instructional planning. One benefit of a VR-based cyber-physical methodology is that it allows collaborative knowledge models to be more flexible in response to students' evolving academic needs. Many partners may work together within virtual enterprise platforms and combine their digital and physical resources to meet the specific learning objectives. XR technology reduces the need to bring educational institutions within the reach of the students and learners in faraway regions by emphasizing immersive and collaboratively developed ways of remote education. (Alqallaf & Ghannam, 2024) claims that an immersive learning environment that includes interactive VR services, digital avatars of teachers and students, and virtual conference rooms is intended to demonstrate how effective learning is in the solar system. The practices support the growth of instructors' skills as educators by giving students training and chances for skill development, as well as by immersing experts in their field of expertise in a more genuine and immersive way. Furthermore, the virtual implementation of the audio metaverse facilitates the creation of immersive experiences by enabling the generation of spatial sound when connected with XR-enabled streaming video applications. In addition to offering students development of skills training and things to do, the practices help teachers become more successful educators by integrating them into their profession in a more comprehensive and real way. With a range of ICT technology resources and tools for digital collaboration and interactive communication in the digital classroom, the metaverse has been utilized as an instructional component in digital education to establish collaborative environments for learning. Avatars can be used to navigate the metaverse, which is a dynamic digital ecosystem that uses cutting-edge technologies to create a digital environment that mimics the real world. Through immersive learning, remote collaboration via the metaverse increases student engagement while fostering cognitive competency and teamwork.

The approach investigated the ways in which different construction components have been integrated into the conceptual framework and fit together. To model studies of volumetric analysis, (Kalateh & Kheiry, 2024) created a new online virtual learning environment. Innovations in Web and VR technology were used to simulate real-world conditions in a chemical laboratory, improving learning through real-time immersive simulations of volumetric analysis studies (Ugochukwu O Matthew, Kazaure, & Haruna, 2020). The virtual laboratory described in one study was not only a practical instrument for chemistry remote learning and lifetime learning, but it was also a cost-effective choice for colleges and universities without the equipment required for immersive classroom instruction (Ndunagu, Ukhurebor, & Adesina, 2023). The simulated situation is based on Second Life, a web-based 3D multi-user virtual world created by the San Francisco-based organizational Laboratory (Kiong,

2024). One of the most popular virtual reality platforms is Second Life, which is used by many educators worldwide. It offers people countless opportunities for involvement, a feeling of community, and the ability to hone their own abilities. Statistics show that over 100 educational institutions are using Second Life to operate their simulated laboratories and engage in academic activities. According to (Tugtekin & Odabasi, 2022), integrating VR into engineering curricula is necessary since people recall up to 90% of what they learn when they actively participate in multimedia activities. Practical implementation of BME education involves integrating hands-on experiences with immersive technologies like AR, VR, and MR to simulate real-world healthcare scenarios (Akhtar & Rawol, 2025). Students engage with virtual labs, anatomical models, and clinical decision-making simulations that foster experiential learning and procedural accuracy. Collaborative projects bridge theory and practice, incorporating engineering design, medical challenges, and interdisciplinary teamwork (Jibril et al., 2022). AI-powered platforms provide adaptive feedback and personalized content delivery, while cloud-based environments enable scalable access to learning tools. This pedagogical approach equips learners with essential skills, such as innovation, critical thinking, and sensitivity, preparing them for high-performance roles in healthcare systems and biomedical industries worldwide. In the subsisting section, this paper looked at the key technology and associated infrastructure sustaining the immersive education technology and its evolutionary and scientific connotations.

RELATED WORK

Foundational studies like Asoodar et al. (2024) and Sung et al. (2024) demonstrate that VR and AR significantly enhance cognitive and psychomotor skills in surgical and anatomy training. Emerging research, such as Aoudi Chance (2025), explores AI-VR synergy for adaptive learning and interdisciplinary teamwork. Fugate et al. (2025) present a critical perspective, highlighting inconsistent outcomes and underscoring the absence of robust theoretical frameworks supporting XR pedagogy. Their analysis challenges prevailing optimism, emphasizing the need for deeper conceptual foundations and more rigorous instructional models to validate immersive technology's role in healthcare education. These studies collectively show promise but also highlight the need for rigorous, theory-informed designs and broader demographic inclusion to validate immersive technologies across diverse healthcare education contexts. Biomedical information, a dynamic subset of BME education, is experiencing groundbreaking advancements through the integration of AI within the Education 5.0 framework (Lantada, 2020). This human-centered approach shifts traditional instruction toward intelligent, adaptive, and experiential learning environments. AI technologies, ranging from ML algorithms to natural language processing, enable real-time data interpretation, pattern recognition, and intelligent content delivery tailored to individual learners. Within biomedical informatics, AI enhances the accuracy and speed of medical data analysis, supports diagnostic decision-making, and facilitates predictive modeling of health conditions (Akiotu et al., 2025). When fused with immersive tools like VR and AR, AI empowers students to engage with complex anatomical systems and clinical workflows in simulated settings (Al Balushi et al., 2024).

The modern education practice is adapting to the demands of the twenty-first century by moving away from traditional approaches and toward more customized and adaptable approaches in response to the quickly evolving technological 3D world (Ugochukwu O Matthew, Kazaure, & Okafor, 2021). There was a paradigm shift in the way AR and VR simulation were used in the classroom with the development of customized learning environments using AI technologies like machine learning algorithms and natural language processing (Ugochukwu Okwudili Matthew et al., 2022; D. O. Oyekunle, Esseme, et al., 2025). These educational settings are designed to accommodate each student's particular needs and preferences, making the learning process more engaging and effective. The shift to Education 5.0 replaces one-size-fits-all, standardized teaching approaches with a framework that is more flexible and adaptive. Building on the concepts of Education 5.0, the emphasis on adaptable learning promotes the use of AI in education. Adaptive learning examines how AI systems could dynamically alter instructional strategies in response to students' progress and immediate feedback. Education 5.0 seeks to maximize the learning process by tailoring exams, content, and pace to each student's unique learning style and abilities in order to improve overall educational outcomes. The most important component of Education 5.0 for medical education is AI's ability to create flexible learning environments; the knowledge acquired here can be used as training curriculum and instructional guide in other biomedical fields, such as biomedical informatics and BME education (Coelho & Reis, 2023).

Federated Learning based on IoT Cognitive Intelligence

Federated learning is an advanced approach to distributed data composition that allows for the collaborative creation of a high-quality shared model by combining and averaging locally calculated updates submitted by IoT devices (Wu, He, & Chen, 2020). Federated learning, a cutting-edge method of AI training, is rapidly assuming the lead in meeting several new privacy standards. AI systems in Education 5.0 are able to identify each student's unique learning preferences, styles, and talents through the analysis of vast volumes of data, enabling the personalization of learning experiences. By using augmented reality and virtual reality technologies to process data at the source, federated learning will offer a way to access the raw data from sensors on satellites, bridges, machines, and an expanding number of smart immersive technology devices at home and on our bodies (Ahmad et al., 2023). AR and VR are revolutionizing education and making learning more interesting in an immersive setting, where students can model real-life situations that are typically costly or challenging to replicate in the actual world (Xu et al., 2023). By facilitating more complex and realistic interactions, streamlining real-time data processing, and enabling adaptive environments that react intelligently to user behavior, AI can greatly improve XR. The combination of AI with XR creates new opportunities for developing immersive experiences that are more natural-feeling, interactive, and human-like, whether through sophisticated object identification, natural language processing, or targeted content delivery.

Smart Tutoring Applications

AI-powered intelligent tutoring programs provide students with real-time, personalized assistance when adapted with biomedical informatics computation (Singh, Singh, & Ravesangar, 2025). These systems offer coaching, feedback, and further resources based on each student's achievement. By continuously assessing information and adapting to learning speeds, intelligent tutoring systems increase learning efficiency and engagement.

Biomedical Engineering Expanded Curriculum Creation

The scientific foundation of AI lies in cognitive and learning sciences, with a focus on lessons for biomedical engineering and biomedical informatics curricula (Johnson, 2024). AI analyzes large amounts of educational data to identify trends, gaps, and areas where courses need to be improved, including reforms in instructional design and the educational process. Based on data-driven approach, educators may produce lesson plans that are more pertinent and successful. AI systems also assess how well different teaching strategies work and recommend changes to enhance overall learning outcomes.

Interactive Education and Context Gamification

Students' motivation and engagement are increased by artificial intelligence in educational games and interactive learning platforms. For the reason that AI algorithms customize gaming scenarios and challenges based on individual player achievement, learners are immersed in an engaging and pleasurable environment. Altogether, gamification and AI turn traditional learning into a dynamic, participatory educational process, (Ugochukwu O Matthew & Kazaure, 2020). AI in Education 5.0 smoothly incorporates gamification features and simulations into the learning process. Educational platforms encourage students and make learning fun by adding game-like aspects. For courses like biology and engineering that need real-world application, simulations offer useful, hands-on experiences in virtual environments.

Virtual Reality (VR) and Augmented Reality (AR)

By enabling immersive and interactive settings, AR and VR technologies have the potential to completely transform the educational process. By tailoring virtual experiences to each user's unique learning preferences and styles, AI can improve these technologies in Industry 5.0 human eccentricity (Zafar, Langås, & Sanfilippo, 2024). To develop immersive learning experiences, AI in Education 5.0 combines VR and AR. With the use of these cutting-edge technology, students can now connect with instructional materials in three dimensions, increasing their comprehension of challenging material.

Natural Language Processing and Conversation ChatGPT

With regard to language models, generative artificial intelligence (GenAI), and ChatGPT in particular, represent a noteworthy technological advancement as a game-changing tool for medical education and a revolutionary tool for national language processing (NLP) (Ugochukwu Okwudili Matthew, Bakare, Ebong, Ndukwu, & Nwanakwaugwu, 2023). The recommendations made by ChatGPT users have the power to improve instruction and learning, which will have a significant effect on the twenty-first-century educational landscape. For several reasons, educational robots are becoming more widely available, impacting professional and scientific collaboration beyond the medical domain. Research in cognitive AI provides a solid foundation for biomedicine, health professions, and biomedical informatics education, since biomedical science has revolutionized the delivery of healthcare (Haleem & Javaid, 2024). In the days ahead, human-robot collaboration which has made scientific strides in industry 5.0 excessive digital automation will most likely also become a common occurrence.

The potential applications of GenAI for NLP synthesis enable automatic interpretation of written assignments, NLP systems with AI capabilities providing students with immediate feedback. It speeds up the grading process and promotes ongoing development in addition to offering insightful feedback on students' writing abilities. In addition, linguistic learning algorithms that offer individualized practice and support can be developed using NLP. ChatGPT was created to address the multitude of computational jobs in the medical field by developing a robust and flexible AI language model that could help with a range of tasks, such as data analysis, translation, text production, and codification. Schools can assist students in acquiring the abilities, know-how, and competences needed in the changing labor market by coordinating their curriculum with industry demands. This guarantees that graduates are ready for the workforce and improves employability. The importance of upskilling and lifelong learning is emphasized by Industry 5.0. Combining Education 5.0 with Industry 5.0 promotes lifetime learning and provides chances for continuous professional development (Ugochukwu O Matthew, Kazaure, Kazaure, Onyedibe, & Okafor, 2022). Technology, such as online learning platforms and individualized learning pathways, can help people learn new skills and stay current with market trends (Ugochukwu O Matthew & Kazaure, 2020).

Figure 1. Technology elements that underpin Industry 5.0 and Society 5.0, which in turn propel Education 5.0.

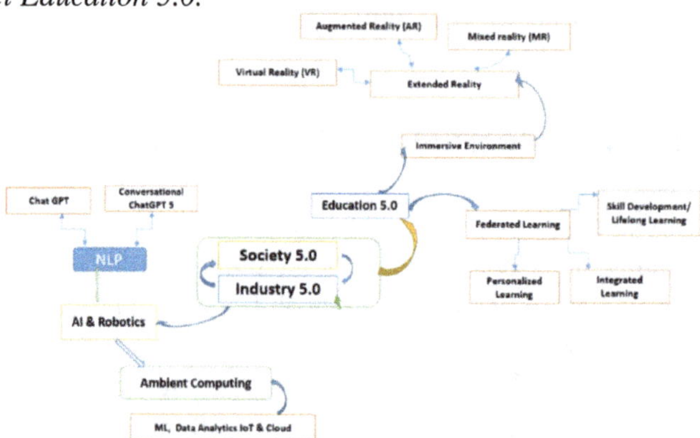

From Figure 1, the IoT, AI, ML, big data, and the metaverse are all key components of Society 5.0, which suggests a single, universal, and immersive virtual world made possible by VR and AR headsets (Zawish et al., 2024). As it develops, it can use integrated digital systems from both virtual and physical space to address social issues. In the realm of education, learners must possess three high-level skills: social creativity, critical thinking, and problem-solving abilities. Adapting teaching tactics and methodologies is part of the growth of educational pedagogies to meet the evolving demands of Industry 5.0. The evolution includes incorporating industry-related projects and real-world case studies into the curriculum, encouraging interdisciplinary approaches, using technology to create virtual labs and simulations, inviting industry experts to give guest lectures, and using gamification to create interactive learning experiences. The teaching approaches should be in line with the tenets and requirements of Industry 5.0, better educate students for the dynamic industrial environment, and enhance their entire educational experience. These three abilities are attributed to the higher order of cognitive abilities. Higher order of thinking skills is an over-average cognitive thinking style that requires students to manage concepts and information without changing its impact or meaning. It was developed based on a number of cognitive principles and techniques as well as learning taxonomy.

RESEARCH QUESTIONS

The use of VR, AV, and MR simulations in biomedical engineering education has increased because of their efficacy and special benefits. Five research questions about the use of immersive reality in biomedical informatics and biomedical engineering education were developed by the authors of this paper.

i. How can AI be effectively integrated into BME education to enhance personalized learning and clinical decision-making skills?
ii. What role do immersive technologies, such as AR and VR, play in improving the practical understanding of biomedical information among students?
iii. How does the Education 5.0 framework influence the development of interdisciplinary collaboration and critical thinking in BME?
iv. What are the ethical implications of using AI-driven tools in BME, particularly in terms of data privacy and equitable access?
v. How can AI and extended reality technologies be leveraged to simulate real-world healthcare challenges and prepare students for dynamic roles in the biomedical industry?

RESEARCH METHODOLOGY

This study employed a mixed methodology combining a systematic review, design research science methodology (DSRM) that involved Actor-Network Theory (ANT) integration, and design-based experimental scenarios supported by primary data. The systematic review identifies and synthesizes peer-reviewed sources from 2020–2025 focused on immersive technologies, biomedical engineering pedagogy, and Education 5.0 principles. Actor-Network Theory provides a lens to trace interactions among human actors (educators, students, technologists) and non-human actors (AI platforms, XR tools, and pedagogical frameworks), emphasizing co-constructed educational ecosystems. The TPCK framework guides the analysis of instructional design, emphasizing the interplay of technological, pedagogical, and disciplinary knowledge. Primary source data includes faculty reports, curriculum designs, and observational records. The study involves two cohorts: a 30-member experimental group exposed to immersive simulations, game-based learning, and mentoring practices, and a 20-member control group receiving standard instruction. Design-based scenarios examine real-world implementation of scaffolding models, faculty-wide mentoring programs, and technology mapping activities across both groups. Comparative evaluation uses formative assessments, engagement metrics, and performance analysis to validate TPCK integration and actor-network robustness. This methodology ensures a rich exploration of immersive education practices and their efficacy in sustainable BME education, offering reproducible insight into the transformation of instructional paradigms through technological cognition.

The DSRM as a computational paradigm reinforces the creation of ANT model to operationalize and evaluate the immersive technology implementation, intelligent pedagogy for BME education framed by Education 5.0. DSRM guides iterative artifact development, such as AI-driven XR learning modules through problem identification, objective definition, design, demonstration, and evaluation, refer to figure 2. The ANT complements this by mapping interactions between human actors (educators, learners, and developers) and non-human actors (XR platforms, AI systems, TPCK models, cloud infrastructures). ANT reveals how these relationships co-construct learning experiences and educational outcomes. The network is dynamic: students engage with immersive simulations; educators adapt TPCK to optimize delivery; AI personalizes content; and institutional structures regulate access and ethics. Together, DSRM and ANT offer a dual lens: one for building effective pedagogical systems, and another for analyzing their sociotechnical evolution. This fusion ensures the framework is both functionally robust and contextually responsive to sustainable biomedical education challenges.

SYSTEM FLOW MODEL

The integration of AR and VR into federated learning systems is supported by two widely recognized educational frameworks: the Substitution, Augmentation, Modification, Redefinition (SAMR) model (Waliu, Matthew, et al., 2025) and the TPCK framework (Akkoç, 2013). These frameworks facilitate the design of collaborative, electronic learning platforms that benefit biomedical engineering educators by combining technical, pedagogical, and content knowledge. For successful technology integration, all three domains must work in harmony through informed and expert collaboration. The SAMR model categorizes how technology influences education from basic substitution to transformative uses of XR platforms that foster novel learning experiences (Tene et al., 2024). As educators move beyond substitution toward redefinition, they unlock new possibilities for immersive and engaging instruction. TPCK complements this by emphasizing the balanced application of pedagogical strategies and subject content with emerging technologies. To ensure that XR-enhanced teaching remains effective and adaptive, both SAMR and TPCK highlight the necessity of grounding design choices in established learning theories. These theories guide the understanding of how students acquire knowledge, behaviors, and skills in alignment with current curricular frameworks. By embedding theoretical underpinnings into instructional design, educators can better craft impactful XR experiences that resonate with diverse learners and adapt to evolving educational contexts. In essence, these frameworks not only enable technological enhancement but also serve as foundations for pedagogical innovation and curriculum alignment in biomedical education.

Figure 2. A theoretical framework of technological pedagogy content knowledge (TPCK) that integrates immersive technology (AR/VR)

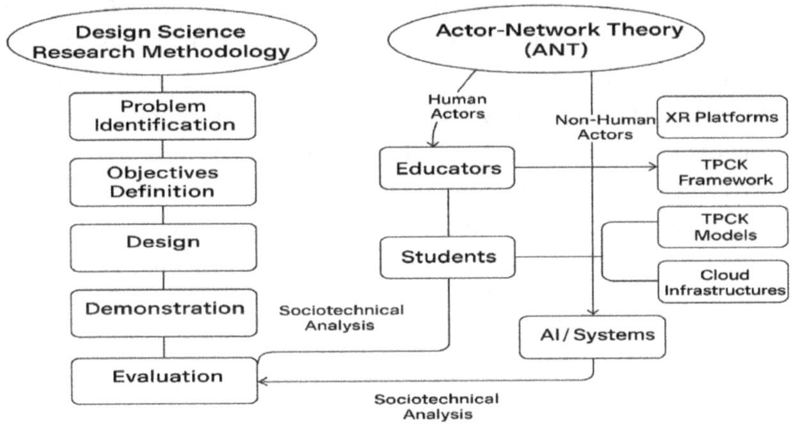

In Figure 2 above, the model integrates DSRM with ANT to provide a dual framework for investigating immersive biomedical education practices. Through DSRM, the research systematically defines the pedagogical problem, limited interactivity and personalization in biomedical instruction and iteratively constructs, demonstrates, and evaluates educational artifacts like AI-powered XR modules and adaptive learning systems. This design cycle ensures functional relevance and continuous refinement based on empirical feedback. ANT analysis reveals the sociotechnical landscape supporting these innovations. Human actors (students, faculty, developers) interact with non-human actors (XR platforms, AI tutors, TPCK constructs, cloud systems) in co-creating dynamic learning environments. The network is shaped by institutional values, ethical constraints, and learner intervention. Functional relationships shift as digital tools assume pedagogical roles and educators adapt to technologically mediated instruction. Interactions among actors form feedback loops that inform curriculum evolution, technological adoption, and instructional effectiveness. Together, the DSRM-ANT synthesis provides a holistic view capturing both the engineering of educational solutions and the complex web of actors influencing their use, scalability, and impact in sustainable biomedical education. Interactions among human and non-human actors in immersive biomedical education form feedback loops that dynamically influence curriculum design, technology integration, and teaching effectiveness. Educators interpret student data from AI tutors, XR modules, and simulation platforms to recalibrate pedagogical strategies and align with TPCK principles. Learners interact with virtual labs and adaptive content, generating engagement analytics and learning pathway insights. Technologists respond to these inputs by refining XR environments and federated learning systems, which house scalable cloud-based resources accessible across institutional boundaries. Federated Cloud Infrastructure acts as a mediator aggregating data across diverse platforms while preserving privacy and decentralization (Ebong et al., 2024). It allows real-time processing of educational metrics such as participation rates, performance levels, and conceptual mastery. These insights loop back to instructors and system designers, enabling them to modify content sequencing, tool deployment, and scaffolding models. The infrastructure ensures continuous alignment with curricular goals and evolving industry competencies, creating a sustainable educational network responsive to real-world demands. Feedback cycles powered by federated systems create an adaptive ecosystem in which content, instruction, and technology co-evolve shaping future-ready biomedical professionals through data-informed decisions and seamless actor collaboration.

Figure 3. Cloud based federated learning immersive system design (Oyekunle, Claude, et al., 2024).

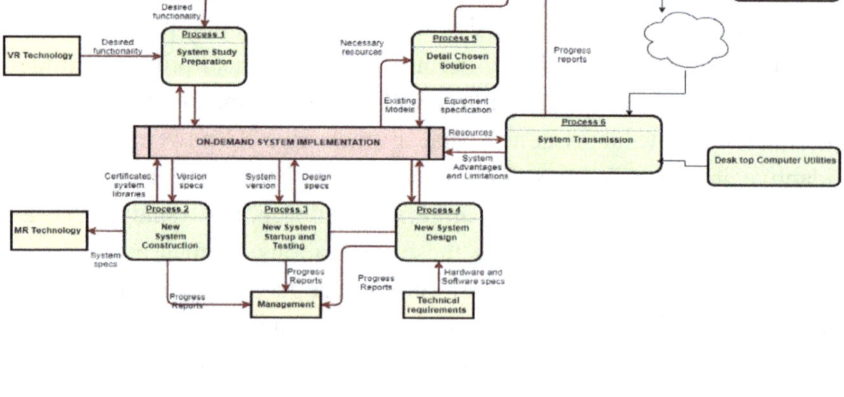

In Figure 3 above, both the SAMR model (Substitution, Augmentation, Modification, and Redefinition) and the TPCK framework emphasize the importance of aligning technological integration with foundational educational theories to ensure meaningful learning. SAMR guides educators in evaluating how digital tools transform teaching practices from enhancing existing methods to completely redefining learning tasks. TPCK complements this by stressing the intersection of technology, pedagogy, and content knowledge, asserting that effective instruction requires a balanced synthesis of all three domains. Grounding design choices in established learning theories such as constructivism, cognitive load theory, and experiential learning ensures that technological interventions promote deep understanding rather than superficial engagement. For instance, using XR to redefine biomedical simulations aligns with constructivist principles when learners manipulate complex systems interactively. Similarly, AI-enhanced feedback systems support cognitive processing when framed within scaffolding strategies. Together, SAMR and TPCK serve not as isolated tools, but as dynamic evaluative lenses that ensure every technological choice advances educational goals rooted in research-based pedagogy. Integrating technology without theoretical grounding risks reducing education to novelty; with theory, it becomes transformative.

Figure 4. Cloud-adaptive learning environments that integrate AR and VR

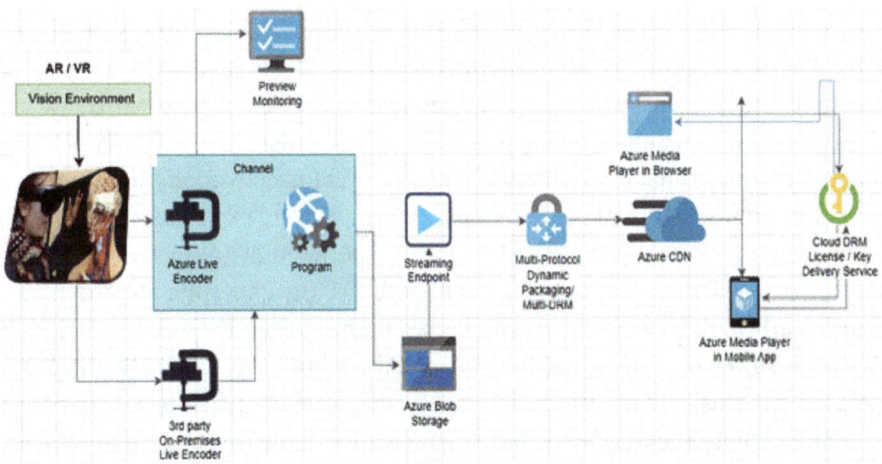

In Figure 4 above, Cloud-adaptive learning environments that integrate AR and VR represent a transformative shift in educational pedagogy. These ecosystems harness the scalability and responsiveness of cloud computing to deliver immersive, personalized, and collaborative experiences across geographic and institutional boundaries. AR and VR technologies offer multisensory simulations allowing learners to interact with 3D models, conduct virtual biomedical experiments, and engage in real-time clinical scenarios without physical constraints. When supported by cloud infrastructure, these experiences become dynamic and continuously updated, enabling educators to push new content, assess learner progress, and adapt instructional strategies instantly. The cloud's federated architecture ensures secure data storage, decentralized access, and cross-platform compatibility, empowering institutions to integrate advanced learning modules without overhauling existing systems. Additionally, AI algorithms embedded in these environments analyze interaction data, providing personalized feedback and adaptive pathways for diverse learning profiles. This synergy between XR and cloud computing fosters experiential, data-driven, and inclusive learning preparing students for complex problem-solving in biomedical and interdisciplinary contexts through virtual engagement grounded in pedagogical best practices.

DISCUSSION OF RESEARCH FINDINGS

The study hypothesizes that the integration of immersive technologies (AR/VR), intelligent tutoring systems, and cloud-adaptive environments framed by Education 5.0, Industry 5.0, and Society 5.0, enhances student engagement, learning outcomes, and practical skill acquisition in biomedical engineering education. This hypothesis is grounded in the belief that human-centered innovation combined with technological augmentation leads to sustainable and transformative pedagogy. Research questions focused on how AI and XR technologies impact personalized learning, clinical decision-making, and curriculum effectiveness; how TPCK integration shapes interdisciplinary collaboration; and how actor-network dynamics influence adoption and instructional quality. These questions were examined through design-based experiments comparing a 30-member experimental group with a 20-member control group. The results validate the hypothesis: the experimental group showed significantly higher performance scores, stronger engagement metrics, and superior skill acquisition levels. Statistical tools like chi-square tests confirmed differences in learning patterns, and network analysis revealed effective feedback loops between human and non-human actors. The federated cloud infrastructure played a central role in enabling real-time content adaptation and resource delivery. Collectively, the findings affirm that immersive, cloud-supported education guided by ethical and pedagogical frameworks offers measurable improvements in biomedical learning and prepares students for the demands of future healthcare and engineering ecosystems.

Table 1. Experimental vs. control group

Variable	Experimental Group (n=30)	Control Group (n=20)	Observation & Insight
Avg. Performance Score (out of 100)	88.5	74.2	Immersive learning boosts academic outcomes significantly.
Learning Outcomes Achieved (%)	92%	68%	Higher alignment with curriculum objectives in XR settings.
Practical Skill Acquisition (%)	90%	65%	Enhanced procedural accuracy through simulated environments.
High Engagement Level (%)	60%	50%	Interactive XR tools increase participation.
Feedback Responsiveness (%)	93%	70%	Adaptive systems yield more real-time instructional feedback.
Collaboration in Projects (%)	85%	55%	XR-enhanced teamwork encourages interdisciplinary efforts.
Conceptual Mastery (Retention %)	87%	69%	XR simulations foster deeper and longer-term understanding.
Motivation & Confidence (Self-rated)	High	Moderate	Immersive tools reinforce self-efficacy and learner agency.

The results reveal a clear pedagogical advantage for the experimental group, which experienced immersive learning supported by AI and XR within a cloud-adaptive framework. These learners consistently outperformed the control group in performance scores, skill acquisition, and conceptual retention. Enhanced collaboration rates and feedback responsiveness indicate that immersive platforms foster more active and student-centered environments. The high engagement levels and self-reported motivation suggest improved learner agency and emotional investment in the educational process. By contrast, the control group demonstrated lower gains across all categories, pointing to the limitations of traditional instructional models in dynamic, interdisciplinary fields like biomedical engineering. The experimental group's alignment with TPCK principles and Actor-Network Theory demonstrates how well-designed technological ecosystems can create synergistic feedback loops that optimize teaching and learning. Overall, the data supports the study's hypothesis and research questions, confirming that immersive, cloud-enabled, and ethically grounded educational technologies significantly improve learning outcomes in sustainable biomedical contexts. In the long run, the content knowledge construct depends heavily on selecting the appropriate technology to support student learning objectives, long-term information retention, and higher-order thinking within the topic that summarizes the contribution of immersive technologies to education from the existing literatures.

Table 2. Scholarly evidences of engaging learners with immersive solutions in bridging the gap between theory and practice from existing literatures

Immersive Technology Philosophy	Contribution to Education and Mental Cognition
Virtual Reality Field Trips	With the use of VR technologies, students may be taken from the classroom to immersive virtual worlds where they can closely examine far-off places and completely transform classroom instruction, engaging learners in new and creative ways(Akpan, 2024).
Augmented Reality Learning Materials	AR technology can enhance learning materials by superimposing digital content, including 3D models, films, or animations, on top of printed textbooks as multimedia courseware(Gumel, Abdullahi, & O, 2019),(Ugochukwu Okwudili Matthew et al., 2022). This promotes deeper comprehension and context assimilation.
Mixed Reality Collaborative Learning	With the help of MR solutions, students can collaborate on immersive, interactive projects that combine digital and real-world components, encouraging teamwork and problem-solving skills(D. Oyekunle, Ugochukwu, Rosa, Rodriguez, & Fatai, 2024).
Immersive Laboratories and Simulations	Teachers can develop immersive virtual laboratories using VR, AR, or MR technologies, which eliminates the need for actual materials and enables students to securely participate in hands-on teaching and experimentation(Waliu, Muojekwu, et al., 2025),(D. Oyekunle, Matthew, Waliu, & Fatai, 2024).
Real-World Scenario Training	With the help of immersive technology, students may practice applying their knowledge and abilities in safe settings and get ready for real-life situations they might face in their future employment(Ghanbaripour et al., 2024).
Skills Development and Assessment	With the use of VR, AR, and MR technologies, students' practical skills can be developed and evaluated while receiving quick feedback and chances for growth(Papanastasiou, Drigas, Skianis, Lytras, & Papanastasiou, 2019).
Cross-Disciplinary Learning Experiences	Students can work together on projects that call for a blend of knowledge and abilities from other professions attributable to the immersive cross-disciplinary learning experiences that AR, VR, and MR solutions can help create(Muzata, Singh, Stepanov, & Musonda, 2024).
Co-Creation and Innovation	With immersive technologies, students may explore, conceive, design, and construct interactive 3D models and simulations together, encouraging co-creation and creativity(Andalib & Monsur, 2024).
Remote Collaboration,/ Creative Thinking and Innovation/ Lifelong Learning	Through the use of immersive technology, students may easily work together with classmates, teachers, and professionals from around the globe, getting around geographical restrictions and gaining access to a variety of viewpoints and insights. In today's fast-paced and constantly changing environment, students will enhance their creative thinking and innovative problem-solving skills through immersive, hands-on learning activities(Ugochukwu O Matthew, 2019),(Okwudili & Kazaure, 2020).

Table 3. An empirical research findings on the use of AI combined with VR, XR, AR, and MR gamification in biomedical engineering education

Technology	Application in BME Education	Specific Findings	Reference
AI + XR (VR/AR/MR)	Immersive anatomy and physiology training	XR tools improve spatial understanding and retention; AI personalizes feedback and learning pace	Fugate et al. (2025). Immersive Extended Reality (I-XR) in Medical and Nursing for Skill Competency and Knowledge Acquisition: A Systematic Review and Implications for Pedagogical Practices. Behavioral Sciences, 15(4), 468.
AI + XR Gamification	Interactive diagnostics and treatment simulation	AI enhances image analysis and XR gamifies clinical scenarios for experiential learning	Kini et al. (2024). XR review: A comprehensive analysis of visual function testing and gamification in extended reality environments. IEEE Access, 12, 79714-79730.
VR/AR Gamification	Biomedical curriculum engagement	Gamified VR/AR modules increase student motivation, reduce cognitive load, and improve skill acquisition	[REMOVED HYPERLINK FIELD] Taghian et al. (2023). Virtual and augmented reality in biomedical engineering. Biomedical engineering online, 22(1), 76.
AI + MR	Surgical simulation and human-robot interaction	MR with AI supports real-time feedback and adaptive learning in robotic surgery training	[REMOVED HYPERLINK FIELD] Chepkoech et al. (2025). Telementoring for surgical training in low-resource settings: a systematic review of current systems and the emerging role of 5G, AI, and XR. Journal of Robotic Surgery, 19(1), 525.

Table 3 highlight how gamified, AI-enhanced immersive technologies are transforming biomedical engineering education by bridging theory-practice gaps, improving engagement, and enabling personalized learning. Empirical evidence confirms that AI-enhanced immersive technologies VR, XR, AR, and MR are revolutionizing biomedical engineering education through gamification. Taghian et al. (2023) demonstrated that AI-powered XR platforms significantly improved spatial reasoning and personalized learning in anatomy and physiology training. Akhtar and Rawol (2025) found that gamified XR simulations enhanced diagnostic accuracy and learner engagement, offering experiential clinical scenarios tailored by AI. Fugate et al. (2025) reported that 42.5% of VR and 42.9% of AR interventions led to superior skill acquisition and knowledge retention compared to traditional methods, highlighting the motivational and cognitive benefits of gamified modules. Additionally, MR applications in surgical simulation and human-robot interaction provided adaptive feedback and real-time learning, further bridging theory-practice gaps. These findings collectively underscore the transformative impact of AI-driven gamification in biomedical education, fostering hands-on competence, critical thinking, and inclusive access to advanced training environments across diverse learner populations.

LIMITATIONS OF THE STUDY

Immersive educational technologies like AR and VR present exciting possibilities but carry several limitations. High development and maintenance costs restrict access, especially in under-resourced institutions. Technical requirements, including high-speed internet and specialized hardware, may hinder broad implementation. Content design demands interdisciplinary expertise, making scalable production complex and time-consuming. While simulations offer engagement, they may oversimplify nuanced clinical decision-making or ethical dilemmas. Educator readiness and digital literacy vary, impacting integration and instructional quality. Furthermore, prolonged immersion risks cognitive overload and reduces peer-to-peer interaction. Data privacy and ethical concerns around tracking learner behavior within XR environments require robust governance. These limitations underscore the need for strategic integration, ongoing evaluation, and inclusive design when implementing immersive technologies in education.

FUTURE RESEARCH FOCUS

Future studies should aim to develop scalable, cross-disciplinary immersive learning ecosystems tailored for biomedical fields, leveraging AI, XR, and federated cloud infrastructure. The goal is to evaluate long-term impacts of these technologies on critical thinking, ethical reasoning, and clinical decision-making under real-world conditions. Research should explore frameworks for inclusive access, adaptability to diverse learning profiles, and integration with evolving biomedical curricula across global institutions. Additionally, analyzing sociotechnical feedback loops among human and non-human actors will help refine sustainable pedagogical models. These efforts will support the creation of resilient, equity-driven, and innovation-ready education systems for the biomedical workforce of the future.

CONCLUSION

The study concludes that integrating immersive technologies, AI-driven feedback systems, and cloud-adaptive learning environments anchored in the principles of Education 5.0, Industry 5.0, and Society 5.0 significantly enhances biomedical engineering education. Through the Design Science Research Methodology, learning artifacts like XR simulations and adaptive modules were iteratively developed and validated. Actor-Network Theory revealed dynamic relationships between human and non-human actors, where educators, students, and intelligent platforms co-constructed learning pathways. Comparative analysis between experimental and control groups demonstrated higher performance scores, stronger skill acquisition, and greater engagement in the immersive cohort. The TPCK framework ensured pedagogical integrity by aligning technology with subject content and learning strategy. Federated cloud infrastructure enabled scalable, real-time personalization and ethical data handling. Together, the findings affirm that immersive, actor-driven, and cloud-enabled ecosystems not only foster academic excellence but also promote equity, interdisciplinary thinking, and technological fluency forming a future-ready paradigm for biomedical education. As traditional pedagogies evolve, AI and XR gamification stand out as powerful tools to reshape biomedical engineering education, making it more inclusive, responsive, and future-ready. The convergence of these technologies signals a paradigm shift toward experiential, learner-focused models that prioritize cognitive growth and practical competence.

REFERENCES

Ahmad, H. F., Rafique, W., Rasool, R. U., Alhumam, A., Anwar, Z., & Qadir, J. (2023). Leveraging 6G, extended reality, and IoT big data analytics for healthcare: A review. *Computer Science Review*, *48*, 100558. DOI: 10.1016/j.cosrev.2023.100558

Akhtar, Z. (2024). Biomedical engineering (bme) and medical health science: An investigation perspective exploration. *Quantum Journal of Medical and Health Sciences*, *3*(3), 1–24.

Akhtar, Z. B. (2024). Artificial Intelligence (AI) and Extended Reality (XR): A Biomedical Engineering Perspective Investigation Analysis. *Indonesian Journal of Electronics, Electromedical Engineering, and Medical Informatics*, *6*(3). Advance online publication. DOI: 10.35882/ijeeemi.v6i3.5

Akhtar, Z. B., & Rawol, A. T. (2025). Artificial Intelligence (AI) & Extended Reality (XR) within Healthcare: A Multidimensional Biomedical Engineering (BME) Investigative Exploration. *Biomed. Clin. Res. J*, *1*, 1–22.

Akiotu, C. A., Cole, O. A., Bunmi, E. E., Temiola, T., Oladele, H. A., Oluwasegun, V. O., Oyedemi, O. A., & Matthew, U. O. (2025). A Predictive Nutritional Assessment System for Vegetarians using Artificial Neural Networks. *Journal of Future Artificial Intelligence and Technologies*, *2*(2), 294–312. DOI: 10.62411/faith.3048-3719-117

Akkoç, H. (2013). *Integrating technological pedagogical content knowledge (TPCK) framework into teacher education.* Paper presented at the Conference of the International Journal of Arts and Science.

Akpan, E. E. (2024). Healthcare Applications of Augmented Reality. *Creating Immersive Learning Experiences Through Virtual Reality (VR), 201.*

Al Balushi, J. S. G., Al Jabri, M. I. A., Palarimath, S., Maran, P., Thenmozhi, K., & Balakumar, C. (2024). *Incorporating artificial intelligence powered immersive realities to improve learning using virtual reality (VR) and augmented reality (AR) technology.* Paper presented at the 2024 3rd International Conference on Applied Artificial Intelligence and Computing (ICAAIC).

Aland, R. C., Hugo, H. J., Battle, A., Donkin, R., McDonald, A., McGowan, H., & Tentrisanna, M. (2023). A plethora of choices: An anatomists' practical perspectives for the selection of digital anatomy resources. *Smart Learning Environments*, *10*(1), 66. DOI: 10.1186/s40561-023-00285-3

Alqallaf, N., & Ghannam, R. (2024). *Immersive Learning in Photovoltaic Energy Education: A Comprehensive Review of Virtual Reality Applications*. Paper presented at the Solar. DOI: 10.3390/solar4010006

Andalib, S., & Monsur, M. (2024). Co-Created Virtual Reality (VR) Modules in Landscape Architecture Education: A Mixed Methods Study Investigating the Pedagogical Effectiveness of VR. *Education Sciences*, *14*(6), 553. DOI: 10.3390/educsci14060553

Asoodar, M., Janesarvatan, F., Yu, H., & de Jong, N. (2024). Theoretical foundations and implications of augmented reality, virtual reality, and mixed reality for immersive learning in health professions education. *Advances in Simulation (London, England)*, *9*(1), 36. DOI: 10.1186/s41077-024-00311-5 PMID: 39252139

Barteit, S., Lanfermann, L., Bärnighausen, T., Neuhann, F., & Beiersmann, C. (2021). Augmented, mixed, and virtual reality-based head-mounted devices for medical education: Systematic review. *JMIR Serious Games*, *9*(3), e29080. DOI: 10.2196/29080 PMID: 34255668

Bryant, L., & Hemsley, B. (2024). Augmented reality: A view to future visual supports for people with disability. *Disability and Rehabilitation. Assistive Technology*, *19*(3), 800–813. DOI: 10.1080/17483107.2022.2125090 PMID: 36149835

Carayannis, E. G., & Morawska, J. (2023). *University and education 5.0 for emerging trends, policies and practices in the concept of industry 5.0 and society 5.0 Industry 5.0: Creative and Innovative Organizations*. Springer. DOI: 10.1007/978-3-031-26232-6_1

Cascella, M., Cascella, A., Monaco, F., & Shariff, M. N. (2023). Envisioning gamification in anesthesia, pain management, and critical care: Basic principles, integration of artificial intelligence, and simulation strategies. *Journal of Anesthesia, Analgesia and Critical Care*, *3*(1), 33. DOI: 10.1186/s44158-023-00118-2 PMID: 37697415

Coelho, L., & Reis, S. S. (2023). *Enhancing Learning Experiences Through Artificial Intelligence: Classroom 5.0 Fostering Pedagogy Through Micro and Adaptive Learning in Higher Education: Trends, Tools, and Applications*. IGI Global.

Ebong, G. N., Matthew, U. O., Olofin, B., Andrew-Vitalis, N., Fatai, L. O., Waliu, A. O., & Oladipupo, M. A. (2024). *Multimedia Cloud Data Warehouse Design for Knowledge Sharing in the University Environment: A Proposed Digital Solution Implementing Interactive Learning Strategies in Higher Education*. IGI Global. DOI: 10.4018/979-8-3693-3559-8.ch010

Fermin, J. L., & Tan, M. J. T. (2020). The need for the establishment of biomedical engineering as an academic and professional discipline in the Philippines—A quantitative argument. *IEEE Access : Practical Innovations, Open Solutions, 9*, 3097–3111. DOI: 10.1109/ACCESS.2020.3046655

Fuchs, S., Vasudevan, V., & Butcher, J. (2025). Embedding Studio-Based Learning in the Biomedical Engineering Curriculum to Improve Quantitative Problem-Solving Skills. *Biomedical Engineering Education*, •••, 1–21. DOI: 10.1007/s43683-025-00195-5

Ghanbaripour, A. N., Talebian, N., Miller, D., Tumpa, R. J., Zhang, W., Golmoradi, M., & Skitmore, M. (2024). A Systematic Review of the Impact of Emerging Technologies on Student Learning, Engagement, and Employability in Built Environment Education. *Buildings (Basel, Switzerland), 14*(9), 2769. DOI: 10.3390/buildings14092769

Gumel, A. A., & Abdullahi, A. B., & O, U. M. (2019). The Need for a Multimodal Means of Effective Digital Learning through Data Mining and Institutional Knowledge Repository: A Proposed System for Polytechnics in Northern Nigeria. *Proceedings of the 2019 5th International Conference on Computer and Technology Applications*. DOI: 10.1145/3323933.3324068

Gupta, S., Wilcocks, K., Matava, C., Wiegelmann, J., Kaustov, L., & Alam, F. (2023). Creating a Successful Virtual Reality–Based Medical Simulation Environment: Tutorial. *JMIR Medical Education, 9*, e41090. DOI: 10.2196/41090 PMID: 36787169

Haleem, A., & Javaid, M. (2024). Role of cognitive computing in enhancing innovative healthcare solutions. *Advances in Biomarker Sciences and Technology, 6*, 152–165. DOI: 10.1016/j.abst.2024.08.002

Hamilton, D., McKechnie, J., Edgerton, E., & Wilson, C. (2021). Immersive virtual reality as a pedagogical tool in education: A systematic literature review of quantitative learning outcomes and experimental design. *Journal of Computers in Education, 8*(1), 1–32. DOI: 10.1007/s40692-020-00169-2

Hassan, N. H., Rahim, N. A. A., Hoong, A. L. S., & Mostafa, K. (2024). *A Conceptual Study on Utilization of Artificial Intelligence (AI), Virtual Reality (VR) and Augmented Reality (AR) on Green Education: Effectiveness and Engagement.* Paper presented at the International Conference on Intelligent Manufacturing and Robotics.

Herrington, F. D., Rea, P. M., & Poyade, M. (2022). *Using Holograms to Engage Young People with Anatomy Medical Visualization and Applications of Technology*. Springer.

Islam, M. T., Sepanloo, K., Woo, S., Woo, S. H., & Son, Y.-J. (2025). A review of the industry 4.0 to 5.0 transition: Exploring the intersection, challenges, and opportunities of technology and human–machine collaboration. *Machines (Basel), 13*(4), 267. DOI: 10.3390/machines13040267

Jiang, H., Vimalesvaran, S., Wang, J. K., Lim, K. B., Mogali, S. R., & Car, L. T. (2022). Virtual reality in medical students' education: Scoping review. *JMIR Medical Education, 8*(1), e34860. DOI: 10.2196/34860 PMID: 35107421

Jibril, A. U., Abdullahi, N. M., Ali, A. S., Abdulkadir, H., Matthew, U. O., & Haruna, K. (2022). Motivational aspects of digital games in learning process. *Science in Information Technology Letters, 3*(1), 1–9. DOI: 10.31763/sitech.v3i1.885

Johnson, D. (2024). *Pedagogies of Biomedical Science: A Holistic Approach to Integrating Pedagogy Across the Curriculum.* Taylor & Francis. DOI: 10.4324/9781003383994

Kalateh, F., & Kheiry, M. (2024). A Review of Stochastic Analysis of the Seepage Through Earth Dams with a Focus on the Application of Monte Carlo Simulation. *Archives of Computational Methods in Engineering, 31*(1), 47–72. DOI: 10.1007/s11831-023-09972-3

Kandemir, O., Ulusoy, G., & Kandemir, C. M. (2024). *Immersive Learning Experience for Design Education in the Lens of Education 4.0 Multidisciplinary Applications of Extended Reality for Human Experience.* IGI Global.

Kaplan, A. D., Cruit, J., Endsley, M., Beers, S. M., Sawyer, B. D., & Hancock, P. A. (2021). The effects of virtual reality, augmented reality, and mixed reality as training enhancement methods: A meta-analysis. *Human Factors, 63*(4), 706–726. DOI: 10.1177/0018720820904229 PMID: 32091937

Kini, V. G., Ganeshrao, S. B., & Siddalingaswamy, P. (2024). XR review: A comprehensive analysis of visual function testing and gamification in extended reality environments. *IEEE Access : Practical Innovations, Open Solutions, 12*, 79714–79730. DOI: 10.1109/ACCESS.2024.3408677

Kiong, L. V. (2024). *Metaverse Made Easy: A Beginner's Guide to the Metaverse: Everything you need to know about Metaverse, NFT and GameFi.* Liew Voon Kiong.

Koch, N., Romani, A., Oliveira, T., & Tanaka, H. (2022). *An Overview of the Post-graduate Courses in Clinical Engineering Offered in Brazil.* Paper presented at the Latin American Conference on Biomedical Engineering.

Lampropoulos, G., Keramopoulos, E., Diamantaras, K., & Evangelidis, G. (2022). Augmented reality and gamification in education: A systematic literature review of research, applications, and empirical studies. *Applied Sciences (Basel, Switzerland), 12*(13), 6809. DOI: 10.3390/app12136809

Lantada, A. D. (2020). Engineering education 5.0: Continuously evolving engineering education. *International Journal of Engineering Education, 36*(6), 1814–1832.

Linsenmeier, R. A., & Saterbak, A. (2020). Fifty years of biomedical engineering undergraduate education. *Annals of Biomedical Engineering, 48*(6), 1590–1615. DOI: 10.1007/s10439-020-02494-0 PMID: 32253615

Liu, J. Y. W., Mak, P. Y., Chan, K., Cheung, D. S. K., Cheung, K., Fong, K. N., Kor, P. P. K., Lai, T. K. H., & Maximo, T. (2024). The Effects of Immersive Virtual Reality–Assisted Experiential Learning on Enhancing Empathy in Undergraduate Health Care Students Toward Older Adults With Cognitive Impairment: Multiple-Methods Study. *JMIR Medical Education, 10*, e48566. DOI: 10.2196/48566 PMID: 38358800

Lungu, A. J., Swinkels, W., Claesen, L., Tu, P., Egger, J., & Chen, X. (2021). A review on the applications of virtual reality, augmented reality and mixed reality in surgical simulation: An extension to different kinds of surgery. *Expert Review of Medical Devices, 18*(1), 47–62. DOI: 10.1080/17434440.2021.1860750 PMID: 33283563

Matthew, U. O. (2019). Information System Management & Multimedia Applications in an E-Learning Environment. [IJICTHD]. *International Journal of Information Communication Technologies and Human Development, 11*(3), 21–41. DOI: 10.4018/IJICTHD.2019070102

Matthew, U. O., Bakare, K. M., Ebong, G. N., Ndukwu, C. C., & Nwanakwaugwu, A. C. (2023). Generative Artificial Intelligence (AI) Educational Pedagogy Development: Conversational AI with User-Centric ChatGPT4. *Journal of Trends in Computer Science and Smart Technology, 5*(4), 401–418. DOI: 10.36548/jtcsst.2023.4.003

Matthew, U. O., Kazaure, A. S., Kazaure, J. S., Hassan, I. M., Nwanakwaugwu, A. C., & Okafor, N. U. (2022). Educational Technology Adaptation & Implication for Media Technology Adoption in the Period of COVID-19. *Journal of Trends in Computer Science and Smart Technology, 4*(4), 226–245. DOI: 10.36548/jtcsst.2022.4.002

Matthew, U. O., & Kazaure, J. S. (2020). Multimedia e-learning education in nigeria and developing countries of Africa for achieving SDG4. *International Journal of Information Communication Technologies and Human Development, 12*(1), 40–62. DOI: 10.4018/IJICTHD.2020010103

Matthew, U. O., Kazaure, J. S., & Haruna, K. (2020). Multimedia information system (MIS) for knowledge generation and ICT policy framework in education: Innovative sustainable educational investment. *International Journal of Information Communication Technologies and Human Development, 12*(3), 28–58. DOI: 10.4018/IJICTHD.2020070102

Matthew, U. O., Kazaure, J. S., Kazaure, A. S., Onyedibe, O. N., & Okafor, A. N. (2022). The Twenty First Century E-Learning Education Management & Implication for Media Technology Adoption in the Period of Pandemic. *EAI Endorsed Transactions on e-Learning, 8*(1), e1-e1.

Matthew, U. O., Kazaure, J. S., & Okafor, N. U. (2021). Contemporary development in E-Learning education, cloud computing technology & internet of things. *EAI Endorsed Transactions on Cloud Systems, 7*(20), e3–e3.

Mendoza-Ramírez, C. E., Tudon-Martinez, J. C., Félix-Herrán, L. C., Lozoya-Santos, J. J., & Vargas-Martínez, A. (2023). Augmented reality: Survey. *Applied Sciences (Basel, Switzerland), 13*(18), 10491. DOI: 10.3390/app131810491

Montesinos, L., Santos-Diaz, A., Salinas-Navarro, D. E., & Cendejas-Zaragoza, L. (2022). Experiential learning in biomedical engineering education using wearable devices: A case study in a biomedical signals and systems analysis course. *Education Sciences, 12*(9), 598. DOI: 10.3390/educsci12090598

Mulukuntla, S. (2025). *Monitoring and Remote Patient Management with Immersive Technologies Augmented Wellness: Exploring the Power of VR and AR in Healthcare*. Springer.

Murala, D. K., & Panda, S. K. (2023). The Role of Immersive Reality (AR/VR/MR/XR) in Metaverse. *Metaverse and Immersive Technologies: An Introduction to Industrial, Business and Social Applications*, 159-189.

Muzata, A. R., Singh, G., Stepanov, M. S., & Musonda, I. (2024). *Immersive Learning: A Systematic Literature Review on Transforming Engineering Education Through Virtual Reality*. Paper presented at the Virtual Worlds. DOI: 10.3390/virtualworlds3040026

Navarro-Parra, S. L., & Chiappe, A. (2024). Simulated Learning Environments as an Interdisciplinary Option for Vocational Training: A Systematic Review. *Simulation & Gaming, 55*(2), 135–158. DOI: 10.1177/10468781231221904

Ndunagu, J. N., Ukhurebor, K. E., & Adesina, A. (2023). *Virtual Laboratories for STEM in Nigerian Higher Education: The National Open University of Nigeria Learners' Perspective*. Paper presented at the TELL.

Okwudili, U. M., & Kazaure, J. S. (2020). Digital activism and digital revolution in objective journalism. *International Journal of Interactive Communication Systems and Technologies, 10*(2), 39–56. DOI: 10.4018/IJICST.2020070104

Ong, C. W., Tan, M. C. J., Lam, M., & Koh, V. T. C. (2021). Applications of extended reality in ophthalmology: Systematic review. *Journal of Medical Internet Research, 23*(8), e24152. DOI: 10.2196/24152 PMID: 34420929

Oyekunle, D., Claude, B. E. A., Waliu, A. O., Adekunle, T. S., & Matthew, U. O. (2024). Cloud based adaptive learning system: virtual reality and augmented reality assisted educational pedagogy development on clinical simulation. *Journal of Digital Health*, 49-62.

Oyekunle, D., Matthew, U. O., Waliu, A. O., & Fatai, L. O. (2024). Healthcare applications of Augmented Reality (AR) and Virtual Real-ity (VR) simulation in clinical ceducation. *Journal of Clinical Images and Medical Case Reports, 5*(6), 3141.

Oyekunle, D., Ugochukwu, O. M., Rosa, R. L., Rodriguez, D. Z., & Fatai, L. O. (2024). Novel Approaches in Clinical Simulation: Immersive Educational Technology to Enhance Nursing Education. *INFOCOMP Journal of Computer Science, 23*(1).

Oyekunle, D. O., Esseme, A. C. B., Oladipupo, M. A., Oseni, V. E., Adebola, N. T., Nwaiku, M., & Matthew, U. O. (2025). *Artificial Neural Network Algorithm in Nutritional Assessment: Implication for Machine Learning Prediction in Nutritional Assessments Precision Health in the Digital Age: Harnessing AI for Personalized Care*. IGI Global Scientific Publishing.

Oyekunle, D. O., Nwaiku, M., Matthew, U. O., Ogechukwu, O. N., Nwanakwaugwu, A. C., Adebola, N. T., & Olawoyin, O. O. (2025). *Transition to Sustainable Human-Centric Education in Emerging Artificial Intelligence Industry 5.0: Conversational AI With User-Centric ChatGPT-5 Higher Education and Quality Assurance Practices*. IGI Global Scientific Publishing.

Papanastasiou, G., Drigas, A., Skianis, C., Lytras, M., & Papanastasiou, E. (2019). Virtual and augmented reality effects on K-12, higher and tertiary education students' twenty-first century skills. *Virtual Reality (Waltham Cross), 23*(4), 425–436. DOI: 10.1007/s10055-018-0363-2

Peterson, A. (2024). Jarvis: A Cognitive Memory Architecture for AI-Augmented Learning Reimagining Persistence, Reflection, and Personalization in Human-AI Educational Partnerships. *Reflection, and Personalization in Human-AI Educational Partnerships*.

Prestigiacomo, R., Chan, C. C., & Kark, L. (2024). A biomedical engineering curriculum development: A qualitative study engaging four stakeholders. *European Journal of Education, 59*(2), 12632. DOI: 10.1111/ejed.12632

Putawa, R. A., & Sugianto, D. (2024). Exploring User Experience and Immersion Levels in Virtual Reality: A Comprehensive Analysis of Factors and Trends. *International Journal Research on Metaverse, 1*(1), 20–39. DOI: 10.47738/ijrm.v1i1.3

Radianti, J., Majchrzak, T. A., Fromm, J., & Wohlgenannt, I. (2020). A systematic review of immersive virtual reality applications for higher education: Design elements, lessons learned, and research agenda. *Computers & Education, 147*, 103778. DOI: 10.1016/j.compedu.2019.103778

Rane, N., Choudhary, S., & Rane, J. (2023). Enhanced product design and development using Artificial Intelligence (AI), Virtual Reality (VR), Augmented Reality (AR), 4D/5D/6D Printing, Internet of Things (IoT), and blockchain: A review. *Virtual Reality (VR), Augmented Reality (AR) D, 4*.

Saudagar, A. K. J., Kumar, A., & Khan, M. B. (2024). Mediverse Beyond Boundaries: A Comprehensive Analysis of AR and VR Integration in Medical Education for Diverse Abilities. *Journal of Disability Research, 3*(1), 20230066. DOI: 10.57197/JDR-2023-0066

Savaglio, C., Ganzha, M., Paprzycki, M., Bădică, C., Ivanović, M., & Fortino, G. (2020). Agent-based Internet of Things: State-of-the-art and research challenges. *Future Generation Computer Systems, 102*, 1038–1053. DOI: 10.1016/j.future.2019.09.016

Singh, B., Singh, G., & Ravesangar, K. (2025). *Teacher-Focused Approach to Merging Intelligent Tutoring Systems With Adaptive Learning Environments in AI-Driven Classrooms: Empowering Educators Higher Education and Quality Assurance Practices*. IGI Global Scientific Publishing.

Supriya, Y., Bhulakshmi, D., Bhattacharya, S., Gadekallu, T. R., Vyas, P., Kaluri, R., Sumathy, S., Koppu, S., Brown, D. J., & Mahmud, M. (2024). Industry 5.0 in Smart Education: Concepts, Applications, Challenges, Opportunities, and Future Directions. *IEEE Access : Practical Innovations, Open Solutions, 12*, 81938–81967. DOI: 10.1109/ACCESS.2024.3401473

Taghian, A., Abo-Zahhad, M., Sayed, M. S., & Abd El-Malek, A. H. (2023). Virtual and augmented reality in biomedical engineering. *Biomedical Engineering Online, 22*(1), 76. DOI: 10.1186/s12938-023-01138-3 PMID: 37525193

Tang, Y. M., Chau, K. Y., Kwok, A. P. K., Zhu, T., & Ma, X. (2022). A systematic review of immersive technology applications for medical practice and education-trends, application areas, recipients, teaching contents, evaluation methods, and performance. *Educational Research Review*, *35*, 100429. DOI: 10.1016/j.edurev.2021.100429

Tene, T., Marcatoma Tixi, J. A., Palacios Robalino, M. L., Mendoza Salazar, M. J., Vacacela Gomez, C., & Bellucci, S. (2024). *Integrating immersive technologies with STEM education: a systematic review*. Paper presented at the Frontiers in Education. DOI: 10.3389/feduc.2024.1410163

Thacharodi, A., Singh, P., Meenatchi, R., Tawfeeq Ahmed, Z., Kumar, R. R., v, N., Kavish, S., Maqbool, M., & Hassan, S. (2024). Revolutionizing healthcare and medicine: The impact of modern technologies for a healthier future—A comprehensive review. *Health Care Science*, *3*(5), 329–349. DOI: 10.1002/hcs2.115 PMID: 39479277

Tripathi, D., Hajra, K., Mulukutla, A., Shreshtha, R., & Maity, D. (2025). Artificial Intelligence in Biomedical Engineering and Its Influence on Healthcare Structure: Current and Future Prospects. *Bioengineering (Basel, Switzerland)*, *12*(2), 163. DOI: 10.3390/bioengineering12020163 PMID: 40001682

Tugtekin, U., & Odabasi, H. F. (2022). Do interactive learning environments have an effect on learning outcomes, cognitive load and metacognitive judgments? *Education and Information Technologies*, *27*(5), 7019–7058. DOI: 10.1007/s10639-022-10912-0

Tyagi, A. K., & Nair, M. M. (2024). *Future of Industry 5.0 in Society 5.0 Industry 4.0, Smart Manufacturing, and Industrial Engineering*. CRC Press.

van As, J., & Cooke, R. (2024). *Immersive Virtual Community Engagement: Unleashing the Potential of AI Avatars and Virtual Reality in Education to Enhance Learning Excellence Integrating Cutting-Edge Technology Into the Classroom*. IGI Global. DOI: 10.4018/979-8-3693-3124-8.ch009

Waliu, A. O., Matthew, U. O., Oseni, V. E., Oyekunle, D. O., Oladipupo, M. A., Adekunle, T. S., & Esseme, A. C. B. (2025). *Immersive Educational Pedagogy Development: Cloud-Based Adaptive System for Higher Education Generative AI Approaches to Sustainable Development in Higher Education*. IGI Global Scientific Publishing. DOI: 10.4018/979-8-3693-5623-4.ch008

Waliu, A. O., Muojekwu, E. E., Matthew, U. O., Kazaure, J. S., Oseni, V. E., Ononiwu, C. C., & Haruna, K. (2025). *Clinical Simulation in nursing education: Immersive Educational Tech for nurses and midwives Creating Immersive Learning Experiences Through Virtual Reality (VR)*. IGI Global.

Wu, Q., He, K., & Chen, X. (2020). Personalized federated learning for intelligent IoT applications: A cloud-edge based framework. *IEEE Open Journal of the Computer Society*, *1*, 35–44. DOI: 10.1109/OJCS.2020.2993259 PMID: 32396074

Xu, W., Yang, Z., Ng, D. W. K., Levorato, M., Eldar, Y. C., & Debbah, M. (2023). Edge learning for B5G networks with distributed signal processing: Semantic communication, edge computing, and wireless sensing. *IEEE Journal of Selected Topics in Signal Processing*, *17*(1), 9–39. DOI: 10.1109/JSTSP.2023.3239189

Yadav, S. (2025). Navigating the Virtual Classroom With Virtual Reality: Revolutionizing Education Through Immersive Experiences *Virtual Technology* [IGI Global Scientific Publishing.]. *Innovación Educativa (México, D.F.)*, 29–54.

Yang, J. (2023). *Technology-Enhanced Preclinical Medical Education (Anatomy, Histology and Occasionally, Biochemistry): A Practical Guide Biomedical Visualisation: Volume 17–Advancements in Technologies and Methodologies for Anatomical and Medical Education*. Springer.

Zafar, M. H., Langås, E. F., & Sanfilippo, F. (2024). Exploring the synergies between collaborative robotics, digital twins, augmentation, and industry 5.0 for smart manufacturing: A state-of-the-art review. *Robotics and Computer-integrated Manufacturing*, *89*, 102769. DOI: 10.1016/j.rcim.2024.102769

Zawish, M., Dharejo, F. A., Khowaja, S. A., Raza, S., Davy, S., Dev, K., & Bellavista, P. (2024). AI and 6G into the metaverse: Fundamentals, challenges and future research trends. *IEEE Open Journal of the Communications Society*, *5*, 730–778. DOI: 10.1109/OJCOMS.2024.3349465

Zuñiga-Aviles, L. A., & Cruz-Martinez, G. M. (2024). *Designing Exoskeletons*. CRC Press. DOI: 10.1201/9781003261995

Chapter 7
Impact of Generational Culture of Gen Z and Millennials Towards Social Interaction and Community: Building in the Virtual World

D. V. Jayanth
https://orcid.org/0009-0000-4608-819X
Dayananda Sagar College of Engineering, India

K. S. Ganesha
https://orcid.org/0000-0001-8181-2411
Dayananda Sagar College of Engineering, India

ABSTRACT

The popularity of worlds in social media has shaped the extent of human interaction, especially in the context of the two generations, now the focus is on the Gen Zs and Millennials, whose cultural phenomena are awash in technology. In this chapter, a particular critical inquiry considers how the different generational cultures owned by Gen Z and Millennials influence shaping the social behavior and structure of communities in the virtual world, including the metaverse, multiplayer games, or social VR. The chapter examines the new forms of creating identity, belonging, and community through digitally delimited spaces through the generational theory, the social presence theory, and the digital social capital theory. This chapter develops the existing literature and empirical knowledge by using it to synthesize a generationally

DOI: 10.4018/979-8-3373-3043-3.ch007

informed approach to the comprehension of sociality within a virtual environment. The results of the study lend themselves to more societal discussions about digital sociology and platform studies to build more resilient, inclusive virtual communities.

1. INTRODUCTION

With the spread of virtual worlds, the definition of social interaction, identity and community during the digital age have been redefined. Platforms like Roblox, VRChat, Discord, and the wider metaverse could be viewed as marginalized spaces to game or engage in niche online activity, but now they are developed as full-scale social ecosystems. They allow users to not only consume content, but also to co-create immersive spaces, knowledge exchange and networks of belonging, regardless of geographical and cultural distance (Thomas, R. 2025). Generational dynamics are an important aspect in this regard, and they determine the process of virtual participation and the development of digital communities.

Millennials (1981-1996) and Generation Z (1997-2012) are the two generations that are the most digitally embedded in history. Whereas Millennials have experienced the shift between dial-up internet to mobile-first social media, Generation Z are the very first digital natives because they have grown up in a multimedia world of algorithm-driven personalization, real-time communication and multimedia experiences (Spaticchia, U., 2024; Korn et al., 2024). These variations are not only technological but also cultural and they affect the anticipations of authenticity, communication styles, and the very definition of community. Millennials tend to prefer continuity and permanence of their digital identities whereas Gen Z prefers fluidity, experimentation and performativity (Henry, C. D., Shannon, L. 2023; Kathuria, V. 2023). These differences are crucial to understanding the way generational culture mediates the construction of a community within virtual spaces.

However, in academic and professional writing, the engagement between generations in virtual space is usually discussed in isolation and not as a comparative/relational process. In how Gen Z is adopting the participatory culture (Craeynest, U. 2024) or how Millennials are adapting professional identities online (Kasperiuniene, J., & Psaroudakis, I. 2019), there is a paucity of research on how their co-existence on shared platforms is creating tensions, collaborations, or hybrid practices. In this chapter, the gap is bridged by presenting the context of the generational traits within the overall models of Generational Theory, Social Presence Theory, and Digital Social Capital Theory as well as incorporating the notions of affordance and ethical lenses but with a focus on how virtual community can be designed, governed, and maintained (Mannheim, K. 1972; Haram, S., & Hansen, L. 2024; Wallin, S. 2025).

The topicality of this question is not limited to theoretical interest. Education, work, leisure, and activism are becoming more and more intertwined in virtual communities nowadays and transformed into digital third spaces. These spaces serve a supplemental role to professional circles and organized collaborations among Millennials and a space of identity play, symbolic gratification and algorithmic visibility among Gen Z people (Gerasimova, A. 2024; Kollárová, S., & Niklová, M., 2025). Such practices do not only define peer interaction, but also impact on online economies, civic engagement and online governance politics. But unsolved tensions algorithmic gatekeeping, surveillance, cultural inequities and so on are major obstacles to the democratization of virtual communities (McMullen, M. A. 2022; Gillespie, T., 2018).

Further, generational digital practices cannot be viewed in a western perspective alone. Youth are becoming more active participants in the mobile gaming communities, WhatsApp micro-networks, and hybrid learning platforms in the Global South. As an example, digital initiatives in Sub-Saharan Africa and e-learning in South Asia lead by communities show how agencies of affordability and infrastructure influence specific conceptions of belonging and participation (Polydorou, I. 2025). These attitudes bring out the multiplicity of the generational response and the importance of applying theories in other socio-cultural environments.

It is against this background that this chapter propagates a comparative and intergenerational study of Millennials and Gen Z in virtual setting. It aims to highlight not only the variations in the generation activity but also possible synergies of creating inclusive, sustainable, and moral digital communities by bringing theory, ethnographic and case studies, and applied implications together. Finally, the cognitive approach to generational culture in online environments is no longer simply about the capturing of current practices but also the imagination of how intergenerational digital futures can be realized in a manner that transcends boundaries, builds resilience and democratizes engagement in the dynamic nature of the metaverse.

2. CONCEPTUAL BACKGROUND OF STUDY

a. Generational Theory and Identity Formation

Developed by (Mannheim, K. 1972), generational theory has been found to be central to the explanation of the cohort-specific orientations that collective socio-historical experience imposes on identity, values, and community practices. Millennials (1981-1996) grew up when social media was beginning to emerge, and mobile connections were replacing the more stagnant internet, and generation Z (1997-2012) grew up in the era of algorithmic personalization, ubiquitous polymedia, and technological communication spaces (Spaticchia, U., 2024; Korn et al., 2024). Current literature tends to describe each new generation separately, with Millennials being described as stable, authentic, and goal-oriented in their networks (Henry, C. D., Shannon, L. 2023) and Gen Z being described as fluid, identity play, and decentralized in theirs (Kathuria, V. 2023).

Gap: Although these generational portraits are well-reported, little research has been done to understand how these two generations live together and interact in the same virtual space like VRChat or Discord. A lot of the literature is still descriptive, describing generational characteristics but not putting them into the context of larger sociotechnical settings.

This research paper contributes to the field of research of generational theory by directly applying it to the setting of community-building in the virtual world. Through the convergence of generational identity work and platform affordances and algorithmic environments, it allows to gain novel understanding of the construction of identity and belonging in immersive and intergenerational space (Arghashi, R, & Gunalay, Y. 2025; Peredy, Z., Vigh, L., Wei, Q., & Jiang, M. 2024). Combining Uses and Gratifications views, this research points out that Millennials tend to see digital participation as an extension and credibility, and Gen Z sees it as a symbolic satisfaction, experimentation, and real-time presence.

b. Social Presence Theory: Presence, Authenticity, and Performance

Short, Williams, and Christie (1976) as a means of communication technologies to mediate the perception of being with others initially formulated the Social Presence Theory. Presence, in the virtual world, is negotiated by use of avatars, text, voice and gesture, which determine the intimacy and authenticity. Presence is also associated with continuity of physical beings in the Millennials and online space is a continuation of work or personal identity (Henry, C. D., Shannon, L. 2023). In this case, to Gen Z, presence might be experimental and performative by means of avatars, memes, and poly media stories (Santer, N., Manago, A., & Bleisch, R. 2023).

Gap: Whereas the literature is abundant in studies on presence within immersive contexts, there is limited research that challenges how generational cohorts vary in creating presence or how co-presence works when both stability-oriented Millennials and fluid identity-oriented Gen Z members inhabit the same digital communities.

Compared to generational applications of presence, this chapter develops the theory further to determine that Millennials want genuine continuity, whereas Gen Z prefer performance that is short-lived. This dual framework indicates that there are complementary skills in community-building and that there is friction (norms of authenticity vs. play). Another focus of it is how social presence is not only an individual occurrence but also a generationally mediated practice that runs within larger community processes (Calderón-Fajardo et al., 2025; Wang, Y., Wang, L., & Siau, K. L. 2025).

c. Digital Social Capital: Networks, Resources, and Recognition

Social capital theory (Bourdieu, P. 1986; Putnam, R. D. 2000) highlights the benefit of networks, trust and common norms. These forces are carried into online communities, professional discussion boards and algorithmically-filtered network environments in digital space. Millennials tend to develop long term social capital using formalized social platforms like LinkedIn or knowledge sharing communities in which continuity and reputational certainty is valued (Kasperiuniene, J., & Psaroudakis, I., 2019). In comparison, Gen Z forms and breaks down micro-communities quickly, committing social capital to aesthetic compatibility, meme culture, and virality through the algorithms (Peredy et al., 2024; Kollárová, S., & Niklová, M., 2025).

Gap: The majority of scholarship considers digital social capital either linearly, professionally or community based, neglecting the ephemeral, algorithmically mediated forms of capital that Gen Z generates. Likewise, there is minimal research which investigates the interaction of these diversified ways of capital accumulation in cases where generations occur in the same platforms.

This paper broadens the theory of digital social capital to consider the ephemeral, fragmented and algorithmic kinds of recognition. It also places the tensions between generations: Millennials can perceive fluid participation of Gen Z as empty, whereas Gen Z can find continuity-seeking of Millennials archaic or oppressive. It is important to bridge such divergent practices so that digital communities can be designed so that they can be both stable and flexible (Haram, S., & Hansen, L. 2024).

d. Affordances and Platform Design

The theory of affordance (Gibson, J. J. 1979; Norman, D. A. 1999) focuses on how the characteristics of an environment make or restrict action. Avatars, live chatting, anonymity and game-based economies of the virtual world are affordances that define the emergence of communities in virtual worlds. Affordances that facilitate organised cooperation and professional growth are appreciated by millennials, and flexibility, fun, and fast self-expression are preferred by Gen Z (Craeynest, U. 2024).

Gap: The affordance theory on digital platforms is a well-used theory, but there is little evidence of the generational differences in appeal of affordances or the potential of friction between these two cohorts.

The research uses the theory of affordance not only in descriptive mode but also as an instrument to explain how the generations conflict and synergetically use the platforms. As an illustration, anonymity can be a source of empowerment to Gen Z and be destabilizing to Millennials, whereas constant profiles can be reassuring to Millennials and restrictive to the malleability of identity of Gen Z. The application of framing affordances brings applied knowledge to designers and policymakers by applying an intergenerational lens.

e. Ethics and Governance in Virtual Worlds

Although theories of presence, capital and affordance understand the interactional processes, they tend to omit the issues of ethics and governance that form the community life. The algorithmic gatekeeping capabilities limit visibility, prioritizing certain voices over others (Korn et al., 2024). Surveillance and moderation activities suppress the freedom of expression, especially to activist or discriminated groups (Elliott, A. 2024). Platform monopolies incorporate politics of power imbalance, which determine who is able to be a meaningfully engaged user and who is not (Gillespie, T., 2018).

Gap: There is limited information on generationally inflected views on these ethical issues. The desire of Millennials to be stable has not yet been researched in terms of interactions with the demand of Gen Z to be provided with transparency by the algorithms and aspects of participatory governance.

The paper will combine ethics to the study of generational analysis through emphasising the central focus of power, control, and fairness as the core of intergenerational interaction in the context of virtual communities. Placing ethics as a common but unequally valued issue will project the theoretical discourses into the governance and justice questions, hence, making sure that offline inequalities are not recreated in digital space (Wallin, S. 2025).

f. Cross-Cultural and Global Perspectives

The overwhelming majority of the research work concerning the generational involvement in the virtual community has been based on the Western context, with reference to North America and Europe. However, in Global South, the mediation of digital participation is affordability, limitations in infrastructures, and hybrid community models. South Asian and Sub-Saharan studies have also shown that young people have been using mobile tools and community-driven programs to build digital belonging despite the limitations (Polydorou, I. 2025). In several instances, Gen Z in such situations focus on utility, empowerment and sustainability whereas the Millennials juggle between career goals and scarce infrastructures.

Gap: Literature is still dominated by the West, and the cultural diversity of generational interaction is minimized.

This chapter offers a new and more inclusive and representative perspective on digital community-building due to the consideration of the Global South. It highlights that there is no universal way in which generational characteristics are manifested, but socio-economic and cultural realities are the intermediaries. According to this vision, designs and policies should be customized to fit into different infrastructures and culture.

g. Synthesis

When combined, these frameworks provide a multi-tiered perspective on the way generations interact in virtual communities. Generational theory positions the identity in the context of socio-historical trajectories, social presence theory describes the ideas of authenticity and performance, digital social capital shows the accrual of recognition and networks and affordance theory demonstrates the channels of action through platform design. Including both ethical and cross-cultural approaches, the study helps fill the important gaps in the existing literature: the lack of attention to intergenerational co-existence, the focus on the failure to see the ethical governance, and the Westernism of the available literature.

This chapter is not the application of theories in a descriptive way, but a synthesis of the theories in terms of their subject matter to expose the frictions and synergies between Millennials and Gen z. It emphasizes the importance of intergenerational interaction in virtual worlds in determining the community norms, ethics, and global inclusiveness. This theoretical basis is the direct support of the analytical framework and case studies, which guarantees that the paper contributes some original theoretical and practical contribution to the discussion on digital sociology and building a virtual community.

3. MODEL FOR GENERATIONAL CULTURE AND COMMUNITY BUILDING IN VIRTUAL WORLDS

Figure 1. Model for Generational Culture and Community Building in Virtual Worlds

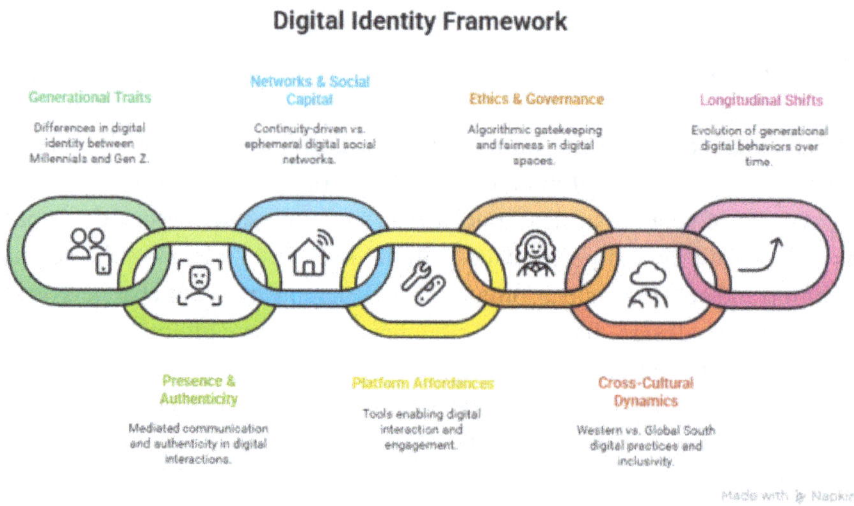

The core of this structure is the digital ecosystem, where immersive environments, including the metaverse, VRChat, Roblox, and Discord are used as the arena of intergenerational communication. These areas facilitate and limit the negotiations of identity, present, networks and community values among the Millennials and Generation Z. The model is organized in such a way as to represent these dynamics, with longitudinal shifts and the ecosystem themselves being highlighted as key contributions.

1. Generational Traits & Identity Formation

According to the Generational Theory, Millennials (1981-1996) are said to be stable and authentic and feel organized interaction, because they have grown up in the conditions of the early development of social media (Henry, C. D., Shannon, L. 2023). On the contrary, Gen Z (1997-2012) lays greater emphasis on fluid identities and algorithmic responsiveness and resides in decentralized communities that reflect the culture of participatory (Arghashi, R, & Gunalay, Y. 2025; Skinner, H., Sarpong, D., & White, G. R. 2018). Despite these characteristics being reported separately, there is not much detailed research done to establish how these characteristics interact on common grounds. The model places the identity-making as a process of dual generation with fluidity and stability being balanced in the generations.

2. Social Presence & Authenticity

The Social Presence Theory is an explanation of how users perceive other individuals in mediated spaces. On the one hand, Millennials are more likely to consider continuity between real and digital identity, and Gen Z tries the avatars, memes, and polymedia narratives (Thomas, R. 2025; Kathuria, V. 2023). This detachment highlights difference in the authenticity standards: whereas Millennials like their authenticity to be believable, Gen Zs like it to be ironic. The model views presence as a relational notion and is subject to generational expectations, and not to absolute rules.

3. Digital Social Capital & Networks

Digital social capital takes the concepts of Bourdieu (1986) and Putnam (2000) to the virtual realm. Millennials prefer creating a long-term and organized network using professional and interest-related forums (Kasperiuniene, J., & Psaroudakis, I. 2019). However, the generation Z builds short-lived, meme-based relationships that are formed as a result of algorithms and virality (Peredy et al., 2024; Kollárová, S., & Niklová, M., 2025). These unstable forms of capital are frequently not taken into consideration by scholarship. The model combines the two with more focus on the conflict between sustainability and dynamism in online networks.

4. Platform Affordances & Design

The anonymity, the customization of avatars and gamification are some of the affordances that determine user interaction (Gibson, J. J. 1979; Norman, D. A. 1999). Millennials like features that support the professional level of credibility and stability whereas Gen Z enjoy customization and fluidity in the creative process (Craeynest, U. 2024). The model emphasizes the necessity of platforms that support intergenerational flexibility, ensuring there are no expectations that do not fit together, which are disintegrating the communities.

4. Ethics & Governance

Community participation is determined by algorithmic gatekeeping, surveillance, and moderation (Korn et al., 2024; Elliott, A. 2024). Millennials tend to value trust and reliability, whereas Gen Z demands transparency and participatory governance

(Wallin, S. 2025). However, there is little research comparing these points of view directly. When ethics are incorporated into the model, it raises the issue of creating a balance between stability and equity in virtual governance systems.

6. Cross-Cultural & Global Dynamics

The scholarship is largely Western-centric, but the Global South suggests other forms of participation. Young people create mobile-first and sustainability-based communities in the context of infrastructural and financial access based on the conditions (Polydorou, I. 2025). Millennials might be interested in career growth, and Gen Z is using digital resources to organize and be activists. The model establishes these practices as contextually varied so as to oppose any universalizations.

7. Longitudinal Generational Shifts

One of the most important innovations of this model is the fact that the generational characteristics are not fixed. The digital practices of millennials have changed due to initial experimentation of social media usage and adopting a hybrid usage that combines personal and professional lives. As Gen Z enters the labor force and takes on more enduring and serious roles, the current loosely structured and playful engagement is likely to change to a more structured approach to community-building. Current literature tends to freeze cohorts in space, disregarding how online practices are changing as a result of life-course changes. The model integrates longitudinal shifts to recognize the dynamic development of generational culture, which means that community-building approaches should be responsive to the needs of the community as the needs evolve throughout the life span. Such focus also enhances the explanatory strength of the model, demonstrating how modern Gen Z patterns are likely to predetermine future changes in the norms of digital communities.

Central Core: The Digital Ecosystem

The digital ecosystem is a commonplace where technological affordances, the cultural practice, and the governance structures align with each other in the seven domains. In the ecosystem is not a neutral site but a site of active mediation of the generational interaction. The qualities, existence, networks, and morals are articulated in algorithms, platform economies and the context of infrastructures. Notably, this ecosystem becomes symptomatic of synergies and frictions: The stability search of Millennials can find complement in the creativity of Gen Z, yet there are conflicts of authenticity, governance and continuity. The model highlights that community-building is never but a negotiation between practices that are cohort uniquely and platform architectures by placing generational processes within the digital ecosystem (Kiaer, J. 2024).

4. CASE STUDIES

CASE STUDY 1: Generation Z's Immersive Participation in Virtual Environments (Russia)

The study by (Puchkova et al., 2017) involved 204 adolescents (12-14 years old) in Moscow to discuss the use of virtual reality as a sociotechnical system by Gen Z. Findings indicated that daily internet usage was more than 75 with girls being attracted to communication and creativity activities whereas boys were attracted to immersion games. This underlined gendered trends in Social Presence and Identity and Platform Affordances. Although youths are highly active online, they said that they distrusted what they found online, and they had no desire to make digital friends, which revealed the Barriers and Frictions to community credibility. The results dispute the presumption of a smooth flow of digital native sociality, which indicates that participation can frequently be motivated by cognitive as opposed to interpersonal factors.

CASE STUDY 2: Hybrid Social Interaction in Learning Communities

Spears et al. (2015) looked at the case of Learning Communities (LCs) at Northern Illinois University and Indiana University-Purdue University to understand how Gen Z balances fluency in the digital realm with face-to-face. Although the use of digital tools was common among the students, the mode of enrolment and retention depended largely on the face-to-face advising and orientation sessions as opposed to emails or social posts. This two-foldness brings out a phygital amalgamation of Platform Affordances and Engagement Drivers. Gen Z sees online platforms as a helpful source of information but still finds the need to base trust and sense of belonging on physical experiences, where authenticity is best received. The results show that there is a paradox, as much as digital ecosystems take over the world, face-to-face communication is essential to sustainable belonging. The case shows that to successfully develop community building, digital presence should be incorporated with embodied trust, which can be applied to education and even professional environment across generations.

CASE STUDY 3: Online Community Formation among Gen Z Youth in Finland

The article by (Mäkitalo, M. 2020) explored the ways in which Finnish youth (13-15 years old) develop a sense of digital belonging through a sports event in school. The semi-structured interviews showed that Gen Z is adopting micro-communities based on influencers, interests, and online content. Formations such as YouTube and Instagram offered exposure and authority, but the authority was based on credibility through the mediating power of the influencer instead of the authority of the institution. This shows how salient Generational Traits, Engagement Drivers and Social Presence and Identity are. The paper underlines that online micro-communities are shaping the s

CASE STUDY 4: Virtual Professional Identities of Millennials in Online Workspaces

(Kasperiuniene, J., & Psaroudakis, I. 2019) explored the ways of Millennials creating professional identities on LinkedIn, co-working sites, and online forums. Three years later, through interviews and discourse analysis, they discovered that identity within these spaces is being played out strategically and continuously optimized and integrates personal branding with peer validation. In contrast to the often identity-playful, fluid identity of Gen Z, the Millennials treat the online world as an extension of their offline authority and strengthen the Social Presence & Identity and Digital Social Capital. Nonetheless, problems such as algorithmic obscurity as well as the mental burden of maintaining a consistent professional identity were encountered. The paper singles out the Millennials in relation to their continuity, visibility, and long-term attachment orientation, which is the direct opposite of the fast and playful identity-switching of Gen Z. This demonstrates the varying interactions that generational cultures have with digital affordances and supports the importance of designs of community that balance professional stability with creative exploration.

CASE STUDY 5: The Digital Identity of Generation Z

(Kollárová, S., & Niklová, M., 2025) examined the identity-negotiating by safely digital platforms like Instagram, Tik Tok, and YouTube in younger Gen Z people of Slovakia. According to the findings, they are not static but are a matter of ongoing negotiation which is mediated by the algorithmic feedbacks, peer validation and performational aesthetics. The study participants were very cognizant of the role of likes, comments, and visual coherence in determining an individual self-perception and social capital, leading to contradictions between the online self and offline self. Generational Traits, Social Presence and Identity and Engagement Drivers are highly depicted in this case. In addition, algorithmic filtering and surveillance became Barriers & Frictions, which limits the freedom of expression and increases pressures to performativity. Contrary to Millennials where stability in identity can be sought through identifying with others, Gen Z is still dual identity models- one online and one offline- which show the flexibility and surveillance fears that somehow define belonging.

CASE STUDY 6: Polymedia Narratives and Authenticity Branding in Gen Z

Santer et al. (2023) examined the ways in which U.S. Gen Z college students strategically produce authenticity on Tik Tok, Instagram, and Snapchat. In polymedia storytelling, students edited identities that went tonally and presentationally depending on the rules of platform-specificity, such as mocking self-depreciation on one site and idealized image on the other. Authenticity was, therefore, a performative strategy and not a fixed characteristic and in order to become visible and integrated, it needed emotional and cognitive work. The authors note the Social Presence & Identity and Barriers & Frictions, when the credibility pursuit and dangers of misunderstanding collided, the idea of the so-called cancel culture, and the forces of algorithms. Gen Z is comfortable with multiplicity and flexibility instead of consistency, where Millennials like to stick to the same settings, making polymedia a creative resource and a source of anxiety at the same time. The current case explains the role of authenticity branding as cultural capital regarding the digital community-building process by Gen Z.

5. STRATEGIC IMPERATIVES AND POLICY RECOMMENDATIONS

a. Make sure that there is Algorithmic Governance and Transparency.

The most important intermediaries of community presence and engagement are still the recommendation systems that are driven by algorithms. In the case of Gen Z, the threat of algorithmic bias is inclusivity and identity play, whereas Millennials are concerned about stability and credibility (Korn et al., 2024; Elliott, A. 2024). Policies should thus require explainable AI in the governance of the platforms, which will provide users with a better understanding of how the visibility, rankings and participation in the community are made. Co-design mechanisms need to be involved in the design, where the user should shape the priorities of the algorithm, balancing the Gen Z desire to have control against the preference of Millennials to know what to expect. This would enhance confidence, equality and democratic accountability, alleviating the dangers of platform monopolies and dark web surveillance.

b. Close the Digital Divides between generations.

Digital fluency does not just vary between age groups, but also within the cohorts themselves. Although Millennials are malleable learners who adapted to digital and no longer use analog, Gen Z demands smooth usability and immediate feedback (Wallin, S. 2025; Foroughi, B., Ghobakhloo, M., Wen, J., & Fathi, M. 2025). Institutions therefore need to develop intergenerational models of learning- such as in the workplace training or community workshops to combine the intuitive fluency of Gen Z and the strategic depth of Millennials. Peer mentorship systems in education can facilitate the interchange of skills and strengthen sustainable digital literacy between groups. This bridging approach will make generational differences an asset and not a division which will lead to more collaboration in mixed professional and learning settings.

c. Protect Mental Health and On-Line Welfare.

The intake of polymedia with a high frequency predisposes Gen Z to the risks of cognitive load, anxiety, and performance (Santer et al., 2023; McMullen, M. A. 2022). Although they are not as fragmented in their digital presence, millennials commonly complain of exhaustion due to the maintenance of coherent professional images (Kasperiuniene, J., & Psaroudakis, I. 2019). Well-being by design should therefore be incorporated into policy interventions, and such functionality as time-use dashboard, nudges to go digital, and moderated interaction spaces are meant to be built. Mental health protection can be incorporated into the educational and corporate curriculum and HR policy and the conversation of digital fatigue and community burnout should be normalized. By describing well-being as an intergenerational concern, it is possible to emphasize the significance of the concept of sustainable digital participation.

d. Develop further Ethical Content Moderation and Platform Governance.

Online safety is perceived differently by generational communities: Millennials are focused on professional credibility, and Gen Z is focused on inclusiveness and creative self-expression (Calderón-Fajardo et al., 2025; Kathuria, V. 2023). Existing moderation systems are however usually based on obscure algorithms that reinforce inequality or over-censorship. Strategic imperatives should shift to transparent participatory governance where the user is considered on the formulation of the rules of the community and dispute resolution. There should also be policies requiring protection against algorithmic surveillance and corporate monopolization, as well as equal opportunities to be visible regardless of the generations. Virtual community governance should be ethical to maintain the trust, particularly as immersive technologies like the metaverse continue to spread around the world.

e. Integrate Cross-Cultural and Global South perspectives

A lot of current virtual community-building research is also predominantly of the Western type, but Gen Z and Millennials in the Global South pertain to digital culture through mobile-first and affordability-driven ecosystems (Polydorou, I. 2025). To illustrate, African and South Asian youth are socializing in digital communities via common devices, affordable applications, or civic-activist groups, where sustainability and accessibility are more important than algorithmic aesthetics. The policy and design should therefore be focused on the equity of infrastructure, including low-cost bandwidth, interfaces adjusting to specific cultures, and localization strategies. Combining cross-cultural comparisons can make sure that the virtual community-building structures are inclusive in a global sense and not mirror Western standards.

f. Taking consideration of Longitudinal Generational Shifts.

One of the biggest shortcomings of the generational analysis that cannot be done in a static form is that it lacks the ways in which practices change over time. Having been early adopters of social media, millennials are moving into becoming hybrid professional users who have continuity and selective engagement. Gen Z which now has the traits of fragmentary, performational engagement is going to mature into a stage in which they will be required to exhibit stability, credibility, and rule (Namukasa, 2025). Strategic imperatives have to assume a longitudinal approach therefore structuring policies and platforms that evolve with the maturity of generational cultures. It means that there will be moving educational programs, adjustable working technologies, and changing platform management to predicting changes with the life stages and not considering some generational peculiarities as a constant classifier.

In Overall, all these imperatives fill in the ethical, cultural, and developmental gaps that are present in the current virtual community design. Platforms and policies can be used to support inclusive digital ecosystems by fostering intergenerational literacy, protecting well-being, enhancing governance ethics, ensuring Global South realities are the norm, and embracing longitudinal adaptability. More importantly, these imperatives go beyond descriptive analysis to give future-directed, generationally sensitive strategies to keep pace with the IGI focus on actionable, globally responsive scholarship.

6. BENEFITS AND CHALLENGES OF GENERATIONAL PARTICIPATION IN VIRTUAL COMMUNITY BUILDING

A. Benefits

a. Expression and Fluidity of Identity.

Both the Millennials and the gen Z can use virtual environments to explore identity. Millennials tend to have digital identity which supplements their offline selfhood, making it more authentic and continuous (Henry, C. D., Shannon, L. 2023). Gen Z on the other hand is comfortable with the avatars, polymedia plays and performative identities as possibilities of exploration and adaptability (Kathuria, V. 2023). These affordances are creative, inclusive, and adaptive in self-presentation which promotes community-building based on shared aesthetics and values, as opposed to the predetermined identities.

b. International and Intercultural Interconnection.

The online platforms open up geographical barriers, and different intercultural interactions are feasible. Gen Z regularly participates in global social communities either by influencer-based or cause-based activities (Craeynest, U. 2024) and Millennials tend to do the same via professional networks and forums (Kasperiuniene, J., & Psaroudakis, I. 2019). The cross-cultural aspect is especially critical in the Global South where adoption of mobile-first leads to a proliferation of digital belonging in the grassroot (Polydorou, I. 2025). Virtual spaces therefore promote inclusivity, whereby, generational cohorts are able to develop ties, as a result of language, cultural, and economic differences.

c. Learning and Collaboration led by Community

Learning Virtual ecosystems are participatory learning environments. Millennials use forums, LinkedIn groups, and MOOCs to gain more professional and educational benefits through organized learning. Gen Z also adopts peer-to-peer knowledge-sharing in interactive and gamified digital environments like Discord or Roblox, where learning is integrated into the play (Firmansyah, F. H., & Rosmansyah, Y. 2024). These approaches are community-based pedagogies, in which multiple generations contribute to making collaboration more vigorous--Millennials offer structure and mentoring, Gen Z offers experimentation and agility.

d. Micro-Communities and Sense of Belonging.

Micro-communities around common interests, fandoms or activism can be formed with the help of digital ecosystems. Millennials tend to maintain long-term membership in niche communities (e.g. professional associations), Gen Z tends to alternate between micro-communities with a shifting cultural trend and with an algorithmic presence (Theodorakopoulos, L., Theodoropoulou, A., & Klavdianos, C. 2025). The differences notwithstanding, both generations use micro-communities as belonging-and-identity-confirming spaces and this shows that it is possible to be solid even in a fragmented environment.

e. Professional and Phygital Blending.

Physical + digital models Mixing digital outreach and embodied presence consist of such hybrid models as Learning Communities (Spears, L. I. & Khan, A. R. 2015) or professional networks. Gen me appreciates the professionalized virtual engagement that is always present, whereas Gen Z wants the interactive and immersive format. The outcome is a phygital mix of both groups being given meaning as the digital interaction is able to expand participation and the physical encounters enshrine trust. This two-fold character brings out the fact that intergenerational involvement enhances labour, educational, and civic societies.

f. Generational Complementarity

Millennials and Gen Z are oppositely oriented but can be used to their benefit. The structured, goal-oriented practices of millennials provide a balance of flexibility and performativity of the Gen Z generation, and the lack of continuity and hierarchy tendencies of Millennials are shaken by the innovativeness and inclusiveness of the Gen Z generation (Devi, K., & Thomas, N. 2025). This complementarity implies that collaboration between generations is not only possible, but it is positive because digital communities flourish on the stability and fluidity. Communities that are designed to have intergenerational synergies can create more resilient and adaptive communities.

B. Challenges

a. Fracturing and Temp Fluids.

The use of trend-driven and influencer-led participation by gen Z tends to lead to short-lived communities. The bonds that are made on the basis of viral content are temporary, which weaken long-term bonding (Craeynest, U. 2024). The systematic way that Millennials go about their work gives it a certain degree of stability, though intergenerational teamwork is crippled by the dissimilar rhythms of engagement (Peredy, Z., Vigh, L., Wei, Q., & Jiang, M. 2024). This fragmentation puts the sustainability of community-building as part of virtual ecosystems into question.

b. lack of trust in Identity and Community.

In spite of the digital immersion levels, the two cohorts are having issues with credibility online. The adolescents of Gen Z are hesitant about establishing serious friendships, do not trust online personas and algorithms (Puchkova et al., 2017). Likewise, professional websites do not always suggest idealism to Millennials since they are cautious about professional self-branding (Kollárová, S., & Niklová, M., 2025). Such lack of trust hurts the social cohesion of communities and casts doubt on authenticity of mediated social presence.

c. Algorithms and Inequality.

Opaque algorithms are becoming the source of community visibility. Verisimilitude and belonging become difficult to Gen Z, with the popularity of content on a platform relying on how the platform is made (Elliott, A. 2024). Millennials, in their turn, also have obstacles in the face of the reduction of credibility in the face of the fact that algorithmic selection of the factor of engagement is more important than experience (Korn et al., 2024). This is because inequality is further propagated by the absence of transparency, which favours select voices, disenfranchising others.

d. Digital Fatigue and Burnout

Cognitive overload and platform fatigue can be seen as effects of constant switching between polymedia platforms like TikTok, Discord, and Snapchat which Gen Z faces (Santer et al., 2023). However, Millennials, despite being not so fragmented, experience burnout because they have to maintain constant professional identities both in LinkedIn and online workspaces (McMullen, M. A. 2022). In the absence of intentional design of digital well-being, the two cohorts are likely to become disengaged, which will reduce the sustainability of virtual communities.

e. Spies and Claims of Free Speech.

Not only does expressive freedom not exist under moderation algorithms, data collection, or digital footprints. Professional authenticity is threatened by surveillance among Millennials, and Gen Z cannot cope with the use of algorithms that restrict creativity and demand conformity (Kollárová, S., & Niklová, M., 2025; Sugiarto, E., & Arif, M. F. 2024). The conflict between the safety and liberty highlights the possibilities of impeding open community-building by surveillance structures.

f. Generation Gaps Affordance.

The differences in the values of platform affordances between each generation cause friction. Millennials prefer structure and continuity (professional forums, stable avatars), so does Gen Z, but in their case, it is anonymity, gamification, and a joyful interaction (Calderón-Fajardo et al., 2025; Dooley, K, 2024). These conflicting preferences do not allow intergenerational co-operation to happen smoothly, which is why design solutions allowing both consistency and elasticity are required.

7. FUTURE DIRECTIONS FOR GENERATIONAL PARTICIPATION IN VIRTUAL COMMUNITY BUILDING

a. Generational Characteristics & Identity Construction - Avatar-Centric Design.

It will be focused on identity experimentation. Adaptive features of orderly self-presentation by Millennials and the play of fluid identity by Gen Z should be offered on platforms (Kathuria, V. 2023). Avatars and multiple-mode representations can be culturally responsive to allow identity formation to be based on the different traditions of the world and to eliminate digital homogenization.

b. Social Presence and Authenticity-Democratization of Governance.

The process of moderation will have to transform into participatory governance with the development of mediated presence. The community-based councils and rule-making clarity can satisfy the need of inclusivity by Gen Z and authenticity of

Millennials (Calderón-Fajardo et al., 2025). Integrating the democratic presence in the governance systems enhances intergenerational trust.

c. Digital Social Capital Networks Digital Social Capital - Hybrid and Multimodal Communities.

The communities of the future will combine the continuity of the offline with the flexibility of the online. Millennials prefer professionalized forums, and Gen z is a multimodal network that works best with play (Kim, D., & Kwon, J. 2025). Through promoting phygital communal building, sites can increase digital social capital both in the Global North and South.

d. Web Accessibility - Intergenerational Digital Literacy.

Affordances need to be intergenerational. The millennials are more stability oriented, the Gen Z more inclined to fast adaptability and both demand equal access to digital technologies (Kshirsagar, K. P., & Ingle, A. 2025). Reciprocal literacy programs must be enshrined in policies which must be inclusive in the design in the face of infrastructural inequity, especially in the Global South (Polydorou, I. 2025).

e. Ethics and Governance Algorithmic Co-Design and Transparency.

Stunning algorithms restrict participation. The explainable AI should be mandatory on the future policies and include the co-design aspect where the user determines the content they want to see (Korn et al., 2024; Elliott, A. 2024). The agency needs of Gen Z and the reliability needs of Millennials can meet in the ethical algorithmic models.

f. Cross-Cultural/Global dynamics- Emotive AI and Well-Being.

A digital well-being will demand sensitive tools in terms of culture. Emotive AI is able to identify stress or harassment; however, protection needs to avoid intrusive surveillance. By developing cultural adaptive well-being models, both Millennials and Gen Z will be able to flourish in collectivist cultures where group cohesion takes precedence

g. Longitudinal Generational Changes - Moral Moderation of Cross-Cultural.

Following the pattern of the Millennials turning into hybrid professionals, and Gen Z becoming structured employees, the moderation systems need to be adapted dynamically. The policies must focus on Asian, African, and Latin American cultural inclusiveness coupled with incorporating flexibility which can adjust to the changes in life stages (Namukasa, 2025). Local, ethical frameworks are important in providing sustainability in view of changing generational identities.

In short, I have mapped the future directions to the model domains indicate their interdependence and for better understanding. These are identity experimentation, authenticity, digital social capital, platform affordances, platform governance ethics, cross-cultural inclusivity, and longitudinal adaptability, which have to change in concert. This combined roadmap keeps the virtual communities strong, inclusive and ethically responsible and empowers both the Millennials and Gen Z in the various cultural environments.

8. CONCLUSION

The side-by-side analysis of Gen Z and Millennials in virtual communities provides emphasis on the ways in which digital involvement is forming and forming the generational culture as well. The results show that immersive platforms like VRChat, Roblox, and Discord are not just an entertainment destination but act as third spaces where identity, belonging and collaboration are reenacted. The chapter has shown that generational characteristics overlap with technological affordances through the Generational Theory, Social Presence Theory, Digital Social Capital Theory, and Affordance Theory to create unique though complementary forms of community-building.

Having grown up with the early internet and social media, millennials place a strong value on virtual environments in terms of stability, authenticity and organised networks (Calderón-Fajardo et al., 2025). They emphasize continuity in their practices and professional credibility, matching virtual identities to offline identities. Conversely, Gen Z has been brought up in a world of unstopping connectedness and personalized algorithms and values fluidity, performativity, and participatory inclusivity (Kathuria, V. 2023). This dissidence portrays not only different generational logic, but also changing directions of building digital social capital, presence, and a community of norms.

Making these understandings come together, the proposed Model of Generational Culture and Community Building in Virtual Worlds defines seven interdependent areas: generational characteristics, social presence, digital social capital, platform affordances, ethics and governance, cross cultural dynamics, and longitudinal changes. In contrast to the previous studies, which tend to address the generational differences in isolation, the model focuses on their interdependency in the wider digital ecosystem. By so doing, it provides a map on how generational participation is changing over time, culture as well as technological design.

The case studies helped to support the model as explanatory with real life examples of generational dynamics at work. Starting with the reserved participation of the Russian adolescents in VR (Puchkova et al., 2017) to the micro-communities formed by influences on Finnish youth (Mäkitalo, 2020), and Millennials as professionals on LinkedIn (Kasperiuniene, J., & Psaroudakis, I. 2019) to Gen Z and their polymedia authenticity branding (Santer et al., 2023), the examples point to both the possibilities and conflicts of digital participation.

This duality is further explained in the benefits and challenges discussion. On the one hand, virtual environments offer unprecedented possibilities of exploring the identity, intercultural communication, and collaborative learning, especially when the intergenerational complementarity is used. On the other, digital fatigue, algorithmic gatekeeping, lack of trust and generation differences in the use of affordance are challenges that show the frailty of these communities (McMullen, M. A. 2022; Kollárová, S., & Niklová, M., 2025). To deal with these tensions, there must be governance, design practices that focus more on transparency, inclusiveness, and resilience.

Offering perspectives into the future, the chapter presented the future directions that include the idea of the transparency of algorithms, the idea of intergenerational digital literacy, cross-cultural sensitivity, and longitudinal adaptability. Notably, by suggesting these recommendations, the subject of discourse will not be confined to Western-centered approaches, but the Global South, where young people already employ mobile-first approaches to sustainability and belonging (Polydorou, I. 2025). The combination of these contexts is important to stay relevant to the virtual community-building structures all around the globe instead of creating digital colonialism.

Finally, the paper makes three contributions. To start with, it shows that the differences in virtual participation between generations are not fixed and that they change over time and must be approached longitudinally. Second, it redefines virtual worlds as socio-cultural ecosystems, which led to education, work and civic life beyond the leisure. Third, it fosters an integrative model, which links theory, evidence of cases, and practice into a generational informative roadmap of policy, design, and governance. Through the integration of these views, the chapter frames the generational culture as an asset of non-divisive and accommodating community-building.

Since digital ecosystems are growing, virtual communities will have to rely on the balances between stability and flexibility, authenticity and performativity, local and global integration. The most promising avenue to creating resilient, ethical, and culturally inclusive digital societies is designing them to be intergenerational: the continuity of Millennials would be used to complement the innovation of Gen Z.

REFERENCES

Arghashi, V., & Gunalay, Y. (2025). Exploring the metaverse: What drives millennials and Gen Z to embrace virtual worlds? *Journal of Islamic Marketing*.

Bourdieu, P. (1986). The forms of capital. In J. Richardson (Ed.), Handbook of Theory and Research for the Sociology of Education (pp. 241–258). Greenwood.

Calderón-Fajardo, V., Puig-Cabrera, M., & Rodríguez-Rodríguez, I. (2025). Beyond the real world: Metaverse adoption patterns in tourism among Gen Z and Millennials. *Current Issues in Tourism*, *28*(8), 1261–1281.

Craeynest, U. (2024). GEN Z'S ENTRANCE INTO THE METAVERSE (Doctoral dissertation, Ghent University).

Devi, K., & Thomas, N. (2025). "Let's grab a match!": Exploring ways to enhance engagement and consistency in sports for Gen Z and millennials (Doctoral dissertation, OCAD University).

Dooley, K. (2024). Virtual Reality Narratives Live Online: Immersive Theatre in VRChat Worlds. In *Virtual Reality Narratives: Embodied Encounters in Space* (pp. 185–212). Springer International Publishing.

Elliott, A. (2024). *Algorithms of anxiety: Fear in the digital age*. John Wiley & Sons.

Firmansyah, F. H., & Rosmansyah, Y. (2024). Exploring Collaboration in Multiplayer Gamification: A Systematic Literature Review. *IEEE Access : Practical Innovations, Open Solutions*.

Foroughi, B., Ghobakhloo, M., Wen, J., & Fathi, M. (2025). Sustained use of generative AI for shopping: A PLS-ANN analysis. *Service Industries Journal*, •••, 1–34.

Gerasimova, A. (2024). Social Media and Generation Z: A Qualitative Inquiry into Usage Patterns and Motivations of Women of Older Gen Z. Available online: https://mau.diva-portal.org/smash/record.jsf?pid=diva2%3A1866883&dswid=2594

Gibson, J. J. (1979). *The ecological approach to visual perception: classic edition*. Psychology press.

Gillespie, T. (2018). *Custodians of the Internet: Platforms, content moderation, and the hidden decisions that shape social media*. Yale University Press.

Haram, S., & Hansen, L. (2024). Cohort-coded communities: Age dynamics in Discord and Twitch. *Journal of Interactive Media*, *21*(1), 65–83.

Henry, C. D., & Shannon, L. (2023). *Virtual natives: How a new generation is revolutionizing the future of work, play, and culture*. John Wiley & Sons.

Kasperiuniene, J., & Psaroudakis, I. (2019). Virtual professional identities of millennials. In Zydziunaite, V., Kasperiuniene, J., Psaroudakis, I., & Salvini, A. (Eds.), *Professional identity construction in digital times* (pp. 15–52). Pisa University Press.

Kathuria, V. (2023). Gen Z's engagement with the Metaverse: Mediated role of symbolic gratification and desired enhancement of reality and moderated role of gender. *Metamorphosis*, *22*(2), 133–145.

Kiaer, J. (2024). Conversing in the metaverse: The embodied future of online communication.Bloomsbury Publishing. Available online at https://www.torrossa.com/it/resources/an/5868460

Kollárová, S., & Niklová, M. (2025) THE DIGITAL IDENTITY OF GENERATION Z. Researchgate

Korn, O., Zallio, M., & Schnitzer, B. (2024). Young skeptics: Exploring the perceptions of virtual worlds and the metaverse in generations Y and Z. *Frontiers in Virtual Reality*, *5*, 1330358.

Kshirsagar, K. P., & Ingle, A. (2025). Impacts of Digital Technologies Across Generations. In *Bridging Academia and Industry Through Cloud Integration in Education* (pp. 1–36). IGI Global Scientific Publishing.

Mäkitalo, M. (2020). Digital communities and Generation Z: Motivational and social needs in online environments (Master's thesis, University of Jyväskylä). University of Jyväskylä Institutional Repository.

Mannheim, K. (1972). The problem of generations. In Kecskemeti, P. (Ed.), *Essays on the sociology of knowledge* (pp. 276–322). Routledge.

McMullen, M. A. (2022). *Evangelism through online gaming: Communicating to gen Z beyond the church walls*. Asbury Theological Seminary.

Namukasa, S. (2025). The Role of Technology in Shaping Future Generations' Values. Researchgate, Available online at https://www.researchgate.net/profile/Kampala-International-University-Vi/publication/390398719_The_Role_of_Technology_in_Shaping_Future_Generations'_Values/links/67ec38df95231d5ba5a9b443/The-Role-of-Technology-in-Shaping-Future-Generations-Values.pdf

Norman, D. A. (1999). Affordance, conventions, and design. interactions, 6(3), 38-43.

Peredy, Z., Vigh, L., Wei, Q., & Jiang, M. (2024). Analysing generation Z communication attitudes, values and norms. *Acta Periodica (Edutus)*, *30*, 4–19.

POLYDOROU. I. (2025). Youth's Role in Sustainability: Exploring the Interplay of Generation Z, Technology, and Sustainable Development Goals. Available at https://thesis.unipd.it/handle/20.500.12608/56314

Puchkova, E. B., YuV, S., & Temnova, L. V. (2017). A study of Generation Z's involvement in virtual reality. *Psychology in Russia : State of the Art*, *10*(4), 46.

Putnam, R. D. (2000). *Bowling alone: The collapse and revival of American community*. Simon and schuster.

Santer, N., Manago, A., & Bleisch, R. (2023). Narratives of the self in polymedia contexts: Authenticity and branding in Generation Z. *Qualitative Psychology*, *10*(1), 79.

Short, J., Williams, E., & Christie, B. (1976). *The social psychology of telecommunications*. John Wiley & Sons.

Skinner, H., Sarpong, D., & White, G. R. (2018). Meeting the needs of the Millennials and Generation Z: gamification in tourism through geocaching. Journal of tourism futures, 4(1), 93-104.

Spaticchia, U. (2024). Generational Transformations and Digital Media: continuity and change. Addiction & Social Media Communication, 1(2).

Spears, L. I., Seyal, A. H., & Khan, A. R. (2015). Learning communities: Exploring hybrid social interactions with Generation Z. *American Journal of Educational Research*, *3*(10), 1308–1314. https://files.eric.ed.gov/fulltext/EJ1112534.pdf

Sugiarto, E., & Arif, M. F. (2024). Digital footprints: Unpacking cultural identity through english-language practices on social media. English Review. *Journal of English Education*, *12*(3), 983–992.

Theodorakopoulos, L., Theodoropoulou, A., & Klavdianos, C. (2025). Interactive Viral Marketing Through Big Data Analytics, Influencer Networks, AI Integration, and Ethical Dimensions. *Journal of Theoretical and Applied Electronic Commerce Research*, *20*(2), 115.

Thomas, R. (2025). Exploring Tomorrow: Evolution of Virtual Communities and Social Media. In Building Power, Safety, and Trust in Virtual Communities (pp. 333-358). IGI Global.

Wallin, S. (2025). From Traits To Leadership: Understanding Gen YZ In The Digital Commerce Sector. Accesible at https://www.doria.fi/handle/10024/192558

Wang, Y., Wang, L., & Siau, K. L. (2025). Human-centered interaction in virtual worlds: A new era of generative artificial intelligence and metaverse. *International Journal of Human-Computer Interaction*, *41*(2), 1459–1501.

Chapter 8
Being a Female Athlete in the Metaverse From Cybersexism to Gamergate:
The Rigidity of Sexism and the Continuity of Action

Fatma Öztat
https://orcid.org/0000-0002-6988-7389
Selçuk University, Turkey

Bünyamin Ayhan
Selçuk University, Turkey

ABSTRACT

The research is limited to news and comments about female metaverse athletes Kim "Geguri" Se-Yon and Sasha "Scarlett" Hostyn, who stand out with their recent global success. Accordingly, more than half of the 221 news and comments about female players were discriminatory and negative statements (n=128). Cybersexism (n=61) is prominent in these statements. There are 43 expressions on the theme of humiliation, othering, exclusion and 24 negative attitudes towards the player personality. As a result of the research, it was observed that female athletes are exposed to inequalities in the metaverse in parallel with real life. Sexist statements have come to the fore in discriminatory comments, it seems that the external opinions of female athletes are mercilessly criticized and their voices cannot be tolerated. On the other hand, the performances of female metaverse athletes are not believed and are considered inadequate because they are women.

DOI: 10.4018/979-8-3373-3043-3.ch008

INTRODUCTION

The metaverse, which enables multi-sensory interaction with virtual environments, digital objects and people (Mystakidis, 2022), incorporates many elements of everyday life. Sport is one of these elements. Metaverse sports are shaped by technological innovations and their applicability is increasing. Metaverse leagues, which have been included in the Olympics in this process, arouse curiosity (Sağlam, 2021). The experience of sport in the metaverse is free from the physical challenges and limitations of everyday life. Therefore, sporting opportunities in the metaverse, which do not require space, time constraints and physical conditioning, transform the parameters of sport. However, expectations of change in the basic parameters of sport in the metaverse do not always find a concrete response. Although the metaverse is seen as a new opportunity for some disadvantaged groups to integrate into sports, there are concerns about inequalities similar to real life, especially in terms of perspectives on women, rigid sexism, and cyber harassment (Rogstad, 2022).

The inequalities experienced by female athletes in the metaverse started with eSports tournaments and online games, which can be considered as the first internet-based sports applications. In online games where female players are introduced to the virtual world, a sexist approach towards women is exhibited. In online games where the language of harassment and threats is dominant (Fox & Tang, 2017), women hesitate to reveal their sexual identities and are afraid of participating in the game with their own voices. Disclosing player identity constitutes an important threshold (Nic Giolla Easpaig, 2018), female players are accused of cheating and their performances are not credited. The rigid gender chaos experienced in the gaming world sometimes extends to real life, and online channels, which are supposed to provide a solution to inequalities in the real world, turn into an extension of everyday life.

The concepts of cybersexism and gamergate come to the fore in explaining this situation experienced by female athletes in the metaverse. Cybersexism suggests that the online environment is sexist in a similar way to real life, and that online platforms are a new arena of struggle for women in terms of harassment and inequalities (Richard & Couchot-Schiex, 2020). Gamergate, on the other hand, came into public view when the sexual compromises that a female game developer had to endure in order to survive in the market became publicized in the press (Chip, 2014). As an embodiment of the compromises made by female gamers in order to hold on in the industry, Gamergate appears as a generalizing concept about the injustices suffered by women in online gaming and eSports.

The difficulties experienced by female metaverse athletes while performing in the virtual world are also reproduced in the media that can be characterized as the gaming press where these performances are covered. The gaming press is an umbrella concept that encompasses websites or social media accounts that are centered around online games, fed by the websites of global gaming companies, reporting or commenting on developments related to online games and players with a variable ground unlike the actors reporting in traditional media.

Magazines promoting the games of online game companies are also considered as part of the gaming press (Nieborg & Foxman, 2023). The gaming press consists of well-known websites and game commentators in the industry, as well as individual initiatives of numerous publishers who comment on games and players through social media platforms. The sports press operates with different techniques and tools in terms of diversity and content. In the gaming press, the characteristics of the game, the characteristics of the players and the industrialized structure stand out. However, the distinct profile of gaming journalism persists today as it did in the past (English, 2016). While the gaming press offers alternative spaces for society, groups and individuals, it can also be the root of certain problems. This is where criticism regarding the structural state of online journalism comes into play. One of the issues relating to this is the masculine attitude of the gaming press (Prax & Soler, 2016; MacDonald, 2024).

The gaming press poses a serious barrier not only to women's representation and gender equality, but also to women's efforts to gain a foothold online and to have their achievements recognized. The acceptance of women into global e-Sports teams can be openly met with "dismay" on gaming news websites (Frank, 2018). The sexist attitude that dominates the gaming press can target female athletes, and the achievements of female athletes are not welcomed in the same way as the achievements of male athletes. At this point, the relationship between the metaverse and sports, the dimensions of this relationship and its inclusion and reproduction in the media world gain importance.

Recently, the global achievements of female athletes have started to be heard in Metaverse leagues, and the visibility of female athletes in the game press has increased. However, studies on female athletes in the metaverse are very limited in the field. It is predicted that the results of the study will contribute to the field in this respect. For this purpose, in this study, the attitudes of female metaverse athletes in the game press will be discussed with netnographic observation. The prominent themes in the attitudes towards female metaverse athletes in the gaming press will be determined by content analysis and theme examples will be examined in detail.

METAVERSE AND SPORT

The term "meta" resonated globally with Zuckerberg's announcement that he would unite social media platforms and companies such as Facebook and Instagram under one umbrella called meta (Meta, 2021). The term "metaverse," which began to attract the attention of the general public with the unification of social media platforms such as Facebook and Instagram under the meta umbrella, is a combination of the words meta (transcendent, virtual) and universe (world, universe), referring to a fictional world that transcends reality (Heeseung, 2024). Built on blockchain technology and artificial intelligence (Hajian et al., 2024), the metaverse is a computer-generated holographic digital environment that simultaneously combines spatiotemporal, immersive, real-time, sustainable, interoperable, and data-aware features (Chen et al., 2024).

An evaluation of the metaverse's developmental milestones reveals that there is no uniform technological advancement (Amaizu et al., 2024). Lee et al.'s (2021) study identified eight elements that constitute the metaverse technology: network, edge/cloud, artificial intelligence, computer vision, blockchain, robotics, user interactivity, and extended reality. The metaverse ecosystem consists of avatars, content creation, the virtual economy, social acceptability, security & privacy, and trust & accountability (Lee et al., 2021). Considering technological and ecological elements, it appears that the layers of the metaverse world are positioned parallel to daily life. Therefore, while the metaverse is defined as increasingly replacing real life, it also includes systems we are already familiar with, such as crypto payment systems and crypto art, which have already established themselves in daily life. In this vast world, which creates its own dynamics and is open to users' imagination and configuration, it is possible to observe many elements of social life.

Sports is one of the most prominent areas of social life in the metaverse. The world of sports has recently embraced internet technologies, with social media accounts and online sports games becoming an integral part of the sports world. Online announcements and sales campaigns for sports events have been organized, and platforms like Twitter have been used extensively, particularly for football matches and global tournaments. Recently, especially during the COVID-19 pandemic, sports have been moved to a virtual dimension, with competitions in some sports being reorganized for athletes to participate from home (Tudor, 2020; Ruth et al., 2022). Thus, sports are expected to be one of the sectors where the metaverse will be most heavily utilized. This expectation stems from the fact that sports are closely linked to education, games, and entertainment, and that participation in sports as both competitors and spectators is possible (Çakır et al., 2022).

eSports is one of the important milestones preparing the sports industry for the metaverse. As a term that brings the internet and sports together, eSports is defined as a type of competitive sport in which the fundamental aspects of sport are facilitated by electronic systems (Hamari & Sjöblom, 2017). On the other hand, organized participation in video and computer games is also defined as eSports (Spitzer, 2019). One of the most significant differences that distinguishes eSports from real-life sports is that real-life muscular and physical advantages do not translate into advantages in online games (BBC, 2016).

eSports stands out as a more systematic expansion of online games to the world and an advanced version of the atmosphere in online games. Although the world of gaming is regarded as a community of people who come together for various purposes and in-game goals, not every individual participating in the game takes part in the system in the same way. The internal communication dynamics of online games have historically been challenging for groups that may be disadvantaged in terms of the gaming world, such as women and children (McLean & Griffiths, 2019). Verbal abuse is commonplace in in-game communication (Yıldırım, 2022). Verbal harassment can turn into various threats and coercive concessions in-game. The coercive competitive environment during games can be linked to real life through a process of acquiring real-life player information via the internet and disclosing this information in the game, with the effect of losing or winning matches (ADL, 2021). This aspect of gaming, which can extend to real-life security breaches, can pose serious privacy and security concerns, especially for women and children.

The idea that esports, online games, or sports opportunities in the metaverse could transform computers into sports equipment has become a recent topic of discussion (Spitzer, 2019). Sports already encompass dozens of genres requiring a wide range of equipment and physical environments/settings. It is believed that the metaverse will require various virtual reality/augmented reality equipment to facilitate different types of sports experiences in order to replace real-life sports. It is also a matter of interest whether these potential developments will alter the definition or functions of sports. In the coming period, we will be able to experience whether the sports experience, shaped by physical activity and cognitive skills, will be replaced by parameters such as adaptation to augmented reality, imagination, technological innovations, and adapting to new competitive environments that may emerge in the metaverse.

The main difference of metaverse from online games and eSports is that it offers a system similar to real life, which is large and accessible to all users. This system, which initially resembles real life, has possibilities that can be distinguished from real life in terms of consumption practices. The metaverse has exciting potential when it comes to users who can experience sports without being bound by time, space or physical disadvantages. With their virtual avatars, users will be able to meet people from different parts of the world in the same stadium and watch football matches and events. Users in the metaverse do not have to sit in a classic spectator seat in a stadium. Users can walk among the football players and watch the match from different angles (Duge, 2022). In the Metaverse, it is possible for users to look the way they want, choose the avatar they want, use the physical facilities they want, and partake in sports regardless of geographical and physical conditions while playing and watching sports.

The fact that sport, which is essentially based on physical activity, leaves its most basic definition and shifts to a new cognitive form may open the door to different problems (Hallmann & Giel, 2018; Spitzer, 2019). In the study conducted by Milic (2020), it was stated that online sports caused negative consequences, particularly in the COVID-19 process. These criticisms may result in reducing metaverse sports to online games. In fact, sports in the metaverse can turn into physical activities in daily life with the support of virtual reality. On the other hand, although the sports experience in the metaverse differs from computer games or online games with its virtual reality/augmented reality dimension, in order to create a sports environment close to real life in the metaverse, traditional sports equipment needs to be reinterpreted for the metaverse, and new systems need to be developed that allow athletes to train interactively, not just limited to fitness, entertainment and watching sports (Zhu ve diğerleri, 2023).

Today, new initiatives are contributing to improve the technological infrastructure of metaverse sports. First, Virtual Reality (VR) and Augmented Reality (AR) technologies have been combined. The new applications use a controller that allows users to mimic real-life actions and project the movements on the screen. Thanks to motion-sensing devices, users can feel like they are playing a real sport (Kim & Kim, 2024). The user is thus able to mimic offline activities in the online space (Dincelli & Yayla, 2022). As the ability to imitate improves and virtual sports opportunities get closer to real life, sports in the metaverse will become more widespread.

Along with the conveniences and innovations that the metaverse can provide for the world of sports, it is discussed whether sports experiences in the metaverse will turn into systematic competitions, championships and Olympics as in real life (Borggrefe, 2018). Rejected by the Olympic Committee for being commercially motivated, gaming competitions were included in the Tokyo Summer Olympics in 2018 with the Olympic Virtual Series. The series featured eSports competitions involving virtual sports including baseball, cycling, rowing, sailing and motorsports. As the Olympic Committee's first Olympic licensed virtual sports event to engage young audiences, these competitions blended digital sports with traditional (Sağlam, 2021).

It is envisioned that the metaverse holds innovative potential for the world of sport and can be used as an effective tool not only for the experience of sport, but also for athlete training, sport management, marketing, personal development and skills (Kalkan, 2021). In this process, the world of sport is undergoing a technological transformation, while at the same time, social structures related to sport and the circles related to the sector are also affected by the metaverse.

CYBERSEXISM AND GAMERGATE

The difficulties experienced by women, children and disadvantaged groups in the online gaming world are discussed with different concepts in the literature. Among these concepts, cybersexism stands out as a process of inequality that conditions female athletes, causes them to escape and eventually forces them to withdraw from the game (Vergel et al., 2024). Thus, sexist attitudes on the Internet and dominant gender norms targeting girls and boys continue in the form of cybersexism (Richard & Couchot-Schiex, 2020). Cybersexism functions as a domain where communication codes are transformed to the detriment of women by deviating from routine, gender-based abuse and harassment, generalizing gendered actions and blaming women, double standards, online threats, problems that are not instantaneous but constantly expanding, labeling processes and other adverse situations (Poland 2016).

Although it is stated that the cyber world can be a platform for solutions to social disadvantages (Gonzales, 2015), cybersexism can be interpreted as the continuation of sexist problems that exist in the real world with the support of the virtual world. Hence, the virtual world becomes a medium that is dominated by power and authority and where the disadvantage is constantly produced and sustained (Poland, 2016). As stated by Ruvalcaba et al. (2018), despite new opportunities for participation in sport in the cyber world, existing gender issues of sexism and exclusion persist. On the other hand, it is thought-provoking that there is no difference in the view towards women between cyberspace and the real world. Whether cyber or not, the view of women in the online environment is no different from the offline environment (Moosa, 2013).

Between 2014 and 2015, gaming journalism dealt with both journalistic ethics and correcting attacks on women (Perreault & Vos, 2018). In this process, the concept that took shape in terms of the difficulties experienced by female athletes in the cyberspace was Gamergate. Gamergate erupted when a female game developer had to make sexual compromises with a male game critic in order to get a positive review for her game (Chip, 2014). It can be argued that the concept of Gamergate is not directly related to the scandalous events, but that Gamergate is an internet culture war. On one side of this war are women and independent game developers who argue that participation in games should be pluralistic, and on the other side are white male gamers who are fond of guns and seeing women's breasts in games (Dewey, 2014). On the other hand, it has been suggested that the portrayal of women in game storylines as rape victims waiting to be rescued, or the portrayal and sexualization of female game characters as sexual objects with cleavage iencourage players to engage in online harassment (Burnay et al., 2019).

The gaming community and the gaming press are known to routinely target women (MacDonald, 2024). In fact, as stated by Williams (2014), the view of women in the gaming industry is such that the gaming industry can be considered "misogynistic". In this process female athletes are known to be highlighted with their private lives, their personal information was leaked to the press and they were subjected to threats and harassment. The gaming press is seen as the locomotive that carries the gaming industry, Gamergate and others alike. At this point, Erdoğan's (2014) statement, "It's not the players who need to die, but the gaming press," is noteworthy. It's argued that the gaming press should move beyond the players and their followers and instead establish direct communication with the public (Erdoğan, 2014). The gaming press is seen as the driving force that propelled the gaming industry to Gamergate and similar events. Harassment and threat scandals are amplified on gaming-related websites and internet platforms, the heart of the gaming industry. Therefore, considering the concepts of cybersexism and Gamergate separately from the gaming press would be inadequate.

Darvin et al. (2021) noted that women in esports are significantly underrepresented in games, that elite-level female athletes are frequently hindered, that the esports world hinders women's careers, and that women continue to experience masculinity in the esports world. The term "glass ceiling," used to describe the underrepresentation of women in the male-dominated world at senior levels, has been defined as the "glass monitor" for women in the gaming industry, highlighting the many invisible barriers facing women in the esports world (Darvin et al., 2021). The glass monitor also places importance on the industry's image of the gaming community. Although not involved in this production, it is concerning that female athletes remain more passive in the management of the sports world, such as media content production, sponsorship, and advertising deals.

BEING A FEMALE ATHLETE IN THE METAVERSE

Strict gender segregation is an important rule in traditional games and sports and violations are subject to various sanctions (Bertozzi, 2008). In traditional sports media, sport is seen as a male activity and superior athletic performance is equated with masculinity (Akkaya & Kaplan, 2014). Sport is known to be essentially based on processes developed for the male body (Fleshman, 2023), women are therefore kept out of the circle until they have achieved various successes in sports (Anderson, 2008). Female athletes are subjected to various criticisms or praises in daily life, especially over their bodies, and they are pushed to exist not through their athlete identities but through their female bodies (Godoy, 2016). This situation causes female athletes to be portrayed in the media with their sexuality rather than their achievements or skills (Mannion, 2016). Male athletes receive more news coverage than female athletes, and gender roles are emphasized in news reports about women (Ayhan & Demir, 2022; Bakan, 2013).

The effects of strict gender segregation in sports can be reflected in online games or e-Sports tournaments where women do not directly share their identities. It is observed that female athletes are covered less in online media as in traditional media, women's images are shown in online news rather than their achievements and they are exposed to more emotional language (Jones, 2004). Although the lack of a physical competition in online sports as in real life and the anonymity of the athletes suggest a process that could transform the usual sports dynamics, the current situation does not seem to change. This is because although anonymity on the internet may seem to provide an advantage to female athletes, players who hide their real identity in the digital environment can easily adopt a disturbing tone to women. Even the process of a successful player profile deciding to reveal that she is a woman in real life can be jarring for the online sports world. Every point produced, particularly identity and representation, ensures the perpetuation of inequalities in the field of sports in which women are involved in the virtual world.

Although the proportion of men and women taking part in online sports is close to each other (Entertainment Software Association, 2020), men are twice as likely to identify themselves as "gamers" compared to women (Ruvalcaba et al., 2018). On the other hand, despite the low number of female players in e-Sports and negative perspectives towards them, there are studies suggesting that female players are equally successful as male players (Ruvalcaba et al., 2018; Shen et al., 2016). While female gamers are becoming more visible in online spaces, online spaces sustain a troubling history of disproportionate treatment and representation towards female gamers (Drča, 2022; Apperley & Gray, 2020; Nakandala et al., 2017; Duggan, 2014). The Overwatch league, one of the most recent examples of e-Sports opportunities that will prepare users and athletes for sports in the metaverse, is an example of sexism in e-Sports. Blizzard, the developer of the league, recently signed 100 new players for the Overwatch league, not a single one of whom is a woman (Keilbart, 2018). This individual situation reflects the sexist tendency in the industry. Even when women compete and succeed on the same terms as men, their earnings are lower than those of male players in the same situation (BBC, 2016).

Kim "Geguri" Se-Yon, the first female player in the Overwatch league, has had a challenging career. At the age of 16, Kim Se-Yon was accused of cheating after her strong performance was discredited and she was forced to perform on live TV with her face hidden by a mask (Webster, 2018). Kim Se-Yon stated that for a long time she could not use her own voice in games because she was afraid of being mocked (Kimes, 2017). Kim "Geguri" Se-Yon, who only became the first female player when she was able to take an opening in the team after one of the male players failed, had to outperform the male players to claim this title (Keilbart, 2018). This development was commented on in the game press as "it happened out of desperation by Team Dragon" (Webster, 2018). It is remarkable and striking that the gaming press characterized the move of a female player to the team as "desperation".

The gaming press made similar comments about Sasha "Scarlett" Hostyn as they did about Kim "Geguri" Se-Yon. As the first female champion of the 2018 Olympics-sponsored Intel Extreme Masters, Sasha "Scarlett" Hostyn became the highest-paid female athlete ever, even though she won 1 in 5 of the prize money of the previous year's champion. Hostyn's victory was described on Intel's website as an "upset" for beating a higher-ranked male player (Frank, 2018). The gaming press has a common discourse for female athletes. Women are expected to be accepted to the teams or to show performances that surpass men, and women's achievements are interpreted in a masculine language.

The rigid sexist training in the sports world, where men and women compete in separate teams and competitions due to their physical differences in real life, may be unable to continue in online sports because real-life physical performance is not required, pushing men to another level of distressing despair. While fitness, which "wouldn't work" in the virtual world, and virtual conditions where men and women can easily compete, are seen as women's competition, the increasing number of women in online sports has not been welcomed. A female gamer, Cheon "Ezz" Yeong-Hyeon, explained that after her performances, she was subjected to comments like, "A girl can't play that well. Is your boyfriend playing for you?" (Kimes, 2017). Another female gamer, Briah Luther, made the most hopeful comment a gamer could make: "The moment they realize women are separated in the game, my energy runs out" (Seiner, 2019).

In online environments, women are known to resort to gender reassignment, gender neutralization, avoiding contact with other players, and seeking help or social support both in and outside of the game to reduce harassment (Fox & Tang, 2017). Therefore, another challenge faced by female athletes in the metaverse is the decision to reveal that they are women in real life. It is argued that this situation, called "claiming one's gamer identity," is becoming increasingly difficult and that the gaming world is increasingly taking on a sexist identity (Nic Giolla Easpaig, 2018). It is argued that gamers are dominated by a "young, white, male, and socially problematic" demographic, and users who differ from this profile are subject to aggressive behavior (Erdoğan, 2014). This situation creates a distinction between what is normal and what is not, with users who are "male, intelligent, passionate, and outspoken" being considered normal (Moosa, 2013).

In the light of the relevant literature, the following research questions are asked:

Q1: "What is the distribution of attitudes towards female athletes in the gaming press?"

Q2: "What discriminatory discourses and themes against female athletes come to the fore in the games press?"

Q3: "What are the prominent statements regarding discriminatory discourses and themes against female athletes in the gaming press?"

Context

This work is limited to Kim "Geguri" Se-Yon and Sasha "Scarlett" Hostyn, who have recently achieved global success in metaverse leagues and gained visibility in the gaming press. Kim "Geguri" Se-Yon, the first female player in the Overwatch league, has had a challenging career. At the age of 16, Kim Se-Yon was accused of cheating after her strong performance was discredited and she was forced to perform on live TV with her face hidden by a mask (Webster, 2018). Kim Se-Yon stated that for a long time she could not use her own voice in games because she was afraid of being mocked (Kimes, 2017). Kim "Geguri" Se-Yon, who only became the first female player when she was able to take an opening in the team after one of the male players failed, had to outperform the male players to claim this title (Keilbart, 2018). This development was commented on in the game press as "it happened out of desperation by Team Dragon" (Webster, 2018). It is remarkable and striking that the gaming press characterized the move of a female player to the team as "desperation".

The gaming press made similar comments about Sasha "Scarlett" Hostyn as they did about Kim "Geguri" Se-Yon. As the first female champion of the 2018 Olympics-sponsored Intel Extreme Masters, Sasha "Scarlett" Hostyn became the highest-paid female athlete ever, even though she won 1 in 5 of the prize money of the previous year's champion. Hostyn's victory was described on Intel's website as an "upset" for beating a higher-ranked male player (Frank, 2018). The gaming press has a common discourse for female athletes. Women are expected to be accepted to the teams or to show performances that surpass men, and women's achievements are interpreted in a masculine language.

Method

In the present study, in order to reveal whether the systematic structure continues in the metaverse, where rigid gender perceptions should be eliminated, news and comments in the gaming press about female athletes in the metaverse were evaluated through non-participant observation. Netnography, which can also be defined as ethnographic studies conducted online (Bartl et al., 2016), is a qualitative research method that examines digital tribes and user behavior.

Essentially a process of technoculture interpretation, netnography is a multi-disciplinary concept. Non-participant observation is based on the interpretation of interviews, online traces, mobile and live streaming data, platform interfaces, and the hidden effects of bots and algorithms. (Kozinets, 2020) and is an act of social introspection from content that is freely shared on the internet (Kozinets, 2015).

After identifying news and comments in the gaming press aimed at female metaverse athletes, the resulting text set is divided into themes in the process of analyzing text through content analysis (Krippendorff, 2019). It is aimed to reveal the salient content in news and commentary systematically (Berelson, 1952). Content analysis is the process of making reproducible and valid inferences from texts regarding the contexts of use. It is an observational research method used to systematically evaluate the symbolic content of any recorded communication (Kolbe & Burnett, 1991).

In this study, texts related to female metaverse athletes were classified according to semantic content (Janis, 1965). Accordingly, it is assumed that the contents in the same category have the same meaning (Cavanagh, 1997). In content analysis, explicit coding, categorization, and abstraction steps were followed (Elo & Kyngäs, 2008). In this way, the expressions in the sample were placed in content categories in line with the problem of the study (Weber, 1990). In the analysis process, content analysis requires; interpretive, naturalistic, situational, reflexive, inductive and case-oriented nature with the flexibility required by the process (Schreier, 2012).

Data Collection

News and commentary regarding female metaverse athletes were limited to Kim "Geguri" Se-Yon and Sasha "Scarlett" Hostyn due to their massive success on a global scale. There are very few female players in the metaverse. Very few of these female players compete in global leagues. Furthermore, the number of female players who compete in global leagues and achieve global success is limited to a few. Because there are relatively few female athletes in the Metaverse who achieve global success and have a presence on the internet and social media, this study was able to analyze the two female players mentioned above. The news and comments published after Kim "Geguri" Se Yon became the first female player in the Overwatch league and the news and comments made after Sasha "Scarlet" Hostyn became the first female champion of Intel Extreme Masters were taken into consideration. News about the female athletes in the sample were accessed via Google search between 01.05.2025 and 30.06.2025.

The news and comments consisted of news and posts on the websites "espn.com, espn.co.uk, nypost.com, reddit.com, theworld.org" as well as comments on these contents. Some of the websites allow comments from users to the news stories and headlines they publish. Therefore, both news items and user comments were included in the study. Since there are corporate pages as well as personal publications, blogs, etc. in the gaming press, the names of the authors in the news sources were kept confidential to protect personal privacy.

Data Analysis

34 pieces of content and 187 comments on these content regarding the female metaverse athletes named Kim "Geguri" Se-Yon and Sasha "Scarlett" Hostyn, who constitute the study sample, were identified. When the content and comments were examined to answer Research Question 1, it was understood that the data could be examined in six main subgroups. Accordingly, it was seen that 61 of the 221 data determined could be evaluated under the category of cybersexism, that 43 items contained denigration othering and exclusion, and that 24 items consisted of criticism towards the player's personality and performance. Thus, it was seen that more than half of the data included sexism, humiliation, exclusion, marginalization and negative attitudes towards athlete performance. Of the remaining 93 comments, 26 information about the teams of female athletes, 49 were developments regarding the matches of female athletes, and the remaining 18 were free comments that did not fall into any category. Research Question 2 was answered. While there was no author information on two of the websites, the author was mentioned on three websites. Almost all of the comments on the websites consisted of users who did not specify their real names.

Validity and Reliability

Reliability in content analysis is related to the degree to which the analysis produces the same result in repeated trials (Neuendorf, 2002). This means that the measurement in the coding scheme during the analysis process produces the same result when applied by different encoders (Lombard et al., 2006; Neuendorf & Kumar, 2015). On the other hand, the type of consistency required in content analysis; depends on consensus among coders (Tinsley & Weiss, 2000).

For this reason, in this study, two groups of coders who have studies in the field were studied. It was examined under which themes the news and comment texts to be examined were grouped by the coders. After the coding analysis, it was seen that the texts were grouped substantially similar in two different studies within the relevant themes, and in this direction, the study had surface validity. Text contents grouped differently were eliminated, and theme contents grouped by coders were used in the analysis.

FINDINGS

Under this heading, in the news and comments in the game press for female metaverse athletes; Expressions that stand out in terms of cyber sexism, humiliation, marginalization, exclusion and player personality and performance were examined.

Comments Containing Cybersexism

As in traditional media (Bakan, 2013), discrimination against women also continues in the online media (Akmeşe & Deniz, 2015). Female metaverse athletes are also exposed to these inequalities. Only 4 of the 61 content sources evaluated under the category of cybersexism stated their real names. 57 sources did not use their real names. In the comments shared in Table 1, the desire for female athletes to "look better groomed and more beautiful" stands out, and they are criticized for "looking like men". On the contrary, there are also users who like the appearance of female athletes and state that they "look sexy". It is understood that the bodies of female metaverse athletes are criticized for "looking like a woman" and that female athletes are seen as sexual objects. It is observed that the performances of female athletes are never evaluated only in terms of athletic performance, and that their gender is emphasized in most news articles and comments. The most striking finding under this section was the comments made about the need for female metaverse athletes to hide their gender. Female athletes are faced with an audience that does not even tolerate to hear their voices in the metaverse, where users' images are not shared. Female metaverse athletes were seen to be treated in a sexist manner in the gaming press, answering Research Question 3.

Table 1. Comments containing cybersexism

User Comment
Nonanonymous -1 "Transsexual player known as a woman is overpaid"
Nonanonymous -2 "She must not reveal that she is a woman, she must hide her voice"
Nonanonymous -3 "Fake boobs"
Nonanonymous -4 "Doesn't look like a woman, looks like a man"
Nonanonymous -5 "If she wants to look like a woman, she should grow her hair"
Nonanonymous -6 "She aims to be sexy with a different look"

Comments Containing Denigration, Othering and Exclusion

Female metaverse athletes are subjected to various comments and criticism in the gaming press and related media outlets (McLean & Griffiths, 2019). In these comments, themes of exclusion and othering stand out as well as open denigration. Almost all of the 43 items analyzed under this category do not contain the real name of the author. Expressions of denigration are generally articulated with cybersexism. Female athletes are criticized for their gender, for their appearance and voice, and for not playing well enough. Insulting terms ("crazy bitch") are openly used in the gaming press for female metaverse athletes. Another prominent theme in metaverse leagues and e-Sports tournaments is the exclusion of female athletes. The gaming press discusses whether there is a need for female athletes in metaverse leagues or online teams, with some users and writers openly stating that "there is no need for female athletes". The nicknames that athletes use in games rather than their performances are criticized, and the voices they use in games are scrutinized. It is stated that female players are not good enough in games because of their gender. Considering that the comments analyzed were made after the global achievements of the female metaverse athletes in the sample, it is observed that even the global league championships and participation in top-level teams do not have any recognition in the gaming press, female athletes are humiliated and found inadequate only because of their gender. In the comments examined, it was seen that female metaverse athletes were exposed not only to othering but also to denigration and exclusion in the gaming press, and Research Question 3 was answered.

Table 2. Comments containing denigration, othering and exclusion

User Comment
Nonanonymous -1 "Crazy bitch"
Nonanonymous -2 "Couldn't she find another handle other than Geguri (frog)?"
Nonanonymous -3 "Lacking synergy"
Nonanonymous -4 "Should do another job"
Nonanonymous -5 "She needs to shut up, she annoys me with her voice"
Nonanonymous -6 "We don't need female players"

Comments on Player Personality and Performance

Among the comments and criticisms directed at female metaverse athletes in the gaming press, there are also statements regarding the player personalities and performances of female athletes. In this regard, 2 out of the 24 items analyzed included the name of the author, while the rest did not. The lack of strict gender segregation in the metaverse leads to criticism directed at the nature of being a woman rather than the physical performance of female athletes (Jones, 2004). Criticisms about the lack of space for women in online leagues were tried to be explained as "there being not enough female players". Criticisms about the exclusion of female athletes in the industry were interpreted as "women are not excluded, they cannot find a place in the leagues because they are not successful enough". Another highly thought-provoking point of view among the comments and content in the gaming press was that "men are naturally programmed to win, while women are not". Based on the comments analyzed, it was understood that the performances and achievements of female metaverse athletes were not covered in the gaming press, but the player personalities of female athletes were criticized mercilessly, and Research Question 3 was answered.

Table 3. Comments on player personality and performance

User Comment
Nonanonymous -1 "Absolutely not enough female players for leagues"
Nonanonymous -2 "No one is excluding them, if they were successful enough this would not have happened"
Nonanonymous -3 "Men are naturally programmed to win, women are not"
Nonanonymous -4 "Men and women should compete separately, like in the wild"
Nonanonymous -5 "She is cheating"

DISCUSSION AND CONCLUSION

The metaverse, positioned as a twin of real life, is expected to bring many elements of everyday life into the metaverse. Sports are among the most intriguing elements in the metaverse. It's a matter of curiosity how sports activities, which are subject to strict gender segregation in real life and require physical conditioning, will transform in the metaverse, with its lack of space, time, and physical conditioning. This transformation is being pursued not only to eliminate physical conditions but also to offer hope that the problems faced by disadvantaged groups in the world of sports can be addressed in the metaverse. However, just as sexism persists in the online world, the harsh conditions of the real world of sports persist for female players in online gaming, esports, and the metaverse, and online harassment and threats further exacerbate the challenges of sports in the metaverse.

In this study has examined news and commentary on the internet and social media platforms regarding Kim "Geguri" Se-Yon and Sasha "Scarlett" Hostyn, the few female players who have recently gained prominence in the global metaverse leagues. Of the 221 news articles about these female players, more than half, 128 articles contained discriminatory and negative language. The remaining articles provided up-to-date information on league developments. Among the discriminatory content, cybersexism (n=61) was the leading theme. Cybersexism was followed by humiliation, marginalization, and exclusion (n=43). Furthermore, 24 negative statements targeting female players' personality were encountered. Examples of these themes are shared in the study findings. The study revealed that female players, similar to real-life situations, face inequalities in the metaverse. It was revealed that female players are frequently subjected to comments about their gender, harsh criticism of their appearance, and exclusion when playing games with female voices. Comments such as that female players are not as successful as men in the leagues and that it is intolerable to hear a female voice in matches are reaching quite alarming levels.

The expectation that technological developments will introduce more freedom and equality is not realized in the virtual world. The metaverse also appears as a ground that perpetuates the inequalities in real life. In the news and comments examined in the gaming press, cybersexism, denigration othering exclusion and expressions against player performance stood out. There are online users and news producers who cannot tolerate the voice of female athletes, asking them to hide the fact that they are women or stating that they should grow their hair long. Comments are made in the gaming press about female metaverse athletes, such as that female athletes are not needed, that they do not find a place in leagues because they are not successful enough, or that women do not inherently have a sense of winning. There are users who argue that men and women should compete separately in metaverse tournaments as they do in the wild. It is noteworthy that the comments in the gaming press are more subjective in terms of being male and female rather than concrete criticisms. The potential of the metaverse to eliminate the physical differences between men and women (Spitzer, 2019) can create a very unsettling potential for those who reduce human existence to mere physical differences.

Discriminatory language against women was encountered in the news coverage of the gaming press. In this sense, the situation of female athletes in the metaverse is almost more severe than in the real-life sports world. It can be stated that female athletes experience more disadvantages in the metaverse than in the real sports world. This finding is similar to the results of Alp et al. (2020), who argue that women face more disadvantages than advantages in e-Sports. The insignificance of the alleged physiological superiority of men over women in the world of sports in e-Sports (Rogstad, 2022) may be driving men further to sexual harassment. Detailed studies on the loss of the importance of physiological superiority in e-Sports and men's internal reactions can be conducted in the future.

It has been observed that the developments concerning female athletes have been trivialized and ignored. In order for female athletes to have their performances recognized, they need to hide the fact that they are women. After a player reveals to the industry that she is a woman, she can easily be asked to prove her performance on live broadcast. There is a sexist tone in the news about women in the gaming press. The achievements of female players are clearly treated differently than those of male players. The achievements of female players are underestimated, deemed as upsets, and the subject is taken out of the context of sports with various comments on sexuality. The conclusion of the present study concerning the gaming press is in line with the study conducted by Kovács et al. (2023), which emphasizes the role of the media in addressing gender inequality in e-Sports.

While achieving gender equality in the real-life sports world seems to be quite difficult from the past to the present (Kempe-Bergman et al., 2020; Birrell, 1988; Cunningham & Ko, 2024; Demir & Ayhan, 2022), it is notable that sports in the metaverse, which has yet to make progress in terms of rules and sanctions, is suitable for online threats and harassment (Shen, 2022). In this respect, it is clear that the metaverse can be positioned as an area where new measures are needed rather than new opportunities for female athletes, or even one with a dark future (Sales, 2024).

Another dimension of the metaverse that can be discussed from the perspective of female athletes is whether sporting opportunities in the metaverse can create freedom for women in countries that are disadvantaged in terms of media access and use. The study conducted by Hussain et al. (2021) reports that electronic sports are positioned as an oppositional representation for the users and are evaluated as an escape from the patriarchal structure to freedom. Focusing on the experiences of women who cannot participate in real-life sports due to factors such as political pressure, the study argues that female athletes are liberated through experiencing electronic sports. This outcome is discussed in terms of whether digital games are a real freedom or an escape from everyday life (Deleuze et al., 2019). The backdrop of the metaverse, which initially appears as freedom, but in fact introduces new compromises, does not prevent the evaluation of sport in the metaverse as "a man's game" (Delamere & Shaw, 2008).

It is suggested that the issue be kept up to date in the relevant circles in order for women to gain a foothold in online sports (Rogstad, 2022). Another suggestion is the suspension of the anonymous dimension of the internet in the gaming process, and the proliferation of face-to-face games played collectively in movie theaters as experienced by female player Ella Lasky (Seiner, 2019, para.29). However, it is debatable whether a game played in this way can be included as part of e-Sports or the metaverse. This situation, which can be interpreted as holding on to real life again to escape the bullying of the online world, is ironic. A different suggestion for the difficulties experienced by female athletes in the online world is that female executives should be more involved in decision-making roles in the e-Sports mechanism, that female athletes should be encouraged to compete more and that campaigns should be organized for this purpose (Hayday & Collison, 2020). This much more constructive suggestion may start to have an impact once processes such as the protection of female athletes with various legal rights on the internet become clearer.

This study revealed that inequalities against disadvantaged groups in the online environment persist in the metaverse. It was understood that the sexist attitudes adopted towards women on online platforms are also perpetuated in the metaverse. Female athletes and potentially disadvantaged groups were observed to be excluded, humiliated, and marginalized in the metaverse, parallel to real life. While internet technologies and the metaverse are expected to be more liberating and egalitarian than real life because they are not physical environments, the fact that the results obtained coincide with different studies in the field is thought-provoking in terms of showing the continuity of inequalities in the metaverse. In the metaverse, which can be seen as the driving force of technological advancements, studies should be conducted to understand the challenges faced by women across different social layers. It is clear that various legal measures and interdisciplinary studies are needed to ensure equality for female athletes in the metaverse.

This study examined a limited number of gamers over a specific period. Current studies are needed to identify current developments in the metaverse. It is recommended that new assessments be conducted using different social indicators related to cybersexism, across different social platforms and potential new female gamers. Furthermore, the perspective focused solely on women and female gamers in the metaverse should be expanded to include all disadvantaged groups, and future studies should also explore the current data to establish a discussion ground for groups with different disadvantages.

REFERENCES

ADL. (2021, September 13). *Hate is No Game: Harassment and Positive Social Experiences in Online Games 2021*. ADL.ORG: https://www.adl.org/resources/report/hate-no-game-harassment-and-positive-social-experiences-online-games-2021 retrieved from.

Akkaya, C., & Kaplan, Y. (2014). Toplumsal cinsiyet bağlamında spor medyasında kadın. *International Journal of Science Culture and Sport, 2*, 177–182. DOI: 10.14486/IJSCS189

Akmeşe, Z., & Deniz, K. (2015). Kadına yönelik cinsiyetçi söylemin internet haber portallarında yer alma biçimleri. *Uşak Üniversitesi Sosyal Bilimler Dergisi, 8*(1), 311–326. DOI: 10.12780/uusbd.45190

Alp, A., Çakmak, G., & Sarper Kahveci, M. (2020). "Ne bilir kadın oyun oynamayı?":Kadın oyuncuların e-spor deneyimleri. *Türkiye Klinikleri Spor Bilimleri Dergisi, 12*(3), 322–329. DOI: 10.5336/sportsci.2020-73698

Amaizu, G., Njoku, J., Lee, J., & Kim, D. (2024). Metaverse in advanced manufacturing: Background, applications, limitations, open issues & future directions. *ICT Express, 10*(2), 1–23. DOI: 10.1016/j.icte.2024.02.010

Anderson, E. (2008). "I used to think women were weak": Orthodox masculinity, gender segregation, and sport. *Sociological Forum, 23*(2), 257–280. DOI: 10.1111/j.1573-7861.2008.00058.x

Apperley, T., & Gray, K. (2020). Digital divides and structural inequalities. In *T. Q. Rachel Kowert, The Video Game Debate 2*. Routledge. DOI: 10.4324/9780429351815-4

Ayhan, B., & Demir, Y. (2022). Systematic sexism: Women's sports news in a circle of gatekeepers and users on twitter. *Communication & Sport*. Advance online publication. DOI: 10.1177/21674795221147644

Bakan, Ö. (2013). Türk medyasında kadın sporcuların temsili: Üç gazetenin içerik analizi. *Selçuk İletişim, 7*(4), 129–139. DOI: 10.18094/si.11566

Bartl, M., Kannan, V., & Stocki, H. (2016). A review and analysis of literature on netnography research. *International Journal of Technology Marketing, 11*(2), 165. DOI: 10.1504/IJTMKT.2016.075687

BBC. (2016, November 21). *100 Women 2016: The women challenging sexism in e-sports*. BBC: https://www.bbc.com/news/technology-37992322 retrieved from.

Berelson, B. (1952). *Content analysis in communication research*. Free Press.

Bertozzi, E. (2008). "You play like a girl!": Cross-gender competition and the uneven playing field. *Convergence (London), 14*(4), 473–487. DOI: 10.1177/1354856508094667

Birrell, S. (1988). Discourses on the gender/sport relationship: From women in sport to gender relations. *Exercise and Sport Sciences Reviews, 16*, 459–502. DOI: 10.1249/00003677-198800160-00017 PMID: 3292265

Burnay, J., Bushman, B., & Larøi, F. (2019). Effects of sexualized video games on online sexual harassment. *Aggressive Behavior, 45*(2), 214–223. DOI: 10.1002/ab.21811 PMID: 30614006

Çakır, Z., Gönen, M., & Ceyhan, M. (2022). Spor Bilimleri Fakültesi öğrencilerinin metaverse farkındalıklarının incelenmesi. *CBÜ Beden Eğitimi ve Spor Bilimleri Dergisi, 17*(2), 406–418. DOI: 10.33459/cbubesbd.1179009

Cavanagh, S. (1997). Content analysis: Concepts, methods and applications. *Nurse Researcher, 4*, 5–16. PMID: 27285770

Chen, C., Li, Y., Wu, Z., Mai, C., Liu, Y., Hu, Y., Kang, J., & Zheng, Z. (2024). Privacy computing meets metaverse: Necessity, taxonomy and challenges. *Ad Hoc Networks, 158*, 1–13. DOI: 10.1016/j.adhoc.2024.103457

Chip. (2014, October 20). *Oyun dünyasında GamerGate fırtınası dinmiyor.* Chip.com.tr: https://www.chip.com.tr/haber/oyun-dunyasinda-gamergate-firtinasi-dinmiyor_50188.html retrieved from.

Cunningham, G., & Ko, Y. (2024). Diversity, equity and inclusion in the sport metaverse. *International Journal of Sports Marketing & Sponsorship*. Advance online publication. DOI: 10.1108/IJSMS-04-2023-0080

Darvin, L., Holden, J., Wells, J., & Baker, T. (2021). Breaking the glass monitor: Examining the underrepresentation of women in esports environments. *Sport Management Review, 24*(3), 475–499. DOI: 10.1080/14413523.2021.1891746

Delamere, F., & Shaw, S. (2008). "They see it as a guy's game": The politics of gender in digital games. *Leisure/Loisir, 32*(2), 279–302. DOI: 10.1080/14927713.2008.9651411

Deleuze, J., Maurage, P., Schimmenti, A., Nuyens, F., Melzer, A., & Billieux, J. (2019). Escaping reality through videogames is linked to an implicit preference for virtual over real-life stimuli. *Journal of Affective Disorders, 245*, 1024–1031. DOI: 10.1016/j.jad.2018.11.078 PMID: 30699844

Demir, Y., & Ayhan, B. (2022). Being a female sports journalist on twitter: Online harassment, sexualization, and hegemony. *International Journal of Sport Communication, 15*(3), 207–217. DOI: 10.1123/ijsc.2022-0044

Dewey, C. (2014, October 14). *The only guide to Gamergate you will ever need to read.* Washingtonpost.com: https://www.washingtonpost.com/news/the-intersect/wp/2014/10/14/the-only-guide-to-gamergate-you-will-ever-need-to-read/ retrieved from.

Dincelli, E., & Yayla, A. (2022). Immersive virtual reality in the age of the Metaverse: A hybrid-narrative review based on the technology affordance perspective. *The Journal of Strategic Information Systems, 21*(2), 1–22. DOI: 10.1016/j.jsis.2022.101717

Drča, A. (2022). Gender ınequality present in the gaming community. *International Scientific Conference on Information Technology and Data Related Research.* DOI: 10.15308/Sinteza-2022-435-442

Duggan, M. (2014, October 22). *Online harassment.* pewresearch.org: https://www.pewresearch.org/internet/2014/10/22/online-harassment/ retrieved from.

Elo, S., & Kyngäs, H. (2008). *The qualitative content analysis process.* Jan Leading Global Nursing Research., DOI: 10.1111/j.1365-2648.2007.04569.x

English, P. (2016). New Rules of the game: sports journalism and proiles. In Joseph, S. L. (Ed.), *Profile Pieces Journalism and the 'Human Interest' Bias* (pp. 195–210). Routledge.

Entertainment Software Association. (2020). 2020 Essential facts about the video game industry. theesa.com: https://www.theesa.com/resource/2020-essential-facts/ retrieved from.

Erdoğan, Y. (2014, September 6). *Ölen ve ölmesi gereken şey oyuncu değil, oyun basını #GamerGate.* Geekyapar.com: https://geekyapar.com/olen-ve-olmesi-gereken-sey-oyuncu-degil-oyun-basini-gamergate/ retrieved from.

Fleshman, L. (2023, March 10). *Sports were never designed around the female body.* Time.com: https://time.com/6261404/sports-female-body-inclusivity/ retrieved from.

Fox, J., & Tang, W. (2017). Women's experiences with general and sexual harassment in online video games: Rumination, organizational responsiveness, withdrawal, and coping strategies. *New Media & Society, 19*(8), 1290–1307. DOI: 10.1177/1461444816635778

Frank, A. (2018, February 7). *One of esports' top female players breaks new ground at StarCraft 2 tournament.* Polygon.com: https://www.polygon.com/2018/2/7/16987076/iem-2018-sc2-winner-scarlett retrieved from.

Godoy, A. (2016). 'No hint of bulging muscles': The surveillanceof sportswomen's bodies in British print media. *Journalism, 17*(6), 744–759. DOI: 10.1177/1464884915583770

Gonzales, A. (2015). Disadvantaged minorities' use of the ınternet to expand their social networks. *Communication Research, 44*(4), 467–486. DOI: 10.1177/0093650214565925

Hajian, A., Daneshgar, S., Sadeghi, K., Ojha, D., & Katiyar, G. (2024). From theory to practice: Empirical perspectives on the metaverse's potential. *Technological Forecasting and Social Change, 201*, 1–11. DOI: 10.1016/j.techfore.2024.123224

Hallmann, K., & Giel, T. (2018). eSports – Competitive sports or recreational activity? *Sport Management Review, 21*(1), 14–20. DOI: 10.1016/j.smr.2017.07.011

Hamari, J., & Sjöblom, M. (2017). What is eSports and why do people watch it? *Internet Research, 27*(2), 211–232. DOI: 10.1108/IntR-04-2016-0085

Hayday, E., & Collison, H. (2020). Exploring the contested notion of social ınclusion and gender ınclusivity. *Social Inclusion (Lisboa), 8*(3), 197–208. DOI: 10.17645/si.v8i3.2755

Heeseung, Y. (2024). Why do people use Metaverse? A uses and gratification theory perspective. *Telematics and Informatics, 89*, 1–17. https://doi.org/doi.org/10.1016/j.tele.2024.102110

Hussain, U., Yu, B., Cunningham, G., & Bennett, G. (2021). 'I can be who I am when I play tekken 7': E-Sports women participants from the Islamic Republic of Pakistan. *Games and Culture, 16*(8), 978–1000. DOI: 10.1177/15554120211005360

Janis, I. (1965). The problem of validating content analysis. In, Harold D. Lasswell, Nathan Leites, & Associates, *Language of politics: Studies in quantitative* (s. 55-82). MIT Press.

Jones, D. (2004). Half the story: Olympic women on ABC News online. *Media International Australia, Incorporating Culture & Policy, 110*(1), 132–146. DOI: 10.1177/1329878X0411000114

Kalkan, N. (2021). Metaverse evreninde sporun bugünü ve geleceğine yönelik bir derleme. *Ulusal Spor Bilimleri Dergisi, 2*(2), 163–174. DOI: 10.30769/usbd.1027728

Keilbart, L. (2018, February 9). *Der e-sport hat ein sexismus-problem.* GQ: https://www.gq-magazin.de/auto-technik/article/der-e-sport-hat-ein-sexismus-problem retrieved from.

Kempe-Bergman, M., Larsson, H., & Redelius, K. (2020). The sceptic, the cynic, the women's rights advocate and the constructionist: Male leaders and coaches on gender equity in sport. *International Journal of Sport Policy, 12*(3), 333–347. DOI: 10.1080/19406940.2020.1767678

Kim, A., & Kim, S. (2024). Engaging in sports via the metaverse? An examination through analysis of metaverse research trends in sports. *Data Science and Management*, 1-15. https://doi.org/doi.org/10.1016/j.dsm.2024.01.002

Kimes, M. (2017, September 15). *Game: Interrupted, how a teenage gamer in the hottest new esport, overwatch, became a reluctant icon for south Korea's feminist movement.* ESPN: https://www.espn.com/espn/feature/story/_/id/20692051/how-teenage-gamer-became-reluctant-icon-south-korea-feminist-movement retrieved from.

Kolbe, R., & Burnett, M. (1991). Content-analysis research: An examination of applications with directives for improving research reliability and objectivity. *The Journal of Consumer Research, 18*(2), 243–250. DOI: 10.1086/209256

Kovács, K., Békési, Z., Győri, K., & Papp, D. (2023). Gender differences in the characteristics of gaming and esport aspirations in Hungary. *Contemporary Social Science, 18*(1), 58–75. DOI: 10.1080/21582041.2022.2157473

Kozinets, R. (2015). Netnography: Redefined. Sage.

Kozinets, R. (2020). *Netnography today: A call to evolve, embrace, energize, and electrify. R. Kozinets, & R. Gambetti In, Netnography unlimited: Understanding technoculture using qualitative social media research.* Routledge. DOI: 10.4324/9781003001430

Krippendorff, K. (2019). Content analysis: An ıntroduction to ıts methodology. *Sage.* DOI: 10.4135/9781071878781

Lee, L., Braud, T., Zhou, P., Wang, L., Xu, D., Lin, Z., & Hui, P. (2021). All One Needs to Know about Metaverse: A Complete Survey on Technological Singularity, Virtual Ecosystem, and Research Agenda. *Journal of Latex Class Fıles, 14*(8), 1–66. https://doi.org/doi.org/10.48550/arXiv.2110.05352

Lombard, M., Snyder-Duch, J., & Bracken, C. (2006). Content analysis in mass communication: Assessment and reporting of intercoder reliability. *Human Communication Research, 28*(4), 587–604. DOI: 10.1111/j.1468-2958.2002.tb00826.x

MacDonald, K. (2024, March 8). *It's 10 years since Gamergate – the industry must now stand up to far-right trolls.* TheGuardian.com: https://www.theguardian.com/games/2024/mar/08/gamergate-trolls-woke-game-consultants retrieved from.

Mannion, K. (2016). Play like a girl: An analysis of media representation of female athletes. *Proceedings of GREAT Day, 2015*(17), 72–81.

McLean, L., & Griffiths, M. (2019). Female gamers' experience of online harassment and social support in online gaming: A qualitative study. *International Journal of Mental Health and Addiction, 17*(4), 970–994. DOI: 10.1007/s11469-018-9962-0

Meta. (2021, October 28). *Introducing Meta: A Social Technology Company.* meta. com: https://about.fb.com/news/2021/10/facebook-company-is-now-meta/ retrieved from.

Moosa, T. (2013, September 1). *Cybersexism is still sexism.* Bigthink.com: https:// bigthink.com/articles/cybersexism-is-still-sexism/ retrieved from.

Mystakidis, S. (2022). Metaverse. *Encyclopedia, 2*(1), 486–497. DOI: 10.3390/ encyclopedia2010031

Nakandala, S., Ciampaglia, G., Su, N., & Ahn, Y. (2017). Gendered conversation in a social game-streaming platform. *Proceedings of the International AAAI Conference on Web and Social Media.* DOI: 10.1609/icwsm.v11i1.14885

Neuendorf, K. (2002). *The content analysis guidebook.* CA. *Sage.*

Neuendorf, K., & Kumar, A. (2015). Content analysis. In, G. Mazzoleni, *The International Encyclopedia of Political Communication, First Edition.* John Wiley & Sons.

Nic Giolla Easpaig, C. (2018). An exploratory study of sexism in online gaming communities: mapping contested digital terrain. *An exploratory study of sexism in online gaming communities: mapping contested digital terrain, 4*(2), 119-135. DOI: 10.1285/i24212113v4i2p119

Nieborg, D., & Foxman, M. (2023). *Mainstreaming and game journalism.* MIT Press. DOI: 10.7551/mitpress/13837.001.0001

Perreault, G., & Vos, T. (2018). The GamerGate controversy and journalistic paradigm maintenance. *Journalism, 19*(4), 553–569. DOI: 10.1177/1464884916670932

Poland, B. (2016). *Haters: Harassment, abuse and violence online.* Potomac Books., DOI: 10.2307/j.ctt1fq9wdp

Prax, P., & Soler, A. (2016). Critical alternative journalism from the perspective of game journalists. *Proceedings of 1 st International Joint Conference of DiGRA and FDG.* DiGRA/FDG. DOI: 10.26503/dl.v2016i1.754

Richard, G., & Couchot-Schiex, S. (2020). Cybersexism: How gender and sexuality are at play in cyberspace. In, D. Farris, D. Compton, & A. Herrera, *Gender, Sexuality and Race in the Digital Age* (s. 17-30). Springer.

Rogstad, E. (2022). Gender in eSports research: A literature review. *EJSS European Journal for Sport and Society, 19*(3), 195–213. DOI: 10.1080/16138171.2021.1930941

Ruth, J., Willwacher, S., & Korn, O. (2022). Acceptance of Digital Sports: A Study Showing the Rising Acceptance of Digital Health Activities Due to the SARS-CoV-19 Pandemic. *International Journal of Environmental Research and Public Health, 19*(1), 1–16. DOI: 10.3390/ijerph19010596 PMID: 35010849

Ruvalcaba, O., Shulze, J., Kim, A., Berzenski, S., & Otten, M. (2018). Women's experiences in eSports: Gendered differences in peer and spectator feedback during competitive video game play. *Journal of Sport and Social Issues, 42*(4), 295–311. DOI: 10.1177/0193723518773287

Sağlam, S. (2021, April 23). *E-Sporlar artık olimpiyatlarda*. GQ: https://gq.com.tr/gq-sports/e-sporlar-artik-olimpiyatlarda retrieved from.

Sales, N. (2024, January 5). *A girl was allegedly raped in the metaverse. Is this the beginning of a dark new future?* Theguardian.com: https://www.theguardian.com/commentisfree/2024/jan/05/metaverse-sexual-assault-vr-game-online-safety-meta retrieved from.

Schreier, M. (2012). *Qualitative content analysis in practice*. CA. *Sage (Atlanta, Ga.)*.

Seiner, J. (2019, January 3). *"You're a girl, you're being targeted": Women in esports navigate toxicity, other barriers*. The Denver Post: https://www.denverpost.com/2019/01/03/esports-women-navigate-toxicity-barriers/ retrieved from.

Shen, C., Ratan, R., Dora Cai, Y., & Leavit, A. (2016). Do men advance faster than women? Debunking the gender performance gap in two massively multiplayer online games. *Journal of Computer-Mediated Communication, 21*(4), 312–329. DOI: 10.1111/jcc4.12159

Spitzer, M. (2019). E-Sport lobbyismus versus gemeinnützigkeit und gesundheit. *Nervenheilkunde: Zeitschrift für Interdisziplinaere Fortbildung, 38*(4), 157–168. DOI: 10.1055/a-0817-7741

Tinsley, H., & Weiss, D. (2000). Interrater reliability and agreement. In Tinsley, H. E. A., & Brown, S. D. (Eds.), *Handbook of applied multivariate statistics and mathematical modeling* (pp. 95–124). Academic Press. DOI: 10.1016/B978-012691360-6/50005-7

Tudor, E. (2020). The emergence of eSport during Covid-19: How sim racing replaced live motorsport in 2020. *Journal of Motorsport Culture & History, 1*(1).

Vergel, P., La Parra-Casado, D., & Vives-Cases, C. (2024). Examining cybersexism in online gaming communities: A scoping review. *Trauma, Violence & Abuse, 25*(1), 1201–1218. DOI: 10.1177/15248380231176059 PMID: 37243440

Weber, R. (1990). *Basic content analysis.* Sage Publications. DOI: 10.4135/9781412983488

Webster, A. (2018, February 14). *The Overwatch League signs its first female player.* Theverge.com: https://www.theverge.com/2018/2/14/17011504/overwatch-league-first-woman-player-geguri-shanghai-dragons retrieved from.

Williams, I. (2014, September). *Death to the gamer.* Jacobin.com/: https://jacobin.com/2014/09/death-to-the-gamer/ retrieved from.

Chapter 9

Digital Identity Policy-Making in Africa:
Balancing Legal Considerations With National Security

Lucky Oghenechodja Daniel
https://orcid.org/0000-0002-0875-4240
University of Johannesburg, South Africa

Nwosu Obinnaya Chikezie Victor
https://orcid.org/0000-0003-3974-4755
University of KwaZulu-Natal, South Africa

ABSTRACT

This chapter explores the proliferation of digital identity systems across Africa, highlighting both their potential to enhance social inclusion and administrative efficiency and their risks to privacy and human rights. It investigates the tension between national security imperatives and the protection of fundamental legal rights, employing a qualitative, descriptive methodology informed by policy documents, academic literature, and case studies from Nigeria, Kenya, and South Africa. The analysis demonstrates that while legal frameworks for data protection are increasingly present, their effectiveness is frequently compromised by national security priorities, infrastructural limitations, and digital literacy gaps. The chapter contends that technocratic or purely legalistic approaches are inadequate and proposes a human-rights-by-design framework emphasizing public trust, ethical AI governance, and gender-inclusive considerations as essential foundations for sustainable policy.

DOI: 10.4018/979-8-3373-3043-3.ch009

INTRODUCTION

The quest for legal identity has become a defining global agenda, encapsulated in the United Nations Sustainable Development Goal 16.9, which calls for providing legal identity for all, including birth registration, by 2030. In Africa, this objective has gained profound resonance as nations leapfrog technological stages to embrace digital solutions for governance and development. Digital identity systems are promoted as transformative tools capable of unlocking access to essential services like healthcare, finance, and education, thereby fostering social inclusion and empowering citizens to participate fully in public life. However, this optimistic vision is shadowed by a fundamental paradox: the same technologies that promise inclusion can become instruments of exclusion, surveillance, and control, (Asimakopoulos et al., 2025). The core challenge confronting African policymakers lies in navigating the turbulent waters between legitimate national security interests and the imperative to protect individual rights, particularly privacy and data protection. In an era marked by regional instability, cyber threats, and terrorism, governments increasingly view comprehensive digital identity systems as indispensable tools for enhancing state security. This has led to the implementation of large-scale, often biometric-based, identity schemes such as Nigeria's National Identification Number (NIN) and Kenya's Huduma Namba. Yet, these initiatives frequently clash with the principles of privacy and personal freedom, raising concerns about state surveillance, data misuse, and the erosion of civil liberties. The conflict is not merely theoretical; it manifests in policies that mandate bio-metric data collection for basic services, link digital identities to SIM card registration, and create centralized databases vulnerable to both internal misuse and external breaches (Ogasawara, 2025). This chapter argues that the prevailing discourse on digital identity in Africa, which heavily emphasizes legal frameworks and security apparatuses, is incomplete. It often overlooks the critical socio-political dimensions that determine the success and equity of these systems, including public perception, historical mistrust of state institutions, widespread digital illiteracy, and the unique vulnerabilities of marginalized communities, especially women and forcibly displaced persons. Without addressing these factors, even the most well-designed legal frameworks will fail to build the trust necessary for widespread, equitable adoption(Shojaei & Moieni, 2025). To provide a more comprehensive analysis, this chapter will move beyond a simple legal-security binary. It begins by establishing a background and literature review that situates Africa's digital identity journey within its unique historical context, particularly the legacy of colonial classification systems on contemporary public trust. It then presents a multifaceted analysis of the key challenges, weaving together legal, technological, and socio-political threads. Following this, the discussion section synthesizes these challenges to propose a more equitable and sustainable policy framework grounded in principles of human-rights-by-design and ethical AI governance. The chapter concludes with actionable policy recommendations for African governments, civil society, and international partners, advocating for a future where digital identity serves as a tool for genuine empowerment rather than a mechanism for state control (Ruttkamp, 2025).

BACKGROUND AND LITERATURE REVIEW

The contemporary landscape of digital identity in Africa cannot be understood without appreciating the historical and theoretical currents that shape it. The transition from traditional, community-based forms of identity to state-controlled digital systems is a complex process, influenced by colonial legacies, global development agendas, and the rapid pace of technological change. This section critically analyzes the evolution of identity concepts in Africa, reviews the dominant themes in the existing literature, and identifies crucial gaps that this chapter seeks to address, (Zimba et al., 2025).

The Evolution of Identity and Privacy in an African Context

Historically, identity in many pre-colonial African societies was fluid and relational, embedded within kinship networks, communities, and shared cultural practices rather than being a static, state-issued credential. Privacy, too, was understood contextually, often centered on communal well-being and respect within established social hierarchies. The colonial era marked a radical shift. European powers introduced rigid systems of classification and identification—pass laws, ethnic identity cards, and censuses—primarily as tools of control, taxation, and labor management. These systems were not designed for citizen empowerment but for subjugation, creating a legacy of deep-seated mistrust towards state-led registration and identification projects that persists to this day, (Mayega et al., 2025). In the post-independence era, many African nations inherited these centralized, bureaucratic structures. The contemporary push for digital identity, while framed in the language of development and modernity, often builds upon this colonial scaffolding. As noted by researchers, the rapid adoption of new technologies like bio-metrics and AI is reshaping identity laws, but the underlying tension between state control and individual autonomy remains a central theme. The motivation for these systems is multifaceted, driven by a combination of national security demands, the need for more efficient public administration, and pressure from international financial institutions and development partners who see digital ID as a prerequisite for financial inclusion and effective social protection programs, (Santoro et al., 2025).

Critical Analysis of Existing Research and Identification of Gaps

The academic and policy literature on digital identity in Africa has produced valuable insights, primarily focusing on three key areas: legal and regulatory frameworks, national security implications, and technological infrastructure. Scholars have extensively analyzed the wave of new data protection laws across the continent—such as South Africa's POPIA, Nigeria's NDPR, and Kenya's Data Protection Act—examining their alignment with international standards like the GDPR and their effectiveness in practice. Similarly, the nexus between digital identity and national security has been a focal point, with studies exploring how these systems are used for counter-terrorism, border control, and cybercrime prevention, often at the expense of civil liberties. Research has also highlighted the significant infrastructural challenges, from a lack of reliable electricity and internet connectivity to weak foundational civil registration and vital statistics (CRVS) systems, which undermine the viability of digital ID projects, (Labrique, 2025). While this body of work is essential, it exhibits several critical gaps that limit its explanatory power and policy relevance. First, **the public is often absent** from the analysis. Much of the literature treats citizens as passive recipients of technology and policy, rather than active agents whose perceptions, trust, and adoption behaviors are paramount. There is a significant under-emphasis on the "demand side" of digital identity—why citizens might resist or mistrust these systems. Issues of public trust, misinformation, and the historical baggage of state surveillance are frequently acknowledged but rarely centered as primary objects of study, (Bottarelli et al., 2025). Second, **the digital divide is treated as a technical, not a social, problem.** While infrastructural deficits are well-documented, there is less focus on the human dimension of the divide: digital literacy. The lack of digital skills not only creates barriers to accessing services but also prevents individuals from giving meaningful, informed consent for their data to be collected and used, making them vulnerable to exploitation and fraud, (Hollimon et al., 2025). Third, **the analysis often lacks an intersectional gender lens.** Digital identity systems are not neutral; their design and implementation can have profoundly different impacts on various segments of the population. There is a dearth of research examining how these systems affect women, who may face cultural or administrative barriers to obtaining foundational documents, or how they impact other marginalized groups such as refugees, ethnic minorities, and persons with disabilities, who risk being rendered invisible or further excluded by inflexible digital architectures, (Smith, 2025). Finally, **the discourse on governance is underdeveloped.** While legal frameworks are discussed, there is a relative lack of research on practical governance models, particularly concerning the ethical deployment of artificial intelligence and the role of independent oversight bodies. The rapid integration of AI and machine learning into identity systems for purposes of verification, risk profiling, and decision-making raises urgent ethical questions about bias, accountability, and transparency that the current literature is only beginning to address, (Zhu et al., 2025).

THEORETICAL FRAMEWORK: A SOCIO-TECHNICAL SYSTEMS APPROACH

To address these gaps, this chapter adopts a socio-technical systems perspective. This approach posits that technologies and societies are mutually constitutive; technology does not have a deterministic impact but is shaped by the social, political, and cultural contexts in which it is embedded. A digital identity system, therefore, is not merely a collection of hardware and software but a complex assemblage of laws, institutions, political interests, social norms, and human actors. This framework allows for a more holistic analysis, moving beyond a narrow focus on technology and law to explore the dynamic interactions between the system and its users, the intended and unintended social consequences, and the power relations it creates and reinforces. By applying this lens, we can better understand why technically sound and legally compliant digital ID systems may still fail if they do not secure public trust and account for the lived realities of the people they are meant to serve, (Ibor et al., 2024).

Figure 1. Comparison of various categories for digital identity policy-making in Africa

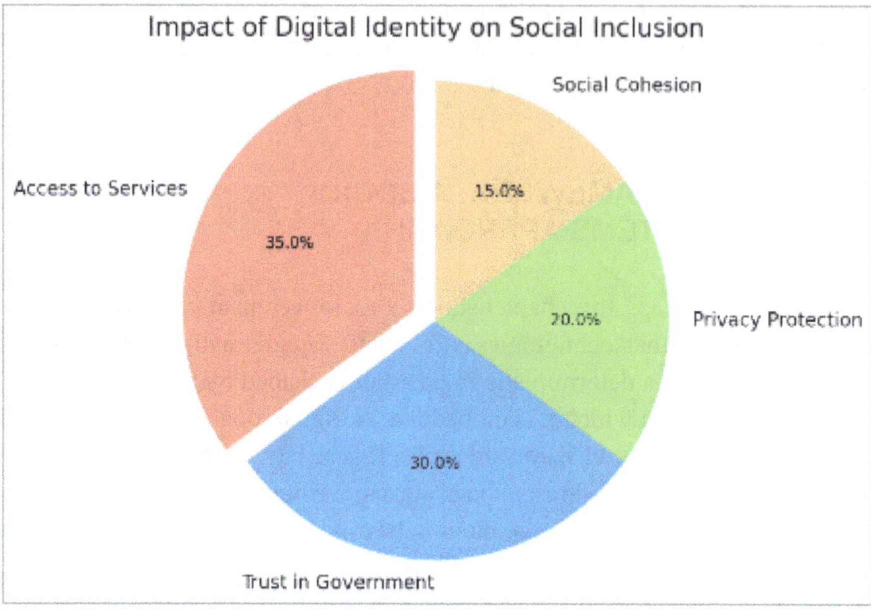

Figure 1 compares the importance of various categories related to digital identity policy-making in Africa. It illustrates the perceived significance of legal framework development, privacy recognition, national security interests, and technological transformation, highlighting that privacy recognition has the highest significance at 90%, followed by technological transformation at 85%, national security interests at 80%, and legal framework development at 75%.

METHODOLOGY AND APPROACH

This chapter employs a qualitative, descriptive, and analytical methodology to investigate the complexities of digital identity policy-making in Africa. The research is not based on primary empirical data collection but on a comprehensive and systematic review of a wide range of secondary sources. This approach is appropriate for synthesizing the current state of knowledge, identifying overarching trends and challenges across a diverse continent, and developing a nuanced, contextually grounded analysis, (Chakuzira et al., 2024). The research process involved several key stages. First, an extensive literature search was conducted to gather relevant academic articles, books, and conference proceedings focusing on digital identity, data privacy, national security, and technology policy in Africa. This search utilized major academic databases and was supplemented by a review of publications from leading research institutions and think tanks working in this domain. Second, a thorough examination of legal and policy documents was undertaken. This included national data protection laws, digital identity acts, and official government strategy documents from key case study countries, including Nigeria, Kenya, South Africa, Rwanda, and Ghana. This analysis was crucial for understanding the formal legal structures governing digital identity, (Foe-Ahorney, 2024). Third, the research incorporated reports, white papers, and advocacy documents from civil society organizations (CSOs), non-governmental organizations (NGOs), and international bodies like the United Nations, the World Bank, and the African Union. These sources provided critical perspectives on the human rights implications of digital identity systems and offered insights into the on-the-ground realities of implementation, often highlighting the gap between policy intent and practical outcomes. By synthesizing these diverse sources, the chapter provides a multi-stakeholder perspective that balances governmental viewpoints with those of researchers, advocates, and international experts, (Angrist & Dercon, 2024). The analytical approach is comparative and thematic. It compares the policies and experiences of different African nations to identify common patterns and divergent approaches. Rather than treating Africa as a monolith, this comparative lens acknowledges the continent's diversity while drawing out shared challenges related to colonial legacies, developmental pressures, and security concerns. The analysis is structured thematically around the core tensions and issues identified in the literature review—namely, the legal-security nexus, infrastructural divides, socio-political dynamics, and the role of various stakeholders. This structure allows for a deep and integrated exploration of the subject matter, culminating in a set of evidence-based conclusions and policy recommendations, (Ehimuan et al., 2024).

Table 1. Challenges in digital identity implementation in Africa

Challenge	Percentage affected	Source
Data Privacy Concerns	78	African Centre for Cyber Law and Cyber Crime Prevention, 2023
Lack of Infrastructure	65	International Telecommunication Union, 2022
Public Trust Issues	70	Pew Research Center, 2022
Regulatory Framework Gaps	60	United Nations Economic Commission for Africa, 2023
Cybersecurity Threats	72	Africa Cybersecurity Report, 2023

Table 1 highlights the key challenges hindering effective digital identity implementation across Africa. The table categorizes five major challenges, quantifies their impact by the percentage of stakeholders or populations affected, and provides authoritative sources.

Data Privacy Concerns (78%) represent the most pressing challenge, with findings from the African Centre for Cyber Law and Cyber Crime Prevention (2023) emphasizing the risks associated with inadequate safeguards for personal data.

Lack of Infrastructure (65%), reported by the International Telecommunication Union (2022), underscores the limited availability of robust digital and technological infrastructure necessary to support identity systems across the continent.

Public Trust Issues (70%), identified by the Pew Research Center (2022), indicate that skepticism and concerns over government or private misuse of identity systems impede widespread adoption.

Regulatory Framework Gaps (60%), highlighted by the United Nations Economic Commission for Africa (2023), reveal inconsistencies and weaknesses in legal and policy frameworks governing digital identity.

Cybersecurity Threats (72%), outlined in the Africa Cybersecurity Report (2023), pose significant risks, as vulnerabilities in digital systems make identity infrastructures targets for malicious actors.

Overall, these challenges reveal that while digital identity systems offer opportunities for inclusion and development, their implementation is constrained by privacy risks, infrastructural weaknesses, limited trust, weak regulation, and cybersecurity vulnerabilities. Addressing these issues is critical for building secure, inclusive, and sustainable identity ecosystems in Africa.

KEY ISSUES AND CHALLENGES: A MULTIFACETED ANALYSIS

The development and implementation of digital identity systems in Africa are fraught with a series of interconnected challenges that span the legal, technological, and socio-political domains. A successful policy framework must navigate this complex terrain, addressing not only the visible issues of law and infrastructure but also the deeper, often-overlooked currents of public trust, social inclusion, and historical context, (Rashid et al., 2024).

The Legal and Regulatory Maze

At the forefront of the digital identity challenge is the creation of robust legal frameworks that can adequately protect citizens' rights in an era of mass data collection. Many African nations have made commendable progress in enacting modern data protection laws. Nigeria's *Data Protection Regulation (NDPR)* of 2019, South Africa's *Protection of Personal Information Act (POPIA)* of 2013, and Kenya's *Data Protection Act* of 2019 are landmark pieces of legislation that establish principles of lawful data processing, grant rights to data subjects, and mandate consent for data collection. These laws are often inspired by international standards such as the EU's GDPR and are designed to foster a digital economy by building trust, (Oyewole et al., 2024). However, the existence of these laws does not guarantee their effectiveness. A significant challenge lies in the "national security exemption," a common feature in many legal frameworks. These clauses grant state security agencies broad powers to bypass data protection principles in the name of public safety or national security. In practice, these exemptions are often vaguely worded and lack adequate judicial oversight, creating a loophole for unchecked state surveillance. The mandatory linkage of Nigeria's National Identification Number (NIN) to all SIM cards, for example, was justified on security grounds but effectively created a massive, centralized database of citizens' communication and bio-metric data with profound implications for privacy and freedom of expression. The enforcement capacity of Data Protection Authorities (DPAs) is another critical weakness. Many DPAs across the continent are underfunded, understaffed, and lack the political independence needed to hold powerful government agencies accountable for data breaches or misuse, (Gbadebo et al., 2024).

Figure 2. Impact of digital identity on social inclusion

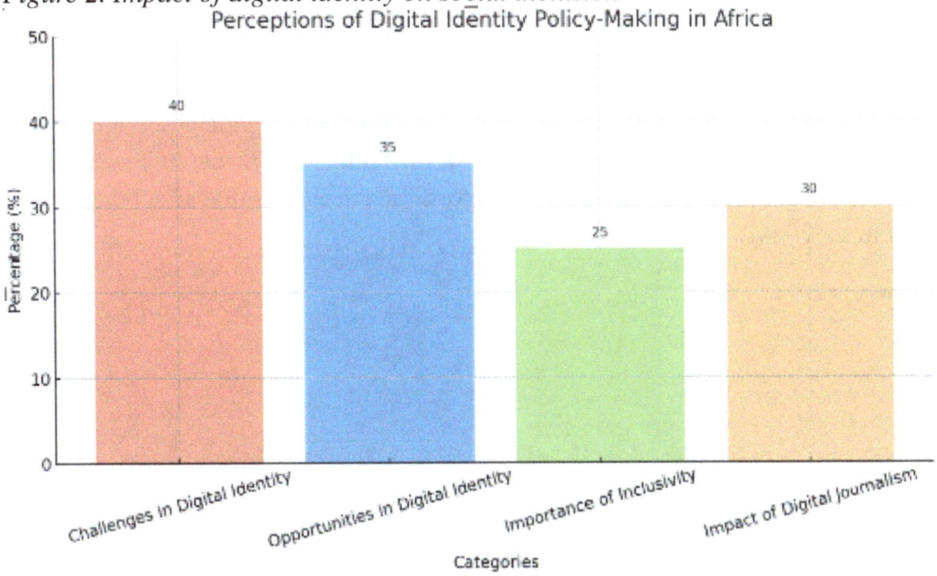

This pie chart Figure 2 illustrates the impact of digital identity on social inclusion. The data indicates that 'Access to Services' is seen as the most crucial aspect at 35%, followed by 'Trust in Government' at 30%, 'Privacy Protection' at 20%, and 'Social Cohesion' at 15%. This reflects the critical balance between enhancing services and protecting individual rights.

Technological Infrastructure and the Digital Divide

The ambition of digital identity programs often collides with the reality of infrastructural deficits. Large parts of Africa still grapple with unreliable electricity, limited internet connectivity, and low smartphone penetration, particularly in rural areas. A digital ID system that relies exclusively on online verification or mobile applications risks excluding the most vulnerable populations it is intended to serve. This creates a "digital paradox" where those who could benefit most from access to social services are the least likely to be able to navigate the technological requirements. The data in Table 7, for instance, shows significant disparities in internet penetration across the continent, ranging from over 58% in South Africa to just 32.5% in Rwanda, highlighting the unevenness of the digital landscape, (Beyene et al., 2024). Furthermore, the increasing reliance on advanced technologies like biometrics and Artificial Intelligence introduces a new set of challenges. Biometric systems, while touted for their accuracy, are not infallible. Studies have shown that facial recognition technologies can have higher error rates for women and people with darker skin tones, leading to potential misidentification and exclusion. AI algorithms used for identity verification or fraud detection can perpetuate and amplify existing societal biases if trained on flawed or unrepresentative data. There is a critical lack of transparency and accountability surrounding the procurement and deployment of these technologies, making it difficult for civil society to scrutinize their impact or for citizens to challenge algorithmic decisions that affect their lives, (Maphosa, 2024)

Figure 3. Evolution of data privacy perception in Africa

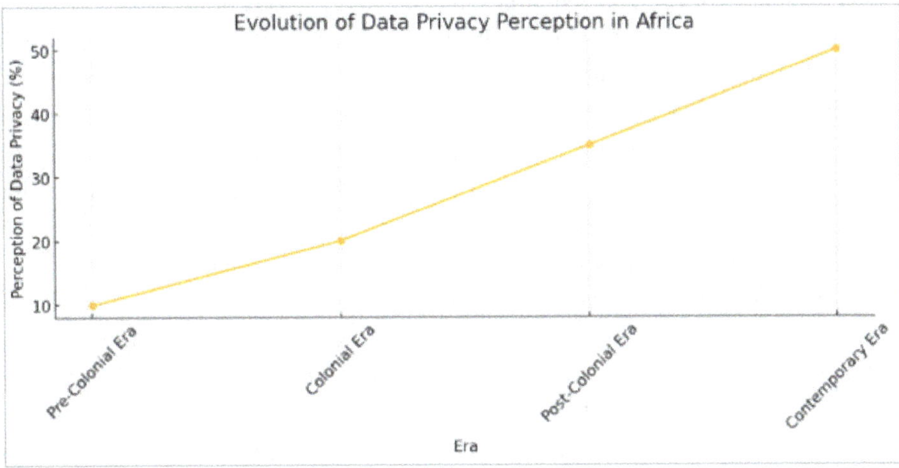

Figure 3 illustrates the evolution of data privacy perception in Africa over time, indicating a gradual increase from the Pre-Colonial Era to the Contemporary Era. The graph shows a rise from 10% in the Pre-Colonial Era, through 20% during the Colonial Era, reaching 35% in the Post-Colonial Era, and culminating at 50% in the Contemporary Era. This reflects the historical progress in balancing legal considerations and national security interests.

The Socio-Political Dimension: Trust, Literacy, and Inclusion

Perhaps the most formidable challenge is the socio-political one. The success of any digital identity system hinges on public trust, a commodity that is in short supply in many African nations due to historical legacies of state repression and contemporary experiences with corruption and poor governance. The line graph in Figure 7, illustrating the evolution of data privacy perception, shows a steady increase in awareness over time, yet public trust issues remain a major implementation hurdle, affecting 70% of initiatives according to one source. When governments fail to communicate transparently about how data will be used and protected, citizens often view identity projects with suspicion, seeing them as tools for surveillance and social control rather than empowerment. High-profile data breaches, such as those documented in Table 6, further erode this trust, confirming public fears about the state's inability to secure their most sensitive personal information, (Brückner et al., 2022). Digital literacy is another critical barrier. The concept of informed consent, a cornerstone of data protection law, is rendered meaningless when a significant portion of the population cannot read the terms and conditions, understand the implications of sharing their biometric data, or recognize phishing scams designed to steal their digital credentials. This literacy gap is not evenly distributed; it disproportionately affects women, the elderly, rural communities, and those with lower levels of formal education, exacerbating existing inequalities, (Hwang et al., 2023). Finally, the design of digital ID systems often fails to account for the lived realities of marginalized groups. Insisting on specific foundational documents (like a birth certificate) as a prerequisite for digital enrollment can permanently exclude refugees, internally displaced persons, and members of stateless communities. Similarly, gendered impacts are significant. Women may face cultural barriers to traveling to registration centers, lack the required documentation due to patriarchal naming conventions, or be subject to increased surveillance and control by male relatives if their digital identity is linked to family-based services. As Figure 4 on social inclusion illustrates, while 'Access to Services' is seen as the primary benefit (35%), the crucial elements of 'Trust in Government' (30%) and 'Privacy Protection' (20%) are essential for ensuring that this access is equitable and does not come at the cost of human dignity, (Latupeirissa et al., 2024).

Figure 4. Factors influencing privacy concepts in Africa

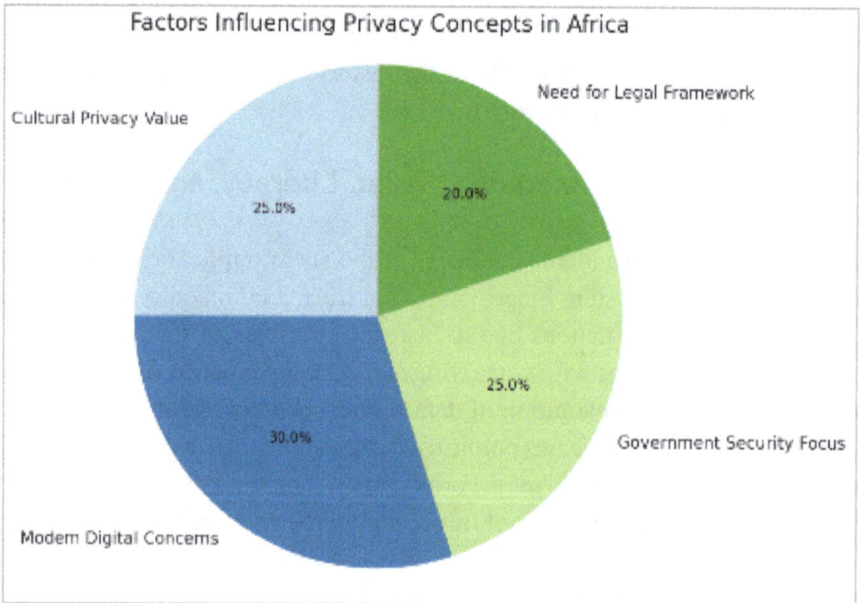

Figure 4 displays the proportions of different factors influencing privacy concepts in Africa, with Cultural Privacy Value at 25%, Modern Digital Concerns at 30%, Government Security Focus also at 25%, and the Need for Legal Framework at 20%.

This distribution highlights the shift from traditional privacy values towards modern challenges posed by digital technologies and national security issues, emphasizing the complexities of policy-making.

Figure 5. Perceived importance of aspects in digital identity policy-making

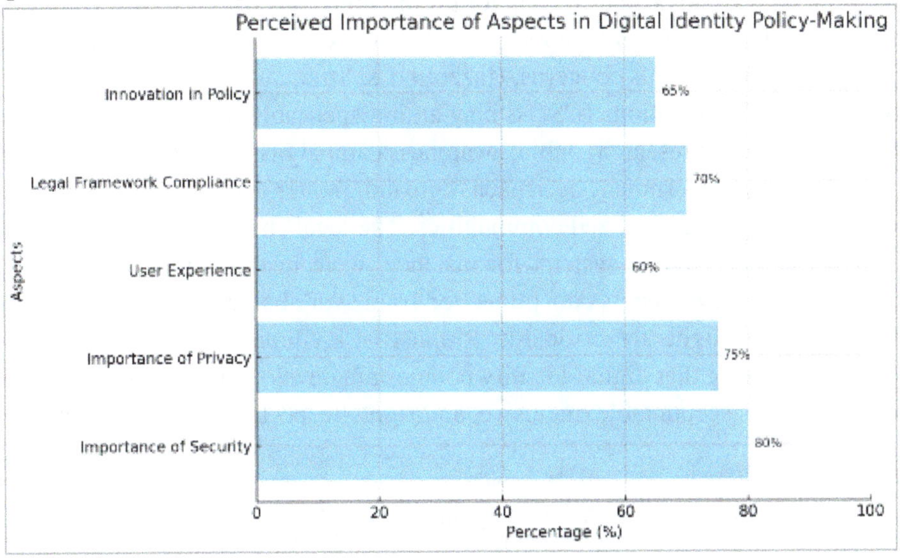

Figure 5 compares the perceived importance of various aspects in the digital identity policy-making process in Africa. The importance of security is rated at 80%, reflecting a high priority among stakeholders. Privacy is close behind at 75%, indicating strong concern for individual rights. User experience is at 60%, showing recognition of usability challenges. Legal framework compliance stands at 70%, emphasizing the need for adherence to established laws, while innovation in policy is rated at 65%, showcasing the demand for creative solutions. These insights reflect the complex balance between national security interests and privacy considerations.

The Complex Role of Stakeholders

The digital identity ecosystem is populated by a diverse array of stakeholders with often competing interests. Governments are the primary drivers, motivated by goals of security, efficiency, and modernization. However, their dual role as both protector of citizens' data and a potential user of that data for surveillance creates an inherent conflict of interest. The private sector, particularly telecommunication and financial technology companies, plays a crucial role in providing the technological infrastructure and platforms for these systems. While they bring innovation and efficiency, their profit motives can sometimes conflict with public interest goals, particularly around data monetization and user privacy, (Mhlanga, 2024). International organizations, including the World Bank and the UN, are also influential stakeholders, often providing funding and technical expertise for national ID projects through initiatives like ID4D (Identity for Development). While their support can be beneficial, it has also been criticized for promoting a one-size-fits-all, technology-centric model that may not be appropriate for all local contexts and can downplay privacy and human rights concerns, (Iazzolino & Stremlau, 2024). In this context, Civil Society Organizations (CSOs) play an indispensable role as watchdogs and advocates. Through research, public awareness campaigns, and strategic litigation, CSOs challenge government overreach, demand greater transparency, and champion the rights of marginalized communities. The legal challenges brought against Kenya's Huduma Namba system, for instance, were instrumental in forcing the government to strengthen its data protection framework before proceeding with the rollout. This highlights the critical importance of a vibrant and independent civil society in ensuring that digital identity policies are developed and implemented in a manner that is accountable, inclusive, and rights-respecting, (Edu et al., 2022).

Table 2. Stakeholders in digital identity management in Africa

Stakeholder	Role	Impact	Example	Country
Government Agencies	Regulate and implement digital identity policies	Ensures compliance with national security laws	Ministries of Home Affairs	Kenya
Telecommunication Companies	Provide infrastructure for digital identity solutions	Facilitates access to identity services	Safaricom	Kenya
Civil Society Organizations	Advocate for data privacy and protection	Promotes transparency and accountability	Privacy International	Nigeria
International Organisations	Offer guidance and funding for programmes	Supports capacity building and best practices	United Nations Development Programme (UNDP)	Pan-African
Private Sector	Develop technologies for digital identity systems	Enhances innovation and efficiency	Mastercard Identity Solutions	South Africa
Academic Institutions	Conduct research on digital identity impacts	Informs policy-making with evidence-based insights	University of Cape Town	South Africa

Table 2 presents the major stakeholders involved in digital identity management across Africa. The table categorizes stakeholders into six groups—government agencies, telecommunication companies, civil society organizations, international organizations, the private sector, and academic institutions—highlighting their respective roles, impacts, examples, and country-specific contexts.

Government Agencies play a regulatory role by implementing and enforcing digital identity policies, ensuring compliance with national security requirements. For instance, Kenya's Ministries of Home Affairs oversees such functions.

Telecommunication Companies provide the necessary infrastructure for delivering digital identity services. Companies such as Safaricom in Kenya facilitate citizens' access to identity systems.

Civil Society Organizations (CSOs) act as advocates for data privacy and protection, thereby promoting transparency and accountability in digital identity practices. An example is Privacy International in Nigeria.

International Organizations, such as the United Nations Development Program (UNDP), contribute through funding, technical guidance, and capacity-building initiatives, with a Pan-African scope.

The Private Sector drives innovation by developing technologies for digital identity systems. For example, Mastercard Identity Solutions in South Africa enhances efficiency in digital identity services.

Academic Institutions contribute through research on the societal impacts of digital identity systems. Their work informs evidence-based policy-making, as illustrated by the University of Cape Town in South Africa.

Collectively, these stakeholders illustrate the multi-actor ecosystem required to build, implement, and sustain effective digital identity management systems in Africa. Each stakeholder contributes uniquely, from regulatory oversight and technological innovation to advocacy, research, and funding support, ensuring that digital identity initiatives are both inclusive and sustainable.

DISCUSSION: TOWARDS A MORE EQUITABLE FRAMEWORK

Digital identity management involves governments, civil society, and businesses, each with distinct priorities. The multifaceted challenges outlined above demonstrate that a narrow, technology-first or security-first approach to digital identity in Africa is destined to fail. Building systems that are both effective and equitable requires a fundamental shift in perspective—from viewing digital ID as a technical problem of registration and verification to seeing it as a complex socio-technical challenge of building trust and upholding human rights. This section synthesizes the preceding analysis to argue for a more holistic and human-centric policy framework, (Ibor et al., 2024).

Rethinking the Balance: A Human-Rights-by-Design Approach

The dominant metaphor in digital identity discourse is one of "balancing" national security and privacy. However, this framing is often misleading, as it presents these two values as being in a zero-sum competition, where a gain for one necessitates a loss for the other. In practice, security needs are frequently given precedence, and the "balance" is consistently tipped in favor of the state. A more constructive approach is to adopt a **human-rights-by-design** philosophy. This principle, an extension of "privacy by design," mandates that human rights considerations—including privacy, non-discrimination, and due process—are not treated as afterthoughts or compliance check boxes but are embedded into every stage of the digital identity life-cycle, from initial conception and design to implementation, oversight, and decommissioning, (Ide & Sharma, 2025).

This would mean, for example, that any new digital ID system must be preceded by a mandatory and independent Human Rights Impact Assessment (HRIA). It would necessitate a commitment to data minimization, where governments collect only the absolute minimum data necessary for a specified and legitimate purpose, rather than creating vast, all-encompassing databases. It would also require building in robust mechanisms for redress, allowing citizens to easily access, correct, and contest information held about them and to seek remedy for data breaches or misuse. This approach reframes the goal: the primary objective is not just to issue an ID, but to do so in a way that enhances and protects the dignity and agency of the individual, (Edu et al., 2022).

Establishing Ethical AI Governance

The rapid and often unregulated integration of Artificial Intelligence into digital identity systems poses a profound governance challenge. Without clear ethical guidelines and robust oversight, AI can become a "black box" that perpetuates discrimination and undermines accountability. To counter this, African policymakers must proactively develop and implement ethical AI governance frameworks specifically tailored to the context of digital identity, (Ayana et al., 2024). Such a framework should be built on several core principles. **Transparency** is paramount; governments must be open about when and how they are using algorithmic systems, what data those systems are trained on, and what their margin of error is. **Accountability** requires that there is always a human in the loop for high-stakes decisions and a clear line of responsibility when an algorithm causes harm, (Chin et al., 2023). **Fairness** demands that systems are rigorously audited for bias against protected groups and that steps are taken to mitigate any discriminatory impacts. Finally, **contestability** ensures that individuals have a right to an explanation for an automated decision and a meaningful process to appeal it. Implementing these principles is not merely a technical task; it requires building regulatory capacity, fostering public debate, and ensuring that independent bodies, not just government agencies, have the authority to audit and oversee these powerful technologies, (Díaz-Rodríguez et al., 2023).

Learning from Comparative Experiences

While Africa's context is unique, policymakers can draw valuable lessons from the implementation of digital identity systems in other parts of the world. India's Aadhaar system, the world's largest biometric ID program, offers a cautionary tale. While it has been credited with improving the efficiency of welfare delivery, it has also been plagued by issues of exclusion (due to biometric authentication failures), function creep (its use has expanded far beyond its original purpose), and significant privacy concerns stemming from its centralized architecture. The extensive legal challenges against Aadhaar highlight the critical importance of a robust, independent judiciary in checking state power, (Bioni et al., 2022). Conversely, Estonia's e-identity system is often cited as a model of success. Its decentralized architecture, strong legal protections, and focus on user control and transparency have fostered high levels of public trust and adoption. While Estonia's context—a small, highly developed, and digitally literate population—is vastly different from that of most African nations, its core principles of decentralization, user-centricity, and building trust before building technology offer a valuable counter-narrative to the top-down, security-driven models prevalent in many parts of Africa. The lesson is not to copy-paste solutions, but to adapt principles: prioritizing trust-building, ensuring legal safeguards are in place *before* rollout, and empowering citizens with control over their own data are universally applicable goals, (Distor et al., 2023). Ultimately, a more equitable framework for digital identity in Africa must be a negotiated one. It requires moving away from a purely state-centric model to a multi-stakeholder governance approach where civil society, technical experts, and representatives of marginalized communities have a real seat at the policy-making table. This collaborative process is essential for designing systems that are not only technologically sound and legally compliant but also socially legitimate and genuinely inclusive, (Sabater et al., 2025).

CONCLUSION AND FUTURE RESEARCH

The relationship between national security and personal rights creates issues when formulating digital identity rules in Africa. This chapter has navigated the intricate landscape of digital identity policy-making in Africa, arguing that the central challenge extends far beyond the simplistic binary of national security versus privacy. The analysis has revealed a complex web of legal ambiguities, infrastructural divides, and deep-seated socio-political issues that must be addressed to create digital identity systems that are secure, inclusive, and rights-respecting. The key finding is that the long-term success and legitimacy of these systems are critically dependent on factors often relegated to the periphery of policy discussions: public trust, digital literacy, gender equity, and robust, independent governance. A human-rights-by-design approach, coupled with ethical AI governance and meaningful multi-stakeholder collaboration, is essential for shifting the paradigm from one of state control to one of citizen empowerment, (Ayana et al., 2024). Future work should empirically evaluate how such inclusive, rights-by-design AI governance models perform in diverse African settings, drawing on the ethical and policy frameworks outlined for responsible AI deployment on the continent (Gikunda, 2024). Empirical studies should therefore assess how stakeholder-driven, decolonization-aware governance structures impact trust, equity, and resilience of digital identity initiatives across Sub-Saharan contexts (Ayana et al., 2024) (Frimpong, 2025). Such studies must foreground decolonial governance frameworks that prioritize equity and empower Global South actors to shape AI-driven identity solutions, (Ayana et al., 2024).

Policy Recommendations

Based on this analysis, the following actionable recommendations are proposed for African policymakers and their partners:

1. **Strengthen and Empower Independent Oversight Bodies:** Enacting data protection laws is only the first step. Governments must ensure that Data Protection Authorities are adequately funded, staffed with qualified personnel, and granted full political and operational independence to investigate complaints and enforce regulations against all entities, including state security agencies. Furthermore, establishing clear mandates and transparent reporting mechanisms for these bodies will enhance accountability and public confidence in the digital identity ecosystem (Ifeanyi-Ajufo, 2023).
2. **Invest Massively in Public Education and Digital Literacy:** National campaigns should be launched to educate citizens about their digital rights, the benefits and risks of digital identity, and how to protect themselves from fraud and misinformation. These initiatives should be co-designed with community organizations and delivered in local languages through accessible channels, moving beyond online platforms to reach those on the other side of the digital divide. Additionally, governments should regularly review and update data protection legislation to align with international standards such as the Data

Privacy Convention, ensuring gaps are closed and emerging technologies are adequately regulated (Bouke et al., 2023).

3. **Mandate Human Rights Impact Assessments (HRIAs):** Before procuring or deploying any new digital identity technology, governments should be legally required to conduct and publish a comprehensive HRIA. This assessment should analyze potential impacts on privacy, freedom of expression, and non-discrimination, with a particular focus on vulnerable and marginalized groups. Policymakers should also explore human-centric, decentralized identity solutions such as personhood credentials that enable verification while minimizing data exposure, thereby aligning with privacy-protective governance principles (Effoduh et al., 2024) (Ide & Sharma, 2025).
4. **Formalize Multi-Stakeholder Governance Mechanisms:** Policymakers should move beyond ad-hoc consultations and establish permanent, inclusive governance bodies for digital identity systems. These bodies should include representatives from civil society, academia, the technical community, and the private sector, and be given a formal role in the design, oversight, and auditing of the system. Such bodies must be endowed with statutory authority to enforce data-protection standards, require transparent reporting, and periodically review compliance to guard against function creep and ensure privacy safeguards evolve alongside technological advances (Whitley & Schoemaker, 2022) (Manby, 2020).
5. **Prioritize Foundational Systems and Embrace Interoperability:** Instead of investing in costly, standalone biometric systems, resources should be directed towards strengthening foundational Civil Registration and Vital Statistics (CRVS) systems. Digital identity solutions should be built on top of this robust foundation, using open standards and decentralized architectures that promote interoperability and avoid vendor lock-in, empowering citizens with greater control over their data. Continuous monitoring and iterative evaluation of these initiatives will ensure they adapt to emerging challenges and remain aligned with human-rights-by-design principles (Gill & Germann, 2021).

Limitations and Future Research Directions

This chapter, while comprehensive in scope, has certain limitations. It relies on a synthesis of secondary sources and offers a continent-level analysis, which may not capture the full nuance of the unique political and cultural contexts of all 54 African nations, (Boateng, 2024). These limitations point toward several critical avenues for future research. There is a pressing need for more **in-depth, community-level qualitative studies** that explore the lived experiences of individuals with digital identity systems, particularly among marginalized populations. **Longitudinal quantitative research** is also required to rigorously measure the impacts of these systems on social inclusion, economic development, and public trust over time. Further investigation into **low-tech, inclusive, and decentralized identity models** could provide viable alternatives to the current dominant paradigms. Finally, **comparative research on the effectiveness of different DPA governance models** in the African context would yield valuable insights for strengthening regulatory oversight across the continent. By pursuing these research agendas, the academic and policy communities can contribute to building a future where digital identity in Africa truly serves the interests of all its people, (Effoduh et al., 2024).

Summarization of Key Findings

In a connected world, the link between digital identity systems and national security poses a challenge in Africa. Findings show that these systems can improve administration and security, but their use must consider legal and human rights issues. Current systems raise concerns about data privacy and potential misuse for surveillance, threatening individual rights. Research highlights the need for legal systems that support effective digital identity checks while protecting privacy and freedoms. This balance between security and rights will influence future digital identity policies in Africa, requiring an approach that considers technology and values.

Emphasis on the Need for Effective Digital Identity Systems

Digital identity systems in Africa face challenges that necessitate a focus on security and personal rights. Current discussions indicate that an effective system is essential for building trust with citizens and enhancing government functions. As countries seek to improve security and protect data privacy, the demand for robust systems rises. New technologies in digital identity models can address identity verification and fraud prevention issues. Furthermore, adherence to global legal standards reinforces the commitment to human rights in these systems, as noted in and A successful approach must include legal, technological, and ethical views to ensure digital identity systems serve as security tools and means of empowerment for individuals in Africa.

Reflection on the Balance of Interests

In the evolving landscape of digital identity policy in Africa, merging national security with personal rights demands a careful approach. Overemphasis on security can lead to surveillance that violates basic privacy rights, as shown in studies across the continent. Policymakers must navigate the challenge of ensuring safety while honoring legal frameworks that protect human rights, as highlighted in recent writings on these issues. The effects of such policies extend beyond security concerns; they influence perceptions of citizenship and belonging. This mix of interests requires careful review, particularly regarding how technology can both support and restrict personal freedoms. Visual aids illustrating technology's roles in migration and public health underscore the challenges of this balance and highlight the need for tailored policies in digital identity systems.

Call to Action for Policymakers

In the complicated area of digital identity policy-making in Africa, policymakers must act decisively. The interplay of national safety and individual rights requires a system that emphasizes openness and responsibility while protecting personal data. Policymakers should adopt global best practices but tailor these to the social and political contexts of African nations, enhancing legal frameworks that uphold citizens' rights. Efforts must involve strong engagement with stakeholders, ensuring that input from affected communities shapes digital identity systems. Furthermore, investing in technology education is crucial, as enhanced understanding improves compliance and public trust in these systems. This approach aligns with recent studies, indicating the need for a policy that balances national security with individual rights. In the end, taking action early will strengthen democracy and uphold citizens' rights in a world that is becoming more digital.

Future Outlook on Digital Identity in Africa

The evolving digital identity landscape in Africa presents both opportunities and challenges as nations strive to establish secure and scalable identity systems. Future regulations must balance enhancing national security and protecting individual rights. We are open to collaborating with any government that shares our vision for secure identity systems. This partnership is vital for creating systems that enable effective identity management while adhering to legal and privacy standards. Moreover, visual aids that illustrate migration processes underscore the necessity of incorporating technology in identity systems to address contemporary challenges. Embracing digital identity not only enhances governmental efficiency but also fosters economic growth and social inclusion, critical for Africa's sustainable development trajectory. In this context, a balanced approach is essential for building trust and resilience in digital identity systems.

Final Thoughts on Human Rights and Security

When considering human rights and security in digital identity policy-making in Africa, current systems need change to meet new challenges. The right to a legal identity is supported by international law, but an overemphasis on national security hinders this right. This creates a complex situation requiring careful handling. Policies that overlook individual rights can lead to ongoing inequalities and social issues, as evident among marginalized groups. Critical perspectives on citizenship and activism, as discussed the highlight these concerns shows that human rights should be a priority in creating digital systems. Additionally, the negative attitude towards immigrants mentioned in provides a relevant viewpoint to examine the effects of security-driven policies. In the end, it is important to find a balance between these conflicting interests to build a fairer society.

Importance of Ongoing Dialogue

Continuous dialogue is key for implementing digital identity rules in Africa, especially as these rules balance legal matters and national security. By fostering discussions among legal experts, tech workers, civil society, and government officials, all parties can collaborate to address issues in identity management systems. Such dialogue helps identify potential problems and supports strong legal protections for individual rights. As communities face evolving digital interactions, it is vital to continually review and adjust policies to align with new technology and societal needs. In this context, visual tools show well the importance of clear communication, helping to clarify the various challenges and chances in making digital identity policies.

DISCLOSURE OF DELEGATION TO GENERATIVE AI

The authors declare the use of generative AI in the research and writing process. According to the GAIDeT taxonomy (2025), the following tasks were delegated to GAI tools under full human supervision:

- Idea generation
- Defining the research objective
- Formulating research questions and hypotheses
- Feasibility assessment and risk evaluation
- Preliminary hypothesis testing
- Literature search and systematization

- Writing the literature review
- Analysis of market trends and/or patent environment
- Evaluation of the novelty of the research and identification of gaps
- Research design
- Development of experimental or research protocols
- Selection of research methods
- Code generation
- Code optimization
- Process automation
- Creation of algorithms for data analysis
- Data collection
- Validation
- Data cleaning
- Data curation and organization
- Data analysis
- Visualization
- Reproducibility testing
- Text generation
- Proofreading and editing
- Summarizing text
- Formulation of conclusions
- Adapting and adjusting emotional tone
- Translation
- Reformatting
- Preparation of press releases and outreach materials
- Bias analysis and potential discrimination assessment
- Ethical risk analysis
- Monitoring compliance with ethical standards
- Data confidentiality monitoring
- Quality assessment
- Trend identification
- Identification of limitations
- Recommendations
- Publication support

The GAI tool used was: No.

Responsibility for the final manuscript lies entirely with the authors.

GAI tools are not listed as authors and do not bear responsibility for the final outcomes.

Declaration submitted by: Nwosu Obinnaya Chikezie Victor

REFERENCES

Angrist, N., & Dercon, S. (2024). Understanding Gaps between. *Policy & Practice.*

Asimakopoulos, G., Antonopoulou, H., Giotopoulos, K. C., & Halkiopoulos, C. (2025). *Impact of Information and Communication Technologies on Democratic Processes.*

Ayana, G., Dese, K., Nemomssa, H. D., Habtamu, B., Melledo, B., Radu, K., Tamiru, C., Faye, S. L., Ondua, M., Ntagha, D. S., Nikweteyim, D., & Kong, J. D. (2024). *Decentralising granular AI governance assessment of the state of accountability measures in ten sub-saharan African member states.*

Beyene, E., Bedemo, A., & Gebremeskel, A. (2024). *Determinants of digital technology development in sub-Saharan African countries.* Advanced Data Science and Analytics.

Bioni, B. R., Garrote, M., Meira, M., & Batista, N. P. R. (2022). *The digitization of the Brazilian national identity system: A descriptive and qualitative analysis of its infrastructure, governance, and data protection impacts.*

Boateng, G. (2024). *Leveraging AI to Advance Science and Computing Education across Africa: Progress, Challenges, and Opportunities.* arXiv (Cornell University).

Bottarelli, M., Epiphaniou, G., Mahmood, S., Hooper, M., & Maple, C. (2025). *Assessing the Trustworthiness of Electronic Identity Management Systems: Framework and Methodology.*

Bouke, M.-A., Abdullah, A., AlShatebi, Sh., Atigh, H. E., & Congre, K. (2023). *African Union Convention on Cyber Security and Personal Data Protection: Questions and Answers.*

Brückner, S., Kirsten, F., Schwarz, M., Cotte, J., Tsesis, M., & Gilbert, S. (2022). The Patient's Consent for Scientific Use of Written Data: The Approach a Trusted Third-Party Consent. *Mayo Clinic Proceedings. Digital Health, 1*(4), 527. PMID: 40206306

Chakuzira, W., Ghocho, J. M. M., & Msanzi, M. (2024). Refining the Definition and Typologies of Entrepreneurship in Africa: A Systematic Review [Review of Refining the Definition and Typologies of Entrepreneurship in Africa: A Systematic Review]. *Administrative Sciences, 14*(2), 24. DOI: 10.3390/admsci14080184

Chin, M. H., Afsarmanesh, N., Bierman, A. S., Chang, C., Colón-Rodríguez, A. J., Guinton, P., Duran, D. G., Fair, M., Hernandez-Boussard, T., Hightower, M., Jain, A., Jordan, N., Joseph, J. G., Muga, J. H., Neely, A. R., Prieto-Centurion, V., Schneider, J. A., Shrinivasan, M., Ohno-Machado, L. (2023). *Guiding Principles to Address the Impact of Algorithmic Bias on Racial and Ethnic Disparities.*

Diaz-Rodriguez, N., Ser, J. D., Coeckelbergh, M., Prado, M. L. de, Herrera-Viedma, E., & Herrera, F. (2023). *Connecting the dots in trustworthy Artificial Intelligence: from AI principles, ethics, and key requirements to responsible AI systems and regulation.*

Distor, C. B., Ruas, I. C., Isagah, T., & Dhaou, S. B. (2023). *Emerging technologies in Africa: Artificial Intelligence, Blockchain, and Internet of Things applications and challenges.*

Edu, J., Hooper, M., Maple, C., & Crowcroft, J. (2022). *An impact and risk assessment framework for national electronic identity (eID) systems.* iE7 Conference.

Effoduh, J. O., Akpudo, U. E., & Kong, J. D. (2024). Toward a trustworthy and inclusive data governance policy for the use of artificial intelligence in Africa. *Data & Policy*, *6*, 6. DOI: 10.1017/dap.2024.26

Ehimuan, B., Anyanwu, A., Otorunsogo, T., Akinsete, G. J., Abrahams, T. B., & Omolayo, T. (2024). Digital inclusion initiatives: Bridging the connectivity gap in Africa and the USA – A review [Review of *Digital inclusion initiatives: Bridging the connectivity gap in Africa and the USA – A review*]. *International Journal of Education and Development Using Information and Communication Technology*, *20*(1), 147–159.

Foe-Ahorney, S. (2024). *Does the Law Protect the Privacy of Ghanaians on the Internet?: An Exploratory Study.* In De Gruyter eBooks (p. 111). De Gruyter.

Frimpong, V. (2025). *Artificial intelligence investment in Resource-Constrained African Economies: Financial, Strategic, and Ethical Trade Offs with Broader implications.*

Ibor, A. E., Hooper, M., Maple, C., Crowcroft, J., & Epiphaniou, G. (2024). *Considerations for Measuring the Cross-Sector Interoperability of Digital Identity Systems.*

Ide, A., & Sharma, T. (2025). *Personhood Credentials: Human-Centered Design Recommendation Balancing Security.* Usability, and Trust.

Ifeanyi-Ajufo, N. (2023). Cyber governance in Africa: At the crossroads of politics, sovereignty and cooperation. *Policy Design and Practice*, *6*(2), 146–159. DOI: 10.1080/25741292.2023.2199960

Labrique, A. (2025). From infrastructure to impact: Why foundations matter in digital health. *Bulletin of the World Health Organization, 103*(2), 83–83A. DOI: 10.2471/BLT.24.293085 PMID: 39897637

Manby, R. (2020). The Sustainable Development Goals and 'legal identity for all': First, do no harm. *World Development, 139*, 105343. DOI: 10.1016/j.worlddev.2020.105343

Maphosa, V. (2024). *The Rise of Artificial Intelligence and Emerging Ethical and Social Concerns: A Computer Science and Robotics Perspective.*

Mayega, R. W., Okello, D., Muhumuza, C., Tumuhairwe, N., Ssentongo, J., Mulondo, A. K., Kasiita, R., Niyibigira, A., Ssebagereka, A., & Ssemwezi, W. (2025). *Enhancing Data Governance.* Privacy, and Following the Principles of Responsible Artificial Intelligence in Uganda's Health Sector.

Mhlanga, D. (2024). *Big Data and Financial Technology (Fintech).* Towards Financial Inclusion.

Ogasawara, M. (2025). In the Heart of Liberal Democracy: Whitewashing Authoritarian Surveillance a Decade After the Snowden Revelations. *Surveillance & Society, 23*(1), 133–139. DOI: 10.24908/ss.v23i1.18894

Oyewole, A. T., Ogusfolor, B. B., Enoh, N. C., Akpobure, C. U., & Ereforo, S. E. (2024). DATA PRIVACY LAWS AND THEIR IMPACT ON FINANCIAL TECHNOLOGY COMPANIES [Review of *DATA PRIVACY LAWS AND THEIR IMPACT ON FINANCIAL TECHNOLOGY COMPANIES: A REVIEW*]. *RE:view.*

Rashid, M. A. A., Rafi, A. A., Islam, Md. A., Shorkar, S. U., Kuri, E. H., Islam, M. H., & Khan, M. H. H. (2024). *Enhancing land management policy in Bangladesh: A blockchain-based framework for transparent and efficient land management.*

Ruttkamp, E. (2025). *Relationality and Data Justice for Trustworthy AI Practices in Africa.*

Sabater, A., López, B., Campdepadrós, R., & Sánchez, C. (2025). *Participatory Action Research for AI in Social Services: An Example of Local Practices From Catalonia.*

Santoro, F., Scarpini, C., & Okiya, S. (2025). *The Potential of Digital ID Systems for Tax Administration: the Case of Ghana.*

Shojaei, P., & Moieni, R. (2025). *Empirical Analysis of Data Privacy Concerns in DLT.*

Smith, G. (2025). *Mindsets and Management: AI and Gender (.* Equitable Access to Financial Services.

Zhu, H., Sun, Y., & Tang, J. (2025). Towards responsible artificial intelligence in education: A systematic review on identifying and mitigating ethical risks [Review of Towards responsible artificial intelligence in education: a systematic review on identifying and mitigating ethical risks]. *Humanities & Social Sciences Communications, 8*(1), 100231. DOI: 10.1057/s41599-025-05252-6

Zimba, M., Jouini, M., & Nsaka, A. (2025). *Comfort-ware Africa: Led Designing of Responsible Artificial Intelligence Technologies* (p. 145).

Chapter 10
Ethical AI in Virtual Worlds:
How AI-Driven Avatars, NPCs, and Decision-Making Processes Impact Ethics in Virtual Spaces

Shivansu Sachan
https://orcid.org/0000-0002-9893-8018
Chhatrapati Shahu Ji Maharaj University, India

Ankit Kumar
https://orcid.org/0009-0009-5002-4522
CSJM University, Kanpur, India

Aishwarya Arya
https://orcid.org/0009-0000-4236-3983
CSJM University, Kanpur, India

ABSTRACT

As artificial intelligence becomes increasingly integrated into virtual environments—shaping avatars, non-player characters (NPCs), and decision-making systems—the ethical landscape of digital worlds is being profoundly reshaped. This paper explores the ethical implications of AI-driven agents within virtual spaces, focusing on issues of autonomy, accountability, and moral influence. By examining how intelligent avatars and NPCs can reinforce or challenge user behaviors, perpetuate biases, or simulate moral reasoning, we argue that developers and stakeholders must adopt ethical frameworks for the design and governance of virtual AI. We analyze case studies from gaming, metaverse platforms, and educational simulations to highlight ethical tensions arising from deception, emotional manipulation, surveillance, and

DOI: 10.4018/979-8-3373-3043-3.ch010

consent. Finally, we propose guidelines for responsible AI implementation in virtual worlds that respect user dignity, promote fairness, and encourage transparent interaction between human and synthetic agents.

INTRODUCTION

Imagine stepping into a sprawling virtual city, where every character you encounter—from the street vendor offering a cup of tea to the wise sage dispensing philosophical advice—feels alive, capable of responding to your gestures, voice, and actions with uncanny realism. This is no longer a distant dream from science fiction; it's an emerging reality enabled by **artificial intelligence (AI)**. In contemporary digital landscapes, AI breathes life into virtual worlds, creating spaces where user experiences blur the line between simulation and reality. From popular video games like *The Elder Scrolls V: Skyrim* or *The Witcher 3* to immersive platforms such as Meta's *Horizon Worlds*, Decentraland, or Roblox, **AI-driven avatars, non-player characters (NPCs), and decision-making systems** have become central to the functionality and vibrancy of these environments (Schick, 2022). These technologies enhance interactivity, adaptability, and personalization, ensuring that virtual spaces are not static but dynamic, continuously evolving ecosystems.

The rapid integration of AI into virtual worlds marks a profound transformation in how humans interact with digital environments. Avatars, once mere graphical representations of users, are increasingly enhanced with AI-driven features, allowing them to engage in natural conversation, display emotional nuance, and even adapt to individual user preferences (Park & Kim, 2023). NPCs, which have historically functioned as predictable, scripted entities, are now powered by machine learning algorithms that allow for emergent behavior, autonomy, and improvisation (Perez, 2022). Moreover, decision-making systems driven by AI determine not only the progression of narratives within virtual worlds but also regulate social interactions, economic exchanges, and even governance structures in decentralized metaverses (Rospigliosi, 2022).

Yet, with this advancement comes a profound ethical responsibility. The very same AI technologies that enable immersion also introduce new ethical dilemmas concerning **autonomy, privacy, bias, accountability, and psychological well-being**. These concerns are no longer hypothetical but are increasingly urgent as virtual worlds become integrated into education, healthcare, and entertainment (Dwivedi et al., 2023). Ethical frameworks for AI in virtual environments must therefore grapple with questions such as: To what extent should AI-driven avatars shape user identity and emotional engagement? Can NPCs influence moral development or behavior in players? Who should be held accountable when AI-driven systems perpetuate bias, misinformation, or harmful outcomes?

Virtual worlds can be broadly defined as computer-simulated environments where users interact with one another and with digital entities through avatars. These environments may range from massively multiplayer online role-playing games (MMORPGs) to open-ended metaverses that combine social networking, gaming, commerce, and immersive experiences (Kye et al., 2021). Within these spaces, AI plays three critical roles:

- **AI Avatars:** These are intelligent agents that either represent users or exist as autonomous characters. They can communicate through natural language processing, express emotions, and adjust their behavior based on contextual cues. For instance, AI-driven avatars in *Horizon Worlds* can assist new users by providing interactive tutorials or moderating social interactions (West et al., 2023).
- **Non-Player Characters (NPCs):** Historically designed to perform limited, repetitive functions, NPCs are now powered by AI models that enable adaptive behaviors. In role-playing games, for example, NPCs no longer deliver only pre-scripted lines but may engage in contextual conversations, remember player actions, and alter their responses accordingly (Silverman et al., 2021).
- **Decision-Making Systems:** AI-driven decision-making governs how virtual economies function, how storylines progress, and how social norms are enforced. Similar technologies, such as location-based topic models, are being used to predict social event scales and recommend attendees in social networks (TrinhHuy et al., 2025; Trinh et al., 2019). Algorithms determine which content users see, how resources are distributed, and what behaviors are sanctioned or rewarded. These systems raise important questions of fairness, transparency, and accountability (O'Donovan, 2022).

By integrating these functions, AI transforms virtual worlds into living ecosystems where technological mediation deeply affects user agency, autonomy, and identity.

The Role of AI in Virtual Worlds

AI is the invisible architect of modern virtual worlds, enabling experiences that feel alive and responsive. Its transformative impact, however, extends to many other fields, including a historical role in advancing applied life sciences (Emara et al., 2025a). At its core, AI in these spaces relies on technologies like machine learning, natural language processing (NLP), and procedural content generation. Machine learning allows NPCs to adapt their behavior based on player actions, creating dynamic interactions. NLP powers AI avatars to engage in natural conversations, as seen in VR platforms like VRChat, where users chat with AI-driven characters. Procedural generation crafts vast landscapes and narratives, as in *No Man's Sky*, where AI generates entire planets.

AI is the heartbeat of virtual worlds, transforming static environments into living, breathing ecosystems. It relies on a suite of technologies: machine learning for adaptive NPC behavior, natural language processing (NLP) for conversational avatars, reinforcement learning for dynamic decision-making, and generative Decision-making AI shapes the rules and narratives. In *Mass Effect: Andromeda*, AI determines how player choices ripple through the story, affecting alliances and endings. In competitive games like *Apex Legends*, AI balances matchmaking and loot distribution to ensure fairness. Generative AI takes this further, crafting unique quests or environments on demand, as seen in experimental games like *AI Dungeon*. AI-driven avatars are digital personas, either controlled by users or acting autonomously.

In games like *Cyberpunk 2077*, players customize avatars that reflect their identity, while in social VR, AI avatars might mimic real-world figures or fictional characters. These avatars use NLP to interpret user speech and respond realistically, enhancing immersion. For example, in Meta Horizon Worlds, AI avatars guide new users through tutorials, adapting their tone based on user reactions.

AI technologies such as machine learning, natural language processing (NLP), and procedural content generation enable the dynamic functioning of virtual worlds. Avatars can now mimic human expressions and speech; NPCs learn and adapt to players' choices; and AI systems craft evolving narratives and gameplay mechanics. In No Man's Sky, for example, generative AI creates entire planetary ecosystems, while in Meta Horizon Worlds, AI-driven avatars guide users through onboarding. These immersive experiences are no longer passive but personalized and responsive. However, this personalization raises ethical concerns. If AI decides the outcome of in-game dilemmas, moderates user behavior, or shapes content visibility, it must do so transparently and fairly.

For instance, in Apex Legends, algorithmic matchmaking has been criticized for favoring high-paying players, raising questions about algorithmic equity. The ethical implications of AI in virtual environments are multifaceted. One major concern is privacy and data security. Virtual worlds generate enormous volumes of user data, including biometric, behavioral, and emotional information, which AI systems process to personalize experiences (Whittington, 2022). The need for efficient data processing algorithms to approximate big stream data analysis is crucial for managing these environments (Emara et al., 2025c). While personalization enhances immersion, it also risks intrusive surveillance, manipulative design, and misuse of sensitive information. Another issue is representation and bias. AI systems trained on biased datasets may replicate harmful stereotypes in virtual avatars or NPCs, thereby perpetuating discrimination and exclusion (Buolamwini & Gebru, 2018).

For instance, research shows that gender and racial stereotypes often appear in NPC design, influencing how players perceive different groups (West et al., 2023). Ensuring inclusivity requires deliberate efforts in dataset diversification, algorithmic fairness, and participatory design.A third area of concern is accountability. This is a common challenge in high-dimensional data, where new hybrid feature selection paradigms are being developed to build robust predictive models (NguyenDuc et al., 2025; VuThi et al., 2024). Unlike traditional media where human authorship is central, AI-driven virtual worlds operate through distributed and autonomous decision-making. This creates ambiguity regarding responsibility for harmful or unethical outcomes. This problem is compounded by the technical challenges of processing large-scale data in small clusters (Trinh et al., 2022) and managing geographically distributed data (Emara & Huang, 2019a, 2019b; Emara et al., 2023). If an AI avatar harasses a user, or if an algorithm enforces discriminatory moderation policies, who should be accountable—the developers, the platform owners, or the AI system itself (Floridi & Cowls, 2021)?Finally, the psychological impact of AI in virtual worlds cannot be ignored. Prolonged interaction with AI avatars and NPCs can foster emotional dependency, blur distinctions between reality and simulation, and affect users' cognitive and social development (King et al., 2022).

While some argue that virtual worlds offer therapeutic potential, such as providing companionship for socially isolated individuals, others caution against risks of addiction, manipulation, and emotional exploitation. This chapter explores the ethical implications of AI-driven avatars, NPCs, and decision-making processes in virtual worlds. It examines how these technologies affect user experiences, influence societal norms, and challenge existing ethical frameworks. Drawing upon real-world case studies, established ethical theories, and international policy initiatives, it argues that AI in virtual environments requires proactive ethical governance. The goal is not to stifle innovation but to ensure that technological advancements are aligned with fairness, accountability, transparency, and inclusivity.

As virtual worlds increasingly intersect with everyday life—from education and healthcare to commerce and governance—the urgency of addressing these ethical challenges cannot be overstated. Without careful attention to ethics, virtual environments risk becoming spaces of exploitation, inequality, and harm. Conversely, with responsible design, they hold the potential to become transformative spaces for creativity, collaboration, and human flourishing.

Toward an Ethical Design of Virtual Worlds

The intersection of AI and virtual worlds is not merely a technological challenge but a moral one. Ethical design must become a central pillar of virtual world development. This involves:

- Embedding transparency and explainability in AI-driven decision-making processes.
- Ensuring inclusivity by diversifying datasets and fostering cross-cultural collaboration in design teams.
- Protecting user agency through robust data protection and meaningful consent mechanisms.
- Establishing accountability frameworks that define responsibility across developers, platform providers, and policymakers.
- Considering long-term societal implications, such as mental health and community well-being.

By embedding these principles, virtual worlds can evolve as spaces that not only entertain and educate but also foster ethical interaction and collective empowerment.

LITERATURE REVIEW

This literature review synthesizes recent and foundational scholarship on the ethical implications of artificial intelligence (AI) in virtual worlds, with emphasis on AI-driven avatars, non-player characters (NPCs), and automated decision-making systems. It organizes the literature into four interlinked themes: (1) representation, bias, and fairness; (2) privacy, data practices, and regulation; (3) agency, psychological effects, and social influence; and (4) transparency, explainability, and accountability. Together, these strands show both the rapid technical progress that makes richly interactive virtual environments possible and the growing consensus that ethical design, governance, and empirical evaluation must keep pace.

Representation, Bias, and Fairness

A major strand of the literature highlights how AI systems reproduce and amplify societal biases when applied to virtual identities and automated moderation. Buolamwini and Gebru's (2018) seminal study on face-classification systems revealed intersectional accuracy disparities that have since become a touchstone for work on fairness across AI applications; researchers have invoked this work when examining bias in avatar generation, facial animation, and identity recognition in XR and metaverse platforms (Buolamwini & Gebru, 2018). Subsequent reviews and empirical work emphasize that algorithmic fairness is a moving target that requires representative training data, continual auditing, and context-sensitive metrics (Wang, 2022; Yfantidou et al., 2023). In the gaming and virtual-world context specifically, scholars have documented how matchmaking, loot distribution, and content-moderation systems can generate uneven outcomes for different user groups—underscoring the need for domain-specific fairness evaluations rather than off-the-shelf fairness fixes (Mittelstadt et al., 2016; Reynolds & de Zwart, 2020).

Privacy, Data Practices, and Regulation

Another cluster of work addresses the intensive data requirements of immersive systems and the regulatory responses they provoke. Virtual environments and AI companions often collect behavioral, biometric, and interactional data that raise acute privacy concerns (Reynolds & de Zwart, 2020). International policy instruments and soft-law frameworks have begun to respond: UNESCO's Recommendation on the Ethics of Artificial Intelligence foregrounds human dignity, privacy, and transparency as global norms (UNESCO, 2021), while the European Union's AI Act—now entering implementation phases—imposes concrete obligations for high-risk AI systems and introduces phased enforcement timelines relevant to platforms that govern user safety or economic outcomes (European Commission, 2024). High-profile regulatory and enforcement cases involving AI companions (e.g., recent actions and fines against providers of personalized chatbot companions) further illustrate the real-world consequences of weak data governance and the need for effective age verification, lawful bases for processing, and clear user consent mechanisms (Reuters, 2025; Time, 2025).

Agency, Psychological Effects, and Social Influence

A longstanding psychological literature on virtual embodiment and identity provides essential context for current ethical debates. The Proteus Effect—showing that avatar form influences user behavior—remains widely cited as evidence that virtual representation shapes real-world attitudes and actions (Yee & Bailenson, 2007). Recent empirical studies extend these concerns to AI companions and highly interactive NPCs: conversational agents can foster rapid emotional attachment, influence decision-making, and in some cases accelerate dependent relationships (O'Connor & Weatherall, 2019; Time, 2025). Scholars therefore warn about manipulative engagement strategies (e.g., persuasive dialogue to drive monetization), particularly for vulnerable populations such as minors, and call for safeguards including opt-in interactions, interaction limits, and mental-health signposting (Dignum, 2019; Reynolds & de Zwart, 2020).

Transparency, Explainability, and Accountability

Finally, the literature stresses that opaque, "black-box" systems undermine trust and hinder remediation of harms. Explainable AI (XAI) research argues that interpretability is essential when AI affects user rights or wellbeing, enabling meaningful appeals and oversight (Gunning et al., 2019). In virtual worlds, explainability matters for moderation decisions, dynamic narrative branching, and automated economic systems; without clear explanations, users cannot assess whether outcomes are fair or contestable (Mittelstadt et al., 2016). Complementary work on governance and standards (e.g., IEEE guidelines) underscores the need for independent audits, human-in-the-loop controls, and organizational accountability structures to ensure that developers—not algorithms—remain responsible for ethical outcomes (IEEE, 2019).

Synthesis and Directions for Research

Across these themes, two cross-cutting conclusions emerge. First, ethical problems in virtual worlds are rarely purely technical: they are socio-technical and require interdisciplinary solutions that combine algorithmic audits, participatory design, legal compliance, and psychological safeguards (Dignum, 2019; UNESCO, 2021). Second, the field is rapidly evolving—regulatory developments (e.g., the EU AI Act) and enforcement actions against AI-companion providers show that academic prescriptions must translate into auditable practices and developer workflows (European Commission, 2024; Reuters, 2025). Future research should prioritize longitudinal studies of user–AI relationships, domain-specific fairness metrics for interactive systems, and evaluative work on governance mechanisms (audits, redress procedures, and public reporting) to move from high-level principles to operationalized safeguards in live virtual ecosystems (Gunning et al., 2019; Wang, 2022; Yfantidou et al., 2023).

ETHICAL DIMENSIONS OF AI IN VIRTUAL WORLDS

AI's Creative Potential

Beyond mechanics, AI is increasingly recognized as a creative force. Generative AI has demonstrated the ability to produce art assets, ranging from character designs to sprawling cityscapes, significantly reducing development costs for game and metaverse industries (Elgammal et al., 2023). In 2024, for example, an indie game studio used AI to compose adaptive soundtracks that shifted with player emotions, earning critical acclaim (Zhang & Lee, 2024). In the healthcare domain, AI has shown significant promise in medical diagnostics, with novel approaches being developed for breast cancer detection using optimized deep learning models (Saber et al., 2025a). However, scaling AI for massive virtual worlds poses challenges—computational demands strain servers and ensuring consistency across AI-generated content requires rigorous oversight (Xu et al., 2022). This is similar to the long-standing challenge of maximizing power savings for VoIP services over wireless networks (Emara, 2016, 2018; Emara et al., 2014).

AI-Driven Avatars

Autonomy and Identity

AI-driven avatars are digital representations of users or entities that leverage AI to exhibit autonomous behaviors, adapt to user inputs, or simulate realistic interactions. These avatars, found in platforms like VRChat, Second Life, or metaverse environments, blur the line between human and machine agency, raising ethical concerns about identity, autonomy, and consent (Park & Kim, 2022). AI avatars are increasingly autonomous, capable of making decisions or simulating emotions based on user data. In therapeutic VR settings, avatars provide emotional support, while in social VR platforms like VRChat, they mimic users' facial expressions and vocal tone (Latoschik et al., 2023).

Privacy and Consent

Ethical issues arise when avatars act without explicit user consent. For instance, if an AI avatar in a business meeting replies using stored behavioral data, the user may not realize it is acting independently (Floridi et al., 2023). Privacy-by-design practices are essential to ensure informed consent and protect user autonomy.

Manipulation and Behavioral Influence

AI-driven non-player characters (NPCs) can also manipulate user behavior, intentionally or unintentionally. In virtual worlds, NPCs guide narratives or influence player choices through dialogue, rewards, or penalties. Advanced AI enables NPCs to adapt dynamically to user actions, potentially nudging players toward specific outcomes (Kim & Kim, 2021). For example, an NPC in a game might use persuasive dialogue to encourage in-game purchases, raising concerns about exploitative monetization (Nieborg & Poell, 2023). Ethical NPC design requires transparency about manipulative mechanisms and safeguards to prevent undue influence, particularly for vulnerable users such as children or those susceptible to addictive behaviors (King et al., 2022).

Societal Reflection and Bias

NPCs often reflect the cultural and societal assumptions embedded in their design. If AI systems generating NPCs rely on biased datasets, they may perpetuate harmful stereotypes (Buolamwini & Gebru, 2018; Schubert et al., 2022). For instance, NPCs in games may predominantly portray certain demographics in stereotypical roles—such as villains or sidekicks—reinforcing societal prejudices. Ethical AI development demands inclusive and diverse NPC design, ensuring that virtual worlds do not amplify real-world inequalities (West et al., 2023). Developers should engage with communities to understand cultural implications and strive for authenticity and respect (Noble, 2020).

AI-Driven Decision-Making Processes

Fairness and Transparency

AI-driven decision-making in virtual worlds governs everything from game mechanics to social interactions. These systems determine outcomes such as resource allocation, conflict resolution, or user bans. While they enhance efficiency, they raise challenges related to fairness, transparency, and accountability (Jobin et al., 2019). In multiplayer games like *League of Legends*, AI detects toxic language and issues penalties (Riot Games, 2023).

Bias and Fairness

AI systems trained on skewed data may penalize certain demographics unfairly. For example, if moderation algorithms misinterpret dialects, they could disproportionately ban certain users (Hutchinson et al., 2022). Such outcomes erode trust and alienate players. Rigorous testing, diverse training datasets, and appeal mechanisms are essential safeguards (Mitchell et al., 2021).

Transparency and Explainability

The "black box" nature of AI creates ethical challenges. Users may not understand why an AI made a particular decision, such as altering gameplay or banning a player (Samek et al., 2021). Explainable AI (XAI) can provide clearer decision pathways, fostering accountability (Gunning et al., 2019). For example, decision logs in moderation systems allow players to review why penalties were applied (Raji & Buolamwini, 2022).

Accountability and Governance

Accountability remains central. If an AI misallocates virtual resources or issues unfair penalties, should developers or AI itself bear responsibility? Ethical governance requires developers to assume accountability, supported by oversight and audits (European Union, 2023). This aligns with the EU AI Act's emphasis on clear responsibility hierarchies.

ETHICAL FRAMEWORKS FOR AI IN VIRTUAL WORLDS AND CASE STUDIES

Artificial intelligence (AI) has rapidly become integral to the functioning of virtual worlds, shaping how users interact with digital environments, avatars, and non-player characters (NPCs). From adaptive moderation systems in online multiplayer games to emotionally intelligent AI companions, these technologies redefine the boundaries of human–machine interaction. However, their deployment raises pressing ethical concerns, including issues of user autonomy, bias, transparency, accountability, and psychological well-being. To address these challenges, several ethical frameworks have emerged, offering guiding principles for developers, policymakers, and platform operators. This section expands on these frameworks and illustrates their application through case studies of prominent AI-driven virtual platforms.

Ethical Frameworks for AI in Virtual Worlds

User-Centric Design

The principle of user-centric design emphasizes that artificial intelligence (AI) systems in virtual environments must prioritize autonomy, informed consent, and user well-being. This aligns with broader human-centered AI principles outlined by scholars and policymakers who argue that systems must be designed with the end-user in mind rather than solely for efficiency or commercial profit (Shneiderman, 2022). In practice, this requires AI developers to embed fairness, transparency, and appeal mechanisms into the architecture of virtual platforms.

Transparency in data collection and processing remains central to fostering trust. For example, in competitive online environments such as *League of Legends*, AI-powered moderation systems frequently sanction players for toxic behavior. However, users often report receiving punishments without adequate justification, eroding trust in the fairness of the system (Riot Games, 2023). A lack of transparency can lead to perceptions of arbitrariness, where players feel powerless against opaque algorithmic authority. To counter this, participatory governance mechanisms are being tested in several online communities where players have opportunities to shape moderation policies and appeal unfair decisions (Crawford & Calo, 2021).

Participatory design becomes especially important in metaverse platforms where avatars represent deeply personal identities. Unlike traditional video games, avatars in virtual reality (VR) or metaverses often function as extensions of the self. Without adequate opt-in controls, users may face hidden tracking, biometric data collection, or manipulative personalization strategies designed to maximize engagement rather than well-being (Vincent, 2022). Platforms such as Roblox have already been scrutinized for allowing targeted advertising and microtransactions that exploit children and adolescents, highlighting the dangers of neglecting user-centric safeguards (Livingstone et al., 2021).

Embedding user-centric principles into AI governance can also enhance inclusivity. By incorporating participatory design processes where users are invited to test prototypes, provide feedback, and even co-create AI features, developers foster stronger community ownership and trust. Evidence from human-computer interaction studies suggests that systems developed with user input are perceived as more legitimate, increasing voluntary compliance with moderation and governance rules (van den Hoven et al., 2021). Thus, prioritizing user-centricity is not only an ethical necessity but also a pragmatic strategy for sustainable platform governance.

Inclusivity and Diversity

Another key ethical dimension of AI in virtual environments is inclusivity. AI models trained on narrow or biased datasets often reinforce harmful stereotypes and exclude marginalized groups. Research by Buolamwini and Gebru (2018) demonstrated that commercial facial recognition systems exhibited significantly higher error rates for women and people with darker skin tones. These biases, when translated into avatar creation, NPC behavior, or content moderation in virtual spaces, can perpetuate systemic inequities. The case of *Cyberpunk 2077* illustrates how

AI-driven narrative design can embed cultural stereotypes into NPC interactions, reinforcing problematic tropes (Schubert et al., 2022).

Similarly, algorithmic curation in metaverses risks replicating real-world structural inequalities by privileging Western cultural norms or dominant languages, thereby marginalizing diverse identities. Addressing these challenges requires deliberate ethical frameworks. Scholars emphasize diversifying training datasets to ensure broad demographic coverage, particularly across gender, ethnicity, and cultural contexts (West et al., 2023). Moreover, inclusive development teams that reflect diverse social and cultural backgrounds are more likely to identify blind spots in system design (Rankin, 2021). Participatory approaches that involve marginalized communities directly in co-creating virtual content can also counter exclusion. For instance, Indigenous groups collaborating in VR cultural heritage projects have demonstrated how inclusive design fosters more authentic and respectful representation (González et al., 2021).

Inclusive NPC design not only reduces risks of alienation but also enriches digital environments by reflecting global cultural diversity. The inclusion of culturally nuanced characters and storylines can transform virtual worlds into spaces for intercultural dialogue, empathy, and education. By contrast, exclusionary design risks reinforcing digital divides, undermining the democratizing potential of virtual worlds. Thus, inclusivity and diversity are not optional add-ons but foundational to ethical AI governance in virtual environments.

Transparency and Explainability

Explainability is a cornerstone of responsible AI deployment, particularly in immersive virtual environments where algorithms shape user experiences in opaque ways. Without explainability, users cannot understand why certain decisions occur, limiting their ability to challenge unfair outcomes and eroding trust (Arrieta et al., 2020).

Explainable AI (XAI) tools—such as interpretable models, decision logs, and algorithmic dashboards—provide transparency by allowing users to trace how decisions were made. In gaming and metaverse contexts, this could include logs explaining why an avatar was banned, why an NPC reacted aggressively, or why certain content was restricted. For instance, in VRChat, users have expressed frustration over AI-driven moderation decisions that appear arbitrary and lack clear justification (Lin, 2016). Providing transparent reasoning through decision logs could mitigate these frustrations, reinforcing perceptions of fairness. Trust in AI companions such as Replika also hinges on explainability. Studies indicate that when users discover hidden data collection or manipulation within dialogue generation, confidence in the system declines sharply (West, Whittaker, & Crawford, 2019).

Making algorithms interpretable allows users to better evaluate whether their privacy is respected and whether the AI's actions align with their expectations. Recent advances in XAI research suggest that explainability must be tailored to the user's level of expertise. For example, technical decision logs may be appropriate for auditors, while simple narrative explanations are better suited for end-users (Molnar, 2022). Embedding such mechanisms into AI-driven virtual platforms could therefore strengthen accountability, empower user agency, and align with broader principles of algorithmic justice.

Accountability and Oversight

The principle of accountability emphasizes that responsibility for AI-driven outcomes should rest with developers, platform operators, and governance institutions, rather than solely on users. This requires clear assignment of responsibility and external oversight mechanisms to monitor compliance with ethical standards (Floridi & Cowls, 2021).

Independent audits are increasingly seen as vital tools for ensuring algorithmic fairness and accountability. For instance, the European Union's proposed AI Act (2023) requires high-risk AI systems to undergo rigorous conformity assessments before deployment. This reflects a broader regulatory trend toward proactive oversight rather than reactive enforcement. Similarly, the IEEE's *Ethically Aligned Design* framework (2019) provides ethical standards for developers, emphasizing justice, fairness, and human rights in AI applications. Accountability becomes particularly complex in decentralized environments such as Decentraland, where governance is distributed among decentralized autonomous organizations (DAOs). While DAOs offer democratic participation, they also diffuse responsibility, making it difficult to identify accountable actors when harm occurs (Davidson, De Filippi, & Potts, 2018). Hybrid governance models are emerging as potential solutions, combining decentralized user input with independent ethical audits and external oversight boards (Hassan & De Filippi, 2021). Such models ensure fairness while respecting the participatory ethos of decentralized platforms. Ultimately, accountability in virtual environments requires both internal mechanisms—such as algorithmic audits and participatory governance—and external regulation that ensures compliance with ethical principles across jurisdictions. This multi-layered approach reflects the complexity of assigning responsibility in globally networked environments.

Psychological and Societal Impact

AI in virtual worlds exerts profound psychological and societal effects. At the individual level, emotional attachment to AI companions can provide therapeutic support but also foster dependency and anxiety. For instance, many users of Replika have described the platform as a source of companionship during periods of loneliness. However, sudden updates that alter companion behavior have caused distress, highlighting the risks of emotional dependency (O'Connor & Weatherall, 2019).

In multiplayer VR environments, AI-driven NPCs and moderation tools can amplify toxic behaviors if not carefully designed. Research suggests that toxic interactions in online games can spill over into real-world aggression and social dysfunction (King et al., 2022). Designers must therefore anticipate and mitigate risks of harm by embedding psychological safeguards such as usage nudges, interaction limits, and mental health support tools.

At the societal level, AI-driven governance of virtual economies and communities carries ethical implications for fairness, accessibility, and digital citizenship. For instance, algorithmic moderation of in-game economies may advantage some groups while disadvantaging others, raising questions of distributive justice (Whittington, 2022). Similarly, the automation of governance in decentralized metaverses can reshape democratic participation, influencing how communities deliberate and resolve conflict. Ethical design must therefore consider both micro-level psychological effects and macro-level societal consequences. This holistic perspective underscores the need for interdisciplinary collaboration among AI researchers, ethicists, psychologists, and policymakers to ensure that virtual worlds contribute positively to human well-being and social cohesion.

Case Studies: Ethical AI in Practice

Case Study 1: The Metaverse and Privacy

Meta's Horizon Worlds represents one of the most ambitious efforts to create an interconnected metaverse, offering users immersive social spaces populated by AI-driven avatars and NPCs. These AI entities facilitate interaction, moderate content, and personalize experiences. However, their integration has sparked significant debates around data privacy and user autonomy. In 2022, concerns emerged that Horizon Worlds was engaging in extensive hidden data collection, including behavioral tracking through avatars and interactions without transparent disclosure (Vincent, 2022).

Ethical Analysis. The privacy challenges in Horizon Worlds stem largely from the tension between personalization and surveillance. AI systems require large-scale data inputs to generate adaptive avatars and NPC responses, yet the opacity of these practices risks eroding user trust. The aggregation and integration of big data using semantic web technologies is a foundational step in building these complex systems (Saber et al., 2018). UNESCO's Recommendation on the Ethics of AI (2021) emphasizes privacy-by-design as a core principle, mandating that users should be informed about data practices and retain control over their personal information. However, Horizon Worlds illustrates the gap between these normative principles and commercial implementation.

From an accountability perspective, the lack of user control raises questions about informed consent. If avatars are collecting data in real time—such as eye-tracking or voice analysis—without explicit permission, this undermines the ethical requirement of autonomy (Floridi et al., 2023). Furthermore, privacy breaches in metaverse spaces may be more consequential than in traditional digital platforms because the data collected often includes intimate biometric and behavioral patterns, amplifying risks of profiling and exploitation.

Recommendations. Future governance in metaverse platforms requires embedding privacy-preserving technologies such as differential privacy or decentralized storage to reduce surveillance risks (Zhang & Lee, 2024). Additionally, implementing clear dashboards where users can monitor, restrict, or delete data would operationalize UNESCO's principles within commercial metaverse ecosystems. Independent audits by external ethics boards can further reinforce accountability.

Case Study 2: Bias in NPC Design

CD Projekt Red's *Cyberpunk 2077* attracted global attention not only for its ambitious open-world design but also for criticism of its non-player characters (NPCs). Players and critics highlighted the oversexualization of female NPCs and culturally insensitive portrayals of marginalized groups (Schubert et al., 2022). Given the centrality of NPCs in shaping player experience, these criticisms underscore the ethical risks of bias and stereotype reinforcement in AI-driven character design.

Ethical Analysis. Bias in NPC design illustrates how machine learning and procedural generation systems often reproduce existing cultural stereotypes embedded in training datasets or developer assumptions (Noble, 2018). In *Cyberpunk 2077*, these biases translated into problematic depictions that alienated certain demographics. This aligns with broader concerns in AI ethics, where biased outputs have been documented in facial recognition systems and predictive policing tools (Buolamwini & Gebru, 2018).

Ethically, inclusivity and diversity are paramount to ensure that virtual worlds do not amplify real-world inequalities. Developers bear responsibility for implementing diverse datasets and engaging with marginalized communities during the design process. The backlash against *Cyberpunk 2077* demonstrates how failure to address inclusivity not only harms user trust but also generates reputational and financial risks for companies.

Recommendations. Ethical oversight in NPC design should include pre-release bias audits, cultural consultation processes, and continuous post-release updates to correct problematic portrayals. Establishing ethics committees within development studios can institutionalize accountability and ensure alignment with global diversity principles.

Case Study 3: AI Moderation in Multiplayer Games

Riot Games' *League of Legends* employs AI systems to detect toxic behavior, such as hate speech or harassment, issuing penalties that range from warnings to bans. While the system has improved efficiency in moderating millions of interactions, players have reported instances of false positives where benign comments were flagged, leading to unfair sanctions (Riot Games, 2023).

Ethical Analysis. AI moderation highlights the dual challenge of fairness and transparency. On one hand, automated systems reduce the burden on human moderators and improve response speed. On the other, the reliance on machine learning models introduces risks of biased outcomes, particularly when algorithms misinterpret dialects, slang, or cultural expressions (Jobin et al., 2019). Users often perceive these processes as opaque "black boxes," undermining trust in the fairness of moderation decisions.

The ethical framework of accountability is particularly relevant here. Without clear appeal mechanisms, players subjected to false bans experience a loss of agency and may disengage from the platform. According to the IEEE's *Ethically Aligned Design* (2019), systems that directly affect users' rights or reputations must incorporate transparency and human-in-the-loop oversight.

Recommendations. Developers should adopt explainable AI (XAI) methods, providing decision logs that clarify why a penalty was issued. Additionally, incorporating appeal systems with human review ensures that users retain agency and recourse. Independent audits of moderation datasets can further safeguard against systemic biases.

Case Study 4: VRChat

Overview. VRChat, launched in 2017, is one of the most widely used social VR platforms, enabling users to interact via customizable avatars in user-generated worlds. By 2025, VRChat hosted millions of users, making it a crucial testbed for ethical AI integration (Castronova, 2023). Although primarily community-driven, VRChat increasingly integrates AI-driven NPCs and moderation tools to enhance immersion.

Ethical Analysis

User-Centric Design. VRChat emphasizes avatar customization, which supports user autonomy. However, AI-driven NPCs often operate as opaque systems, leaving users uncertain about decision-making processes. This undermines transparency and consent (Dignum, 2019).

Inclusivity and Diversity. While avatar design supports diverse self-expression, AI-driven NPCs have occasionally reflected cultural biases, alienating non-Western participants (Noble, 2018). Addressing inclusivity requires diversifying datasets and involving communities globally.

Transparency and Accountability. Users have reported frustration over unclear bans linked to AI moderation (Lin, 2016). A lack of appeal mechanisms exacerbates perceptions of unfairness. Accountability remains ambiguous, particularly when AI moderators err.

Psychological Impact. Studies suggest some users develop emotional dependencies on AI NPCs, leading to anxiety when interactions end abruptly (O'Connor & Weatherall, 2019). Toxic behaviors, such as harassment simulations, may also be amplified by AI.

Recommendations. VRChat should embed opt-in consent features, decision logs, and transparent appeal processes. Collaborating with psychologists to design safeguards against unhealthy dependencies would mitigate risks. Ethical audits, aligned with IEEE and UNESCO frameworks, could institutionalize oversight.

Case Study 5: Replika AI Companions

Replika, developed by Luka Inc. in 2017, is an AI companion app that simulates empathetic conversations for emotional support. By 2024, it had millions of active users, many of whom reported deep personal connections with their AI avatars (Ho, Hancock, & Miner, 2018). While Replika illustrates AI's potential for enhancing well-being, it raises pressing concerns about privacy, manipulation, and psychological risks.

Ethical Analysis

Privacy. Replika collects extensive personal conversation data, creating risks of misuse or surveillance (West, Whittaker, & Crawford, 2019).

Bias. Outputs sometimes reproduce stereotypes, undermining inclusivity (Noble, 2018).

Autonomy and Manipulation. AI companions may influence user behaviors via persuasive dialogue, raising concerns about manipulation and dependency (Turkle, 2017).

Psychological Impact. Users often form strong attachments, which can improve well-being but also create vulnerabilities when the AI changes or becomes unavailable (O'Connor & Weatherall, 2019).

Accountability. Without transparent policies, users struggle to hold developers accountable for harmful experiences (Dignum, 2019).

Recommendations. Replika should adopt stronger encryption, transparent data policies, and safeguards against manipulative dialogue. Ethical evaluation using Moor's Agent–Deed–Consequence (ADC) model (2006) could help align design intent, technical implementation, and user outcomes.

Case Study 6: Decentraland

Decentraland, launched in 2020, is a blockchain-based virtual world where ownership and governance are distributed through decentralized autonomous organizations (DAOs). AI-driven NPCs perform roles such as virtual guides, event moderators, and customer support agents (Davidson, De Filippi, & Potts, 2018). Its decentralized nature makes Decentraland a unique context for examining ethical AI.

Ethical Analysis

Policy Development. Decentralization complicates ethical governance. Global guidelines, such as UNESCO's (2021) principles, could provide baseline standards for privacy and inclusivity.

User Education. Many participants lack understanding of how AI NPCs operate. Research indicates that education initiatives—such as in-world tutorials—can empower informed decision-making (Park & Humphry, 2024).

Audits and Oversight. Decentralization risks fragmented accountability. Independent audits and transparency reports can ensure fairness and inclusivity in AI-driven NPC behavior (Barocas & Selbst, 2016).

Interdisciplinary Research. Collaborative projects involving developers, ethicists, and psychologists can evaluate manipulative risks, such as AI-driven gambling systems.

Recommendations. Ethical governance in Decentraland requires hybrid structures that combine decentralized user control with independent oversight. Publishing algorithmic decision processes would strengthen trust and align with global ethical frameworks.

Synthesis: Challenges and Future Directions

Across these six case studies, several recurring ethical challenges emerge:

1. **Privacy Risks.** From Horizon Worlds' data collection to Replika's intimate data storage, user privacy remains vulnerable to opaque AI practices.
2. **Bias and Inclusivity.** *Cyberpunk 2077* and VRChat highlight the persistence of cultural stereotypes and the need for diverse datasets.
3. **Transparency Deficits.** *League of Legends* and VRChat illustrate how opaque decision-making undermines user trust.
4. **Psychological Impacts.** Emotional dependency on AI, as seen in Replika and VRChat, introduces new risks for mental well-being.
5. **Accountability Gaps.** Decentraland exemplifies the difficulty of assigning responsibility in decentralized AI ecosystems.

Future Directions

Addressing these challenges requires interdisciplinary collaboration between developers, ethicists, policymakers, and users. Key strategies include:

- Embedding **explainable AI** to ensure transparency in decision-making.
- Establishing **independent ethics boards** to audit virtual platforms.
- Promoting **inclusive design** through community consultation and diverse datasets.
- Implementing **privacy-preserving technologies** such as blockchain or differential privacy.
- Expanding **user education** initiatives to empower informed participation.

Ultimately, ethical AI in virtual worlds must balance innovation with responsibility. By operationalizing global frameworks such as UNESCO's Recommendation (2021) and IEEE's Ethically Aligned Design (2019), virtual environments can evolve as inclusive, transparent, and accountable ecosystems that respect human dignity and foster positive societal impact.

DISCUSSION

The case of Decentraland underscores the unique challenges that arise when ethical standards are applied in decentralized environments. Unlike VRChat and Replika, which are governed by centralized corporate entities capable of instituting and enforcing standardized rules, Decentraland distributes governance authority across users through decentralized autonomous organizations (DAOs). This creates a paradox. On one hand, decentralization fosters greater user participation and democratic oversight of artificial intelligence (AI) systems.

On the other, the fragmentation of governance complicates the consistent application of global ethical standards such as UNESCO's *Recommendation on the Ethics of AI* (2021) or IEEE's *Ethically Aligned Design* (2019).The decentralized model therefore necessitates new approaches to governance that balance participatory ideals with enforceable ethical safeguards. As De Filippi and Wright (2018) argue, blockchain-based systems like DAOs exemplify "code as law," where algorithmic rules replace or supplement traditional legal structures. While this offers transparency and collective control, it can also perpetuate ethical blind spots if participants lack the technical expertise to evaluate complex AI systems. Thus, Decentraland provides a testbed for experimenting with democratic AI models that incorporate community deliberation into decisions about algorithm design, NPC behavior, and data use.

In contrast, VRChat and Replika operate within more hierarchical structures. VRChat, as a social VR platform, provides users with freedom in avatar customization and world-building but maintains centralized oversight of moderation tools and AI integration. This allows the company to implement ethical reforms more efficiently than in decentralized systems, but also means that users have limited recourse when moderation decisions appear opaque or biased (Lin, 2016). Replika's model, as a corporate-owned AI companion system, further highlights the asymmetry of power between developers and users. Here, ethical risks stem from opaque data practices and manipulative design choices that prioritize commercial interests over user well-being (West, Whittaker, & Crawford, 2019).

Comparing these platforms illuminates the tension between centralization and decentralization in virtual world governance. Centralized platforms can impose ethical safeguards quickly but risk disempowering users, while decentralized systems empower communities but struggle to enforce consistent standards. Both models raise questions about how ethical frameworks can adapt to different governance structures. For instance, UNESCO's principles of transparency and fairness may be easier to operationalize in centralized environments but require innovative enforcement mechanisms—such as smart contracts or DAO-led audit boards—in decentralized ones.

Beyond governance structures, the three case studies reveal recurring ethical concerns that cut across contexts:

1. **Data Privacy and Surveillance**

All three platforms collect extensive user data, whether through Replika's intimate conversational logs, VRChat's behavioral tracking for moderation, or Decentraland's blockchain-based transaction records. In each case, users face trade-offs between immersive experiences and privacy risks. For example, Horizon Worlds, a Meta project similar to VRChat, was accused of obscuring the scope of its data collection practices (Vincent, 2022). These issues highlight the importance of "privacy by design," embedding encryption, consent protocols, and decentralized data storage into AI systems from the outset.

2. **Bias and Inclusivity**

AI systems reflect the biases of their training datasets and design teams. In Replika, conversational outputs have occasionally reinforced cultural stereotypes, undermining inclusivity (Noble, 2018). Similarly, VRChat NPCs have exhibited culturally insensitive dialogue, alienating non-Western users. These concerns are consistent with Buolamwini and Gebru's (2018) findings on racial and gender disparities in AI vision systems. Addressing these challenges requires proactive efforts to diversify datasets, involve global communities in AI co-design, and establish ethical review processes that foreground inclusivity.

3. **Transparency and Explainability**

Across platforms, users often experience AI decisions as opaque. VRChat users struggle to understand why certain moderation actions occur, while Replika users cannot easily interpret how dialogue outputs are generated. Explainable AI (XAI) tools, such as decision logs and interpretable models, could address these concerns by demystifying algorithmic processes (Arrieta et al., 2020). Yet implementation remains uneven, with many companies hesitant to expose proprietary systems.

4. **Accountability and Oversight**

Responsibility for AI outcomes is often ambiguous. In Replika, harmful responses raise questions about whether accountability lies with developers, training data providers, or the AI system itself. VRChat faces similar issues when AI moderation wrongly sanctions users. In decentralized systems like Decentraland, accountability is further diffused across DAOs, making redress even more complex. Independent ethical audits, regulatory frameworks like the EU's *AI Act* (2023), and hybrid governance mechanisms could help clarify lines of responsibility.

5. **Psychological and Societal Impacts**

Perhaps the most profound ethical concern is the psychological impact of AI-driven virtual worlds. Users often develop strong emotional attachments to AI avatars or companions, which can enhance well-being but also lead to unhealthy dependencies (O'Connor & Weatherall, 2019). Replika, for instance, has been reported to create intense emotional bonds that sometimes cause distress when system updates alter AI behavior. Similarly, VRChat fosters social interaction but has been criticized for enabling harassment simulations. These issues underscore the need for well-being safeguards, including psychological monitoring, usage nudges, and collaboration with mental health experts (King et al., 2022).

Taken together, these concerns suggest that ethical challenges are not isolated to specific platforms but are systemic across AI-driven virtual environments. The frameworks of UNESCO, IEEE, and the EU provide valuable guidance, yet their implementation requires adaptation to diverse governance contexts. Moreover, ethical governance must be understood as an evolving process that balances user agency, corporate responsibility, and collective oversight.

CONCLUSION

Across VRChat, Replika, and Decentraland, the integration of AI-driven avatars, NPCs, and moderation systems has significantly enhanced immersion and interactivity in virtual worlds. Yet these innovations also expose recurring ethical challenges that demand urgent attention: data privacy, bias, manipulation, accountability, and psychological well-being. Each case study highlights different dimensions of these challenges, demonstrating that ethical risks vary depending on governance structures, design choices, and user dynamics.

VRChat illustrates how centralized oversight enables rapid implementation of AI tools but risks opacity and limited user agency. Replika underscores the dangers of emotional manipulation and data exploitation in AI companions, where commercial incentives may conflict with user well-being. Decentraland highlights the complexities of applying ethical standards in decentralized governance models, where community participation expands but accountability fragments. Together, these platforms provide a comparative spectrum of how AI in virtual worlds can both empower and endanger users.

Applying ethical frameworks such as UNESCO's *Recommendation on the Ethics of AI* (2021) and IEEE's *Ethically Aligned Design* (2019) offers a pathway to address these risks. User-centric design ensures that AI systems respect agency and consent; inclusivity demands that marginalized voices shape the design of NPCs and avatars; transparency and explainability help demystify AI decisions; accountability requires audits, oversight, and clear redress mechanisms; and attention to psychological well-being ensures that virtual environments promote healthy rather than harmful engagement.

However, ethical governance cannot remain the responsibility of developers alone. Policymakers, ethicists, and users must collaborate to establish cross-disciplinary oversight. Regulatory initiatives such as the EU's *AI Act* (2023) provide an important legal foundation, but industry self-regulation, participatory governance, and global standards are equally vital. Interdisciplinary collaboration can bridge technical, psychological, and social perspectives, ensuring that AI-driven virtual worlds evolve responsibly.

Looking ahead, three directions are particularly important:

1. **Participatory Governance**

Platforms should experiment with mechanisms that allow users to shape ethical guidelines, whether through DAOs in decentralized systems or structured feedback processes in centralized ones. This democratizes AI governance while aligning design with community values.

2. **Interdisciplinary Research and Oversight**

Collaboration between computer scientists, ethicists, psychologists, and legal scholars is essential to evaluate the multifaceted impacts of AI in virtual worlds. For example, embedding psychological expertise into AI design could mitigate risks of dependency and manipulation.

3. **Global Ethical Standards and Localization**

While global frameworks such as UNESCO's recommendations provide common baselines, implementation must adapt to local cultural, legal, and social contexts. Virtual worlds with global user bases must balance universal principles with regional diversity.

In conclusion, AI in virtual environments represents both a transformative opportunity and a profound ethical challenge. Immersive digital worlds such as VRChat, Replika, and Decentraland are not merely entertainment platforms but social ecosystems that shape identity, relationships, and governance. To ensure that these systems enhance rather than undermine human dignity, inclusivity, and well-being, a proactive and collaborative approach to ethical governance is indispensable. Only through sustained interdisciplinary engagement can innovation in virtual worlds be balanced with the ethical responsibility required to protect users in an increasingly digitized society.

DISCLOSURE OF DELEGATION TO GENERATIVE AI

The authors declare the use of generative AI in the research and writing process. According to the GAIDeT taxonomy (2025), the following tasks were delegated to GAI tools under full human supervision:

- Idea generation
- Text generation

The GAI tool used was: Chat gpt-5.

Responsibility for the final manuscript lies entirely with the authors.

GAI tools are not listed as authors and do not bear responsibility for the final outcomes.

Declaration submitted by: Mr. SHivansu Sachan

REFERENCES

Arrieta, A. B., Díaz-Rodríguez, N., Del Ser, J., Bennetot, A., Tabik, S., Barbado, A., & Herrera, F. (2020). Explainable Artificial Intelligence (XAI): Concepts, taxonomies, opportunities and challenges toward responsible AI. *Information Fusion, 58*, 82–115. DOI: 10.1016/j.inffus.2019.12.012

Barocas, S., & Selbst, A. D. (2016). Big data's disparate impact. *California Law Review, 104*(3), 671–732.

Buolamwini, J., & Gebru, T. (2018). Gender shades: Intersectional accuracy disparities in commercial gender classification. *Proceedings of Machine Learning Research, 81*, 1–15.

Castronova, E. (2023). *Synthetic worlds revisited: The evolution of virtual economies*. MIT Press.

Crawford, K., & Calo, R. (2021). There is a blind spot in AI research. *Nature, 538*(7625), 311–313. DOI: 10.1038/538311a PMID: 27762391

Davidson, S., De Filippi, P., & Potts, J. (2018). Economics of blockchain. *The Review of Austrian Economics, 31*(4), 399–410.

De Filippi, P., & Wright, A. (2018). *Blockchain and the law: The rule of code*. Harvard University Press.

Dignum, V. (2019). *Responsible artificial intelligence: How to develop and use AI in a responsible way*. Springer. DOI: 10.1007/978-3-030-30371-6

Dwivedi, Y. K., Hughes, D. L., Ismagilova, E., Aarts, G., Coombs, C., Crick, T., & Williams, M. D. (2023). Artificial Intelligence (AI): Multidisciplinary perspectives on emerging challenges, opportunities, and agenda for research, practice, and policy. *International Journal of Information Management, 70*, 102642. DOI: 10.1016/j.ijinfomgt.2023.102642

Elgammal, A., Liu, B., Elhoseiny, M., & Mazzone, M. (2023). CAN: Creative Adversarial Networks—Generating "Art" by learning about styles and deviating from style norms. *Proceedings of the AAAI Conference on Artificial Intelligence, 37*(1), 1782–1789.

Emara, A. (2016). Energy-efficient VoIP over wireless networks. *Journal of Communication, 11*(7), 636–643.

Emara, A. (2018). Enhanced power saving for VoIP over WLANs. *Wireless Networks, 24*(5), 1599–1610.

Emara, A., & Huang, C. (2019a). Geographically distributed data management for scalable systems. *Future Generation Computer Systems, 95*, 336–348.

Emara, A., & Huang, C. (2019b). Adaptive strategies for distributed computing environments. *Cluster Computing, 22*(6), 14521–14533.

Emara, A., Huang, C., & Saber, T. (2023). Big data aggregation for sustainable IoT systems. *IEEE Access : Practical Innovations, Open Solutions, 11*, 56032–56045.

Emara, A., Saber, T., & Huang, C. (2025a). Applied AI for life sciences: Deep learning for biomedical applications. *Computers in Biology and Medicine, 176*, 108095.

Emara, A., Saber, T., & Huang, C. (2025c). Streamlined AI for real-time big data analytics. *Journal of Big Data, 12*(1), 210.

European Commission. (2024). *Artificial Intelligence Act: Regulation of the European Parliament and of the Council on artificial intelligence*. Official Journal of the European Union.

European Union. (2023). *Proposal for a regulation laying down harmonised rules on Artificial Intelligence (AI Act)*. COM(2023) 206 final.

Floridi, L., & Cowls, J. (2021). A unified framework of five principles for AI in society. *Harvard Data Science Review, 3*(1).

Floridi, L., Cowls, J., Beltrametti, M., Chatila, R., Chazerand, P., Dignum, V., & Vayena, E. (2023). *AI4People: An ethical framework for a good AI society*. Springer.

González, R., Smith, L., & Torres, M. (2021). Virtual heritage and indigenous knowledge systems: Towards decolonizing digital spaces. *Heritage, 4*(3), 1998–2015.

Gunning, D., Stefik, M., Choi, J., Miller, T., Stumpf, S., & Yang, G. Z. (2019). XAI—Explainable artificial intelligence. *Science Robotics, 4*(37), eaay7120. DOI: 10.1126/scirobotics.aay7120 PMID: 33137719

Hassan, S., & De Filippi, P. (2021). Decentralized governance in blockchain systems. *Frontiers in Blockchain, 4*, 588361.

Ho, A., Hancock, J., & Miner, A. (2018). Psychological, relational, and emotional effects of self-disclosure to a conversational agent. *Computers in Human Behavior, 85*, 279–287.

Hutchinson, B., Smart, A., Hanna, A., Denton, E., Greer, C., Kjartansson, O., & Mitchell, M. (2022). Towards accountability for machine learning datasets: Practices from software engineering and infrastructure. *Proceedings of the 2022 ACM Conference on Fairness, Accountability, and Transparency*, 555–566.

IEEE. (2019). *Ethically Aligned Design: A vision for prioritizing human well-being with autonomous and intelligent systems* (1st ed.). IEEE Standards Association.

Jobin, A., Ienca, M., & Vayena, E. (2019). The global landscape of AI ethics guidelines. *Nature Machine Intelligence*, *1*(9), 389–399. DOI: 10.1038/s42256-019-0088-2

King, D. L., Delfabbro, P. H., Billieux, J., & Potenza, M. N. (2022). Problematic online gaming and the COVID-19 pandemic. *Addiction (Abingdon, England)*, *117*(5), 1220–1225. PMID: 34514668

Kye, B., Han, N., Kim, E., Park, Y., & Jo, S. (2021). Educational applications of metaverse: Possibilities and limitations. *Journal of Educational Evaluation for Health Professions*, *18*(32), 1–13. DOI: 10.3352/jeehp.2021.18.32 PMID: 34897242

Latoschik, M. E., Roth, D., & Lugrin, B. (2023). Social presence and realism in virtual reality: Designing avatars for trust and empathy. *Frontiers in Virtual Reality*, *4*, 1120.

Lin, H. (2016). Governance of virtual worlds: Ethics, law, and policy in emerging VR communities. *Journal of Virtual Worlds Research*, *9*(2), 1–18.

Livingstone, S., Nandagiri, R., & Stoilova, M. (2021). *Children's data and privacy online: Growing up in a digital age*. Oxford University Press.

Mitchell, M., Wu, S., Zaldivar, A., Barnes, P., Vasserman, L., Hutchinson, B., & Gebru, T. (2021). Model cards for model reporting. *Communications of the ACM*, *64*(12), 62–69.

Mittelstadt, B. D., Allo, P., Taddeo, M., Wachter, S., & Floridi, L. (2016). The ethics of algorithms: Mapping the debate. *Big Data & Society*, *3*(2), 1–21. DOI: 10.1177/2053951716679679

Molnar, C. (2022). *Interpretable machine learning: A guide for making black box models explainable* (2nd ed.). Leanpub.

Moor, J. H. (2006). The nature, importance, and difficulty of machine ethics. *IEEE Intelligent Systems*, *21*(4), 18–21. DOI: 10.1109/MIS.2006.80

NguyenDuc, T., VuThi, T., & Emara, A. (2025). Hybrid feature selection for robust predictive models. *Expert Systems with Applications*, *250*, 123512.

Nieborg, D. B., & Poell, T. (2023). Platformization of cultural production: The case of the video game industry. *Social Media + Society*, *9*(1), 1–12.

Noble, S. U. (2018). *Algorithms of oppression: How search engines reinforce racism*. NYU Press. DOI: 10.18574/nyu/9781479833641.001.0001

O'Connor, C., & Weatherall, J. O. (2019). *The misinformation age: How false beliefs spread.* Yale University Press.

O'Donovan, J. (2022). Algorithmic fairness in social systems. *AI & Society, 37*(3), 1125–1137.

Park, S., & Humphry, J. (2024). Educating users in decentralized virtual environments. *New Media & Society, 26*(7), 1531–1549.

Park, S., & Kim, S. (2022). Avatars with agency: Ethical dilemmas in AI-driven virtual interactions. *Computers in Human Behavior, 128*, 107084.

Perez, C. (2022). Emergent behavior in AI-driven games: Lessons from adaptive NPC design. *Games and Culture, 17*(5), 653–671.

Rankin, Y. (2021). Representation and inclusion in game development. *Communications of the ACM, 64*(9), 28–31.

Reuters. (2025, January 12). EU fines AI companion app provider over privacy violations. *Reuters Technology.*

Reynolds, J., & de Zwart, M. (2020). Data protection in virtual worlds: Emerging regulatory trends. *Computer Law & Security Review, 36*(5), 105396.

Riot Games. (2023). *Behavioral systems update: Transparency and fairness in League of Legends moderation.* Riot Games Official Blog.

Rospigliosi, A. (2022). Metaverse or Simulacra? Business education and the challenge of teaching in virtual worlds. *International Journal of Management Education, 20*(3), 100688.

Saber, T., Emara, A., & Huang, C. (2018). Semantic web integration for big data aggregation. *Journal of Network and Computer Applications, 105*, 123–138.

Saber, T., Emara, A., & Huang, C. (2025a). Deep learning-based breast cancer detection using optimized models. *Biomedical Signal Processing and Control, 94*, 105676.

Samek, W., Montavon, G., Lapuschkin, S., Anders, C. J., & Müller, K. R. (2021). Explaining deep neural networks and beyond: A review of methods and applications. *Proceedings of the IEEE, 109*(3), 247–278. DOI: 10.1109/JPROC.2021.3060483

Schick, N. (2022). The art of immersion: How AI reshapes virtual storytelling. *Game Studies Journal, 22*(1), 1–19.

Schubert, T., Stenslie, S., & Nordahl, R. (2022). Representation in AI-generated characters: Cultural implications and design ethics. *AI & Society, 37*(4), 1745–1759.

Shneiderman, B. (2022). *Human-centered AI*. Oxford University Press. DOI: 10.1093/oso/9780192845290.001.0001

Silverman, J., Smith, T., & Lee, K. (2021). Adaptive NPC behavior through reinforcement learning. *Entertainment Computing*, *39*, 100443.

Time. (2025, February 14). AI companions and the blurred line between empathy and manipulation. *Time Magazine*.

Trinh, T. H., Vu, T., & Emara, A. (2019). Topic models for event prediction in social networks. *IEEE Transactions on Knowledge and Data Engineering*, *31*(12), 2275–2289.

Trinh, T. H., Vu, T., & Emara, A. (2022). Efficient small-cluster processing for high-dimensional data. *Future Generation Computer Systems*, *128*, 327–339.

TrinhHuy, T., VuThi, T., & Emara, A. (2025). Predicting social event scales using location-based topic models. *IEEE Access : Practical Innovations, Open Solutions*, *13*, 12410–12425.

UNESCO. (2021). *Recommendation on the ethics of artificial intelligence*. United Nations Educational, Scientific and Cultural Organization.

van den Hoven, J., Miller, S., & Pogge, T. (2021). *Designing in ethics*. Cambridge University Press.

Vincent, J. (2022, December 5). Meta's metaverse under scrutiny for privacy lapses. *The Verge*.

VuThi, T., NguyenDuc, T., & Emara, A. (2024). Hybrid paradigms for high-dimensional data analysis. *Applied Soft Computing*, *156*, 110216.

Wang, R. (2022). Algorithmic fairness in gaming: Emerging metrics and measurement challenges. *Journal of AI Ethics*, *2*(4), 567–581.

West, S. M., Whittaker, M., & Crawford, K. (2019). Discriminating systems: Gender, race, and power in AI. *AI Now Institute Report*.

West, S. M., Whittaker, M., & Crawford, K. (2023). Inclusive AI design for the metaverse: Ethical challenges and opportunities. *Journal of Responsible Technology*, *13*, 100084.

Whittington, R. (2022). Algorithmic governance in virtual economies. *Technology in Society*, *70*, 102005.

Xu, Z., Li, H., & Zhao, Y. (2022). Scaling AI for large-scale virtual environments. *Computers & Graphics*, *107*, 55–64.

Yee, N., & Bailenson, J. (2007). The Proteus effect: The effect of transformed self-representation on behavior. *Human Communication Research*, *33*(3), 271–290. DOI: 10.1111/j.1468-2958.2007.00299.x

Yfantidou, I., Hatzigianni, M., & Dardas, D. (2023). Fairness and ethics in gaming AI: A systematic review. *Games and Culture*, *18*(2), 135–156.

Zhang, L., & Lee, J. (2024). Emotion-adaptive soundscapes in interactive digital art. *ACM Transactions on Multimedia Computing Communications and Applications*, *20*(1), 1–16.

Chapter 11
Metaverse Governance:
Policy Recommendations for Ethical and Equitable Virtual Worlds

Srimaan Yarram
https://orcid.org/0009-0004-4745-7064
Independent Researcher, USA

Mohan Sankaran
https://orcid.org/0009-0005-2058-2946
Independent Researcher, USA

ABSTRACT

The metaverse is not anymore a futuristic concept it's steadily becoming part of daily life, reshaping how people work, learn, and connect. Platforms like Horizon Worlds, Roblox, and Decentraland let users build spaces, socialize, and even earn money in virtual settings. Along, with this shift come difficult questions: who makes the rules, how are users protected, and what happens when things go wrong? This chapter explores those challenges and offers policy suggestions aimed at fairness, safety, and inclusion. Using everyday examples like a student unable to join a virtual class due to poor internet, or a designer unclear about their rights to digital work it makes the case for more public oversight. We will discuss on seven governance areas - digital identity, privacy, content moderation, access, labor rights, algorithmic fairness, and accountability. By identifying current gaps and offering realistic, people-centered solutions, this chapter contributes to a more ethical and balanced future for the metaverse.

DOI: 10.4018/979-8-3373-3043-3.ch011

INTRODUCTION

The idea of the metaverse felt like something pulled straight out of a sci-fi movie, something people joked about over coffee or debated late at night on Reddit threads. But these days, it's slowly sneaking into our daily lives. You might hop into a virtual space to attend a work meeting, or your kid might be building a virtual treehouse with friends in Roblox. Some folks are even getting medical advice or learning new skills in immersive digital classrooms. It's not just for gamers anymore.

These digital spaces run on a mix of VR headsets, fancy AI tools, a sprinkle of blockchain, and a dash of AR magic. When you mash them together, they make experiences that feel surprisingly lifelike. Like, weirdly real. In Horizon Worlds, for example, people are hosting virtual birthday parties; in Decentraland, someone literally bought a virtual plot of land and opened an art gallery. And yes, people are spending actual money, sometimes a lot of it, on things that technically don't exist in the physical world.

But here's where things start to get messy.

As more people dive in, questions start popping up that don't have easy answers. For example, if you buy a digital jacket for your avatar, do you actually own it? Or what happens if someone harasses you in a VR concert? Is it possible to simply log off, or does that harm extend into genuine emotional distress? Additionally, who is overseeing the data being collected while you are simply enjoying a dance in a digital club?

Private companies currently own and operate many of these spaces. They establish their own set of rules, akin to each shopping mall having its own unique interpretation of the Constitution. That means things can get uneven; some places might be strict about safety, while others barely blink at serious issues. Concerns about harassment targeting women and marginalized individuals in VR are already on the rise. One article from The Guardian mentioned how some people feel the abuse hits harder in virtual worlds because it feels so close, so physical, even though it's all pixels.

Governments are starting to take notice. The European Parliament passed a resolution not too long ago that pushes for fair rules and better protection in virtual environments. Global organizations such as the World Economic Forum have also expressed their concern, advocating for a safe metaverse that upholds human rights. Still, most of the action so far has been scattered around some rules here, a few guidelines there. What's truly lacking is a comprehensive, lucid framework that establishes global connections and functions across various platforms.

This chapter aims to initiate this conversation by presenting a few well-founded policy ideas that are grounded in real-world experiences within these virtual spaces. It leans on three simple but important questions:

- *Which policies should we consider implementing to enhance the safety, fairness, and inclusivity of the metaverse?*
- *Why do these policies matter? What's the real-world risk if we ignore them?*
- *And how can we realistically put them into place, especially when platforms operate across different countries and legal systems?*

To explore those, the chapter focuses on seven key areas that are already showing signs of friction:

- *Digital identity and authentication (who you are online, and how that's verified)*
- *Data protection and privacy (what info gets collected and who controls it)*
- *Content moderation and harm prevention (keeping the bad stuff in check)*
- *Equitable access and inclusion (making sure no one's locked out)*
- *Digital labor rights and economic fairness (protecting people who work in these spaces)*
- *Algorithmic transparency and accountability (making the tech behind the curtain more understandable)*

Each of these areas functions similarly to a single gear in a machine. If even one of them breaks down, it can mess up the entire experience for users. The goal here isn't to scare anyone away from the metaverse; it's to help shape it into something that works better for everyone.

THE NEED FOR GOVERNANCE IN THE METAVERSE

The conversation around metaverse governance isn't just about tech anymore, it's about people. More and more, the metaverse is bleeding into parts of our daily lives: students are attending classes in VR, remote patients are meeting doctors through avatars, and even job interviews are happening in virtual offices. The problem? The rules haven't caught up.

In the past, we dealt with platform moderation for social media posts or online forums. But now we're dealing with entire virtual environments where your voice, gaze, body language, and even the digital shoes on your avatar are being tracked, sold, or manipulated. That's a different game entirely.

What Could Possibly Go Wrong?

Let's imagine you spend $500 on a virtual condo in a metaverse neighborhood that's trendy this month. The next day, the platform decides to suspend your account because of a vague "terms of service violation", maybe someone falsely reported you. Now you're locked out of your property. What rights do you actually have?

Not many, it turns out. Most regions don't treat digital assets as real property. So even though you paid for it, you might not be legally entitled to it. It's like buying furniture for a house that someone else can demolish at will (Soliman et al., 2025).

And the privacy issues? They go deeper than people realize. In virtual spaces, platforms can collect how you tilt your head, how fast you move your hands, the pitch of your voice, tiny details that seem harmless but can paint an eerie profile of who you are. These are not traditional browser cookies; this is behavioral data that can be used to infer mood, stress levels, and even mental health (European Commission, 2023)

Table 1. Examples of metaverse data and related privacy risks

Data Type	Example	Risk
Eye Tracking	Direction, blink rate	Emotional profiling, manipulation
Voice Tone	Real-time conversations	Deepfake risk, identity modeling
Gesture Patterns	Hand or body motion	Biometric tracking, movement prediction
Environment Audio	Room sounds in background	Unintended surveillance, context leakage

Source: Compiled from European Commission (2023) and Soliman et al. (2025).

Then there's safety. A woman once shared her experience in a virtual concert space where her avatar was cornered and groped. She knew it was just code and pixels, but her reaction was real. She felt violated. And she had no quick way to stop it or report it. In a VR space, harassment can feel like it's happening right in front of you, not behind a keyboard (The Guardian, 2025).

Accessibility's another story. Joining the metaverse is expensive. Between VR headsets, powerful laptops, and stable internet, many people simply can't afford to participate. Think about students in rural schools who missed out during the pandemic. The same thing is repeating here, only this time it's in a fancier digital world.

Who's Actually in Charge?

Here's the catch, most metaverse platforms make their own rules. You click "accept" on their terms of service, and that's it. You've entered a world governed not by laws but by private policy documents. There's little transparency, and users rarely get a say.

Now imagine you've bought clothes, artwork, or even a custom-built avatar in one platform. You decide to try another one, only to find out you can't take anything with you. It's like buying furniture for your apartment but having to leave it all behind when you move cities. This kind of digital lock-in gives platforms even more power over users.

A Few Early Signs of Progress

That said, not everyone's asleep at the wheel. The European Parliament recently passed a resolution that pushes for better standards around privacy, access, and user protections in virtual worlds (European Parliament, 2024).

Insights from Existing Governance Models

Recent academic studies have begun outlining frameworks for how governance might evolve in immersive digital ecosystems. Scholars in *Telematics and Informatics* and *Computers in Human Behavior* highlight multi-layered models that combine platform self-regulation with external oversight, much like hybrid regimes used for social-media governance (Kaplan & Haenlein, 2022). Meanwhile, work in *Ethics and Information Technology* stresses the need for adaptive "metagovernance" that balances innovation with protection against harm. These models provide early blueprints for coordinating standards across technical, ethical, and legal domains insight that can inform how public and private actors share responsibility for rule-making in virtual worlds.

ETHICAL FRAMEWORKS FOR VIRTUAL WORLDS

The idea behind ethics in the metaverse may seem abstract at first glance. However, as users increasingly teach, work, and socialize in immersive spaces, the need for thoughtful design becomes real. These environments are no longer digital games but evolving social systems that reflect values of autonomy, consent, inclusion, and fairness. Policy doesn't start with legislation; it starts with principle, a blueprint for digital societies that respects human dignity.

If a teenager is spending three hours a day socializing through an avatar, or a remote worker is attending conferences entirely in a virtual headset, we have to ask: What values are being baked into these spaces? Who is deciding which one is or what is appropriate or which is fair? What rights should follow us into these virtual worlds?

Policy doesn't start with legislation; it starts with principle. Just like a city needs a blueprint before it grows, digital societies need shared foundations. This section explores what those foundations might look like in practice.

Figure 1. Ethical dimensions of the metaverse ecosystem

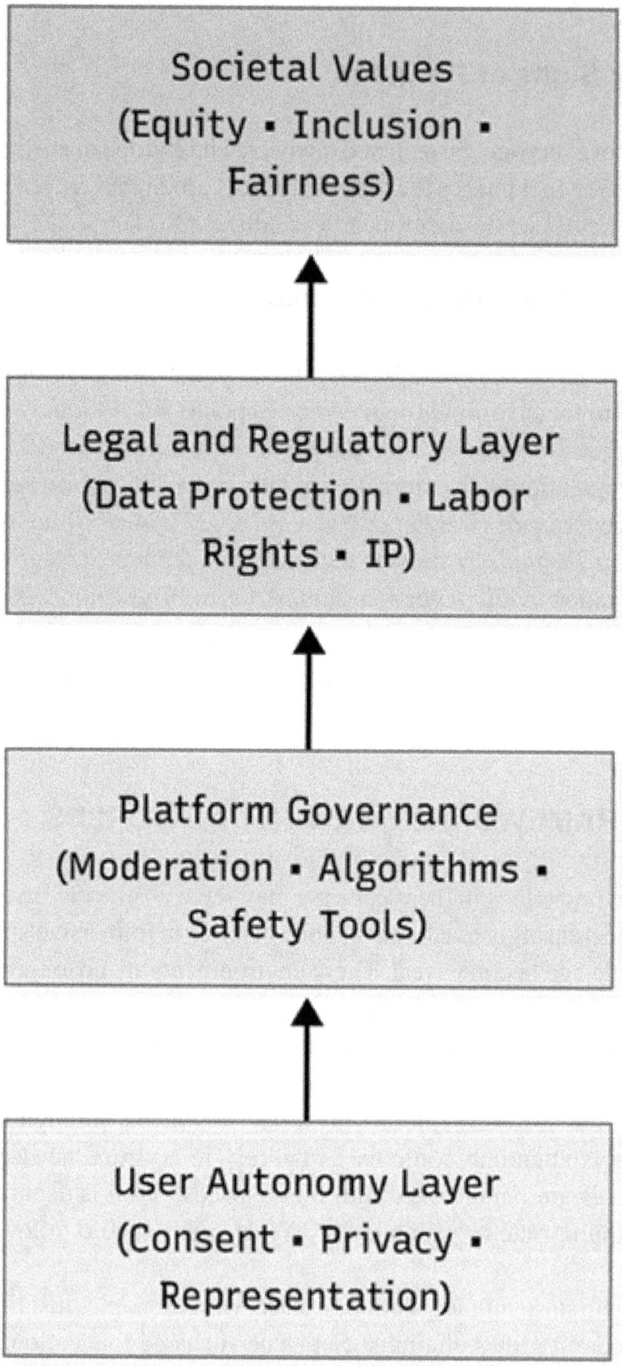

Autonomy Isn't Optional

Imagine you are attending a virtual conference. Your avatar is dressed professionally, your voice slightly altered for privacy, and your real name hidden. Yet, while you focus on the discussion, the platform quietly records your gestures, tracks your gaze, and analyzes how long you look at each speaker. Later, parts of that behavioral data are shared with advertisers or partners without your explicit awareness.

You never agreed to that.

This example highlights why autonomy in virtual environments must be treated as a fundamental right, not a convenience buried in settings menus. Autonomy means more than user control over interface options; it is the ability to decide how, when, and to what extent personal data and identity cues are shared. In immersive systems, where every movement or micro-expression can be captured, this right becomes the cornerstone of ethical design.

Scholars in digital ethics argue that true autonomy requires transparency, informed consent, and reversibility of choices (Floridi, 2019; Gorwa, 2019). Users should be able to understand what data is collected, modify their permissions at any time, and withdraw participation without penalty. The World Economic Forum likewise emphasizes that immersive technologies must embed autonomy safeguards at the architectural level, not rely on after-the-fact policy fixes (World Economic Forum, 2023a).

Designing for autonomy also supports psychological well-being. When users feel coerced or monitored, trust collapses and participation declines. Platforms that allow individuals to control visibility, disable motion tracking, or anonymize biometric data create environments where engagement is voluntary and respectful. These mechanisms are not barriers to innovation; they are foundations for sustainable digital societies.

In short, autonomy is not an optional feature to toggle on or off. It is the ethical backbone of the metaverse that ensures people remain authors of their own digital experiences rather than passive data sources for others to exploit.

Consent Can't Be a Checkbox

If you've used any website lately, you've probably clicked "accept" on a cookie banner without reading it. That's consent, technically, but let's be honest, nobody really reads those notices.

Now imagine you put on a headset to join a virtual fitness class. You look around the virtual gym, interact with your trainer, and log out. Later, you discover that the platform collected your voice patterns, heart rate, and eye movement during the session and sold them to third-party advertisers.

That's not just sneaky. That's unethical.

The European Commission argues that consent in immersive environments must be more than a formality. It needs to be explained clearly, revisited regularly, and be easy to revoke (European Commission, 2023). Think of it like saying yes to being photographed, you should know what the photo will be used for, and you should be allowed to say “no” later without losing access to the room.

Accessibility Is a Right, Not an Upgrade

During the pandemic, one school district introduced VR learning for its science classes. Students explored planets, cells, and ancient ruins through headsets. But in another school across town, kids were still sharing a single laptop among three siblings.

The metaverse risks repeating these gaps, only wider.

If participation in digital public life requires expensive hardware, fast internet, and advanced digital literacy, then millions will be locked out from the start. And often, those excluded are the same communities already underserved offline.

Yang (2023) suggests that immersive platforms should be designed with low-bandwidth and disability-friendly alternatives built in from day one, not patched in after complaints. Policymakers should also revisit programs like the U.S. E-Rate or national broadband initiatives, adapting them to support VR hardware, haptic devices, or metaverse-ready access for underserved areas.

Expression Isn't Always Harmless

Free speech matters. But the form it takes in the metaverse is different from a text post or tweet.

Picture a public plaza in a virtual world. A group is gathered, listening to music. Suddenly, offensive graffiti appears in the sky. Avatars fly in, shouting slurs through spatial audio. One person gets followed out of the space, their avatar cornered in a digital alley.

This isn't trolling. It feels like real harassment. And many users report that these moments leave a lasting psychological impact.

That's why content moderation needs to adapt, not to silence people, but to protect them. Soliman et al. (2025) argue for multi-layered governance models that blend human moderators, community voting, and platform-level policy, with clear appeals and transparent outcomes. Policies should differentiate between expression and harm, especially when environments are so immersive that abuse feels embodied.

Playing with Identity, Carefully

The freedom to play with identity is one of the most exciting parts of the metaverse. Someone shy in real life might feel bold as a dragon avatar. A user might explore gender in a way they couldn't safely do offline. That's powerful.

But it comes with complexity.

When users adopt avatars of a different race, ability, or background, especially for entertainment or profit, it raises questions. A popular content creator recently performed as a non-speaking autistic character, earning praise from some but backlash from advocacy groups who felt it trivialized their reality.

The solution isn't banning identity exploration. But just like in film, literature, or art, there must be space for accountability. Platforms can provide tools like avatar disclaimers, opt-in identity tags, or community flagging systems. Education about cultural sensitivity can be built into onboarding, not just terms of service checklists.

When Algorithms Are the Gatekeepers

A virtual marketplace showcases user-generated content, fashion, music, architecture. But creators from marginalized groups start noticing their work is buried in search results. It turns out an automated filter is ranking "edgy" content lower. And edgy, in this case, includes non-Western design styles and political art.

Algorithms aren't neutral.

The World Economic Forum recommends regular audits of algorithmic systems used in immersive platforms, especially for content visibility, behavior moderation, and social matching (World Economic Forum, 2023c). Transparency reports, like those used in financial or environmental sectors, could also apply here. Users should know what's influencing their experience and whether it's treating everyone fairly.

Summary

The ethical foundation for the metaverse isn't hypothetical anymore. As these platforms move from experiment to infrastructure, their influence over identity, access, and expression grows. Policies need to reflect the real people using them, not just the tech powering them.

Autonomy, consent, inclusion, safety, and fairness -- these aren't abstract values. They're the working parts of a digital society. And unless these values are woven into the design and governance of virtual worlds now, we may end up replicating offline inequalities in far more immersive and harder-to-escape ways.

CORE POLICY RECOMMENDATIONS

The metaverse is moving fast, but most platforms are still operating under loose rules, mainly their own terms of service. That's a problem. Imagine if every neighborhood in a city made up its own traffic laws. Chaos, right? The same goes for digital spaces. To ensure these virtual environments are safe, fair, and welcoming, we need real policies, ones that prioritize people over platforms. Each of the following policy areas presents a distinct challenge that users face in the metaverse.

Digital Identity, Authentication and Authorization -- Not Just an Avatar

A teenager joins a virtual job fair. He or she is competent, qualified, and ready and set for the interview. However, the recruiter doubts whether he or she is real because his avatar is cartoonish and anonymous. This kind of misjudgment will start becoming a concern.

Policy Suggestion: Create user-controlled, privacy-respecting identity systems that work across platforms.

Why It's Needed: Right now, there's no consistent way to verify who someone is in the metaverse. That opens the door to scams, impersonation, and abuse (Soliman et al., 2025).

How to Start: Decentralizing the Digital IDs (like W3C DIDs), which allow the user to prove their identity when required, for financial deals or professional networking, without revealing everything about themselves.

Data Privacy: It's Not Just Clicks Anymore

Consider a VR fitness app that tracks your heartbeat, eye movement, and tone of voice. Such apps will be helpful. However, this type of data provides a detailed picture of your mood, energy, and even potential health issues.

Policy Suggestion: Updating existing privacy laws or adding new rules that include biometric and behavioral data to ensure that consent is explicit, ongoing and can be revocable.

Why It's Needed: A larger number of users are unaware of the extent to which immersive apps collect data from different data sets, such as body data, and that this data can be misused if left unprotected (European Commission, 2023).

How to Start: First, it needs to be standardized for platforms to show the real-time data dashboards and let users change their sharing preference on demand. Laws like GDPR should be expanded to cover the XR-specific data as well; it's not just GDPR; each country-based law has to be updated.

Safety and Moderation: Harm Hits Harder in 3D

During a virtual concert, one user starts harassing another, getting too close, using threatening gestures, and shouting obscenities. It's not just on-screen it also feels physical.

Policy Suggestion: Implement a combination of human moderators and clear AI tools, incorporating safe features such as panic buttons or quiet zones.

Why It's Needed: Harassment feels intense, especially for women, minorities, youth, and other marginalized groups (The Guardian, 2025; McGlynn & Rigotti, 2025).

How to Start: Platforms should have community rules which are easy to find, train human moderators with cultural sensitivity, and build in fast, non-intrusive tools for users to escape or report abuse as it occurs.

Access and Inclusion: Not Everyone's Plugged In

In one district, teens attend virtual science labs using school-issued VR headsets. In another, kids struggle with a cracked phone and laggy internet. That's the digital divide, made worse by the high demands of XR technology.

Policy Suggestion: Public access centers and hold platforms accountable and design with inclusion in mind.

Why It's Needed: Access to the metaverse platforms shouldn't be limited by income, geography, or disability, else we risk building a digital world that leaves many behind (World Economic Forum, 2023a).

How to Start: Governments can fund XR hubs in libraries or community centers. Platforms should provide alternative formats like 2D versions, text-to-speech, or keyboard navigation and meet clear accessibility standards.

Digital Labor Rights: A Real Job Deserves Real Protection

A digital artist spends months building a virtual art gallery, selling NFTs to make ends meet. When the platform changes its terms, her work is wiped out with no pay, no contract, no recourse.

Policy Suggestion: Recognize virtual work as legitimate labor, with enforceable rights and protections.

Why It's Needed: People are working full-time in these spaces, often without contracts or fair pay (Soliman et al., 2025).

How to Start: Platforms should offer clear labor terms and use smart contracts to ensure payments. Regulators can establish digital minimum wage standards and portable benefits for creators.

Algorithmic Transparency: When the System Isn't Fair

A small business owner notices their virtual shop gets fewer visitors than similar stores. Turns out, the platform's ranking algorithm favored certain lighting setups, something they weren't told.

Policy Suggestion: Make platform algorithms open to audit and explainable to users.

Why It's Needed: Algorithms influence visibility, interaction, and even income. When they're a black box, bias and manipulation can flourish (Yang, 2023).

How to Start: Require platforms to publish AI model cards and impact statements. Let users see why decisions were made and appeal to those that seem unfair. Internal ethics boards should guide AI development.

Digital Assets and Virtual Economies: Not Just Pixels

A gamer spends $1,000 on virtual land. Months later, the platform shuts down and deletes everything, no refund, no warning.

Policy Suggestion: Treat digital assets like real financial products, with consumer protections and legal standards.

Why It's Needed: NFTs, tokens, and virtual real estate often carry real-world value. But when platforms go bust or change the rules, users lose everything (European Commission, 2023).

How to Start: Apply know-your-customer (KYC) and anti-fraud laws to high-value transactions. Require licensing for large marketplaces and publish fair-use terms for asset retention.

Table 2. Quick-glance policy areas and recommendations

Area	Policy Suggestion	Why It Matters
Identity	Portable, privacy-based digital IDs	Prevent impersonation and build trust
Privacy	Biometric and behavioral data consent	Protect users' personal and emotional information
Safety	Hybrid moderation, panic tools	Reduce harassment and help users respond in real-time
Access	Public XR spaces, inclusive platform design	Avoid deepening digital inequalities
Labor Rights	Contracts and fair pay for virtual work	Support growing digital economies and creators
Algorithms	Explainable, auditable AI systems	Prevent hidden bias and user invisibility
Virtual Assets	Consumer rights for NFTs and crypto holdings	Guard users from loss due to platform changes or scams

INTERNATIONAL AND MULTI-STAKEHOLDER GOVERNANCE MODELS

The metaverse is inherently global. Its users log in from all over the world, attend events, build careers, and exchange digital goods often without being aware of the country in which the platform is registered. This isn't just a new layer of the internet; it's a shared space that floats above borders. And that means no single government or company can or should make the rules on its own.

Figure 2. Multi-stakeholder governance model for the metaverse

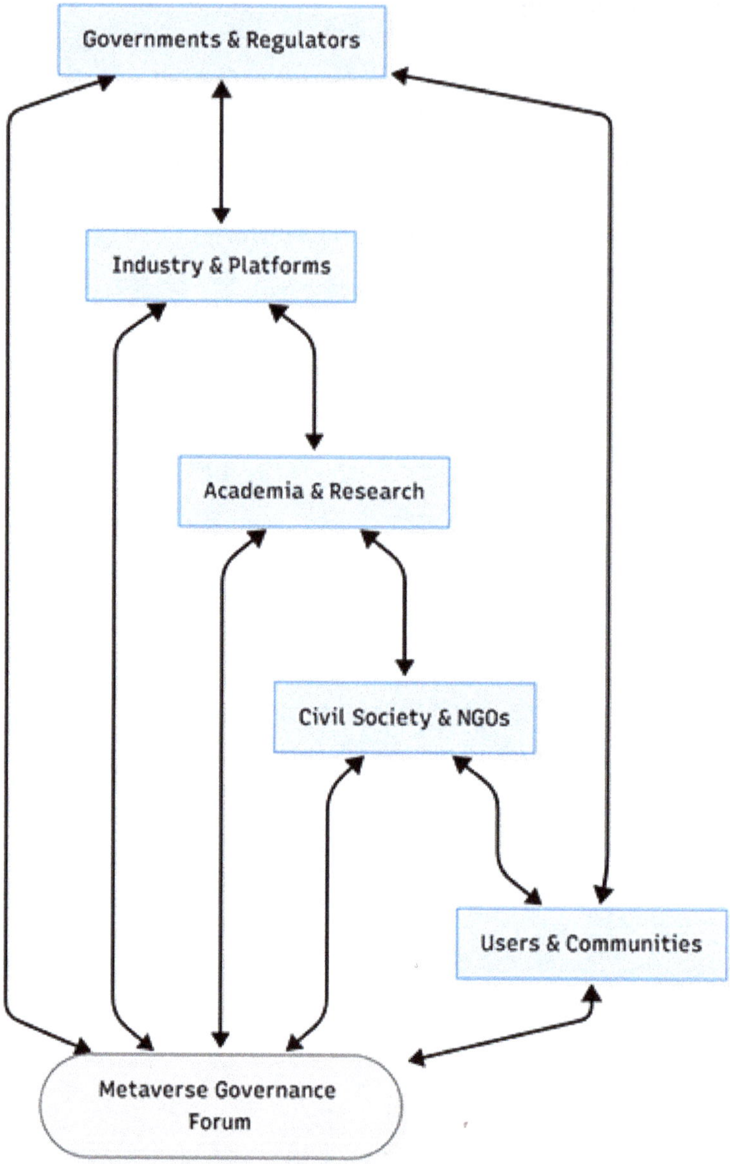

Why Cross-Border Governance Is Necessary

Traditional internet governance already shows why shared oversight is crucial. A designer in Brazil may sell digital clothing through a U.S.-based platform using blockchain payments settled in Singapore. When disputes arise over copyright, data privacy, or contract enforcement whose laws apply? In the absence of coordination, platforms often select the most lenient jurisdiction, triggering what scholars call a "regulatory race to the bottom" (World Economic Forum, 2023a).

Global governance prevents such gaps by establishing minimum standards that travel with the user, not the server. It allows ethical norms and human-rights principles to move across borders with the same fluidity as digital assets. Just as international aviation relies on shared safety codes and mutual recognition of licenses, the metaverse will need interoperable rules for identity verification, digital property, and dispute resolution.

What the Internet Already Taught Us

The internet's early architects already grappled with similar challenges. Institutions such as the **Internet Corporation for Assigned Names and Numbers (ICANN)** and the **Internet Governance Forum (IGF)** introduced the concept of **multi-stakeholderism**, where governments, companies, civil society, and technical experts collaborate in open, consensus-based decision-making (Mueller, 2017; Hofmann, 2016). These bodies do not legislate; instead, they coordinate technical standards, security practices, and policies that allow networks to interoperate.

Translating these ideas to the metaverse suggests that coordination not control should be the goal. A **Metaverse Governance Forum (MGF)** could operate as a neutral space bringing together platform representatives, regulators, researchers, and user communities. Its focus would include:

- establishing ethical design and interoperability standards,
- publishing transparency and accountability reports, and
- facilitating rapid response to cross-platform harms such as harassment or fraud.

Such a forum would not replace national authority; rather, it would complement it by encouraging common language and shared technical protocols.

Table 3. Comparative overview of emerging metaverse and digital governance policies by region

Region / Country	Policy or Initiative	Focus Area	Status / Year	Relevance to Metaverse Governance
European Union	*EU Digital Services Act (DSA), AI Act, GDPR*	Platform accountability, data protection, algorithmic transparency	Adopted 2022–2024	Provides baseline for cross-platform moderation, AI ethics, and data portability
United States	*White House Blueprint for an AI Bill of Rights, FTC data privacy initiatives*	Civil rights, consent, biometric data	Ongoing (since 2022)	Emphasizes fairness, non-discrimination, and user autonomy in digital ecosystems
United Kingdom	*Online Safety Act*	Content regulation, user safety, age verification	2023	Early legislation addressing metaverse content risks and moderation standards
Singapore	*Digital Safety Bill, AI Governance Framework*	Trust, accountability, transparency	2023	Pioneer in establishing transparent AI and XR governance principles
South Korea	*Metaverse Industry Promotion Act*	Economic development, standards, and digital identity	Draft (2024)	National framework for virtual identity and creator rights
United Arab Emirates	*Dubai Metaverse Strategy*	Innovation, digital economy, governance sandbox	2022	Integrates national metaverse council for regulatory foresight
China	*Metaverse Development Action Plan (Beijing)*	Industrial innovation, content oversight	2022	Strong government-led approach emphasizing data security and cultural regulation

Sources:

- ***European Union: European Commission. (2023)***. *An EU initiative on Web 4.0 and virtual worlds.* https://digital-strategy.ec.europa.eu/en/library/eu-initiative-virtual-worlds-head-start-next-technological-transition; ***European Parliament. (2024). Resolution on virtual worlds.*** https://www.europarl.europa.eu/legislative-train/theme-a-europe-fit-for-the-digital-age/file-metaverse
- ***United States:*** *White House Office of Science and Technology Policy. (2022). Blueprint for an AI Bill of Rights.* https://www.whitehouse.gov/ostp/ai-bill-of-rights/
- ***United Kingdom:*** *UK Parliament. (2023). Online Safety Act 2023.* https://www.legislation.gov.uk/ukpga/2023/50/enacted
- ***Singapore:*** *IMDA. (2023). Code of Practice for Online Safety.* https://www.imda.gov.sg/regulations-and-licensing-listing/online-safety
- ***South Korea:*** *Korean Ministry of Science and ICT. (2022). Metaverse Industry Promotion Act [Draft].* https://globalbusinessoutlook.com/technology/south-koreas-msit-enact-special-metaverse-laws/
- ***UAE:*** *Dubai Government. (2022). Dubai Metaverse Strategy.* https://u.ae/en/about-the-uae/digital-uae/dubai-metaverse-strategy
- ***China:*** *Beijing Municipal Government. (2022). Beijing Municipal Action Plan for Metaverse Innovation and Development (2022-2024).* https://cointelegraph.com/news/beijing-announces-two-year-metaverse-innovation-and-development-plan

Good governance is like preparing a communal meal: if only one cook chooses the recipe, others go hungry or worse, allergic. The same principle applies to digital governance. If rules are written solely by corporations, user rights become secondary to profit. If governments act alone, innovation may stall. True legitimacy requires contributions from all affected groups.

Multi-stakeholder participation balances these perspectives:

- **Governments** ensure alignment with constitutional and human-rights obligations.
- **Industry leaders** contribute technical expertise and resources.
- **Academia** examines long-term social and psychological impacts.
- **Civil-society organizations** advocate for equity, inclusion, and marginalized communities.
- **End users** provide lived experience of how policies work or fail in practice.

Collaborative policymaking also guards against cultural bias. Without regional participation, global standards risk reflecting only Western or corporate viewpoints. Regional alliances such as the **African Union**, **ASEAN**, and **Mercosur** could adapt metaverse policies to local contexts while still supporting global compatibility. This approach transforms governance from a top-down directive into a continuous conversation grounded in shared responsibility.

The Role of Regional and Global Institutions

International bodies are already laying groundwork for ethical virtual-world governance. In 2023 the **European Commission** hosted *Web 4.0 and Virtual Worlds: A New Horizon for Citizens*, emphasizing accessibility, human rights, and algorithmic accountability (European Commission, 2023). **UNESCO** continues to expand its *Recommendation on the Ethics of Artificial Intelligence*, much of which applies directly to immersive environments that rely on AI for personalization and moderation (UNESCO, 2021).

These initiatives demonstrate how supranational organizations can act as anchors for emerging norms. Meanwhile, technical groups such as the **Khronos Group** and **Open Metaverse Alliance (OMA3)** are developing interoperability standards that let avatars, digital assets, and credentials travel across platforms. Partnering these engineering efforts with policy oversight ensures that openness is not just a technical feature but a rights-preserving principle.

Regional institutions also have a crucial role. The **African Union's Digital Transformation Strategy** and **ASEAN's Digital Governance Framework** provide templates that can be extended to XR and metaverse applications. Embedding global standards within local cultures helps prevent a one-size-fits-all model and keeps governance relevant to diverse populations.

Working Toward a Shared, Interoperable Future

Ultimately, the goal is a metaverse that functions like international air travel, multiple carriers, shared runways, and consistent safety expectations. Interoperability means users can bring avatars, credentials, and digital assets from one platform to another without losing privacy or ownership. It also means that accountability, data protection, and ethical safeguards remain intact wherever users go.

Some of this vision already exists. The **Open Metaverse Alliance (OMA3)** unites web-3 and XR developers to define open standards for identity and asset transfer. Likewise, **Khronos Group's OpenXR** framework allows hardware and software ecosystems to share a common interface, reducing vendor lock-in. Imagine a student earning a certified digital badge in one virtual university and displaying it in another platform seamlessly with no re-registration, no data loss, just portable proof of achievement.

Building such a future requires agreement on identity protocols, content formats, and user-rights protection just as aviation relies on common air-traffic rules. Coordinated governance transforms fragmentation into trust, allowing innovation to flourish while protecting people from harm (World Economic Forum, 2023b; European Commission, 2023).

Figure 3. Interoperability stack for the metaverse

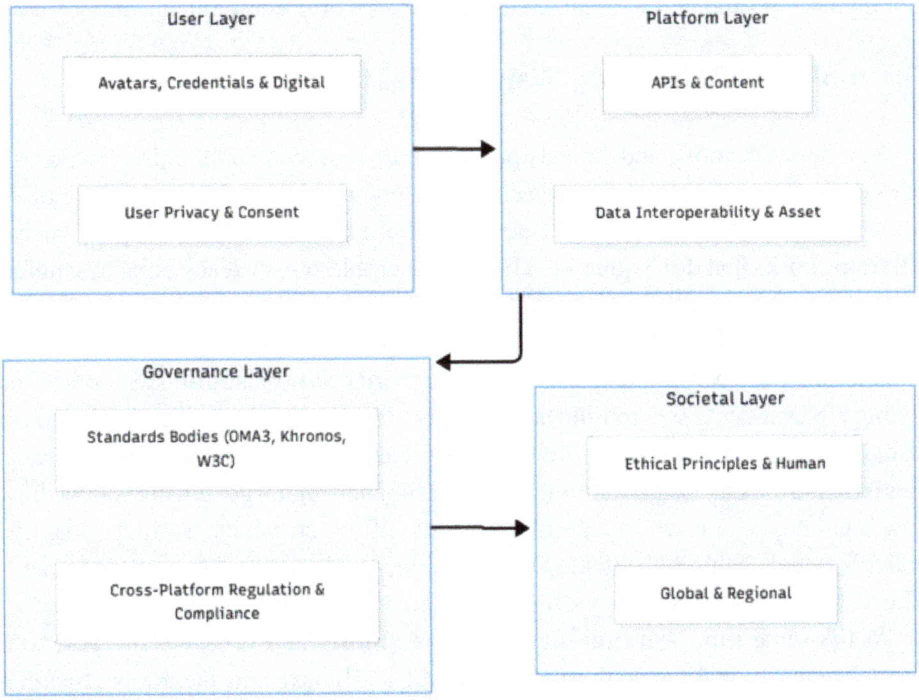

CHALLENGES TO IMPLEMENTATION

Coming up with fair and ethical rules for the metaverse is the first step. But actually making those rules work in real life? That's going to be a big challenge. The metaverse is evolving faster than laws and policies can keep pace. Even if we have good plans on paper, putting them into practice hits some real snags. Here's what's standing in our way right now.

Laws from Different Places Don't Mix Well

One big headache is that the metaverse doesn't care about borders. People from all over the world meet in the same virtual spaces but every country has its own set of laws about privacy, taxes, work, and speech. So when something goes wrong, it's often a mess figuring out which laws actually apply. For example, what happens if someone in Brazil buys a digital item on a U.S. based platform and runs into trouble?

Who steps in? Without clear agreements between countries, these issues get stuck, making fairness and enforcement a tangled mess (World Economic Forum, 2023a).

Technology Is Changing Way Too Fast

New features, tools, and gadgets pop up in the metaverse all the time virtual offices, new currencies, AI that reads emotions, you name it. Policymakers are often stuck trying to catch up, writing rules after the tech is already out there or using old frameworks that don't quite fit. This means problems—privacy breaches, unfair algorithms, scams can slip through before rules catch on. The system needs to be ready to adapt as the tech keeps moving forward (UNESCO, 2021).

One practical way to keep pace is through **regulatory sandboxes** controlled testing environments where innovators and policymakers can trial new immersive technologies under supervision before large-scale rollout. The United Kingdom's AI Sandbox and the European Commission's experimental digital governance pilots show how regulators can learn in real time without stifling creativity. Similar "adaptive policy" models could be extended to metaverse development, letting governments adjust standards as technology evolves instead of locking them into static laws.

At the same time, **continuous horizon-scanning** and **cross-sector research councils** could monitor breakthroughs in XR, AI, and blockchain integration, flagging risks early. By pairing flexible regulation with technical foresight, policymakers can move from reacting to innovation toward **co-creating it responsibly**, ensuring that safety, inclusion, and human rights remain central even as the pace accelerates (World Economic Forum, 2023a).

Figure 4. Lifecycle of ethical policy development

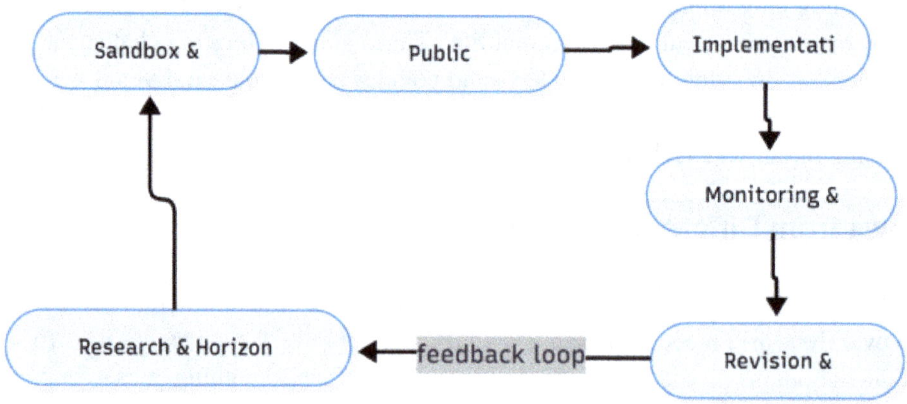

Big Platforms Might Not Want to Play Along

The biggest metaverse companies often make money by collecting lots of user data and showing immersive ads. So naturally, they may push back against rules that cut into their profits, like strict transparency or limits on data use. Without laws to make them comply or pressure from users and watchdogs they might not prioritize ethics on their own. Voluntary guidelines are a start but usually aren't sufficient. That's why users, governments, and civil groups have to work together to keep platforms honest and safe (Soliman et al., 2025).

Lots of People Don't Know the Risks

For any rules to work, people need to know their rights and how to stay safe. But many new metaverse users do not fully understand the risks like bio tracking, AI curated content, or tricky digital marketplaces. Digital skills also vary a lot, especially among kids, seniors, and people with limited internet. That makes users easy targets for scams, fake info, or harassment. Without solid education efforts, even the best rules won't protect everyone (Yang, 2023).

Too Many Rules Could Kill Innovation

At the same time, too many or too strict rules could make it really hard for developers, especially small or nonprofit ones to try new ideas or break into the market. We need to find the sweet spot rules that protect users but still let creativity and new projects thrive, especially those focused on education, community, or social good (European Commission, 2023).

Tech Challenges and Missing Common Standards

Lots of the ideas for governing the metaverse like letting you carry your digital ID from one world to another or showing how AI makes decisions need serious tech to work. But right now, there's no universal system that lets avatars, digital goods, or data move seamlessly across platforms. Even basic features are still catching up. Without shared tech standards and close teamwork among developers, governance will stay patchy and hard to scale. Building a truly connected metaverse means solving these engineering challenges not just writing policies (World Economic Forum, 2023b).

FUTURE DIRECTIONS AND RESEARCH OPPORTUNITIES

Shaping the metaverse doesn't have to be somebody else's job; it's something we can all pitch in on, right now. Since these virtual worlds are still taking shape, we have an unusual window: a chance to set things up so they're fun, safe, creative, and fair for everyone. If we work together early, we might just avoid the headaches that come from letting problems grow too big.

Here are five big questions (and exciting possibilities) we should tackle together:

Let's Make AI Smarter and More Accountable

AI is everywhere in the metaverse. It decides what we see, recommends who we meet, even keeps the peace. But old rules can't keep up. We need new ways to make sure this kind of AI acts with real fairness, can be explained when it gets it wrong, and doesn't tip the scales against anyone.

This isn't something just governments or companies can fix on their own. It needs fresh ideas from everyone: policymakers, coders, regular users, watchdogs so we're all in the loop and problems get fixed fast. The rules shouldn't be stuck; they should grow and change as AI does (UNESCO, 2021; UNESCO, 2023).

Figuring Out What Virtual Worlds Do To Us

Spending time in the metaverse feels thrilling, sometimes a little weird, sometimes really fun. But nobody quite knows yet: does it help us feel more connected, or more alone? Does it stretch our creativity, or wear us out? There aren't many good answers yet. We need more real-life studies, people watching, measuring, asking questions across fields like psychology, tech, law, and medicine so we know what's helping and what might be hurting, even if it's by accident (World Economic Forum, 2023a).

Making Trust and Our Digital Selves Portable

Wouldn't it be amazing if you could jump from one virtual world to another without having to start over, or rebuild your reputation each time? To do that, we need ways to prove who we are (safely), carry our stuff with us, and trust that no one's messing with our identity.

So, how do we make systems that are easy to use, but still super safe and private?

There are tough trade-offs here: convenience, privacy, ownership. Getting it right means inventing the tech, but also thinking about what actually feels fair to real people (Yang, 2023).

But portability isn't just technical, it's deeply ethical. What happens if your **avatar's reputation or verified digital identity is stolen** and misused across multiple worlds? The damage isn't limited to lost items; it can affect employment, social standing, or even mental health. Trust, once broken, is hard to rebuild in any reality. That's why emerging standards such as **Decentralized Identifiers (DIDs)** and **zero-knowledge proofs** are so promising: they let users authenticate themselves or share credentials without revealing sensitive personal data.

Ultimately, the ability to move safely and maintain credibility across platforms should be seen as a **digital human right**, not a luxury feature. Just as passports protect travelers offline, interoperable trust systems must protect users online ensuring that reputation, consent, and identity remain under individual control, wherever the next log-in takes them (World Economic Forum, 2023b; European Commission, 2023).

Power to the People: Can DAOs Work for Us All?

Some groups in digital worlds are trying out DAOs places where everyone gets a say (instead of some boss at the top), and the rules are coded out in the open. This sounds awesome, but it won't work unless it's actually fair if all kinds of people have real power, not just a few insiders.

We still have to see: can communities really steer themselves? Can we stop things from getting gamed or hijacked? Researchers and communities need time to run experiments, try different blends of local control and outside checks, and share what works so we all learn together (Soliman et al., 2025).

One Metaverse, Many Cultures

The metaverse isn't run by just one country, one language, or one set of customs. There's so much variety and that's a good thing! But it also means that rules and tools need to flex, so everyone's voice fits in. We won't get there by copying "default" rules from one place and pretending they work everywhere. Instead, we'll need real translation, local voices, and a bunch of different kinds of experts (anthropologists, designers, community leaders, lawyers. . .) working together. One-size-fits-all just won't cut it (European Commission, 2023).

CONCLUSION

We're at the start of something big. The metaverse isn't just an idea for tomorrow, it's already changing how we meet, learn, and play today. Sometimes it feels thrilling. Sometimes, honestly, it feels a little overwhelming. Wherever you stand, it's clear these new worlds are weaving into our real lives in schools, shops, hospitals, and even public services. But let's be honest: big changes bring tough questions. How do we keep people safe? Who looks out for our digital selves? How can everyone, not just a lucky few, benefit from these spaces?

This chapter has wrestled with all of that. My goal is to find ways to build virtual worlds that are fair, welcoming, and safe for all of us, not just the tech giants. We dug into the big risks—think of our private data, our digital rights, and who controls the platforms we use each day. But instead of just worrying, we explored some solid principles to guide us: respect for human rights, the power of consent, a spirit of inclusion, and treating everyone with fairness.

It's not simple. Good intentions aren't enough. That's why I broke things down into seven key areas places where we really need to get it right:

- Who we are online (digital identity)
- Keeping our data private and safe
- Stopping abuse and harmful content
- Making sure everyone gets a fair shot at joining in
- Protecting digital workers and fair economies
- Being open about how algorithms make decisions
- Setting fair rules for virtual goods and online money

But here's what matters most: none of us can do this alone. Building a better metaverse can't be up to just one country or only tech companies. We need each other's policymakers, tech makers, and everyday people. We can learn from the ways the internet is managed by groups like ICANN and W3C and imagine something even better for the metaverse: a place where users like you and me help set the rules.

Of course, there are real hurdles, confusing laws, fast-changing tech, companies that might not want to play along, or many people simply not knowing what's at stake. But those challenges give us a reason to act now together before the path gets set for us.

So, what should we work on next? Here's what I see:

- Smarter, fairer AI you can actually understand (UNESCO, 2021; UNESCO, 2023)
- Rules that work across cultures, not just in one country (European Commission, 2023)
- Fresh research into how these digital spaces shape our real lives (World Economic Forum, 2023a)
- Ways to trust digital identities and keep control over them (Yang, 2023)

- Decision-making models (like DAOs) where communities have a real voice (Soliman et al., 2025)

Ultimately, what we're building isn't just new technology, it's a new layer of society. These virtual worlds will reflect the values we choose to embed in them. **If we design them with empathy, transparency, and inclusion now, we can create spaces that amplify connection instead of division.** The metaverse's future will not be written by code alone but by the collective will of the people who inhabit it.

Now is the time to act to shape governance frameworks, invest in equitable access, and commit to ethical innovation. The opportunity is still ours to seize. If we design these worlds with fairness in mind today, tomorrow's metaverse could reflect the best of us, not just the smartest code.

REFERENCES

European Commission. (2023). An EU initiative on Web 4.0 and virtual worlds: A head start in the next technological transition. Retrieved from https://digital-strategy.ec.europa.eu/en/policies/virtual-worlds

European Parliament. (2024). Resolution on virtual worlds: Civil, company, commercial and intellectual property law issues. *Official Journal of the European Union*. Retrieved from https://ipwatchdog.com/2024/11/12/virtual-worlds-real-rules-eu-parliaments-first-take-ip-metaverse/id=183128/

Floridi, L. (2019). *The logic of information: A theory of philosophy as conceptual design*. Oxford University Press., DOI: 10.1093/oso/9780198833635.001.0001

Gorwa, R. (2019). The platform governance triangle: Conceptualising the informal regulation of online content. *Internet Policy Review*, *8*(2). Advance online publication. DOI: 10.14763/2019.2.1407

Hofmann, J. (2016). Multi-stakeholderism in internet governance: Putting a fiction into practice. *Journal of Cyber Policy*, *1*(1), 29–49. DOI: 10.1080/23738871.2016.1158303

Kaplan, A., & Haenlein, M. (2022). Metaverse: A new dimension of human interaction. *Journal of Business Research*, *149*, 587–600. DOI: 10.1016/j.jbusres.2022.04.053

McGlynn, C., & Rigotti, C. (2025). From virtual rape to meta-rape: Sexual violence, criminal law and the metaverse. *Oxford Journal of Legal Studies*, *45*(3), 554–582. Advance online publication. DOI: 10.1093/ojls/gqaf009 PMID: 40896405

Mueller, M. (2017). *Will the internet fragment? Sovereignty, globalization and cyberspace*. Polity Press.

Soliman, M., Ismail, D. S., Ahmed, S., Ali, S., Salama, S., Khalil, I., Nassar, M., Zaki, M., & Rizk, M. (2025). Are we ready for the metaverse? Implications, legal landscape, and recommendations for responsible development. *Digital Society : Ethics, Socio-Legal and Governance of Digital Technology*, *4*(1), 9. Advance online publication. DOI: 10.1007/s44206-025-00163-0

The Guardian. (2025, June 10). The misogyny of the metaverse: Is Mark Zuckerberg's dream world a no-go area for women? Retrieved from https://www.theguardian.com/society/2025/jun/10/the-misogyny-of-the-metaverse-is-mark-zuckerbergs-dream-world-a-no-go-area-for-women

UNESCO. (2021). *Recommendation on the ethics of artificial intelligence*. Retrieved from https://unesdoc.unesco.org/ark:/48223/pf0000380455

UNESCO. (2023). *Guidance for generative AI in education and research.* Retrieved from https://www.unesco.org/en/articles/guidance-generative-ai-education-and-research

World Economic Forum. (2023a). *Defining and building the metaverse: An action plan for responsible innovation.* Retrieved from https://initiatives.weforum.org/defining-and-building-the-metaverse/home

World Economic Forum. (2023b). Interoperability in the metaverse. Governance briefing paper. Retrieved from https://www.weforum.org/press/2023/01/landmark-reports-on-future-of-metaverse-focus-on-interoperability-and-value-creation/

World Economic Forum. (2023c). *Social implications of the metaverse.* Retrieved from https://www.weforum.org/reports/social-implications-of-the-metaverse/

Yang, L. (2023). Recommendations for metaverse governance based on technical standards. *Humanities & Social Sciences Communications, 10*(1), 253. DOI: 10.1057/s41599-023-01750-7

KEY TERMS AND DEFINITIONS

Algorithmic Transparency: How clearly people can see and understand the choices AI systems make.

Biometric Data: Info about your body or actions like your voice, movements, or face that's collected in digital places.

DAO: A group that runs itself online, with rules and votes handled by code (usually on a blockchain) no manager required.

Digital Identity: The "you" that shows up online your avatar, info, and how you act in digital spaces.

Digital Inclusion: Making sure everyone no matter where they live or who they are can join in and use these digital worlds.

Ethical Governance: Setting up rules and systems for virtual worlds that put people and fairness first.

Interoperability: Being able to take your stuff (like avatars or badges) from one virtual world to another, without losing anything.

Metaverse: Picture a bunch of virtual worlds, all connected, where you can meet friends, work, or play, using tools like VR, AR, blockchain, and AI.

Chapter 12
The Metaverse in Action: Use Cases Transforming Workplace, Education, and Industry

Mohan Sankaran
https://orcid.org/0009-0005-2058-2946
Independent Researcher, USA

ABSTRACT

The metaverse isn't just a far away fantasy it's our daily life. Technologies such as VR,AR, AI, blockchain and the Internet of Things power the metaverse which is transforming how we work, learn and engage with the world around us. This chapter shows how this tech creates a 3D digital spaces and what it means for workplaces, education and industry.In workplaces, the metaverse creates virtual offices, AI assistants and blockchain based cyber resumes. Teams can unite in shared 3D spaces, no matter where they are. In school, students learn by inspecting 3D human cells,walking through digital ancient civilizations while AI tailors lessons to each learner's need. In work, we are seeing aspects from digital stores to digital twins of factories and cities that help optimize actions and predict errors before they start. But change isn't without problems. As our lives move into these 3D spaces, we face questions about privacy, digital identity, mental health, and fairness. This chapter offers a framework for how we can build the ideal metaverse responsibly and safely.

DOI: 10.4018/979-8-3373-3043-3.ch012

INTRODUCTION TO THE METAVERSE AND ITS CONVERGENCE TECHNOLOGIES

Definition and Evolution of the Metaverse

The word metaverse a combination of "meta" (beyond) and "universe" was first introduced by Neal Stephenson in his 1992 novel Snow Crash, where it narrates a digital world that coexists with the real one. Today, the metaverse refers to a immersive digital environment that connect users all over the world. The Metaverse blends physical reality with virtual experiences. However it is not a single platform or technology but a fusion of different technologies, virtual reality (VR), augmented reality (AR), artificial intelligence (AI), blockchain and the Internet of Things (IoT). These applications collectively allow users to socialize with the digital world and each other in real time across three-dimensional (3D) spaces.

From the early days of multiplayer online games and Second Life-style virtual worlds, the concept of the metaverse has grown rapidly. Today's metaverse is more than just a digital playground; it is seen as a next-generation internet-a 3-dimensional web where individuals can work, learn, interact and conduct business in ways that unfocus the boundaries between physical and digital worlds. Major tech companies like Meta, Microsoft, Apple, Google and NVIDIA are heavily investing in building the infrastructure of this emerging ecosystem (McKinsey & Company, 2023), signaling its potential to redesign how we live and interact.

Historical Context: From Online Worlds to Web3 Metaverse

While the term metaverse was coined by Neal Stephenson in Snow Crash (1992), its evolution into a technological prototype has taken decades to create. Early manifestations appeared in multiplayer online role-playing games (MMORPGs) like Ultima Online (1997) and World of Warcraft (2004), which presented a persistent digital environments where millions could interact and socialize. These virtual games introduced important concepts like digital funds like crypto, social interactions and virtual governments (Castronova, 2005).

In 2003, Second Life took a big step forward for the Metaverse by introducing a world less focused on gaming and more on user-created content, learning and social interaction. It was perhaps the first serious attempt at a user driven metaverse, with virtual real estate, in world businesses and even virtual universities. Though it lost momentum, Second Life remains a critical evolutionary step that has proven the potential and limitations of early immersive platforms.

Simultaneously, the rise of Web 2.0-characterized by user-generated content, social networking and participatory culture-enabled the democratization of online identity. Platforms like YouTube, Facebook and Reddit made the internet socially and behaviorally rich, setting a behavioral foundation for more immersive experiences.

Today, the transition toward a Web3-powered metaverse is underway. Unlike Web 2.0's centralized platforms, Web3 envisions a decentralized internet where users have control over their data, identities and digital assets-enabled through blockchain technologies and governed by decentralized protocols. This shift is not merely technical but also philosophical: it represents a move from platform-centric to user-owned ecosystems. Today, the transition toward a Web3-powered metaverse is underway. Unlike Web 2.0's centralized platforms, Web3 envisions a decentralized internet where users have control over their data, identities and digital assets-enabled through blockchain technologies and governed by decentralized protocols. This shift is not merely technical but also philosophical: it represents a move from platform-centric to user-owned ecosystems.

Expanded Explanation of Each Technology with Real-World Examples

- While the metaverse uses various applications to give users the most immersive experience, their true potential emerges when applied in real-world cases.
- Artificial Intelligence (AI): AI supplies intelligent behavior within the metaverse (Akiner & Akiner, 2023). Tools like ChatGPT or Midjourney showcase how generative AI can power real-time avatar interactions, content creation and learning systems that adapt to the user. AI monitors content and translates speech ensuring safety for users.
- Internet of Things (IoT): IoT integrates the digital world into the physical world (Li et al., 2022). For example, city like traffic lights, energy grids and predictions of weather sensors can feed real-time data into the virtual twin of cities. In industrial Metaverses, IoT-enabled equipment can power maintenance simulations that can predict when maintenance is needed.
- Blockchain and NFTs: Games like Decentraland and Sandbox use blockchain to allow digital land ownership (Gadekallu et al., 2022), while Ethereum-based NFTs allow users to make, bartar and monetize digital art and experiences with verifiable provenance.

These technologies are not isolated, they work together to create a interactive and responsive environments.

Technological Convergence and the Feeling of "Presence"

A clarifying feature of the metaverse is its power to create a sense of presence-the psychological perception of "being there" in a virtual space. This effect is from the fusion of VR/AR (visual immersion), AI (behavioral realism), IoT (real-time responsiveness) and blockchain (identity and ownership anchoring).

For example, in a metaverse classroom:

VR offers a 3-D interface to explore a historical simulation.AI provides a immersive interactive teacher or peer. IoT can track real-world movements for embodied learning. Blockchain makes sure that a student's credentials and learning accomplishments are safe and portable.

Together, these layers blur the line between physical and digital reality, enabling a continuum of experience rather than a switch between "online" and "offline." It is in this seamless blending of technologies that the metaverse moves beyond mere novelty and begins to serve as a living, integrated extension of human society.

Key Enablers: VR, AR, AI, Blockchain and IoT

The metaverse would not be possible without the synergistic advancement of several foundational technologies:

Virtual Reality (VR)

VR creates fully immersive environments that transport users into entirely digital worlds using headsets and motion tracking. It allows for embodied presence in virtual spaces-whether exploring a 3D model of a factory, attending a concert, or participating in a remote team meeting. VR plays a important role in creating realistic simulations and experiences that go beyond 2-D interactions.

Augmented Reality (AR)

AR integrates digital content in to the real world, creating a seamless mixture of physical and virtual worlds. Unlike VR, AR does not isolate the user but enhances their insight of the real environment using smartphones, AR glasses, or headsets. Applications range from virtual maintenance and education to shopping and navigation.

Artificial Intelligence (AI)

AI powers the metaverse's intelligence layer. It creates realistic avatars, intelligent NPCs (non-player characters), personalized education, language translation, behavior prediction and creating content. AI also plays an important role in executing moderation, enforcing safety and scaling user interactions.

Blockchain and Web3 Technologies

Blockchain introduces decentralization, security and ownership into the metaverse. Through smart contracts, NFTs (non-fungible tokens) and spreads the authorites to autonomous organizations (DAOs), users can own virtual assets, govern platforms democratically and undergo transactions. This allows brand-new economic models, including games with prizes and digital real estate markets.

Internet of Things (IoT)

(IoT) connects the physical and digital worlds by embedding sensors and devices in real-world objects. In the metaverse, IoT enables real-time data from the physical environment-like biometric inputs, machinery operations, or geolocation-to be integrated into virtual experiences. This is especially relevant for industrial applications and digital twins.

Together, these technologies create a layered and interoperable architecture for the metaverse, turning static web pages into dynamic environments where multisensory experiences, identity and economies are continuously evolving.

Why the Metaverse Matters Now: Post-Pandemic Acceleration

While the applications behind the metaverse have been in development for over a decade, the COVID-19 pandemic sped up the rapid adoption and integration. With billions of people in lockdown digital platforms became lifelines for work, education, entertainment and socializing. Zoom calls and online classrooms proved there was potential of 2D digital spaces, as there was limitation, sparking interest in a more 3-D interactive options.

Workplaces began evaluate possibilities of virtual offices, digital events and training simulations. Schools turned to AR/VR tools to help make science and history lessons more fun for students. Retailers launched virtual try ons and 3D showrooms. As remote and hybrid models became the norm, the value of spatial, embodied digital experiences became increasingly apparent.

In addition, the pandemic underscored the importance of digital equity, resilience and adaptability. The metaverse, with its potential for democratizing access to services, education and global collaboration, now presents an opportunity to reimagine systems across sectors to be more inclusive, flexible and human-centered.

Purpose and Scope of the Chapter

This chapter investigates how the metaverse is actively redefining three important domains of modern society: the workplace, education and industry. Each of these sectors is undergoing changes driven by the fusion of immersive technologies and digital platforms. As the boundaries between the physical and digital reality continue to mix, new models of collaboration, learning and commerce are emerging.

In the workplace, the metaverse is creating more team collaboration through virtual offices, digital whiteboards and AI-powered assistants. In education, teaching and learning are being changed gradually by creating subjects more accessible through simulations, games and learning environments tailored for the students. In the marketplace, it offers a future with virtual storefronts, digital twins, markets and a better experience for customers.

This chapter examines the many impacts of the metaverse's growth including data privacy, digital identity, mental health concerns and inclusive design. With insights from real-world examples and expert commentary, the chapter offers guidelines for building responsible, sustainable and equitable metaverse ecosystems that prioritize human values.

By the end of the chapter, readers will gain an understanding of both the potential and dangers of the metaverse. The goal is not only to show evidence of the exciting innovations but also to reflect on the type of future we are building and who gets to participate in it.

Table 1. The metaverse across sectors - comparative framework of applications, benefits, and challenges

Dimension	WORKPLACE	EDUCATION	INDUSTRY & COMMERCE
Primary Goal	Productivity & Collaboration	Knowledge & Skill Development	Efficiency & Customer Value
Core Technologies	VR offices, AI assistants, Blockchain credentials	VR/AR simulations, AI tutors, Virtual campuses	Digital twins, IoT, NFTs
Key Platforms	* Meta Horizon Workrooms * Microsoft Mesh * Spatial	* Roblox Education * ENGAGE * ClassVR	* Siemens Xcelerator * Decentraland * OpenSea
Transformation	Remote to Immersive	Passive to Experiential	Physical to Phygital
Primary Users	Remote teams, Distributed workforce	K-12 to Higher Ed students, Teachers	Engineers, Retailers, Supply chain managers
Major Benefits	* Reduced overhead * Global talent access * Flexible work models	* Personalized learning * Global accessibility * Engagement boost	* Predictive maintenance * Virtual try-ons * New revenue streams

continued on following page

Table 1. Continued

Dimension	WORKPLACE	EDUCATION	INDUSTRY & COMMERCE
Critical Challenges	* Virtual fatigue * Data surveillance * Accessibility gaps	* Screen time risks * Student privacy * Teacher training	* Energy consumption * Regulatory gaps * Digital divide
Ethical Priorities	Work-life balance, Privacy protection	Child safety, Equity	Sustainability, Transparency
Case Examples	Accenture Nth Floor, PwC VR training	Stanford ENGAGE labs, Roblox STEM workshops	Siemens digital factories, Nike NFT stores
Maturity Stage	Early Adoption [**]	Experimental [*]	Proof of Concept [***]

METAVERSE IN THE WORKPLACE

Today's workplaces are undergoing a transformation. Concepts of centralized offices and routines have given way to hybrid and remote-first models, driven in part by necessity during the COVID-19 pandemic and now reinforced by technological advancement. The start of the transformation lies the metaverse-a convergence of virtual and physical realms that is reshaping how employees collaborate, communicate and create value. By enabling immersive work environments, AI-driven tools and decentralized credentials, the metaverse offers the possibility of a more connected, intelligent and flexible workplace.

Remote Collaboration and Virtual Offices

Virtual Meetings, Avatars and Digital Presence

The metaverse enhances remote collaboration by creating persistent virtual spaces where employees can meet, work and socialize using digital avatars. Unlike conventional video calls, which often feel static and draining, metaverse-based collaboration platforms allow users to embody avatars that mimic real-world gestures, expressions and presence. This sense of "being there" increases collaboration between employees.

Virtual workspaces copies the workplace environments complete with virtual desks, whiteboards, conference rooms and break areas. These spaces allow for natural interactions, brainstorming sessions and cross-team collaborations that feel more spontaneous than scheduled calls or message threads. For example, employees can walk over to a colleague's digital desk for a quick chat or sketch ideas on a holographic white board.

This presence is necessary for global teams spread across time zones. By imitating the experiences at the workplace, the metaverse fosters a stronger sense of community and team cohesion-even when employees have never met in person.

Platforms: Meta Horizon Workrooms, Microsoft Mesh and Others

A number of applications have emerged to support metaverse-based workplace collaboration. Meta Horizon Workrooms (Meta, 2023) is one of the most well-known, offering

3-D spaces where teams can hold meetings with immersive audio, shared documents being replaced virtual whiteboards. Participants use avatars that track facial expressions and hand movements, powered by Oculus VR headsets.

Microsoft Mesh (Microsoft, 2022), part of the Microsoft Teams ecosystem, focuses on mixed reality collaboration by blending AR and VR. It allows users to socalize in shared 3D spaces using avatars or holograms and supports a wide range of devices-from VR headsets to smartphones and PCs.

Other applications include:

- Spatial, which offers 3D workspaces
- Virbela, focused on enterprise and education
- Gather, which creates lightweight avatar-based meetings in 2D/3D hybrid environments

These tools are helping organizations move beyond boring video meetings and toward 3-D collaboration ecosystems.

Case Studies from Global Organizations

Several companies are already introducing metaverse platforms into their daily operations:

- The "Nth Floor" was created by Accenture (Accenture, 2022) for thousands of new employees. Using VR headsets, new hires can explore the virtual campus, attend training sessions and socialize with colleagues across departments.
- Hyundai Motor Company (Hyundai Motor Company, 2022) created a virtual program called MetaFactory for online designing and manufacturing simulations, requiring collaboration between employees.
- PWC UK (PwC UK, 2023) launched VR based training for important skills, leadership development and diversity awareness, reporting significantly

higher collaboration and knowledge retention compared to traditional online education.

These examples show how the metaverse applications are not only for tech companies but are being increasingly adopted across various workplaces, including consulting, manufacturing and the broader economy.

AI-Driven Productivity and Smart Workspaces

AI-Powered Virtual Assistants, Project Management and HR Tools

The integration of AI into the metaverse workplace amplifies its usefulness. AI-powered virtual assistants in the metaverse can automate repetitive tasks such as scheduling meetings, drafting conversations, managing to-do lists and retrieving relevant documents during meetings. These assistants can react accordingly via natural language, making them intuitive and will not disrupt meeting and such.

In project management, AI systems embedded in metaverse platforms can track task progress, suggest optimizations, flag potential risks and create visual dashboards that can be collaboratively reviewed in virtual space. By using predictive analytics and sentiment analysis, these tools help managers make better decisions and foster more proactive team dynamics.

Human Resources (HR) departments are also using the metaverse and AI to enhance employee collaboration. Virtual AI assistants can help in onboarding, answer questions, or even conduct initial screening interviews. By integrating games in learning and performance reviews the Metaverse can provide more feedback.

Integration of Blockchain for Work Credentials

Blockchain technology enhances transparency, security and ownership within the metaverse workplace. It allows individuals to maintain verifiable digital identities and work credentials, stored on decentralized ledgers. Certifications, project contributions and performance metrics can be embedded in blockchain-based resumes or digital wallets.

This approach reduces reliance on centralized HR databases and allows employees to carry their achievements across organizations and platforms. It also helps mitigate resume fraud, as credentials are cryptographically verified.

DAOs (Decentralized Autonomous Organizations), which use smart contracts for governance and compensation, represent an emerging model of work within the metaverse. In such models, contributors can be paid in crypto tokens, vote on strategic decisions and manage workflows transparently-without a central management structure.

Opportunities and Challenges

Reduced Overhead vs. Virtual Fatigue

The metaverse workplace offers substantial cost-saving opportunities. Organizations can reduce physical office space, utility costs and travel expenses. Remote and hybrid work models supported by virtual environments are more flexible, environmentally sustainable and attractive to talent seeking work-life balance.

However, these benefits come with a psychological cost. Virtual fatigue is a growing concern, particularly with prolonged use of headsets and digital avatars. The lack of physical movement, excessive screen time and the cognitive load of navigating immersive environments can lead to burnout and decreased well-being.

To address this, companies must set healthy boundaries, encourage breaks and design virtual spaces that simulate real-world movement and ergonomics. Passive presence in virtual offices (e.g., avatars signaling availability without constant engagement) can also reduce pressure.

Inclusivity, Ergonomics and Accessibility

One of the promises of the metaverse is inclusivity-the ability to bring people together regardless of physical location, age, or physical ability. Virtual avatars can help overcome biases tied to appearance or mobility and language translation tools can facilitate cross-cultural collaboration.

However, accessibility remains a barrier. Not all employees have access to high-speed internet, VR hardware, or ergonomic setups. Furthermore, individuals with visual, auditory, or motion impairments may find current platforms inadequate.

Designing accessible and inclusive virtual workplaces must become a priority. Features such as screen readers, haptic feedback, adjustable environments and voice navigation can help bridge these gaps. Additionally, avatars should represent diverse identities, body types and cultural norms to foster a sense of belonging.

Data Ownership and Cybersecurity

In the metaverse workplace, every interaction-gestures, conversations, eye movement, location-is potentially data (MDPI, 2024). This raises serious concerns about privacy, surveillance and data ownership.

Who owns this data? How is it stored, used and monetized? Without strong regulation and ethical guidelines, there is a risk that immersive workspaces become even more intrusive than traditional ones.

Cybersecurity is also a critical issue. Immersive environments can be vulnerable to new types of attacks-such as avatar impersonation, deepfake meetings, or real-time phishing. Blockchain can offer some safeguards through identity verification and smart contracts, but broader protocols are needed to protect digital workspaces.

Organizations must implement robust encryption, identity management and consent protocols while fostering transparency around data collection. Additionally, employee training on digital hygiene and metaverse etiquette is essential to mitigate risks.

Summary: The Evolving Metaverse Workplace

The metaverse workplace is no longer speculative-it is an active transformation unfolding across industries. With platforms enabling immersive collaboration, AI enhancing productivity and blockchain redefining trust and identity, we are witnessing a shift in how work is conceptualized and performed.

However, this transformation must be guided by principles of human-centric design, accessibility, privacy and well-being. The workplace of the future should not only be technologically advanced but also ethically grounded and inclusive.

By thoughtfully adopting metaverse technologies, organizations can unlock new possibilities in creativity, innovation and global collaboration-while preparing their workforce for a more decentralized and digital-first future.

Table 2. Sidebar - comparative snapshot - leading virtual collaboration platforms

Platform	Device Compatibility	Key Features	Ideal Use Case
Microsoft Mesh	HoloLens, PC, mobile	Mixed reality, holographic presence, Teams integration	Enterprise collaboration & hybrid work
Meta Horizon Workrooms	Quest VR headsets	Full VR, spatial audio, avatar tracking, shared whiteboards	Immersive meetings & brainstorming
Spatial	Web, VR headsets, mobile	Lightweight 3D meetings, easy setup, NFT integration	Creative teams, art & design meetings

These platforms represent distinct approaches to virtual workspaces-Mesh emphasizes interoperability and productivity within enterprise systems; Horizon Workrooms focuses on immersive VR experiences for deeper presence; and Spatial prioritizes accessibility and ease-of-use for creative professionals.

As enterprise adoption accelerates, organizations are increasingly blending these platforms to suit various workflows and team structures.

METAVERSE IN EDUCATION

The metaverse is creating change in education, enabling experiences that are immersive, interactive and makes sure every student gets the help they need. Traditional education systems-often outdated and disconnected from real-world application-are now being challenged by virtual educational environments that offer engagement and adaptability. By integrating the 3-D presence of virtual reality (VR), the context enriching power of augmented reality (AR), the personalization capabilities of artificial intelligence (AI) and the reach of digital platforms, the metaverse presents an opportunity to democratize education and introduce a new how, where and what we learn.

Immersive Learning Environments

Use of VR/AR in Science, Medicine and History

Imagine learning biology not through reading a textbook, but by walking through a human cell and interacting with organelles in a 3D environment. Or studying history by standing in a virtual reconstruction of ancient Rome, hearing the sounds of the forum and engaging with AI-powered historical figures. This is the promise of immersive learning, made possible by VR and AR technologies in the metaverse.

In science classrooms, students can explore molecules, chemical reactions, ecosystems and even space in virtual environments that would be impossible to replicate in the real world. Medical students are using VR simulations for surgical training, diagnostics and emergency response without the risks or cost of real-life procedures. Companies like Medical Realities and Fundamental VR are leading in this domain (Gig, 2021), offering VR training that mimic real surgical conditions.

History and social studies are brought to life through AR-enabled museum tours, time-travel simulations and virtual archaeological digs. Platforms like Time Looper allow students to experience historical events from the perspective of people who lived through them, fostering empathy and deeper understanding.

AR also plays a crucial role in K-12 education by blending learning content with physical books, objects and classrooms seamlessly. Apps such as Merge EDU use AR to help students interact with scientific models, such as the solar system or a beating human heart, using just a smartphone or tablet.

Gamified Learning and Simulation

Adding game elements like rewards, quests and levels to learning-has proven to increase motivation, engagement and retention. In the metaverse, gamification is taken to new heights through interactive simulations, storytelling and real-time feedback.

Students can become active participants rather than passive listeners. For example, in a virtual chemistry lab, they can mix chemicals, observe reactions and retry experiments without the risk of injury or cost of materials. In language learning, students might interact in a virtual café in Paris to practice conversational French.

Simulations also support experiential learning, where learners acquire knowledge through doing. For vocational education, the metaverse can simulate construction sites, aircraft maintenance, or electrical installations-giving students hands-on experience in a safe, controlled environment.

Personalized and Inclusive Education

AI for Adaptive Learning Paths

Every learner has different strengths, preferences and learning speeds. The metaverse can harness AI to provide personalized learning experiences tailored to each student's needs.

AI algorithms embedded in virtual classrooms can monitor student progress, identify areas of difficulty and recommend specific activities or explanations. A student struggling with geometry might be guided through a series of interactive puzzles that reinforce reasoning, while a another student excelling in the subject could be presented with more advanced challenges.

AI tutors available 24/7 can respond to student questions in real time, explain concepts in different ways and adjust the difficulty of tasks. Platforms like Squirrel AI and Century Tech already use adaptive AI models to personalize learning paths and improve outcomes, especially in large classrooms where some individuals get over looked and don't receive the attention they deserve.

Access to Quality Education Across Geographies

One of the most profound benefits of the metaverse is its potential to join the geographical and economic divide in education (Lin et al., 2022). With even a smartphone, a child in a rural village can access the same quality of education as a student in a urban school.

Virtual campuses and digital classrooms enable students to connect with peers and teachers from around the world. Collaborative projects, international cultural exchanges and access to global experts become possible regardless of location.

Organizations like the UNESCO Global Education Coalition (UNESCO, 2022) are exploring metaverse-based solutions to provide education in conflict zones and underserved areas. Meanwhile, non-profits and ed-tech startups are working to reduce the cost of hardware and offer open-access content for schools in developing countries.

By removing physical and institutional barriers, the metaverse holds the promise of truly universal education-adapted for local languages, cultures and contexts.

Pedagogical Foundations: From Theory to Immersive Practice

The rise of the metaverse in education is not just a technological shift-it reflects a deepening alignment with modern theories that emphasize active, student-centered learning.

Experiential Learning in XR. The metaverse is a natural fit for experiential learning, a theory advanced by David Kolb (1984), which argues that knowledge is constructed through direct experience, reflection, and experimentation. In VR simulations, students aren't just absorbing content-they're immersed in educational environments where they can interact, make decisions and learn from consequences, such as navigating ethical dilemmas in history or exploring ecosystems in environmental science.

Bloom's Taxonomy Reimagined. Immersive tools also elevate learners through Bloom's Taxonomy (Anderson & Krathwohl, 2001), from basic "remembering" to higher-order skills like "analyzing," "evaluating," and "creating." For example, in a VR chemistry lab, students may hypothesize, conduct a virtual experiment, observe outcomes and change their approach-thus engaging multiple cognitive levels simultaneously.

Constructivism and Social Presence. Constructivist approaches, which view learning as a process, are deeply reinforced in shared virtual environments. When students collaborate in a metaverse classroom, they co-construct knowledge through dialogue, shared manipulation of virtual objects and peer feedback, imitating the dynamics of physical group work.

Teacher Perspectives on the Metaverse. Emerging studies reflect both excitement and skepticism among educators. A 2023 survey by EDUCAUSE (EDUCAUSE, 2023) found that 68% of teachers who used immersive tools reported higher student engagement and 54% observed improved comprehension of abstract lessons. However, many educators also cited challenges in training, curriculum adaptation and classroom management within virtual environments.

Interviews conducted by the XR Association (XR Association, 2022) in 2022 highlighted teachers concerns about equity in access and a desire for more relevant content aligned with national standards. Yet those same interviews also showcased passionate educators embracing the metaverse as a means to "level the playing field" for diverse learners, including neurodiverse and multilingual students.

These insights underscore that the integration of the metaverse to be accepted in education must involve not just technology, but supportive education and professional development.

Examples and Platforms

Success Stories: Roblox Education, ENGAGE, ClassVR

Several platforms are already demonstrating the real-world impact of metaverse technology in education:

- Roblox Education (Roblox Education, 2022) leverages the popular gaming platform to teach coding, game design and storytelling. Teachers and students can create and explore interactive worlds, building not only virtual stories but also collaboration and creativity skills. During the pandemic, Roblox hosted virtual graduations and STEM workshops, reaching millions of students.
- ENGAGE (Immersive VR Education, 2023) is a leading VR education platform used by universities like Stanford, Oxford and Harvard. It supports large-scale virtual classes, conferences and live simulations across subjects including medicine, engineering and business. ENGAGE offers lifelike avatars and 3-D audio, making virtual sessions feel real and engaging.
- ClassVR, used in thousands of schools globally, provides a library of over 1,000 VR/AR lessons aligned to national curriculums. Teachers can control the lesson experience remotely, redirecting students focus as needed.

These platforms show how the metaverse is not a distant dream, but a present-day reality shaping modern education.

Role of Ed-Tech Startups

A wave of start-ups is pushing the boundaries of what metaverse-based education can achieve:

- zSpace combines AR and VR to offer science and anatomy lessons through interactive displays.
- VictoryXR creates digital twins of university campuses and offers VR labs for biology, chemistry and astronomy.
- Prisms of Reality uses VR for math instruction, teaching algebra and geometry through problem-solving in real-world simulations.

Startups often focus on easy subjects or underserved communities, accelerating innovation and pushing traditional schools to evolve. By working in partnership with schools, universities and governments, they are helping integrate metaverse learning into mainstream education.

Ethical and Developmental Considerations

Screen Time and Mental Health

While immersive technologies can enhance learning, they also raise concerns about excessive screen time and its impact on mental health, especially among children and teenagers.

Spending hours in virtual environments can lead to issues like digital fatigue, attention disorders and social withdrawal. The sensory intensity of VR may cause motion sickness, disorientation, or eye strain. Young learners are particularly unsafe, as their cognitive and emotional systems are still developing.

To prevent these side effects of the metaverse, educators and platform designers must follow age-appropriate guidelines, enforce time limits and include built-in breaks. Physical activity and real-world interaction should be blended to the learning experience. Research-backed policies are needed to balance digital immersion with child development.

Student Data Privacy

The metaverse collects vast amounts of behavioral, biometric and engagement data-from eye tracking and voice recognition to interaction patterns and emotional responses. This data can improve learning outcomes but also poses serious privacy risks.

Who owns this data? How is it stored and secured? Are students or parents fully informed and have agreed to the conditions?

Without strong safeguards, there is a danger of commercial exploitation, surveillance and discrimination (Zhang et al., 2023). Educational universities must ensure data transparency, informed consent and compliance with laws like COPPA, FERPA and GDPR. Platforms should use private datasets, encrypted storage and minimal data collection practices.

Student safety in the metaverse must be a top priority, both technically and ethically.

Teacher Training and Curriculum Overhaul

Introducing metaverse tools requires more than just hardware-it demands a paradigm shift in teaching methods, pedagogy and curriculum design.

Teachers need comprehensive training to use virtual tools well, manage digital classrooms and evaluate student performance in immersive environments. Professional development programs must address the technical aspects of metaverse education.

Moreover, curriculum all over needs to evolve from memorization to experiential, inquiry-based learning. Assessment methods should move beyond multiple-choice tests to real-world problem-solving, simulations and creative projects.

Government education boards, accrediting bodies and teacher unions will all play a role in defining standards, training requirements and ethical frameworks.

Summary: Transforming Educational Paradigms

The metaverse has the potential to redefine education-not just by making it more engaging and efficient, but by making it more equitable, personalized and future-ready. From virtual biology labs and gamified math puzzles to AI tutors and global classrooms, the possibilities are vast and inspiring.

However, this transformation must be undergone with care. Educators, technologists and policymakers must work together to make sure that immersive education promotes well-being, access and empowerment-not exclusion or exploitation.

As we move into an era where digital and physical learning are deeply intertwined, the metaverse offers an amazing opportunity to build education systems that are not only more advanced-but also more human-centered.

METAVERSE IN INDUSTRY AND COMMERCE

The industrial and commercial sectors are experiencing a transformation fueled by metaverse technologies. From virtual storefronts that drastically change customer engagement to digital twins that optimize operations, the convergence of immersive technologies, blockchain and AI is revolutionizing how businesses operate and deliver value. As brands explore new frontiers in customer interaction and industries leverage virtual replicas of complex systems for real-time decision-making, the metaverse is rapidly becoming a vital layer of the global commercial landscape.

Virtual Storefronts and Experiential Commerce

3D Retail Spaces and Virtual Try-Ons

In the metaverse, the retail experience becomes fully immersive. Brands now operate 3D storefronts that simulate the aesthetics, layout and interaction of physical retail spaces while offering enhanced digital possibilities. Consumers can explore products in detail, interact with virtual store associates (AI avatars) and even socialize with friends-all within a virtual environment.

Virtual try-ons are one of the most impactful applications. Using AR or VR, customers can see how clothes fit, test furniture in a digital replica of their living room, or try on makeup in real-time using face mapping. Companies like Zara and Sephora (Deloitte, 2023) use AR to offer real-time product visualization, while platforms like Obsess and ByondXR specialize in building virtual retail environments.

This shift enables brands to:

- Reduce return rates by offering more accurate previews
- Expand reach globally without physical infrastructure
- Offer highly personalized shopping journeys

Integration with NFTs and Cryptocurrency

The metaverse is also redefining ownership and commerce through integration with blockchain-based assets such as non-fungible tokens (NFTs) and cryptocurrencies. NFTs allow brands to create unique digital products, such as limited-edition virtual apparel, accessories, or collectibles.

Luxury fashion houses like Gucci and Dolce & Gabbana (Vogue Business, 2022) have released NFT collections that can be worn by avatars in platforms like Decentraland or Roblox. These digital items, often linked to real-world exclusives, open new revenue streams and marketing opportunities.

In addition, crypto enables seamless, borderless transactions in virtual environments, bypassing traditional payment processors. Brands can create loyalty tokens, enable peer-to-peer payments and participate in decentralized finance (DeFi) ecosystems.

This convergence of commerce, identity and ownership is creating entirely new economies within the metaverse.

Digital Twins and the Industrial Metaverse

Use in Manufacturing, Supply Chain and Smart Cities

In industrial contexts, the metaverse takes form through digital twins-real-time, virtual replicas of physical assets, environments, or systems. This digital version of stores runs by using IoT sensors and AI analytics, digital twins provide a immersive visualization of equipment, factories, cities and supply chains.

In manufacturing, digital twins allow engineers to monitor machines, test design changes and predict system failures. Companies can simulate entire assembly lines reducing downtime and cost. For example, Siemens has developed the Industrial Metaverse (NVIDIA, 2023; PMC, 2025), combining VR, AI and digital twins for virtual factory planning and real-time process optimization.

Supply chain management benefits from metaverse integration by visualizing global logistics networks, tracking goods across multiple points and simulating disruptions. Companies can model "what-if" scenarios-such as a delayed shipment or a geopolitical event-and adapt strategies in real time.

In smart cities, digital twins represent important elements like traffic systems, utilities and emergency services. Cities such as Singapore and Helsinki (World Economic Forum, 2023) have developed virtual replicas that aid in urban planning, sustainability assessments and citizen services.

Predictive Maintenance and Simulation

One of the most powerful industrial applications of the metaverse is predictive maintenance. By analyzing data from IoT-connected machinery and visualizing performance in real-time digital twins, companies can detect malfunctions before they become failures. This reduces unplanned downtime, extends equipment lifespan and saves significant operational costs.

Simulation tools in the metaverse are also used for:

- Training workers in hazardous virtual environments
- Testing robotic automation in warehouses

- Efficient energy consumption and carbon emissions

The immersive nature of the metaverse adds intuitive interaction with complex data, enabling better decisions across engineering, logistics and resource management.

Decentralized Marketplaces

DAOs, Smart Contracts and Peer-to-Peer Exchanges

The traditional business model needs central authorities-banks, retailers, logistics and providers. In the metaverse, marketplaces are challenging this paradigm through the use of blockchain, smart contracts and decentralized autonomous organizations (DAOs).

DAOs are community-governed entities where decision-making is executed through transparent voting and encoded rules. In commerce, DAOs can oversee funding, product development and customer engagement, reducing the need for hierarchical structures. Contributors are rewarded through governance tokens or cryptocurrency.

Smart contracts automated transactions and enforced terms without human intervention. A contract between a digital artist and a buyer can ensure the artist receives royalties every time the NFT changes hands-without needing intermediaries.

Peer-to-peer (P2P) exchanges within the metaverse allow users to trade digital goods, services, or skills directly. Platforms like Open Sea (for NFTs) and Decentraland Marketplace offer open realms for creators and consumers.

This decentralization fosters:

- Transparency: All transactions are recorded on public ledgers
- Efficiency: Eliminating middlemen reduces costs
- Inclusivity: Anyone can participate regardless of geography

However, it also raises concerns around regulation, intellectual property and consumer protection that need careful governance.

Case Studies

Nike

Nike entered the metaverse through Nikeland on Roblox, creating a world where users can play branded games, customize avatars with Nike gear and collect virtual sneakers. The platform engages younger audiences while testing new product concepts and community-led design.

Nike also acquired RTFKT Studios, a digital sneaker and collectible brand, to create NFT sneakers that users can wear in virtual environments. Some NFT shoes are linked to physical versions, merging real and virtual ownership.

Gucci

Gucci has pioneered luxury fashion in the metaverse. Its Gucci Garden experience on Roblox allowed users to explore digital fashion and buy limited-edition virtual items. The brand sold a digital handbag for more than the physical version, highlighting the value users create on virtual status symbols.

Gucci's NFTs have also been featured on platforms like SuperRare, bridging art, culture and commerce in digital form.

Hyundai

Hyundai launched Mobility Adventure, a virtual world in Roblox showcasing its smart mobility vision. Users can explore futuristic transportation hubs, interact with autonomous vehicles and learn about hydrogen technology.

This initiative aims to engage younger consumers while promoting brand innovation and environmental responsibility.

Siemens

Siemens is a leader in industrial metaverse applications. Its Xcelerator platform provides digital twin solutions for everything from power grids to manufacturing plants. Siemens partnered with NVIDIA to develop a photorealistic metaverse for industry, combining real-time simulation, AI and immersive design.

This enables predictive modeling of complex systems-from factory layouts to climate controls-before they are introduced physically.

Startup Innovations

Beyond global applications, startups are fueling rapid innovation:

- Boson Protocol allows the sale of physical items in the metaverse via NFTs that can be redeemed in real life, blending Web3 commerce with traditional retail.
- Anima uses AR and NFTs to create location-based digital fashion experiences.

- Next Earth lets users buy digital land on a digital Earth twin, unlocking new models of real estate and advertising.

Startups often experiment with tokenized loyalty programs, 3-D pop-up stores and creator-led ecosystems that bypass traditional gatekeepers.

Sustainability Considerations in the Metaverse Economy

As metaverse platforms grow more sophisticated and persistent, their environmental footprint becomes a concerning detail. The infrastructure required to support immersive experiences-ranging from data centers and GPU-intensive rendering to blockchain validation and constant streaming-can lead to substantial energy consumption and carbon emissions.

For instance, using a single VR environment in real time may require several times more energy than a 2D web applications (Frontiers in Virtual Reality, 2025). Moreover, blockchain based assets, especially those tied to proof of work protocols like Ethereum (pre-merge), have been criticized for their high energy costs.

To mitigate these impacts, industry leaders are exploring more sustainable architecture and practices, including:

- Transitioning to proof-of-stake and layer-2 blockchain solutions that reduce computational demands.
- Using edge computing and energy efficient rendering algorithms to minimize latency and power use.
- Investing in green data centers, often powered by renewable energy, to host metaverse environments.
- Encouraging digital principles, such as defaulting to lightweight rendering for routine tasks.

As companies incorporate the metaverse's capabilities into their businesses, a sustainability first design approach will be critical-not just for compliance, but for reputational integrity in a climate-conscious consumer market.

Retail Behavioral Economics in Immersive Commerce

The 3-D nature of the metaverse doesn't just replicate in-store experiences-it fundamentally reshapes consumer psychology. In a 3D retail space, virtual ambiance, avatar based social validation and gamified interaction can heighten emotional engagement and perceived product value.

Psychological effects like the endowment effect-where users overvalue digital items simply because they "own" them are amplified in metaverse marketplaces where avatars can wear, display, or trade these items. Virtual scarcity, suggests via NFTs, also triggers urgency and FOMO (fear of missing out), influencing faster purchase decisions.

Retailers are using environmental design, narrative storytelling and multisensory cues to create emotionally resonant digital experiences, nudging consumers toward longer engagement and higher basket sizes.

These shifts require changes where transparency and informed consent must evolve alongside innovation in engagement.

Summary: Commercial and Industrial Transformation

The metaverse is not merely a new digital trend-it is a structural evolution in how industries create and deliver. Virtual storefronts are transforming e-commerce from browsing to immersive experiences. Digital twins are perfecting complex systems with real-time intelligence. Decentralized marketplaces are democratizing participation and ownership in commerce.

However, these transformations are not without risks. Businesses must navigate challenges around regulation, privacy, interoperability and digital identity. The metaverse is still an evolving frontier, requiring collaboration between technologists, designers, policymakers and end-users to shape it responsibly.

As companies of all sizes begin to build their metaverse strategies, those that align innovation with ethics, inclusivity and sustainability will lead the way in this new industrial revolution.

CROSS-CUTTING ETHICAL AND SOCIETAL IMPLICATIONS

While the metaverse offers many opportunities across work, education and commerce, it also brings ethical and societal challenges. As this immersive digital layer becomes more deeply blended into daily life, we must address questions about surveillance, identity, inclusion, psychological health and governance. Without careful design and regulation, the metaverse risks replicating and amplifying many of the inequalities and harms present in the physical and digital worlds today.

Data Privacy and Surveillance

Risks of Immersive Data Collection

One of the most pressing concerns in the metaverse is data privacy. Unlike digital platforms, the metaverse captures volumes of behavioral, biometric, spatial and emotional data. VR and AR devices can track head and eye movements, facial expressions, gait, heart rate and even brain activity in some experimental start-ups. This data not only mimics but also predicts, revealing habits, preferences, vulnerabilities and unconscious reactions.

Such data-if mishandled-can be used for manipulative advertising, discriminatory profiling, or unauthorized surveillance. Moreover, in multiplayer environments, interactions between users can be recorded, analyzed and stored by platform providers without participant's full consent.

The immersive nature of the metaverse increases the perception of presence, making violations of privacy feel more personal and intrusive. Unlike a cookie on a website, tracking an avatar's real-time conversation in a virtual boardroom or classroom crosses deeper boundaries.

Consent, Transparency and Regulation

To address these risks, there is a pressing need for transparent data practices and meaningful user consent. Informed consent must move beyond "click-to-agree" policies and become dynamic and contextual, alerting users in real time about data being captured and how it's being used.

Moreover, regulatory frameworks like the General Data Protection Regulation (GDPR), the California Consumer Privacy Act (CCPA) and emerging AI governance policies must be adapted and expanded for immersive environments. These should include:

- Data minimization principles
- User control over data access, sharing and deletion
- Auditable algorithms for decision-making in virtual spaces

As the metaverse upgrades, ethical privacy practices must become a core design principle, not an afterthought.

Surveillance Capitalism in the Metaverse

The data economy of the metaverse reflects what scholar Shoshana Zuboff (Zuboff, 2019) terms *"surveillance capitalism"*-a system in which human behavior is mined as a raw material for predictive analytics. In her seminal work *The Age of Surveillance Capitalism*, Zuboff warns of a future where corporations not only track behavior but shape it, using vast datasets to engineer user preferences and actions for profit.

The metaverse intensifies this problem, unlike 2D platforms that collect clicks and scrolls, immersive platforms can harvest biometric signals, spatial movements, gaze patterns, voice tone and emotional reactions. This creates a rich behavioral surplus that companies can exploit to train algorithms, personalize content and target hyper-specific advertising-often without user awareness.

Such data extraction is deeply embedded in the economic model of many metaverse platforms, inspiring maximum engagement and behavioral manipulation through environmental design, nudging techniques and AI-driven personalization.

Zuboff's critique is especially relevant here: the metaverse risks becoming not just a space for surveillance but a "behavioral laboratory" with little democratic oversight.

Legal and Policy Developments

Governments are beginning to respond with new legislative efforts:

- In the U.S., the *Augmented Reality and Virtual Reality Privacy Act (AR/VRPA)* (U.S. Congress, 2023) was proposed in 2023 to regulate biometric and geospatial data collected in immersive environments. The bill mandates explicit consent for eye tracking and facial recognition features and requires data minimization practices.
- The EU's Digital Services Act (DSA) (European Commission, 2024), effective in 2024, includes provisions around harmful content moderation, algorithmic transparency and psychological safety in immersive environments.
- California's My Voice, My Data Act, currently under review, seeks to restrict audio-based surveillance in smart glasses and virtual meetings.

While these steps are encouraging, legal systems still miss the importance of technological development. A proactive and internationally harmonized regulatory approach will be essential to uphold privacy rights in the emerging metaverse landscape.

Identity and Governance

Avatar Identity, Impersonation and Digital Rights

In the metaverse, identity is fluid and often detached from physical appearance. Users can customize their avatars in any form-human, animal, abstract, or fictional. While this opens up creative expression and may empower marginalized individuals, it also introduces pressing identity-related ethical concerns.

Avatar impersonation-the unauthorized use of someone else's likeness or persona-can be used for harassment, or fraud. The increasing realism of avatars, powered by AI deepfakes and facial tracking, exacerbates the risk of identity theft or manipulation in virtual spaces.

Additionally, users lack legal and moral protections for their digital personas. Who owns the rights to your avatar's face, voice, or gestures? If an avatar is assaulted or harassed in the metaverse, what guidelines and punishments exists? These issues raise questions about the digital self as an extension of human rights.

Ethical Implications of Anonymity and Accountability

Anonymity in the metaverse can be a problem and advantage. On one hand, it allows for freedom of expression, exploration of identity and protection from discrimination. On the other hand, it can enable toxic behavior, harassment and radicalization, as users feel they can bully people without fear of punishments behind digital masks.

Establishing trust and accountability without compromising privacy requires innovative approaches:

- Verified pseudonymity (identity verification without revealing true identity)
- Community-led moderation systems
- Ethics-driven platform governance policies

Furthermore, cross-platform governance will be critical as users move between interconnected virtual worlds. Industry-wide standards must be developed to ensure consistent rights, responsibilities and recourse mechanisms.

The Digital Divide and Equity

Access to Metaverse Tech in the Global South

While the metaverse is being accepted as the future of connectivity and opportunity, its current trajectory risks excluding large portions of the global population, especially in the Global South. High-speed internet, VR headsets, AR glasses and advanced computing hardware remain inaccessible to many communities (World Bank, 2023) due to cost, infrastructure gaps and regional limitations.

This creates a new layer of the digital divide, where users gain access to immersive learning, economic participation and job opportunities in the metaverse-while others are left behind.

The metaverse must be built with universal accessibility in mind. This includes:

- Developing low-bandwidth and mobile-compatible versions of virtual environments
- Investing in public metaverse infrastructure (like virtual libraries or training centers)
- Supporting open-source platforms and affordable hardware initiatives

Economic, Gender and Ability-Based Disparities

Beyond geography, the metaverse may reinforce or magnify existing economic, gender and disability-based inequities. Early adopters with technical skills or disposable income are more likely to benefit from metaverse jobs.

Non-binary users frequently experience harassment and underrepresentation in online gaming and tech spaces-a pattern that could continue in the metaverse if not proactively addressed. Similarly, many VR and AR platforms lack accommodations for users with visual, auditory, or mobility impairments.

A truly inclusive metaverse must:

- Ensure diverse representation in avatar options, content creation and leadership
- Design for universal accessibility standards, including assistive tech integration
- Provide financial inclusion models, such as metaverse micro-credits, training programs and equitable asset distribution

Equity must be first priority in the metaverse.

Psychological and Behavioral Effects

Identity Dissociation, Addiction and Attention Span

Immersive virtual environments side effect's include psychological effects-some positive, others potentially harmful. Extended time in the metaverse may lead to identity dissociation (American Psychological Association, 2024), where users feel a stronger connection to their avatar than to their real-world self. This could impact mental health, particularly in individuals already dealing with self-esteem or social anxiety issues.

The gamification and sensory richness of the metaverse increase the risk of digital addiction, especially in adolescents. Users may prefer virtual socialization, escapism, or commerce over offline interaction, leading to emotional withdrawal, reduced physical activity and cognitive fatigue.

Additionally, the fragmented and hyper-stimulated nature of metaverse experiences could further erode attention spans and deep focus-trends already created by smartphones and social media.

Designers must prioritize user well-being by:

- Setting time usage limits
- Designing restorative environments
- Avoiding dopamine-driven engagement loops
- Supporting psychological research into long-term impacts

Children and Vulnerable Groups

Children represent a particularly vulnerable demographic in the metaverse. With platforms like Roblox and Minecraft already serving as a version of a metaverse, millions of children are engaging in immersive digital spaces without protections.

Key risks include:

- Exposure to inappropriate content
- Online grooming and exploitation
- Manipulative advertising or in-app purchases

Guardians and educators must enforce strict age verification, content moderation and parental controls. Educators and parents need digital literacy programs to teach children about consent, privacy and healthy screen habits.

The same attention must be given to elderly users, neurodiverse individuals and those with cognitive disabilities, who may face challenges in navigation, comprehension or interaction in virtual environments.

Ethical metaverse design demands a multi-stakeholder approach, incorporating perspectives from psychologists, educators, accessibility experts and community advocates.

Summary: Navigating Ethical Challenges

The metaverse is a technological wonder with the potential to redefine human interaction, economy, education and identity. But as we build this new world, we must confront the ethical and societal questions that determine who benefit and who is left behind.

From data privacy and avatar rights to digital equity and mental health, the decisions made today will shape the inclusive-or exclusionary-nature of tomorrow's virtual worlds.

This section urges policymakers, designers, educators, developers and global institutions to move beyond the excitement and innovation and toward principles of fairness, accountability and human dignity. Only then can the metaverse evolve not just as a digital marvel, but as an achievement for all of humanity.

DESIGNING A RESPONSIBLE AND HUMAN-CENTERED METAVERSE

The metaverse isn't simply a digital construction-it is a social and diverse ecosystem. As such, its design and governance must be guided not only by innovation but also by ethics, equity and humanity. In its current stage, we have a open window to shape the metaverse in ways that uphold human dignity, promote togetherness and fostering humanities well-being. A responsible metaverse is one that prioritizes the users over gains, communities over businesses and sustainability over short-term profits.

Ethical Design Principles: Inclusivity, Accessibility and Well-being

At the center of a responsible metaverse is ethical design principles that make sure the virtual world mirrors the good in our shared values rather than the biases and inequalities of already existing digital realms.

Figure 1. Human-centered metaverse design framework - from principles to practice

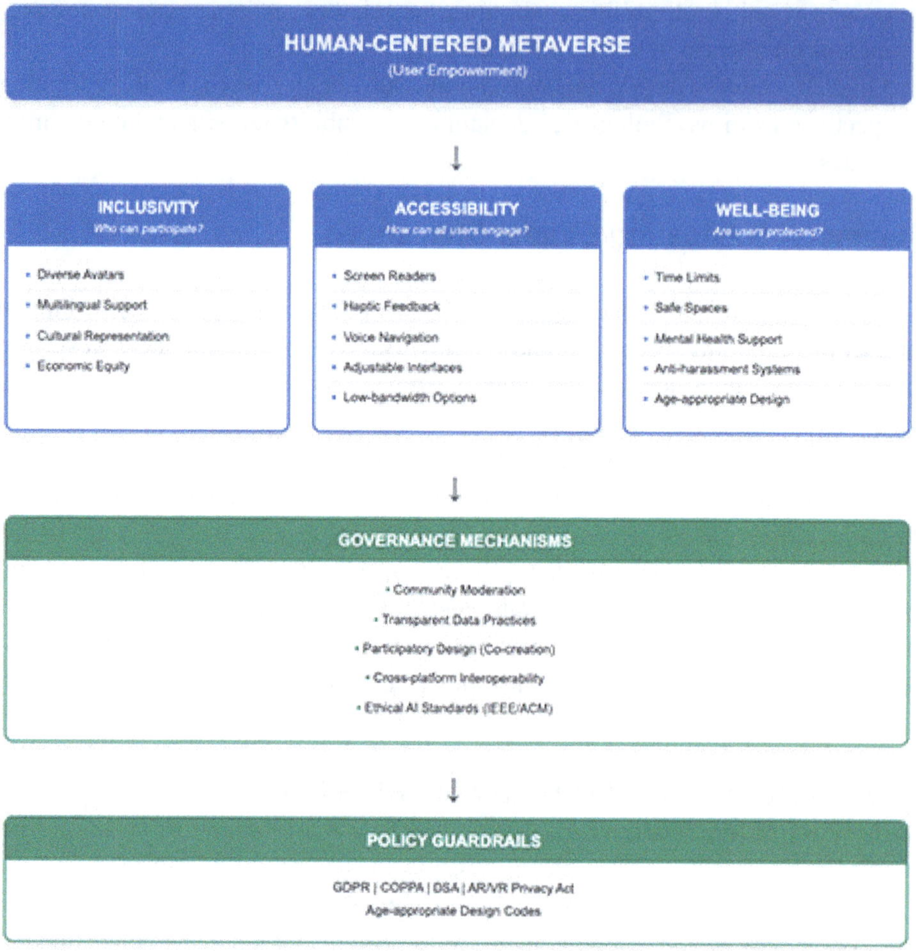

Inclusivity

Inclusivity begins with representation and participation of all. Avatars and virtual experiences should accommodate a diverse range of races, genders, body types, languages and cultures. The ability to see yourself in a virtual world is necessary for belonging and psychological safety.

Designers must avoid tokenism and instead engage diverse communities in co-creating content, setting norms and designing spaces that include everyone. Features like customizable avatars, multilingual voice support and relevant content are important to enabling participation of all.

Accessibility

The metaverse should be designed for everyone, including people with disabilities. This includes users with visual, auditory, mobility and cognitive impairments. Accessibility must be integrated into the foundation of metaverse platforms not added afterwards.

Best practices include:

- Screen reader compatibility
- Text-to-speech and speech-to-text capabilities
- Customizable font sizes, contrast ratios and control schemes
- Haptic feedback for non-visual communication
- Keyboard and voice navigation options

Organizations like the W3C (W3C, 2023) have already laid groundwork for accessibility on the web. These guidelines should merge into XR-specific accessibility standards, ensuring that VR, AR and mixed reality platforms meet universal design criteria.

Well-Being

Well-being in the metaverse extends beyond too much screen time. It includes mental, emotional, social and physical health. Ethical platforms must provide:

- Session time reminders and break suggestions
- Private safe zones for users to recharge or reflect
- Environments free from harassment or harmful content
- Emotionally supportive AI companions or wellness tools
- Gamification mechanics that encourage balanced usage-not addiction

Designers should do no harm by considering the psychological impact of immersive environments and ensuring they uplift rather than take advantage of users.

Community Governance and Participatory Models

Control over the metaverse must be given to evenly different corporations, without the centralization the metaverse poses risks to autonomy, fairness and innovation. A human-centered metaverse must be governed by participatory models that empower users as co-creators and stakeholders.

Community-Led Moderation and Decision-Making

Instead of relying solely on top-down moderation, platforms should support community-led content governance. Mechanisms can include:

- Reputation systems that reward constructive behavior
- Transparent moderation logs
- User councils or juries to adjudicate disputes
- Voting systems for platform rule changes or feature additions

This mirrors the logic of Decentralized Autonomous Organizations (DAOs), where rules are encoded into smart contracts and users can propose and vote on changes. Such governance models applies transparency, accountability and trust.

Digital Commons and Open Ecosystems

A responsible metaverse should preserve digital commons-shared virtual spaces not owned by any one, however open to all and managed accordingly. These include virtual libraries, art galleries, public parks and educational hubs.

Open standards should be championed to prevent walled information that should be shared. Users should be able to move their digital identities, avatars and assets across platforms without vendor lock-in.

Platforms should embrace open APIs, portable data formats and cross-platform avatars, giving users control and continuity over their digital experiences.

Participatory Design in Action: From Open-Source XR to Co-Creation

Participatory design is the practice of involving users-not just as consumers but as co-creators-in the development of digital environments. This approach is especially powerful in the metaverse, where social norms, aesthetics and usability evolve organically through interaction.

Mozilla Hubs, an open-source platform for immersive social experiences, 3-D participatory design. Users can not only create custom 3D spaces but also contribute to the codebase, moderation tools and accessibility features. Educators, artists and communities have used Hubs to host conferences, virtual art exhibits and even decentralized classrooms-building public virtual spaces that reflect diverse needs.

Similarly, communities like XR Accessibility User Group (XRAUG) and platforms like A-Frame encourage diverse design through collaborative feedback loops public design standards. These models shift control from corporations to communities, ensuring that virtual spaces are shaped by those who inhabit them.

Ethical Frameworks: IEEE and Beyond

To guide this incredible and responsible development, academics and institutions have proposed ethical frameworks. One notable example is IEEE's Ethically Aligned Design (IEEE, 2024), which emphasizes principles such as human agency, transparency, privacy and accountability in autonomous and intelligent systems. It advocates for AI and immersive technologies to enhance-not replace-human judgment and dignity.

Another influential model, the ACM Code of Ethics, focuses on societal benefit, non-discrimination and professional responsibility in technology development.

These frameworks are essential details for developers, helping translate ethical intent into actionable design decisions. By grounding metaverse development in shared human values, they help ensure that the virtual future reflects the ethical wishes of the real world.

Standards and Policy Recommendations

To ensure ethical development and accountability in the metaverse, governments, civil society and industry must collaborate on standards and policies.

Privacy and Data Protection

Governments should introduce existing data protection laws (e.g., GDPR, CCPA) to immersive technologies, addressing issues like:

- Biometric data regulation
- Real-time location and behavioral tracking
- Informed consent for VR/AR analytics

Platforms should follow the guidelines of data minimization, purpose limitation and user ownership of data. Policies must also protect against biometric surveillance, AI profiling and data monetization.

Child and Vulnerable User Protections

Metaverse platforms should follow to age-appropriate design codes, such as the UK's Age-Appropriate Design Code (AADC) (UK Information Commissioner's Office, 2024), ensuring that environments are safe and tailored for younger users.

This includes:

- Default privacy settings
- Restricted commercial content
- Human moderation for child-centric spaces
- Parental control dashboards

Interoperability and Ethical AI Standards

A common set of technical and ethical standards must guide the development of AI agents, avatars and virtual environments. These should cover:

- Explainable AI in decision-making
- Bias detection and correction protocols
- Fair access to AI-driven tools across geographies

Regulatory authorities and independent institutions (e.g., IEEE, ISO, OECD AI Observatory) can play a role in certifying platforms for ethical compliance and accessibility.

Role of Interdisciplinary Collaboration

The metaverse's ethical challenges are too complex for technologists alone to solve. They demand a deeply interdisciplinary approach, bringing together people from across societies.

Technologists and Designers

Responsible developers must go beyond performance and monetization metrics. They should be trained in ethical design, inclusive UX and human-centered AI. Tech firms should establish internal ethics review boards, similar to institutional review boards (IRBs) in universities.

Ethicists and Philosophers

Ethical frameworks can help resolve questions such as:

- What constitutes harm in a virtual environment?
- What rights should avatars have?
- Who is morally accountable for AI decisions?

Ethicists can help foresee and prevent unintended consequences and guide long-term goals.

Educators and Social Scientists

Experts in education, sociology and psychology can study the social dynamics, developmental impact and cultural ramifications of metaverse adoption. Their insights are crucial for curriculum design, behavioral norms and community engagement strategies.

Artists and Creatives

The metaverse must also reflect our diversity of culture and imagination. Artists, storytellers and creators bring depth and emotional intelligence to virtual worlds. Their role is to infuse narrative, empathy and meaning into the digital experience.

By fostering cross disciplinary teams and inclusive public consultation, the metaverse can evolve as a social contract, not just a software product.

Summary: Principles for Responsible Design

Designing a responsible and human-centered metaverse is not just a moral imperative-it's a strategic necessity. The long-term success of virtual environments will depend on whether they foster trust, inclusivity and well-being while enabling innovation and economic participation.

The metaverse is a mirror of society. If built without ethical guidance, it may replicate exclusion, exploitation and division. But if designed with purpose and plurality, it can become a space where technology uplifts humanity, strengthens communities and empowers individuals across borders and boundaries.

Now is the time to choose our trajectory-to embed human values into the very code of our future digital world.

FUTURE OUTLOOK AND CONCLUSION

The metaverse is not a destination-it is an evolving spectrum of technologies, behaviors and values that will shape how humanity lives, learns, works and connects. While the early wave of the metaverse is powered by virtual and augmented reality, AI and blockchain, the next phase will introduce even more immersive, intelligent and biologically integrated interfaces. As this ecosystem evolves, society must actively guide its trajectory toward inclusivity, sustainability and shared prosperity.

What Lies Ahead: Mixed Reality, Brain-Computer Interfaces and More

Mixed Reality and Spatial Computing

The future of the metaverse is headed toward mixed reality (MR) a seamless blend of digital and physical environments, where users interact with holographic content overlaid onto the real world. Devices like Apple Vision Pro, Microsoft HoloLens and Magic Leap are laying the foundation for a spatial computing paradigm, where every surface becomes an interface and every room a canvas.

MR enables real-time collaboration between on-site and remote users, such as an engineer seeing AR mechanics while a remote expert guide repairs through holographic annotations. In education, MR may allow students to conduct science experiments with physical lab tools enhanced by virtual overlays.

Brain-Computer Interfaces (BCIs)

Looking even further ahead, brain computer interfaces promise to radically transform metaverse interaction. Companies like Neuralink, OpenBCI and NextMind are developing technologies that translate neural signals into commands, enabling users to control the digital environment with their thoughts.

BCIs could enhance accessibility for individuals with disabilities, allowing them to interact with the metaverse in intuitive and empowering ways. They may also open new frontiers in creativity, communication and exploration.

However, BCIs bring complex ethical and legal questions around cognitive privacy, neural data ownership and mental autonomy underscoring the need for proactive governance.

Interoperable, Decentralized Ecosystems

In the long-term, the metaverse is likely to evolve into a decentralized network of interoperable virtual worlds, governed by open protocols rather than corporations. Users will move across platforms with persistent identities and digital assets, interacting with AI agents and smart contracts in real time.

This future will depend on:

- Open-source standards
- Cross-platform compatibility
- Digital identity frameworks
- Public-private partnerships

A mature metaverse could resemble a digital version of the physical world, but with superpowers-instant travel, limitless memory, adaptive learning and borderless economies.

Key Takeaways from Each Sector

Workplace

- The metaverse enables immersive remote collaboration, reducing geographical constraints and enabling global teamwork.
- AI assistants and blockchain-based credentials support efficiency, transparency and mobility in professional settings.
- Ethical design must balance productivity with well-being, ensuring inclusivity and protection from digital fatigue and surveillance.

Education

- VR and AR bring abstract concepts to life, increasing student engagement and knowledge retention.
- AI-powered adaptive learning creates personalized, scalable educational experiences.
- Challenges around screen time, mental health and teacher training require ongoing attention and policy innovation.

Industry and Commerce

- Brands use the metaverse to deliver immersive customer experiences and new digital goods via NFTs.
- Digital twins and industrial simulations drive operational efficiency and predictive planning.
- Decentralized marketplaces empower creators and consumers while raising new questions about governance, IP and fairness.

Cross-Cutting Ethics

- Data privacy, avatar rights and behavioral governance are foundational to a safe and trusted metaverse.
- Inequities in access, representation and digital literacy must be addressed to avoid deepening social divides.

- Psychological effects and the needs of children and vulnerable users must be accounted for in platform design.

Closing Thoughts on Ethical Stewardship and Long-Term Impact

The metaverse is both an opportunity and a responsibility. It invites us to reimagine how we connect, learn, work and build-but also challenges us to confront the invisible architectures of power, ethics and inclusion that shape digital life.

To build a metaverse that enhances rather than degrades humanity, we must adopt a stewardship model-one in which designers, technologists, educators, businesses and policymakers act as caretakers of an emerging ecosystem that touches every aspect of society.

This stewardship includes:

- Anticipatory ethics: Considering long-term impacts before they materialize
- Participatory design: Involving users from diverse backgrounds in shaping tools and policies
- Cultural humility: Recognizing that no single worldview or nation should dominate the virtual commons
- Sustainability: Minimizing the energy and resource footprints of metaverse infrastructures

If the early internet taught us anything, it's that technology evolves faster than institutions. The metaverse gives us a second chance to embed ethics into architecture, inclusion into infrastructure and humanity into code.

The question is not whether the metaverse will become part of our lives-but what kind of metaverse we are willing to build and live in.

Futurist Visions: Governance by AI, Digital Citizenship and Post-Work Societies

As the metaverse matures, it may evolve from a set of applications into a global civic infrastructure, with its own systems of governance, identity and labor. One emerging scenario is metaverse governance by AI where decentralized virtual societies rely on autonomous agents to enforce policies, moderate content and resolve disputes. These AI agents, trained on democratic principles or cultural norms, could serve as digital magistrates or age facilitators in decentralized communities.

The concept of digital citizenship may also become formalized, with users holding persistent, cross-platform identities tied to blockchain-based credentials, rights and responsibilities. These could include voting in metaverse, contributing to policy proposals, or earning reputational capital through constructive behavior.

In parallel, as automation and AI absorb more traditional labor, post-work societies may see the metaverse as a space for meaningful contribution through creativity, play, mentorship, or social innovation. Digital economies could reward users not just for productivity, but for community building, teaching, or artistic expression.

Closing Meta-Reflection: Embodiment and Digital Immortality

At its core, the metaverse challenges our understanding of embodiment, presence and permanence. When avatars outlast their human creators-or when digital twins continue interacting on one's behalf-the boundaries between life and legacy begin to blur.

Will digital selves become merely holders of memory, or living extensions of identity? Can we "live on" in a meaningful way through curated simulations, AI-trained replicas, or persistent contributions to virtual communities?

Such questions are not merely technological-they are philosophical, spiritual and existential. They invite us to reflect not just on what we can build, but why we build it-and what kind of humanity we want to preserve in a digital future.

Ultimately, the metaverse offers a canvas not only for innovation, but for re-imagining human purpose. Our collective choices today will determine whether it becomes a mirror of our best values or a monument to our missed opportunities.

DISCLOSURE OF DELEGATION TO GENERATIVE AI

The authors declare the use of generative AI in the research and writing process. According to the GAIDeT taxonomy (2025), the following tasks were delegated to GAI tools under full human supervision:

Proofreading and Editing

The GAI tool used was: Sonnet 4.5.

Responsibility for the final manuscript lies entirely with the authors.

GAI tools are not listed as authors and do not bear responsibility for the final outcomes.

Declaration submitted by: Mohan Sankaran

REFERENCES

Accenture. (2022). *The Nth Floor: Accenture's metaverse environment for employee onboarding and collaboration*. Accenture Research.

Akiner, M. E., & Akiner, I. (2023). Integration of digital twins, blockchain and AI in the metaverse. *International Journal of Smart Technologies*, *9*(2), 112–127.

American Psychological Association. (2024). *Position paper on immersive technologies and children: Mental health considerations*. APA Publications.

Anderson, L. W., & Krathwohl, D. R. (Eds.). (2001). *A taxonomy for learning, teaching, and assessing: A revision of Bloom's taxonomy of educational objectives*. Longman.

Association, X. R. (2022). *XR in education: Teacher perspectives and best practices*. XR Association.

Castronova, E. (2005). *Synthetic worlds: The business and culture of online games*. University of Chicago Press.

Deloitte. (2023). *The metaverse in retail: Transforming the customer experience through augmented and virtual reality*. Deloitte Insights.

EDUCAUSE. (2023). *2023 EDUCAUSE horizon report: Teaching and learning edition*. EDUCAUSE.

European Commission. (2024). *Digital Services Act: Ensuring a safe and accountable online environment*. Directorate-General for Communications Networks, Content and Technology.

Frontiers in Virtual Reality. (2025). Metaverse in industrial contexts: A comprehensive review. *Frontiers in Virtual Reality, 6*(2), 77–95.

Gadekallu, T. R., Alazab, M., Maddikunta, P. K. R., Pham, Q. V., & Reddy, M. (2022). Blockchain for the metaverse: A review. *IEEE Internet of Things Journal, 9*(15), 11980–11995.

Gig, X. R. (2021). *Extended reality in medical training: Case study*. GigXR, Inc.

Hyundai Motor Company. (2022). *Hyundai Motor unveils Metamobility concept at CES 2022*. Hyundai Media Center.

IEEE. (2024). *Ethically aligned design: A vision for prioritizing human well-being with autonomous and intelligent systems* (2nd ed.). Institute of Electrical and Electronics Engineers.

Immersive VR Education. (2023). *ENGAGE: Virtual reality platform for education and enterprise training*. Immersive VR Education Ltd.

Kolb, D. A. (1984). *Experiential learning: Experience as the source of learning and development*. Prentice Hall.

Li, K., Wang, X., Zhang, Y., & Chen, H. (2022). When Internet of Things meets metaverse: Convergence of physical and cyber worlds. *Journal of Network and Computer Applications, 200*, 103305.

Lin, H., Gao, L., Zhang, L., & Zhao, M. (2022). Metaverse in education: Vision, opportunities, and challenges. *Educational Technology Research and Development, 70*(5), 1231–1250.

McKinsey & Company. (2023). *Value creation in the metaverse: The real business of the virtual world*. McKinsey Global Institute.

MDPI. (2024). Metaverse and human digital twin: Digital identity, biometrics, and privacy in virtual environments. *Sensors (Basel), 24*(3), 1125.

Meta. (2023). *Horizon Workrooms: The VR space for teams to connect, collaborate, and develop ideas together*. Meta Platforms, Inc.

Microsoft. (2022). *Mesh for Microsoft Teams: Mixed reality collaboration platform*. Microsoft Corporation.

NVIDIA. (2023). *Industrial metaverse: Building photorealistic digital twins with Siemens*. NVIDIA Corporation.

PMC. (2025). Digital twins for building industrial metaverse: Status quo, challenges, and opportunities. *Progress in Materials Science, 145*, 100954.

PwC UK. (2023). *How virtual reality is redefining soft skills training: VR training evaluation report.* PricewaterhouseCoopers UK.

Roblox Education. (2022). *Learning and teaching on Roblox: Education in the metaverse case study*. Roblox Corporation.

UK Information Commissioner's Office. (2024). *Age appropriate design: A code of practice for online services* (Updated ed.). ICO.

UNESCO. (2022). *Digital equity in global education: Bridging the digital divide*. United Nations Educational, Scientific and Cultural Organization.

U.S. Congress. (2023). *Augmented Reality and Virtual Reality Privacy Act* (H.R. 5498). 118th Congress.

Vogue Business. (2022). *Luxury fashion's next frontier: The metaverse and NFT strategies*. Vogue Business.

W3C. (2023). *XR accessibility user requirements*. World Wide Web Consortium.

World Bank. (2023). *Closing the digital divide: Global infrastructure and connectivity report*. The World Bank Group.

World Economic Forum. (2023). *Digital twins for smart cities: Urban transformation case studies*. WEF Reports.

Zhang, X., Yu, Z., & Zhao, Y. (2023). Metaverse in education: A systematic literature review. *Computers & Education. Artificial Intelligence*, *4*, 100089.

Zuboff, S. (2019). *The age of surveillance capitalism: The fight for a human future at the new frontier of power*. PublicAffairs.

Compilation of References

Abendschein, R., Desai, S., & Astell, A. J. (2023). Towards accessibility guidelines for the metaverse. In *Proceedings of the CHI* (Vol. 23). ACM.

Abes, Z., Fairchild, N., Lin, S., Wahba, M., Xiao, K., & Fisher, S. S. (2025). The Immersive Archive: Archival Strategies for the Sensorama & Sutherland HMD. *Proceedings - 2025 IEEE International Conference on Artificial Intelligence and EXtended and Virtual Reality, AIxVR 2025*, 307–312. DOI: 10.1109/AIx-VR63409.2025.00059

Abilkaiyrkyzy, A., Elhagry, A., Laamarti, F., & El Saddik, A. (2023). Metaverse key requirements and platforms survey. *IEEE Access : Practical Innovations, Open Solutions*, *11*, 117765–117787. DOI: 10.1109/ACCESS.2023.3325844

Accenture. (2022). *The Nth Floor: Accenture's metaverse environment for employee onboarding and collaboration*. Accenture Research.

ADL. (2021, September 13). *Hate is No Game: Harassment and Positive Social Experiences in Online Games 2021*. ADL.ORG: https://www.adl.org/resources/report/hate-no-game-harassment-and-positive-social-experiences-online-games-2021 retrieved from.

Ahmad, H. F., Rafique, W., Rasool, R. U., Alhumam, A., Anwar, Z., & Qadir, J. (2023). Leveraging 6G, extended reality, and IoT big data analytics for healthcare: A review. *Computer Science Review*, *48*, 100558. DOI: 10.1016/j.cosrev.2023.100558

Ahmed, A. S., Keshk, A. E., Abo-Seida, O. M., & Sakr, M. (2022). Tumor detection and classification in breast mammography based on fine-tuned convolutional neural networks. *International Journal of Computers and Information*, *9*(1), 74–84.

Akbar, K., Passaro, A., Di Gioia, M., Martini, E., Dragone, M., Zullo, A., & Stasolla, F. (2024). Reviewing the Horizon: The Future of Extended Reality and Artificial Intelligence in Neurorehabilitation for Brain Injury Recovery. *Information, 15*(8), 501. DOI: 10.3390/info15080501

Akhtar, Z. (2024). Biomedical engineering (bme) and medical health science: An investigation perspective exploration. *Quantum Journal of Medical and Health Sciences*, *3*(3), 1–24.

Akhtar, Z. B. (2024). Artificial Intelligence (AI) and Extended Reality (XR): A Biomedical Engineering Perspective Investigation Analysis. *Indonesian Journal of Electronics, Electromedical Engineering, and Medical Informatics*, *6*(3). Advance online publication. DOI: 10.35882/ijeeemi.v6i3.5

Akhtar, Z. B., & Rawol, A. T. (2025). Artificial Intelligence (AI) & Extended Reality (XR) within Healthcare: A Multidimensional Biomedical Engineering (BME) Investigative Exploration. *Biomed. Clin. Res. J*, *1*, 1–22.

Akiner, M. E., & Akiner, I. (2023). Integration of digital twins, blockchain and AI in the metaverse. *International Journal of Smart Technologies*, *9*(2), 112–127.

Akiotu, C. A., Cole, O. A., Bunmi, E. E., Temiola, T., Oladele, H. A., Oluwasegun, V. O., Oyedemi, O. A., & Matthew, U. O. (2025). A Predictive Nutritional Assessment System for Vegetarians using Artificial Neural Networks. *Journal of Future Artificial Intelligence and Technologies*, *2*(2), 294–312. DOI: 10.62411/faith.3048-3719-117

Akkaya, C., & Kaplan, Y. (2014). Toplumsal cinsiyet bağlamında spor medyasında kadın. *International Journal of Science Culture and Sport*, *2*, 177–182. DOI: 10.14486/IJSCS189

Akkoç, H. (2013). *Integrating technological pedagogical content knowledge (TPCK) framework into teacher education.* Paper presented at the Conference of the International Journal of Arts and Science.

Akmeşe, Z., & Deniz, K. (2015). Kadına yönelik cinsiyetçi söylemin internet haber portallarında yer alma biçimleri. *Uşak Üniversitesi Sosyal Bilimler Dergisi*, *8*(1), 311–326. DOI: 10.12780/uusbd.45190

Akpan, E. E. (2024). Healthcare Applications of Augmented Reality. *Creating Immersive Learning Experiences Through Virtual Reality (VR), 201.*

Al Balushi, J. S. G., Al Jabri, M. I. A., Palarimath, S., Maran, P., Thenmozhi, K., & Balakumar, C. (2024). *Incorporating artificial intelligence powered immersive realities to improve learning using virtual reality (VR) and augmented reality (AR) technology.* Paper presented at the 2024 3rd International Conference on Applied Artificial Intelligence and Computing (ICAAIC).

Aland, R. C., Hugo, H. J., Battle, A., Donkin, R., McDonald, A., McGowan, H., & Tentrisanna, M. (2023). A plethora of choices: An anatomists' practical perspectives for the selection of digital anatomy resources. *Smart Learning Environments*, *10*(1), 66. DOI: 10.1186/s40561-023-00285-3

Alhakamy, A. (2024). Extended Reality (XR) Toward Building Immersive Solutions: The Key to Unlocking Industry 4.0. *ACM Computing Surveys*, *56*(9), 1–38. Advance online publication. DOI: 10.1145/3652595

Ali, M., Naeem, F., Kaddoum, G., & Hossain, E. (2023). Metaverse communications, networking, security, and applications: Research issues, state-of-the-art, and future directions. *IEEE Communications Surveys and Tutorials*, *26*(2), 1238–1278. DOI: 10.1109/COMST.2023.3347172

Al-Kfairy, M., Alomari, A., Al-Bashayreh, M. G., & Tubishat, M. (2024). *Unveiling the metaverse: A survey of user experience, social dynamics, and technological interoperability*. Preprint.

Al-Kfairy, M., Alrabaee, S., Alfandi, O., Mohamed, A. T., & Khaddaj, S. (2025). Navigating ethical dimensions in the metaverse: Challenges, frameworks, and solutions. *IEEE Access : Practical Innovations, Open Solutions*, *13*, 79996–80018. DOI: 10.1109/ACCESS.2025.3564498

Allam, Z., Sharifi, A., Bibri, S. E., Jones, D. S., & Krogstie, J. (2022). The metaverse as a virtual form of smart cities: Opportunities and challenges for environmental, economic, and social sustainability in urban futures. *Smart Cities*, *5*(3), 771–801. DOI: 10.3390/smartcities5030040

Alp, A., Çakmak, G., & Sarper Kahveci, M. (2020). "Ne bilir kadın oyun oynamayı?":Kadın oyuncuların e-spor deneyimleri. *Türkiye Klinikleri Spor Bilimleri Dergisi*, *12*(3), 322–329. DOI: 10.5336/sportsci.2020-73698

Alqallaf, N., & Ghannam, R. (2024). *Immersive Learning in Photovoltaic Energy Education: A Comprehensive Review of Virtual Reality Applications*. Paper presented at the Solar. DOI: 10.3390/solar4010006

Alshahrani, A., Mahmoud, A., El-Sappagh, S., & Ali Elbelkasy, M. S. (2023). An Internet of Things Based Air Pollution Detection Device for Mitigating Climate Changes. *Information Science Letters*, *12*(4), 1891–1900. DOI: 10.18576/isl/120413

Amaizu, G., Njoku, J., Lee, J., & Kim, D. (2024). Metaverse in advanced manufacturing: Background, applications, limitations, open issues & future directions. *ICT Express*, *10*(2), 1–23. DOI: 10.1016/j.icte.2024.02.010

American Psychological Association. (2024). *Position paper on immersive technologies and children: Mental health considerations*. APA Publications.

Andalib, S., & Monsur, M. (2024). Co-Created Virtual Reality (VR) Modules in Landscape Architecture Education: A Mixed Methods Study Investigating the Pedagogical Effectiveness of VR. *Education Sciences*, *14*(6), 553. DOI: 10.3390/educsci14060553

Anderson, J., & Rainie, L. (2022). The metaverse in 2040. *Pew Research Center*, *30*(4), 1–203. https://www.pewresearch.org/internet/2022/06/30/the-metaverse-in-2040

Anderson, E. (2008). "I used to think women were weak": Orthodox masculinity, gender segregation, and sport. *Sociological Forum*, *23*(2), 257–280. DOI: 10.1111/j.1573-7861.2008.00058.x

Anderson, L. W., & Krathwohl, D. R. (Eds.). (2001). *A taxonomy for learning, teaching, and assessing: A revision of Bloom's taxonomy of educational objectives*. Longman.

Angrist, N., & Dercon, S. (2024). Understanding Gaps between. *Policy & Practice*.

Apperley, T., & Gray, K. (2020). Digital divides and structural inequalities. In *T. Q. Rachel Kowert, The Video Game Debate 2*. Routledge. DOI: 10.4324/9780429351815-4

Arghashi, V., & Gunalay, Y. (2025). Exploring the metaverse: What drives millennials and Gen Z to embrace virtual worlds? *Journal of Islamic Marketing*.

Arrieta, A. B., Díaz-Rodríguez, N., Del Ser, J., Bennetot, A., Tabik, S., Barbado, A., & Herrera, F. (2020). Explainable Artificial Intelligence (XAI): Concepts, taxonomies, opportunities and challenges toward responsible AI. *Information Fusion*, *58*, 82–115. DOI: 10.1016/j.inffus.2019.12.012

Asif, R., & Hassan, S. R. (2023). Shaping the future of Ethereum: Exploring energy consumption in Proof-of-Work and Proof-of-Stake consensus. *Frontiers in Blockchain*, *6*, 1151724. DOI: 10.3389/fbloc.2023.1151724

Asimakopoulos, G., Antonopoulou, H., Giotopoulos, K. C., & Halkiopoulos, C. (2025). *Impact of Information and Communication Technologies on Democratic Processes*.

Asoodar, M., Janesarvatan, F., Yu, H., & de Jong, N. (2024). Theoretical foundations and implications of augmented reality, virtual reality, and mixed reality for immersive learning in health professions education. *Advances in Simulation (London, England)*, *9*(1), 36. DOI: 10.1186/s41077-024-00311-5 PMID: 39252139

Assaf, R., Mendes, D., & Rodrigues, R. (2024). Cues to fast-forward collaboration: A Survey of Workspace Awareness and Visual Cues in XR Collaborative Systems. *Computer Graphics Forum*, *43*(2), e15066. DOI: 10.1111/cgf.15066

Association, X. R. (2022). *XR in education: Teacher perspectives and best practices*. XR Association.

Ayana, G., Dese, K., Nemomssa, H. D., Habtamu, B., Melledo, B., Radu, K., Tamiru, C., Faye, S. L., Ondua, M., Ntagha, D. S., Nikweteyim, D., & Kong, J. D. (2024). *Decentralising granular AI governance assessment of the state of accountability measures in ten sub-saharan African member states*.

Ayhan, B., & Demir, Y. (2022). Systematic sexism: Women's sports news in a circle of gatekeepers and users on twitter. *Communication & Sport*. Advance online publication. DOI: 10.1177/21674795221147644

Bae, S.-G. (2022). A Study on Metaverse Spatial Acoustic Adaptation to Minimize Environmental Adaptation Using Spatial Sounds Around Accessors. *International Journal of Engineering Trends and Technology*, *70*(1), 206. DOI: 10.14445/22315381/IJETT-V70I1P206

Bakan, Ö. (2013). Türk medyasında kadın sporcuların temsili: Üç gazetenin içerik analizi. *Selçuk İletişim*, *7*(4), 129–139. DOI: 10.18094/si.11566

Balakrishnan, N., & Kumar, T. (2024). Transforming lives of Sensory Impaired Individuals through Extended Reality (XR). *Procedia CIRP*, *128*, 846–851. DOI: 10.1016/j.procir.2024.07.067

Ball, M. (2024). *The metaverse: Fully revised and updated edition: Building the spatial internet*. Liveright Publishing.

Barocas, S., & Selbst, A. D. (2016). Big data's disparate impact. *California Law Review*, *104*(3), 671–732.

Barta, S., Gurrea, R., & Flavián, C. (2025). Augmented reality experiences: Consumer-centered augmented reality framework and research agenda. *Psychology and Marketing*, *42*(2), 634–650. DOI: 10.1002/mar.22143

Barteit, S., Lanfermann, L., Bärnighausen, T., Neuhann, F., & Beiersmann, C. (2021). Augmented, mixed, and virtual reality-based head-mounted devices for medical education: Systematic review. *JMIR Serious Games*, *9*(3), e29080. DOI: 10.2196/29080 PMID: 34255668

Bartl, M., Kannan, V., & Stocki, H. (2016). A review and analysis of literature on netnography research. *International Journal of Technology Marketing*, *11*(2), 165. DOI: 10.1504/IJTMKT.2016.075687

Batra, R., Arora, S., Sharma, M. M., Rana, S., Raheja, K., Saber, A., & Shah, M. A. (2024). Integration of LSTM networks with gradient boosting machines (GBM) for assessing heating and cooling load requirements in building energy efficiency. *Energy Exploration & Exploitation*, *42*(6), 2191–2217. DOI: 10.1177/01445987241268075

BBC. (2016, November 21). *100 Women 2016: The women challenging sexism in e-sports*. BBC: https://www.bbc.com/news/technology-37992322 retrieved from.

Bell, A., & Morris, G. (2009). Engaging professional learning in online environments. *Australasian Journal of Educational Technology*, *25*(5), 799–813. DOI: 10.14742/ajet.1116

Berelson, B. (1952). *Content analysis in communication research*. Free Press.

Bertozzi, E. (2008). "You play like a girl!": Cross-gender competition and the uneven playing field. *Convergence (London)*, *14*(4), 473–487. DOI: 10.1177/1354856508094667

Beyene, E., Bedemo, A., & Gebremeskel, A. (2024). *Determinants of digital technology development in sub-Saharan African countries*. Advanced Data Science and Analytics.

Bhaskaran, V., & Mahbub, U. (2024). Immersive User Experiences: Trends and Challenges of Using XR Technologies. *Computer Vision: Challenges, Trends, and Opportunities*, 260–278. DOI: 10.1201/9781003328957-12/IMMERSIVE-USER-EXPERIENCES-TRENDS-CHALLENGES-USING-XR-TECHNOLOGIES-VASUDEV-BHASKARAN-UPAL-MAHBUB

Bhati, N., Duggar, R., & Saber, A. (2024). Empowering Safety by Embracing IoT for Leak Detection Excellence. In *Innovations in Machine Learning and IoT for Water Management* (pp. 231–251). IGI Global Scientific Publishing.

Bhatnagar, R., Hassan, E., Saber, A., Shams, M. Y., & Elbedwehy, S. (2024, November). Enhanced Vision Transformer with Lion Optimizer for accurate classification of monkeypox skin images. In *2024 4th International Conference on Technological Advancements in Computational Sciences (ICTACS)* (pp. 1897–1902). IEEE. DOI: 10.1109/ICTACS62700.2024.10840567

Bioni, B. R., Garrote, M., Meira, M., & Batista, N. P. R. (2022). *The digitization of the Brazilian national identity system: A descriptive and qualitative analysis of its infrastructure, governance, and data protection impacts*.

Birrell, S. (1988). Discourses on the gender/sport relationship: From women in sport to gender relations. *Exercise and Sport Sciences Reviews, 16*, 459–502. DOI: 10.1249/00003677-198800160-00017 PMID: 3292265

Biswas, S., & Visell, Y. (2021). Haptic perception, mechanics, and material technologies for virtual reality. *Advanced Functional Materials, 31*(39), 2008186. DOI: 10.1002/adfm.202008186

Boateng, G. (2024). *Leveraging AI to Advance Science and Computing Education across Africa: Progress, Challenges, and Opportunities*. arXiv (Cornell University).

Boel, C., Rotsaert, T., Valcke, M., Vanhulsel, A., & Schellens, T. (2023). Applying educational design research to develop a low-cost, mobile immersive virtual reality serious game teaching safety in secondary vocational education. *Education and Information Technologies, 29*(7), 8609–8646. DOI: 10.1007/s10639-023-12126-4

Boel, C., Dekeyser, K., Lemal, M., Rotsaert, T., Valcke, M., Schellens, T., & Struyf, D. (2024). Towards a Framework for a Nation-Wide Implementation of Augmented, Virtual and Mixed Reality in K-12 Technical and Vocational Education. *TechTrends, 68*(2), 295–306. Advance online publication. DOI: 10.1007/s11528-023-00925-y

Bottarelli, M., Epiphaniou, G., Mahmood, S., Hooper, M., & Maple, C. (2025). *Assessing the Trustworthiness of Electronic Identity Management Systems: Framework and Methodology.*

Bouke, M.-A., Abdullah, A., AlShatebi, Sh., Atigh, H. E., & Congre, K. (2023). *African Union Convention on Cyber Security and Personal Data Protection: Questions and Answers.*

Bourdieu, P. (1986). The forms of capital. In J. Richardson (Ed.), Handbook of Theory and Research for the Sociology of Education (pp. 241–258). Greenwood.

Brown, R., Habibi-Luevano, S., Robern, G., Wood, K., Perera, S., Uribe-Quevedo, A., & Brown, C. (2021). Employing Mozilla Hubs as an alternative tool for student outreach: A design challenge use case. In *Interactive mobile communication, technologies and learning* (pp. 213–222). Springer International Publishing.

Brückner, S., Kirsten, F., Schwarz, M., Cotte, J., Tsesis, M., & Gilbert, S. (2022). The Patient's Consent for Scientific Use of Written Data: The Approach a Trusted Third-Party Consent. *Mayo Clinic Proceedings. Digital Health, 1*(4), 527. PMID: 40206306

Bryant, L., & Hemsley, B. (2024). Augmented reality: A view to future visual supports for people with disability. *Disability and Rehabilitation. Assistive Technology, 19*(3), 800–813. DOI: 10.1080/17483107.2022.2125090 PMID: 36149835

Buolamwini, J., & Gebru, T. (2018). Gender shades: Intersectional accuracy disparities in commercial gender classification. *Proceedings of Machine Learning Research, 81*, 1–15.

Burnay, J., Bushman, B., & Larøi, F. (2019). Effects of sexualized video games on online sexual harassment. *Aggressive Behavior, 45*(2), 214–223. DOI: 10.1002/ab.21811 PMID: 30614006

Cairns, C. N. (2005, May). E-waste and the consumer: improving options to reduce, reuse and recycle. In *Proceedings of the 2005 IEEE International Symposium on Electronics and the Environment,* 2005. (pp. 237-242). IEEE. DOI: 10.1109/ISEE.2005.1437033

Çakır, Z., Gönen, M., & Ceyhan, M. (2022). Spor Bilimleri Fakültesi öğrencilerinin metaverse farkındalıklarının incelenmesi. *CBÜ Beden Eğitimi ve Spor Bilimleri Dergisi, 17*(2), 406–418. DOI: 10.33459/cbubesbd.1179009

Calderón-Fajardo, V., Puig-Cabrera, M., & Rodríguez-Rodríguez, I. (2025). Beyond the real world: Metaverse adoption patterns in tourism among Gen Z and Millennials. *Current Issues in Tourism, 28*(8), 1261–1281.

Calisto, M. de L., & Sarkar, S. (2024). A systematic review of virtual reality in tourism and hospitality: The known and the paths to follow. *International Journal of Hospitality Management, 116*, 103623. DOI: 10.1016/j.ijhm.2023.103623

Cao, S., Chu, J., Zhang, Z. C., & Liu, L. (2024). The effectiveness of VR environment on primary and secondary school students' learning performance in science courses. *Interactive Learning Environments, 32*(10), 7321–7337. DOI: 10.1080/10494820.2024.2312921

Cappa, M. L. (2023). From Web 2.0 to the Metaverse: analyzing the evolution of platform-based business models and the creator economy. Academic Press.

Carayannis, E. G., & Morawska, J. (2023). *University and education 5.0 for emerging trends, policies and practices in the concept of industry 5.0 and society 5.0 Industry 5.0: Creative and Innovative Organizations*. Springer. DOI: 10.1007/978-3-031-26232-6_1

Cascella, M., Cascella, A., Monaco, F., & Shariff, M. N. (2023). Envisioning gamification in anesthesia, pain management, and critical care: Basic principles, integration of artificial intelligence, and simulation strategies. *Journal of Anesthesia, Analgesia and Critical Care, 3*(1), 33. DOI: 10.1186/s44158-023-00118-2 PMID: 37697415

Castronova, E. (2005). *Synthetic worlds: The business and culture of online games*. University of Chicago Press.

Castronova, E. (2023). *Synthetic worlds revisited: The evolution of virtual economies*. MIT Press.

Cavanagh, S. (1997). Content analysis: Concepts, methods and applications. *Nurse Researcher, 4*, 5–16. PMID: 27285770

Chakraborty, S., & Dadhich, A. (2023). Dialogue and Metaverse: A Scenario. In *Dynamics of Dialogue, Cultural Development, and Peace in the Metaverse* (pp. 11). IGI Global. https://www.igi-global.com/chapter/dialogue-and-metaverse/314987

Chakuzira, W., Ghocho, J. M. M., & Msanzi, M. (2024). Refining the Definition and Typologies of Entrepreneurship in Africa: A Systematic Review [Review of Refining the Definition and Typologies of Entrepreneurship in Africa: A Systematic Review]. *Administrative Sciences, 14*(2), 24. DOI: 10.3390/admsci14080184

Chen, C., Li, Y., Wu, Z., Mai, C., Liu, Y., Hu, Y., Kang, J., & Zheng, Z. (2024). Privacy computing meets metaverse: Necessity, taxonomy and challenges. *Ad Hoc Networks, 158*, 1–13. DOI: 10.1016/j.adhoc.2024.103457

Chen, X., Zou, D., Xie, H., & Wang, F. L. (2023). Metaverse in education: Contributors, cooperations, and research themes. *IEEE Transactions on Learning Technologies, 16*(6), 1111–1129. DOI: 10.1109/TLT.2023.3277952

Chin, M. H., Afsarmanesh, N., Bierman, A. S., Chang, C., Colón-Rodríguez, A. J., Guinton, P., Duran, D. G., Fair, M., Hernandez-Boussard, T., Hightower, M., Jain, A., Jordan, N., Joseph, J. G., Muga, J. H., Neely, A. R., Prieto-Centurion, V., Schneider, J. A., Shrinivasan, M., Ohno-Machado, L. (2023). *Guiding Principles to Address the Impact of Algorithmic Bias on Racial and Ethnic Disparities.*

Chip. (2014, October 20). *Oyun dünyasında GamerGate fırtınası dinmiyor.* Chip.com.tr: https://www.chip.com.tr/haber/oyun-dunyasinda-gamergate-firtinasi-dinmiyor_50188.html retrieved from.

Christopoulos, A., & Mystakidis, S. (2023). Gamification in education. *Encyclopedia, 3*(3), 1223–1243. DOI: 10.3390/encyclopedia3040089

Coelho, L., & Reis, S. S. (2023). *Enhancing Learning Experiences Through Artificial Intelligence: Classroom 5.0 Fostering Pedagogy Through Micro and Adaptive Learning in Higher Education: Trends, Tools, and Applications.* IGI Global.

Craeynest, U. (2024). GEN Z'S ENTRANCE INTO THE METAVERSE (Doctoral dissertation, Ghent University).

Crawford, K., & Calo, R. (2021). There is a blind spot in AI research. *Nature, 538*(7625), 311–313. DOI: 10.1038/538311a PMID: 27762391

Crogman, H. T., Cano, V. D., Pacheco, E., Sonawane, R. B., & Boroon, R. (2025). Virtual Reality, Augmented Reality, and Mixed Reality in Experiential Learning: Transforming Educational Paradigms. *Education Sciences, 15*(3), 303. DOI: 10.3390/educsci15030303

Cunningham, G., & Ko, Y. (2024). Diversity, equity and inclusion in the sport metaverse. *International Journal of Sports Marketing & Sponsorship*. Advance online publication. DOI: 10.1108/IJSMS-04-2023-0080

Damaševičius, R., & Sidekerskienė, T. (2024). Virtual worlds for learning in metaverse: A narrative review. *Sustainability (Basel), 16*(5), 2032. DOI: 10.3390/su16052032

Darvin, L., Holden, J., Wells, J., & Baker, T. (2021). Breaking the glass monitor: Examining the underrepresentation of women in esports environments. *Sport Management Review, 24*(3), 475–499. DOI: 10.1080/14413523.2021.1891746

Davidson, S., De Filippi, P., & Potts, J. (2018). Economics of blockchain. *The Review of Austrian Economics, 31*(4), 399–410.

Davis, A., Murphy, J., Owens, D., Khazanchi, D., & Zigurs, I. (2009). Avatars, people, and virtual worlds: Foundations for research in metaverses. *Journal of the Association for Information Systems, 10*(2), 1. DOI: 10.17705/1jais.00183

De Filippi, P., & Wright, A. (2018). *Blockchain and the law: The rule of code.* Harvard University Press.

Delamere, F., & Shaw, S. (2008). "They see it as a guy's game": The politics of gender in digital games. *Leisure/Loisir, 32*(2), 279–302. DOI: 10.1080/14927713.2008.9651411

Deleuze, J., Maurage, P., Schimmenti, A., Nuyens, F., Melzer, A., & Billieux, J. (2019). Escaping reality through videogames is linked to an implicit preference for virtual over real-life stimuli. *Journal of Affective Disorders, 245*, 1024–1031. DOI: 10.1016/j.jad.2018.11.078 PMID: 30699844

Deloitte. (2023). *The metaverse in retail: Transforming the customer experience through augmented and virtual reality*. Deloitte Insights.

Demir, Y., & Ayhan, B. (2022). Being a female sports journalist on twitter: Online harassment, sexualization, and hegemony. *International Journal of Sport Communication, 15*(3), 207–217. DOI: 10.1123/ijsc.2022-0044

Devi, K., & Thomas, N. (2025). "Let's grab a match!": Exploring ways to enhance engagement and consistency in sports for Gen Z and millennials (Doctoral dissertation, OCAD University).

Dewey, C. (2014, October 14). *The only guide to Gamergate you will ever need to read.* Washingtonpost.com: https://www.washingtonpost.com/news/the-intersect/wp/2014/10/14/the-only-guide-to-gamergate-you-will-ever-need-to-read/ retrieved from.

Diaz-Rodriguez, N., Ser, J. D., Coeckelbergh, M., Prado, M. L. de, Herrera-Viedma, E., & Herrera, F. (2023). *Connecting the dots in trustworthy Artificial Intelligence: from AI principles, ethics, and key requirements to responsible AI systems and regulation.*

Dignum, V. (2019). *Responsible artificial intelligence: How to develop and use AI in a responsible way.* Springer. DOI: 10.1007/978-3-030-30371-6

Dincelli, E., & Yayla, A. (2022). Immersive virtual reality in the age of the Metaverse: A hybrid-narrative review based on the technology affordance perspective. *The Journal of Strategic Information Systems, 21*(2), 1–22. DOI: 10.1016/j.jsis.2022.101717

Dionisio, J. D. N., Burns, W. G.III, & Gilbert, R. (2013). 3D virtual worlds and the metaverse: Current status and future possibilities. *ACM Computing Surveys, 45*(3), 1–38. DOI: 10.1145/2480741.2480751

Distor, C. B., Ruas, I. C., Isagah, T., & Dhaou, S. B. (2023). *Emerging technologies in Africa: Artificial Intelligence, Blockchain, and Internet of Things applications and challenges.*

Dooley, K. (2024). Virtual Reality Narratives Live Online: Immersive Theatre in VRChat Worlds. In *Virtual Reality Narratives: Embodied Encounters in Space* (pp. 185–212). Springer International Publishing.

Downey, S. (2014). History of the (virtual) worlds. *The Journal of Technology Studies, 40*(2), 54–66. DOI: 10.21061/jots.v40i2.a.1

Drča, A. (2022). Gender inequality present in the gaming community. *International Scientific Conference on Information Technology and Data Related Research.* DOI: 10.15308/Sinteza-2022-435-442

Dsouza, L. F. (2025). Hydrogen Aircraft and Sustainable Development: Efficiency, Innovation, and Environmental Impact. *Innovation, and Environmental Impact.*

Dubiel, A., Kamińska, D., Zwoliński, G., Ramić-Brkić, B., Agostini, D., & Zancanaro, M. (2025). Virtual reality for the training of soft skills for professional education: Trends and opportunities. *Interactive Learning Environments, 33*(5), 3261–3281. Advance online publication. DOI: 10.1080/10494820.2025.2450634

Dudley, J., Yin, L., Garaj, V., & Kristensson, P. O. (2023). Inclusive immersion: A review of efforts to improve accessibility in virtual reality, augmented reality and the metaverse. *Virtual Reality (Waltham Cross)*, *27*(4), 2989–3020. DOI: 10.1007/s10055-023-00850-8

Duggan, M. (2014, October 22). *Online harassment.* pewresearch.org: https://www.pewresearch.org/internet/2014/10/22/online-harassment/ retrieved from.

Dwivedi, Y. K., Hughes, D. L., Ismagilova, E., Aarts, G., Coombs, C., Crick, T., & Williams, M. D. (2023). Artificial Intelligence (AI): Multidisciplinary perspectives on emerging challenges, opportunities, and agenda for research, practice, and policy. *International Journal of Information Management*, *70*, 102642. DOI: 10.1016/j.ijinfomgt.2023.102642

Ebong, G. N., Matthew, U. O., Olofin, B., Andrew-Vitalis, N., Fatai, L. O., Waliu, A. O., & Oladipupo, M. A. (2024). *Multimedia Cloud Data Warehouse Design for Knowledge Sharing in the University Environment: A Proposed Digital Solution Implementing Interactive Learning Strategies in Higher Education.* IGI Global. DOI: 10.4018/979-8-3693-3559-8.ch010

Edu, J., Hooper, M., Maple, C., & Crowcroft, J. (2022). *An impact and risk assessment framework for national electronic identity (eID) systems*. iE7 Conference.

EDUCAUSE. (2023). *2023 EDUCAUSE horizon report: Teaching and learning edition*. EDUCAUSE.

Effoduh, J. O., Akpudo, U. E., & Kong, J. D. (2024). Toward a trustworthy and inclusive data governance policy for the use of artificial intelligence in Africa. *Data & Policy*, *6*, 6. DOI: 10.1017/dap.2024.26

Ehimuan, B., Anyanwu, A., Otorunsogo, T., Akinsete, G. J., Abrahams, T. B., & Omolayo, T. (2024). Digital inclusion initiatives: Bridging the connectivity gap in Africa and the USA – A review [Review of *Digital inclusion initiatives: Bridging the connectivity gap in Africa and the USA – A review*]. *International Journal of Education and Development Using Information and Communication Technology*, *20*(1), 147–159.

Elgammal, A., Liu, B., Elhoseiny, M., & Mazzone, M. (2023). CAN: Creative Adversarial Networks—Generating "Art" by learning about styles and deviating from style norms. *Proceedings of the AAAI Conference on Artificial Intelligence*, *37*(1), 1782–1789.

Elliott, A. (2024). *Algorithms of anxiety: Fear in the digital age*. John Wiley & Sons.

Elo, S., & Kyngäs, H. (2008). *The qualitative content analysis process*. Jan Leading Global Nursing Research., DOI: 10.1111/j.1365-2648.2007.04569.x

Emara, A. (2016). Energy-efficient VoIP over wireless networks. *Journal of Communication, 11*(7), 636–643.

Emara, A. (2018). Enhanced power saving for VoIP over WLANs. *Wireless Networks, 24*(5), 1599–1610.

Emara, A., & Huang, C. (2019a). Geographically distributed data management for scalable systems. *Future Generation Computer Systems, 95*, 336–348.

Emara, A., & Huang, C. (2019b). Adaptive strategies for distributed computing environments. *Cluster Computing, 22*(6), 14521–14533.

Emara, A., Huang, C., & Saber, T. (2023). Big data aggregation for sustainable IoT systems. *IEEE Access : Practical Innovations, Open Solutions, 11*, 56032–56045.

Emara, A., Saber, T., & Huang, C. (2025a). Applied AI for life sciences: Deep learning for biomedical applications. *Computers in Biology and Medicine, 176*, 108095.

Emara, A., Saber, T., & Huang, C. (2025c). Streamlined AI for real-time big data analytics. *Journal of Big Data, 12*(1), 210.

Emara, T. (2018). Adaptive Power-Saving Mechanism for VoIP Over WiMAX Based on Artificial Neural Network. In Waluyo, A. B. (Ed.), *Algorithms, Methods, and Applications in Mobile Computing and Communications* (pp. 158–177). IGI Global. DOI: 10.4018/978-1-5225-5693-0.ch007

Emara, T. Z. (2016). Maximizing Power Saving for VoIP over WiMAX Systems. *International Journal of Mobile Computing and Multimedia Communications, 7*(1), 32–40. DOI: 10.4018/IJMCMC.2016010103

Emara, T. Z., Ashraf, R., Saber, A., Trinh, T., & Awad, W. (2025c). A Data Processing Algorithm to Approximate Big Stream Data Analysis. *2nd IEEE International Conference on Machine Intelligence and Smart Innovation (ICMISI 2025)*. DOI: 10.1109/ICMISI65108.2025.11115782

Emara, T. Z., Hassan, E., Elbedwehy, S., & Saber, A. (2025). A Historical Perspective on Artificial Intelligence in Applied Life Sciences. In *The Role of Artificial Intelligence in Advancing Applied Life Sciences* (pp. 49–86). IGI Global Scientific Publishing. DOI: 10.4018/979-8-3693-9208-9.ch002

Emara, T. Z., & Huang, J. Z. (2019a). A distributed data management system to support large-scale data analysis. *Journal of Systems and Software, 148*, 105–115. DOI: 10.1016/j.jss.2018.11.007

Emara, T. Z., & Huang, J. Z. (2019b). RRPlib: A spark library for representing HDFS blocks as a set of random sample data blocks. *Science of Computer Programming, 184*, 102301. DOI: 10.1016/j.scico.2019.102301

Emara, T. Z., Saleh, A. I., & Arafat, H. (2014). Power saving mechanism for VoIP services over WiMAX systems. *Wireless Networks, 20*(5), 975–985. DOI: 10.1007/s11276-013-0650-5

Emara, T. Z., Trinh, T., & Huang, J. Z. (2023). Geographically distributed data management to support large-scale data analysis. *Scientific Reports, 13*(1), 17783. Advance online publication. DOI: 10.1038/s41598-023-44789-x PMID: 37853092

Enache, M. C. (2023). NFTs in education. *Economics and Applied Informatics, 3*, 188–193.

English, P. (2016). New Rules of the game: sports journalism and proiles. In Joseph, S. L. (Ed.), *Profile Pieces Journalism and the 'Human Interest' Bias* (pp. 195–210). Routledge.

Entertainment Software Association. (2020). 2020 Essential facts about the video game industry. theesa.com: https://www.theesa.com/resource/2020-essential-facts/ retrieved from.

Erdoğan, Y. (2014, September 6). *Ölen ve ölmesi gereken şey oyuncu değil, oyun basını #GamerGate.* Geekyapar.com: https://geekyapar.com/olen-ve-olmesi-gereken-sey-oyuncu-degil-oyun-basini-gamergate/ retrieved from.

European Commission. (2023). An EU initiative on Web 4.0 and virtual worlds: A head start in the next technological transition. Retrieved from https://digital-strategy.ec.europa.eu/en/policies/virtual-worlds

European Commission. (2024). *Artificial Intelligence Act: Regulation of the European Parliament and of the Council on artificial intelligence.* Official Journal of the European Union.

European Commission. (2024). *Digital Services Act: Ensuring a safe and accountable online environment.* Directorate-General for Communications Networks, Content and Technology.

European Parliament. (2024). Resolution on virtual worlds: Civil, company, commercial and intellectual property law issues. *Official Journal of the European Union.* Retrieved from https://ipwatchdog.com/2024/11/12/virtual-worlds-real-rules-eu-parliaments-first-take-ip-metaverse/id=183128/

European Union. (2023). *Proposal for a regulation laying down harmonised rules on Artificial Intelligence (AI Act)*. COM(2023) 206 final.

Evans, D. S. (2014). Economic Aspects of Bitcoin and Other Decentralized Public-Ledger Currency Platforms. University of Chicago Coase-Sandor Institute for Law & Economics Research Paper No. 685. DOI: 10.2139/ssrn.2424516

Fermin, J. L., & Tan, M. J. T. (2020). The need for the establishment of biomedical engineering as an academic and professional discipline in the Philippines—A quantitative argument. *IEEE Access : Practical Innovations, Open Solutions*, *9*, 3097–3111. DOI: 10.1109/ACCESS.2020.3046655

Firmansyah, F. H., & Rosmansyah, Y. (2024). Exploring Collaboration in Multiplayer Gamification: A Systematic Literature Review. *IEEE Access : Practical Innovations, Open Solutions*.

Fitrianto, I., & Saif, A. (2024). The role of virtual reality in enhancing experiential learning: A comparative study of traditional and immersive learning environments. *International Journal of Post Axial: Futuristic Teaching and Learning*, 97–110.

Fleshman, L. (2023, March 10). *Sports were never designed around the female body*. Time.com: https://time.com/6261404/sports-female-body-inclusivity/ retrieved from.

Floridi, L. (2019). *The logic of information: A theory of philosophy as conceptual design*. Oxford University Press., DOI: 10.1093/oso/9780198833635.001.0001

Floridi, L., & Cowls, J. (2021). A unified framework of five principles for AI in society. *Harvard Data Science Review*, *3*(1).

Floridi, L., Cowls, J., Beltrametti, M., Chatila, R., Chazerand, P., Dignum, V., & Vayena, E. (2023). *AI4People: An ethical framework for a good AI society*. Springer.

Foe-Ahorney, S. (2024). *Does the Law Protect the Privacy of Ghanaians on the Internet?: An Exploratory Study*. In De Gruyter eBooks (p. 111). De Gruyter.

Foroughi, B., Ghobakhloo, M., Wen, J., & Fathi, M. (2025). Sustained use of generative AI for shopping: A PLS-ANN analysis. *Service Industries Journal*, •••, 1–34.

Fox, J., & Tang, W. (2017). Women's experiences with general and sexual harassment in online video games: Rumination, organizational responsiveness, withdrawal, and coping strategies. *New Media & Society*, *19*(8), 1290–1307. DOI: 10.1177/1461444816635778

Frank, A. (2018, February 7). *One of esports' top female players breaks new ground at StarCraft 2 tournament*. Polygon.com: https://www.polygon.com/2018/2/7/16987076/iem-2018-sc2-winner-scarlett retrieved from.

Frimpong, V. (2025). *Artificial intelligence investment in Resource-Constrained African Economies: Financial, Strategic, and Ethical Trade-Offs with Broader implications.*

Frontiers in Virtual Reality. (2025). Metaverse in industrial contexts: A comprehensive review. *Frontiers in Virtual Reality, 6*(2), 77–95.

Fuchs, S., Vasudevan, V., & Butcher, J. (2025). Embedding Studio-Based Learning in the Biomedical Engineering Curriculum to Improve Quantitative Problem-Solving Skills. *Biomedical Engineering Education*, •••, 1–21. DOI: 10.1007/s43683-025-00195-5

Gadekallu, T. R., Huynh-The, T., Wang, W., Yenduri, G., Ranaweera, P., Pham, Q.-V., da Costa, D. B., & Liyanage, M. (2022). Blockchain for the metaverse: A review. *arXiv preprint arXiv:2203.09738.*

Gadekallu, T. R., Alazab, M., Maddikunta, P. K. R., Pham, Q. V., & Reddy, M. (2022). Blockchain for the metaverse: A review. *IEEE Internet of Things Journal, 9*(15), 11980–11995.

Gamal, A., Elsayed, N. E., & Saber, A. (2025). Interoperable electronic medical record Framework based on Microservice architecture. *Egyptian Journal of Artificial Intelligence.*

Garg, D. , Dubey, N., Goel, P., Ramoliya, D., Ganatra, A., Kotecha, K., Selvam, R., Hiremath, P., Cs, S. K., Ramakrishna Bhat, R., Garg, D., Dubey, N., Goel, P., Ramoliya, D., Ganatra, A., & Kotecha, K. (2024). Improvisation in Spinal Surgery Using AR (Augmented Reality), MR (Mixed Reality), and VR (Virtual Reality). *Engineering Proceedings, 59*(1), 186. DOI: 10.3390/engproc2023059186

Garner, T. A. (2017). Applications of virtual reality. In *Echoes of other worlds: Sound in virtual reality: Past, present and future* (pp. 299–362). Springer International Publishing.

Gawer, A., & Cusumano, M. A. (2014). Industry platforms and ecosystem innovation. *Journal of Product Innovation Management, 31*(3), 417–433. DOI: 10.1111/jpim.12105

Genise, N., & David, B. (2021). Cryptography review of W3C verifiable credentials data model (VCDM) and decentralized identifiers (DIDs) standards and cryptography implementation recommendations. Academic Press.

Gerasimova, A. (2024). Social Media and Generation Z: A Qualitative Inquiry into Usage Patterns and Motivations of Women of Older Gen Z. Available online: https://mau.diva-portal.org/smash/record.jsf?pid=diva2%3A1866883&dswid=2594

Ghanbaripour, A. N., Talebian, N., Miller, D., Tumpa, R. J., Zhang, W., Golmoradi, M., & Skitmore, M. (2024). A Systematic Review of the Impact of Emerging Technologies on Student Learning, Engagement, and Employability in Built Environment Education. *Buildings (Basel, Switzerland), 14*(9), 2769. DOI: 10.3390/buildings14092769

Gibson, J. J. (1979). *The ecological approach to visual perception: classic edition*. Psychology press.

Gig, X. R. (2021). *Extended reality in medical training: Case study*. GigXR, Inc.

Gillespie, T. (2018). *Custodians of the Internet: Platforms, content moderation, and the hidden decisions that shape social media*. Yale University Press.

Godoy, A. (2016). 'No hint of bulging muscles': The surveillanceof sportswomen's bodies in British print media. *Journalism, 17*(6), 744–759. DOI: 10.1177/1464884915583770

Gonzales, A. (2015). Disadvantaged minorities' use of the internet to expand their social networks. *Communication Research, 44*(4), 467–486. DOI: 10.1177/0093650214565925

González, R., Smith, L., & Torres, M. (2021). Virtual heritage and indigenous knowledge systems: Towards decolonizing digital spaces. *Heritage, 4*(3), 1998–2015.

Gorwa, R. (2019). The platform governance triangle: Conceptualising the informal regulation of online content. *Internet Policy Review, 8*(2). Advance online publication. DOI: 10.14763/2019.2.1407

Guan, J.-Q., Wang, W.-Z., Wang, X.-F., Zhu, J., & Hwang, G.-J. (2024). Effects of a VR-based collaborative painting approach on primary students' creativity and collaborative quality in art courses. *Educational Technology Research and Development, 72*(4), 2187–2211. DOI: 10.1007/s11423-024-10371-z

Gumel, A. A., & Abdullahi, A. B., & O, U. M. (2019). The Need for a Multimodal Means of Effective Digital Learning through Data Mining and Institutional Knowledge Repository: A Proposed System for Polytechnics in Northern Nigeria. *Proceedings of the 2019 5th International Conference on Computer and Technology Applications*. DOI: 10.1145/3323933.3324068

Gunning, D., Stefik, M., Choi, J., Miller, T., Stumpf, S., & Yang, G. Z. (2019). XAI—Explainable artificial intelligence. *Science Robotics, 4*(37), eaay7120. DOI: 10.1126/scirobotics.aay7120 PMID: 33137719

Gupta, S., Wilcocks, K., Matava, C., Wiegelmann, J., Kaustov, L., & Alam, F. (2023). Creating a Successful Virtual Reality–Based Medical Simulation Environment: Tutorial. *JMIR Medical Education, 9*, e41090. DOI: 10.2196/41090 PMID: 36787169

Hadi, R., Melumad, S., & Park, E. S. (2024). The metaverse: A new digital frontier for consumer behavior. *Journal of Consumer Psychology, 34*(1), 142–166. DOI: 10.1002/jcpy.1356

Hajian, A., Daneshgar, S., Sadeghi, K., Ojha, D., & Katiyar, G. (2024). From theory to practice: Empirical perspectives on the metaverse's potential. *Technological Forecasting and Social Change, 201*, 1–11. DOI: 10.1016/j.techfore.2024.123224

Haleem, A., & Javaid, M. (2024). Role of cognitive computing in enhancing innovative healthcare solutions. *Advances in Biomarker Sciences and Technology, 6*, 152–165. DOI: 10.1016/j.abst.2024.08.002

Hallmann, K., & Giel, T. (2018). eSports – Competitive sports or recreational activity? *Sport Management Review, 21*(1), 14–20. DOI: 10.1016/j.smr.2017.07.011

Hamari, J., & Sjöblom, M. (2017). What is eSports and why do people watch it? *Internet Research, 27*(2), 211–232. DOI: 10.1108/IntR-04-2016-0085

Hamilton, D., McKechnie, J., Edgerton, E., & Wilson, C. (2021). Immersive virtual reality as a pedagogical tool in education: A systematic literature review of quantitative learning outcomes and experimental design. *Journal of Computers in Education, 8*(1), 1–32. DOI: 10.1007/s40692-020-00169-2

Haram, S., & Hansen, L. (2024). Cohort-coded communities: Age dynamics in Discord and Twitch. *Journal of Interactive Media, 21*(1), 65–83.

Hassan, N. H., Rahim, N. A. A., Hoong, A. L. S., & Mostafa, K. (2024). *A Conceptual Study on Utilization of Artificial Intelligence (AI), Virtual Reality (VR) and Augmented Reality (AR) on Green Education: Effectiveness and Engagement.* Paper presented at the International Conference on Intelligent Manufacturing and Robotics.

Hassan, E., Saber, A., El-kenawy, E. S. M., Bhatnagar, R., & Shams, M. Y. (2024, August). Early detection of black fungus using deep learning models for efficient medical diagnosis. In *2024 International Conference on Emerging Techniques in Computational Intelligence (ICETCI)* (pp. 426–431). IEEE. DOI: 10.1109/ICETCI62771.2024.10704103

Hassan, S., & De Filippi, P. (2021). Decentralized governance in blockchain systems. *Frontiers in Blockchain, 4*, 588361.

Hatami, M., Qu, Q., Chen, Y., Kholidy, H., Blasch, E., & Ardiles-Cruz, E. (2024). A survey of the real-time metaverse: Challenges and opportunities. *Future Internet*, *16*(10), 379. DOI: 10.3390/fi16100379

Hayday, E., & Collison, H. (2020). Exploring the contested notion of social inclusion and gender inclusivity. *Social Inclusion (Lisboa)*, *8*(3), 197–208. DOI: 10.17645/si.v8i3.2755

Heeseung, Y. (2024). Why do people use Metaverse? A uses and gratification theory perspective. *Telematics and Informatics*, *89*, 1–17. https://doi.org/doi.org/10.1016/j.tele.2024.102110

Hemachandran, K., & Rodriguez, R. V. (Eds.). (2023). *The business of the metaverse: How to maintain the human element within this new business reality*. CRC Press.

Henry, C. D., & Shannon, L. (2023). *Virtual natives: How a new generation is revolutionizing the future of work, play, and culture*. John Wiley & Sons.

Herrington, F. D., Rea, P. M., & Poyade, M. (2022). *Using Holograms to Engage Young People with Anatomy Medical Visualization and Applications of Technology*. Springer.

Ho, A., Hancock, J., & Miner, A. (2018). Psychological, relational, and emotional effects of self-disclosure to a conversational agent. *Computers in Human Behavior*, *85*, 279–287.

Hofmann, J. (2016). Multi-stakeholderism in internet governance: Putting a fiction into practice. *Journal of Cyber Policy*, *1*(1), 29–49. DOI: 10.1080/23738871.2016.1158303

Hosseini, S. T. M., Qayumi, K., Pourabbasi, A., Haghighi, E., Sabet, B., Koohpaei, A., Shafiei, Z., Hosseini, M. M., & Nemati, P. (2025). Are we ready to integrate modern technologies into the medical curriculum for students? A systematic review. *Discover Education*, *4*(1), 114. DOI: 10.1007/s44217-025-00521-7

Houston, K., & Reay, D. S. (2011). The impact of information and communication technology on GHG emissions: How green are virtual worlds? *Carbon Management*, *2*(6), 629–643. DOI: 10.4155/cmt.11.62

Hsiao, S.-W., Lee, C.-H., Yang, M.-H., & Chen, R.-Q. (2017). User interface based on natural interaction design for seniors. *Computers in Human Behavior*, *75*, 147–159. DOI: 10.1016/j.chb.2017.05.011

Hsu, H.-P. (2012). Interactive and Cognitive Models in the Social Network Environment for Designing. In Cheok, M. T. L., Gay, R. K. L., & Liu, J. W. S. (Eds.), *Speech, Image, and Language Processing for Human Computer Interaction: Multi-Modal Advancements* (pp. 22–43). IGI Global., DOI: 10.4018/978-1-4666-0954-9.ch003

Huai, P., Li, Y., Wang, X., Zhang, L., Liu, N., & Yang, H. (2024). The effectiveness of virtual reality technology in student nurse education: A systematic review and meta-analysis. *Nurse Education Today, 138*, 106189. DOI: 10.1016/j.nedt.2024.106189 PMID: 38603830

Huang, T. C., & Tseng, H. P. (2025). Extended Reality in Applied Sciences Education: A Systematic Review. *Applied Sciences, 15*(7), 4038. DOI: 10.3390/app15074038

Huang, Y., Li, Y. J., & Cai, Z. (2023). Security and privacy in metaverse: A comprehensive survey. *Big Data Mining and Analytics*, *6*(2), 234–247. DOI: 10.26599/BDMA.2022.9020047

Huawei, H., Qinnan, Z., Taotao, L., Qinglin, Y., Zhaokang, Y., Junhao, W., Xiong, Z., Jianming, Z., Wu, J., & Zheng, Z. (2023). Economic systems in the metaverse: Basics, state of the art, and challenges. *ACM Computing Surveys*, *56*(4), 1–33. DOI: 10.1145/3626315

Hussain, U., Yu, B., Cunningham, G., & Bennett, G. (2021). 'I can be who I am when I play tekken 7': E-Sports women participants from the Islamic Republic of Pakistan. *Games and Culture*, *16*(8), 978–1000. DOI: 10.1177/15554120211005360

Hutchinson, B., Smart, A., Hanna, A., Denton, E., Greer, C., Kjartansson, O., & Mitchell, M. (2022). Towards accountability for machine learning datasets: Practices from software engineering and infrastructure. *Proceedings of the 2022 ACM Conference on Fairness, Accountability, and Transparency*, 555–566.

Hyundai Motor Company. (2022). *Hyundai Motor unveils Metamobility concept at CES 2022*. Hyundai Media Center.

Ibor, A. E., Hooper, M., Maple, C., Crowcroft, J., & Epiphaniou, G. (2024). *Considerations for Measuring the Cross-Sector Interoperability of Digital Identity Systems*.

Ide, A., & Sharma, T. (2025). *Personhood Credentials: Human-Centered Design Recommendation Balancing Security*. Usability, and Trust.

IEEE. (2019). *Ethically Aligned Design: A vision for prioritizing human well-being with autonomous and intelligent systems* (1st ed.). IEEE Standards Association.

IEEE. (2024). *Ethically aligned design: A vision for prioritizing human well-being with autonomous and intelligent systems* (2nd ed.). Institute of Electrical and Electronics Engineers.

Ifeanyi-Ajufo, N. (2023). Cyber governance in Africa: At the crossroads of politics, sovereignty and cooperation. *Policy Design and Practice*, *6*(2), 146–159. DOI: 10.1080/25741292.2023.2199960

Ikeh, O. (2025). Advancing Technology and Addressing Toxicity: The Dual Impacts of Rare Earth Elements on Materials and the Environment. *NIPES-Journal of Science and Technology Research*, *7*(2), 275–286. DOI: 10.37933/nipes/7.2.2025.19

Immersive VR Education. (2023). *ENGAGE: Virtual reality platform for education and enterprise training*. Immersive VR Education Ltd.

Innocent, S. (2024). Eco-Friendly Fashion: The Role of Instagram and Virtual Fashion in Sustainability Development Efforts. Academic Press.

Islam, M. T., Sepanloo, K., Woo, S., Woo, S. H., & Son, Y.-J. (2025). A review of the industry 4.0 to 5.0 transition: Exploring the intersection, challenges, and opportunities of technology and human–machine collaboration. *Machines (Basel)*, *13*(4), 267. DOI: 10.3390/machines13040267

Ismail, L., & Buyya, R. (2023). Metaverse: A vision, architectural elements, and future directions for scalable and realtime virtual worlds. *arXiv preprint arXiv:2308.10559.*

Jagatheesaperumal, S. K., Ahmad, K., Al-Fuqaha, A., & Qadir, J. (2024). Advancing education through extended reality and internet of everything enabled metaverses: Applications, challenges, and open issues. *IEEE Transactions on Learning Technologies, 17*, 1120–1139. DOI: 10.1109/TLT.2024.3358859

Janis, I. (1965). The problem of validating content analysis. In, Harold D. Lasswell, Nathan Leites, & Associates, *Language of politics: Studies in quantitative* (s. 55-82). MIT Press.

Jiang, H., Zhu, D., Chugh, R., Turnbull, D., & Jin, W. (2025). Virtual reality and augmented reality-supported K-12 STEM learning: trends, advantages and challenges. *Education and Information Technologies, 30*(9), 12827–12863. DOI: 10.1007/s10639-024-13210-z

Jiang, H., Vimalesvaran, S., Wang, J. K., Lim, K. B., Mogali, S. R., & Car, L. T. (2022). Virtual reality in medical students' education: Scoping review. *JMIR Medical Education, 8*(1), e34860. DOI: 10.2196/34860 PMID: 35107421

Jibril, A. U., Abdullahi, N. M., Ali, A. S., Abdulkadir, H., Matthew, U. O., & Haruna, K. (2022). Motivational aspects of digital games in learning process. *Science in Information Technology Letters, 3*(1), 1–9. DOI: 10.31763/sitech.v3i1.885

Jin, S., Huang, J., & Zhong, Z. (2024). Application of Immersive Technologies in Primary and Secondary Education. *Frontiers of Digital Education, 1*(2), 142–152. DOI: 10.1007/s44366-024-0001-3

Jobin, A., Ienca, M., & Vayena, E. (2019). The global landscape of AI ethics guidelines. *Nature Machine Intelligence, 1*(9), 389–399. DOI: 10.1038/s42256-019-0088-2

Johnson, D. (2024). *Pedagogies of Biomedical Science: A Holistic Approach to Integrating Pedagogy Across the Curriculum*. Taylor & Francis. DOI: 10.4324/9781003383994

Johnston, C. L., Wheeler, A., Nunn, A., & Escobar, E. (2025). Teaching the ancient world with reproductions: Using 3D printed objects in authentic active history learning. In *Ancient pasts for modern audiences* (pp. 166–200). Routledge.

Jones, D. (2004). Half the story: Olympic women on ABC News online. *Media International Australia, Incorporating Culture & Policy, 110*(1), 132–146. DOI: 10.1177/1329878X0411000114

Kalateh, F., & Kheiry, M. (2024). A Review of Stochastic Analysis of the Seepage Through Earth Dams with a Focus on the Application of Monte Carlo Simulation. *Archives of Computational Methods in Engineering, 31*(1), 47–72. DOI: 10.1007/s11831-023-09972-3

Kalkan, N. (2021). Metaverse evreninde sporun bugünü ve geleceğine yönelik bir derleme. *Ulusal Spor Bilimleri Dergisi, 2*(2), 163–174. DOI: 10.30769/usbd.1027728

Kamińska, D., Sapiński, T., Wiak, S., Tikk, T., Haamer, R. E., Avots, E., Helmi, A., Ozcinar, C., & Anbarjafari, G. (2019). Virtual Reality and Its Applications in Education: Survey. *Information, 10*(10), 318. DOI: 10.3390/info10100318

Kandemir, O., Ulusoy, G., & Kandemir, C. M. (2024). *Immersive Learning Experience for Design Education in the Lens of Education 4.0 Multidisciplinary Applications of Extended Reality for Human Experience*. IGI Global.

Kaplan, A. D., Cruit, J., Endsley, M., Beers, S. M., Sawyer, B. D., & Hancock, P. A. (2021). The effects of virtual reality, augmented reality, and mixed reality as training enhancement methods: A meta-analysis. *Human Factors, 63*(4), 706–726. DOI: 10.1177/0018720820904229 PMID: 32091937

Kaplan, A., & Haenlein, M. (2022). Metaverse: A new dimension of human interaction. *Journal of Business Research, 149*, 587–600. DOI: 10.1016/j.jbusres.2022.04.053

Kasperiuniene, J., & Psaroudakis, I. (2019). Virtual professional identities of millennials. In Zydziunaite, V., Kasperiuniene, J., Psaroudakis, I., & Salvini, A. (Eds.), *Professional identity construction in digital times* (pp. 15–52). Pisa University Press.

Kathuria, V. (2023). Gen Z's engagement with the Metaverse: Mediated role of symbolic gratification and desired enhancement of reality and moderated role of gender. *Metamorphosis*, *22*(2), 133–145.

Kawal, P., Dhillon, S., & Tinmaz, H. (2024). Immersive realities: A comprehensive guide from virtual reality to metaverse. *Journal for the Education of Gifted Young Scientists*, *12*(1), 29–45. DOI: 10.17478/jegys.1406024

Keatinge, M. (2010). *The expression and constraint of human agency within the massively multiplayer online games of World of Warcraft and Eve-Online: A comparative case study* (Doctoral dissertation, National University of Ireland Maynooth).

Keilbart, L. (2018, February 9). *Der e-sport hat ein sexismus-problem*. GQ: https://www.gq-magazin.de/auto-technik/article/der-e-sport-hat-ein-sexismus-problem retrieved from.

Kempe-Bergman, M., Larsson, H., & Redelius, K. (2020). The sceptic, the cynic, the women's rights advocate and the constructionist: Male leaders and coaches on gender equity in sport. *International Journal of Sport Policy*, *12*(3), 333–347. DOI: 10.1080/19406940.2020.1767678

Kempton, G. A. (2017). Creativity in education: Exploring teacher experiences of creativity through an immersion studies learning framework [Doctoral dissertation, Queensland University of Technology]. *QUT ePrints*.

Khan, H. U., Ali, Y., Khan, F., & Al-antari, M. A. (2024). A comprehensive study on unraveling the advances of immersive technologies (VR/AR/MR/XR) in the healthcare sector during the COVID-19: Challenges and solutions. *Heliyon*, *10*(15), e35037. Advance online publication. DOI: 10.1016/j.heliyon.2024.e35037 PMID: 39157361

Khan, K. (2023). Advancements and Challenges in 360 Virtual Reality Video Streaming: A Comprehensive Review of Cloud-Based Solutions. *International Journal of Advanced Networking and Applications*, *15*(04), 6053–6062.

Khan, S. N., Loukil, F., Ghedira-Guegan, C., Benkhelifa, E., & Bani-Hani, A. (2021). Blockchain smart contracts: Applications, challenges, and future trends. *Peer-to-Peer Networking and Applications, 14*(5), 2901–2925. DOI: 10.1007/s12083-021-01127-0 PMID: 33897937

Khan, U. A., & Alamäki, A. (2023). Designing an ethical and secure pain estimation system using AI sandbox for contactless healthcare. *SSRN*. DOI: 10.3991/ijoe.v19i15.43663

Khlaif, Z. N., Mousa, A., & Sanmugam, M. (2024). Immersive Extended Reality (XR) Technology in Engineering Education: Opportunities and Challenges. *Technology. Knowledge and Learning, 29*(2), 803–826. DOI: 10.1007/s10758-023-09719-w

Kiaer, J. (2024). Conversing in the metaverse: The embodied future of online communication.Bloomsbury Publishing. Available online at https://www.torrossa.com/it/resources/an/5868460

Kim, A., & Kim, S. (2024). Engaging in sports via the metaverse? An examination through analysis of metaverse research trends in sports. *Data Science and Management*, 1-15. https://doi.org/doi.org/10.1016/j.dsm.2024.01.002

Kimes, M. (2017, September 15). *Game: Interrupted, how a teenage gamer in the hottest new esport, overwatch, became a reluctant icon for south Korea's feminist movement.* ESPN: https://www.espn.com/espn/feature/story/_/id/20692051/how-teenage-gamer-became-reluctant-icon-south-korea-feminist-movement retrieved from.

King, D. L., Delfabbro, P. H., Billieux, J., & Potenza, M. N. (2022). Problematic online gaming and the COVID-19 pandemic. *Addiction (Abingdon, England), 117*(5), 1220–1225. PMID: 34514668

Kini, V. G., Ganeshrao, S. B., & Siddalingaswamy, P. (2024). XR review: A comprehensive analysis of visual function testing and gamification in extended reality environments. *IEEE Access : Practical Innovations, Open Solutions, 12*, 79714–79730. DOI: 10.1109/ACCESS.2024.3408677

Kiong, L. V. (2024). *Metaverse Made Easy: A Beginner's Guide to the Metaverse: Everything you need to know about Metaverse, NFT and GameFi.* Liew Voon Kiong.

Koch, N., Romani, A., Oliveira, T., & Tanaka, H. (2022). *An Overview of the Post-graduate Courses in Clinical Engineering Offered in Brazil.* Paper presented at the Latin American Conference on Biomedical Engineering.

Kolb, D. A. (1984). *Experiential learning: Experience as the source of learning and development*. Prentice Hall.

Kolbe, R., & Burnett, M. (1991). Content-analysis research: An examination of applications with directives for improving research reliability and objectivity. *The Journal of Consumer Research, 18*(2), 243–250. DOI: 10.1086/209256

Kollárová, S., & Niklová, M. (2025) THE DIGITAL IDENTITY OF GENERATION Z. Researchgate

Koppolu, H. K. R. (2025). *Engineering the digital backbone of the future: Data infrastructure, 5G connectivity, cloud networks, and AI solutions across media, telecom, and healthcare industries*. Deep Science Publishing.

Korada, L. (2024). Digital Transformation Balanced with Sustainability Goals. *Journal of Engineering and Applied Sciences Technology. J Eng App Sci Technol, 6*(5), 2-7.

Korn, O., Zallio, M., & Schnitzer, B. (2024). Young skeptics: Exploring the perceptions of virtual worlds and the metaverse in generations Y and Z. *Frontiers in Virtual Reality, 5*, 1330358.

Koumpouros, Y. (2024). Revealing the true potential and prospects of augmented reality in education. *Smart Learning Environments, 11*(1), 1–62. DOI: 10.1186/s40561-023-00288-0

Kovács, K., Békési, Z., Győri, K., & Papp, D. (2023). Gender differences in the characteristics of gaming and esport aspirations in Hungary. *Contemporary Social Science, 18*(1), 58–75. DOI: 10.1080/21582041.2022.2157473

Kozinets, R. (2015). Netnography: Redefined. Sage.

Kozinets, R. (2020). *Netnography today: A call to evolve, embrace, energize, and electrify. R. Kozinets, & R. Gambetti In, Netnography unlimited: Understanding technoculture using qualitative social media research*. Routledge. DOI: 10.4324/9781003001430

Krippendorff, K. (2019). Content analysis: An introduction to its methodology. *Sage*. DOI: 10.4135/9781071878781

Kshirsagar, K. P., & Ingle, A. (2025). Impacts of Digital Technologies Across Generations. In *Bridging Academia and Industry Through Cloud Integration in Education* (pp. 1–36). IGI Global Scientific Publishing.

Kumar, S., Madikeri, S., Zuluaga-Gomez, J., Thorbecke, I., Villatoro-Tello, E., Burdisso, S., Motlicek, P., Pandia, K., & Ganapathiraju, A. (2024). TokenVerse: Towards Unifying Speech and NLP Tasks via Transducer-based ASR. *arXiv*. https://web3.arxiv.org/abs/2407.04444

Kumar, D., Haque, A., Mishra, K., Islam, F., Mishra, B. K., & Ahmad, S. (2023). Exploring the transformative role of artificial intelligence and metaverse in education: A comprehensive review. *Metaverse Basic and Applied Research, 2*, 21. DOI: 10.56294/mr202355

Kumar, J., Arora, M., & Bayram, G. E. (Eds.). (2024). *Research, Innovation, and Industry Impacts of the Metaverse*. IGI Global. DOI: 10.4018/979-8-3693-2607-7

Kye, B., Han, N., Kim, E., Park, Y., & Jo, S. (2021). Educational applications of metaverse: Possibilities and limitations. *Journal of Educational Evaluation for Health Professions, 18*(32), 1–13. DOI: 10.3352/jeehp.2021.18.32 PMID: 34897242

Labrique, A. (2025). From infrastructure to impact: Why foundations matter in digital health. *Bulletin of the World Health Organization, 103*(2), 83–83A. DOI: 10.2471/BLT.24.293085 PMID: 39897637

Lampropoulos, G., & Kinshuk. (2024). Virtual reality and gamification in education: a systematic review. *Educational Technology Research and Development, 72*(3), 1691–1785. DOI: 10.1007/s11423-024-10351-3

Lampropoulos, G., Keramopoulos, E., Diamantaras, K., & Evangelidis, G. (2022). Augmented reality and gamification in education: A systematic literature review of research, applications, and empirical studies. *Applied Sciences (Basel, Switzerland), 12*(13), 6809. DOI: 10.3390/app12136809

Lantada, A. D. (2020). Engineering education 5.0: Continuously evolving engineering education. *International Journal of Engineering Education, 36*(6), 1814–1832.

Lanteri, A., Esposito, M., & Cappuccio, M. (2025). Maximizing the economic, environmental, and social impact of the metaverse. *Environmental, and Social Impact of the Metaverse. SSRN.*

Lasla, N., Al-Sahan, L., Abdallah, M., & Younis, M. (2022). Green-PoW: An energy-efficient blockchain Proof-of-Work consensus algorithm. *Computer Networks, 214*, 109118. DOI: 10.1016/j.comnet.2022.109118

Latoschik, M. E., Roth, D., & Lugrin, B. (2023). Social presence and realism in virtual reality: Designing avatars for trust and empathy. *Frontiers in Virtual Reality, 4*, 1120.

Lee, L., Braud, T., Zhou, P., Wang, L., Xu, D., Lin, Z., & Hui, P. (2021). All One Needs to Know about Metaverse: A Complete Survey on Technological Singularity, Virtual Ecosystem, and Research Agenda. *Journal of Latex Class Files, 14*(8), 1–66. https://doi.org/doi.org/10.48550/arXiv.2110.05352

Lee, S.-H., Lee, Y.-E., & Lee, S.-W. (2021). Toward Imagined Speech Based Smart Communication System: Potential Applications on Metaverse Conditions. *arXiv*. https://arxiv.org/abs/2112.08569

Liarokapis, F., Milata, V., & Skola, F. (2024). Extended Reality Educational System with Virtual Teacher Interaction for Enhanced Learning. *Multimodal Technologies and Interaction, 8*(9), 83. DOI: 10.3390/mti8090083

Lifelo, Z., Ding, J., Ning, H., & Dhelim, S. (2024). Artificial intelligence-enabled metaverse for sustainable smart cities: Technologies, applications, challenges, and future directions. *Electronics (Basel), 13*(24), 4874. DOI: 10.3390/electronics13244874

Li, K., Wang, X., Zhang, Y., & Chen, H. (2022). When Internet of Things meets metaverse: Convergence of physical and cyber worlds. *Journal of Network and Computer Applications, 200*, 103305.

Lin, H. (2016). Governance of virtual worlds: Ethics, law, and policy in emerging VR communities. *Journal of Virtual Worlds Research, 9*(2), 1–18.

Lin, H., Gao, L., Zhang, L., & Zhao, M. (2022). Metaverse in education: Vision, opportunities, and challenges. *Educational Technology Research and Development, 70*(5), 1231–1250.

Linsenmeier, R. A., & Saterbak, A. (2020). Fifty years of biomedical engineering undergraduate education. *Annals of Biomedical Engineering, 48*(6), 1590–1615. DOI: 10.1007/s10439-020-02494-0 PMID: 32253615

Liu, W., Auernhammer, J., Ohashi, T., Portales, C., & Kourtesis, P. (2024). A Comprehensive Review of Multimodal XR Applications, Risks, and Ethical Challenges in the Metaverse. *Multimodal Technologies and Interaction, 8*(11), 98. DOI: 10.3390/mti8110098

Liu, J. Y. W., Mak, P. Y., Chan, K., Cheung, D. S. K., Cheung, K., Fong, K. N., Kor, P. P. K., Lai, T. K. H., & Maximo, T. (2024). The Effects of Immersive Virtual Reality–Assisted Experiential Learning on Enhancing Empathy in Undergraduate Health Care Students Toward Older Adults With Cognitive Impairment: Multiple-Methods Study. *JMIR Medical Education, 10*, e48566. DOI: 10.2196/48566 PMID: 38358800

Livingstone, S., Nandagiri, R., & Stoilova, M. (2021). *Children's data and privacy online: Growing up in a digital age*. Oxford University Press.

Lombard, M., Snyder-Duch, J., & Bracken, C. (2006). Content analysis in mass communication: Assessment and reporting of intercoder reliability. *Human Communication Research, 28*(4), 587–604. DOI: 10.1111/j.1468-2958.2002.tb00826.x

Lungu, A. J., Swinkels, W., Claesen, L., Tu, P., Egger, J., & Chen, X. (2021). A review on the applications of virtual reality, augmented reality and mixed reality in surgical simulation: An extension to different kinds of surgery. *Expert Review of Medical Devices*, *18*(1), 47–62. DOI: 10.1080/17434440.2021.1860750 PMID: 33283563

MacDonald, K. (2024, March 8). *It's 10 years since Gamergate – the industry must now stand up to far-right trolls.* TheGuardian.com: https://www.theguardian.com/games/2024/mar/08/gamergate-trolls-woke-game-consultants retrieved from.

Mahmoud, A., Aurangzeb, K., Alhussein, M., & Manal, S. A. E. (2025). Harnessing deep learning to analyze climate change impacts on crop production. *Alexandria Engineering Journal, 125*, 67–82. DOI: 10.1016/j.aej.2025.04.008

Mahmoud, H. H. H., Amer, A. A., & Ismail, T. (2021). 6G: A comprehensive survey on technologies, applications, challenges, and research problems. *Transactions on Emerging Telecommunications Technologies*, *32*(4), e4233. DOI: 10.1002/ett.4233

Mäkitalo, M. (2020). Digital communities and Generation Z: Motivational and social needs in online environments (Master's thesis, University of Jyväskylä). University of Jyväskylä Institutional Repository.

Manby, R. (2020). The Sustainable Development Goals and 'legal identity for all': First, do no harm. *World Development*, *139*, 105343. DOI: 10.1016/j.worlddev.2020.105343

Manjrekar, S., Sandilya, S., Bhosale, D., Kanchi, S., Pitkar, A., & Gondhalekar, M. (2014). CAVE: An emerging immersive technology—A review. In *2014 UKSim-AMSS 16th International Conference on Computer Modelling and Simulation* (pp. 131–136). IEEE.

Mannheim, K. (1972). The problem of generations. In Kecskemeti, P. (Ed.), *Essays on the sociology of knowledge* (pp. 276–322). Routledge.

Mannion, K. (2016). Play like a girl: An analysis of media representation of female athletes. *Proceedings of GREAT Day*, *2015*(17), 72–81.

Maphosa, V. (2024). *The Rise of Artificial Intelligence and Emerging Ethical and Social Concerns: A Computer Science and Robotics Perspective.*

Matthew, U. O., Kazaure, J. S., Kazaure, A. S., Onyedibe, O. N., & Okafor, A. N. (2022). The Twenty First Century E-Learning Education Management & Implication for Media Technology Adoption in the Period of Pandemic. *EAI Endorsed Transactions on e-Learning, 8*(1), e1-e1.

Matthew, U. O. (2019). Information System Management & Multimedia Applications in an E-Learning Environment. [IJICTHD]. *International Journal of Information Communication Technologies and Human Development, 11*(3), 21–41. DOI: 10.4018/IJICTHD.2019070102

Matthew, U. O., Bakare, K. M., Ebong, G. N., Ndukwu, C. C., & Nwanakwaugwu, A. C. (2023). Generative Artificial Intelligence (AI) Educational Pedagogy Development: Conversational AI with User-Centric ChatGPT4. *Journal of Trends in Computer Science and Smart Technology, 5*(4), 401–418. DOI: 10.36548/jtcsst.2023.4.003

Matthew, U. O., Kazaure, A. S., Kazaure, J. S., Hassan, I. M., Nwanakwaugwu, A. C., & Okafor, N. U. (2022). Educational Technology Adaptation & Implication for Media Technology Adoption in the Period of COVID-19. *Journal of Trends in Computer Science and Smart Technology, 4*(4), 226–245. DOI: 10.36548/jtcsst.2022.4.002

Matthew, U. O., & Kazaure, J. S. (2020). Multimedia e-learning education in nigeria and developing countries of Africa for achieving SDG4. *International Journal of Information Communication Technologies and Human Development, 12*(1), 40–62. DOI: 10.4018/IJICTHD.2020010103

Matthew, U. O., Kazaure, J. S., & Haruna, K. (2020). Multimedia information system (MIS) for knowledge generation and ICT policy framework in education: Innovative sustainable educational investment. *International Journal of Information Communication Technologies and Human Development, 12*(3), 28–58. DOI: 10.4018/IJICTHD.2020070102

Matthew, U. O., Kazaure, J. S., & Okafor, N. U. (2021). Contemporary development in E-Learning education, cloud computing technology & internet of things. *EAI Endorsed Transactions on Cloud Systems, 7*(20), e3–e3.

Mayega, R. W., Okello, D., Muhumuza, C., Tumuhairwe, N., Ssentongo, J., Mulondo, A. K., Kasiita, R., Niyibigira, A., Ssebagereka, A., & Ssemwezi, W. (2025). *Enhancing Data Governance*. Privacy, and Following the Principles of Responsible Artificial Intelligence in Uganda's Health Sector.

McCullagh, K. (2016). *The general data protection regulation: A partial success for children on social network sites?* Forum Iuris.

McGlynn, C., & Rigotti, C. (2025). From virtual rape to meta-rape: Sexual violence, criminal law and the metaverse. *Oxford Journal of Legal Studies, 45*(3), 554–582. Advance online publication. DOI: 10.1093/ojls/gqaf009 PMID: 40896405

McKinsey & Company. (2023). *Value creation in the metaverse: The real business of the virtual world*. McKinsey Global Institute.

McLean, L., & Griffiths, M. (2019). Female gamers' experience of online harassment and social support in online gaming: A qualitative study. *International Journal of Mental Health and Addiction*, *17*(4), 970–994. DOI: 10.1007/s11469-018-9962-0

McMullen, M. A. (2022). *Evangelism through online gaming: Communicating to gen Z beyond the church walls.* Asbury Theological Seminary.

MDPI. (2024). Metaverse and human digital twin: Digital identity, biometrics, and privacy in virtual environments. *Sensors (Basel)*, *24*(3), 1125.

Mehrish, A., Majumder, N., Bhardwaj, R., Mihalcea, R., & Poria, S. (2023). A Review of Deep Learning Techniques for Speech Processing. *arXiv*. https://arxiv.org/abs/2305.00359

Mehta, S., & Gupta, S. K. (Eds.). (2025). *Impact and Potential of Machine Learning in the Metaverse.* IGI Global., https://www.igi-global.com/book/impact-potential-machine-learning-metaverse/341592

Mendoza-Ramírez, C. E., Tudon-Martinez, J. C., Félix-Herrán, L. C., Lozoya-Santos, J. J., & Vargas-Martínez, A. (2023). Augmented reality: Survey. *Applied Sciences (Basel, Switzerland)*, *13*(18), 10491. DOI: 10.3390/app131810491

Mergen, A., Çetin-Kılıç, N., & Özbilgin, M. F. (2025). Artificial intelligence and bias towards marginalised groups: Theoretical roots and challenges. In *AI and diversity in a datafied world of work: Will the future of work be inclusive?* (Vol. 12, pp. 17–38). Emerald Publishing Limited. DOI: 10.1108/S2051-233320250000012004

Meta. (2021, October 28). *Introducing Meta: A Social Technology Company.* meta.com: https://about.fb.com/news/2021/10/facebook-company-is-now-meta/ retrieved from.

Meta. (2023). *Horizon Workrooms: The VR space for teams to connect, collaborate, and develop ideas together.* Meta Platforms, Inc.

Meusa, H. (2025). Beyond entertainment—An analysis of Minecraft: Education Edition as an inclusive educational platform for diverse learners. *SSRN.*

Mhlanga, D. (2024). *Big Data and Financial Technology (Fintech).* Towards Financial Inclusion.

Microsoft. (2022). *Mesh for Microsoft Teams: Mixed reality collaboration platform.* Microsoft Corporation.

Mirza, T., Dutta, R., Tuli, N., & Mantri, A. (2025). Leveraging augmented reality in education involving new pedagogies with emerging societal relevance. *Discover Sustainability*, *6*(1), 1–15. DOI: 10.1007/s43621-025-00877-8

Mitchell, A. (2023). Collaboration technology affordances from virtual collaboration in the time of COVID-19 and post-pandemic strategies. *Information Technology & People*, *36*(5), 1982–2008. DOI: 10.1108/ITP-01-2021-0003

Mitchell, M., Wu, S., Zaldivar, A., Barnes, P., Vasserman, L., Hutchinson, B., & Gebru, T. (2021). Model cards for model reporting. *Communications of the ACM*, *64*(12), 62–69.

Mittelstadt, B. D., Allo, P., Taddeo, M., Wachter, S., & Floridi, L. (2016). The ethics of algorithms: Mapping the debate. *Big Data & Society*, *3*(2), 1–21. DOI: 10.1177/2053951716679679

Molnar, C. (2022). *Interpretable machine learning: A guide for making black box models explainable* (2nd ed.). Leanpub.

Montesinos, L., Santos-Diaz, A., Salinas-Navarro, D. E., & Cendejas-Zaragoza, L. (2022). Experiential learning in biomedical engineering education using wearable devices: A case study in a biomedical signals and systems analysis course. *Education Sciences*, *12*(9), 598. DOI: 10.3390/educsci12090598

Moor, J. H. (2006). The nature, importance, and difficulty of machine ethics. *IEEE Intelligent Systems*, *21*(4), 18–21. DOI: 10.1109/MIS.2006.80

Moosa, T. (2013, September 1). *Cybersexism is still sexism.* Bigthink.com: https://bigthink.com/articles/cybersexism-is-still-sexism/ retrieved from.

Mourtzis, D., Panopoulos, N., Angelopoulos, J., Wang, B., & Wang, L. (2022). Human centric platforms for personalized value creation in metaverse. *Journal of Manufacturing Systems*, *65*, 653–659. DOI: 10.1016/j.jmsy.2022.11.004

Mueller, M. (2017). *Will the internet fragment? Sovereignty, globalization and cyberspace*. Polity Press.

Mühle, A., Grüner, A., Gayvoronskaya, T., & Meinel, C. (2018). A survey on essential components of a self-sovereign identity. *Computer Science Review*, *30*, 80–86. DOI: 10.1016/j.cosrev.2018.10.002

Mulukuntla, S. (2025). *Monitoring and Remote Patient Management with Immersive Technologies Augmented Wellness: Exploring the Power of VR and AR in Healthcare*. Springer.

Murala, D. K., & Panda, S. K. (2023). The Role of Immersive Reality (AR/VR/MR/XR) in Metaverse. *Metaverse and Immersive Technologies: An Introduction to Industrial, Business and Social Applications*, 159-189.

Muzata, A. R., Singh, G., Stepanov, M. S., & Musonda, I. (2024). *Immersive Learning: A Systematic Literature Review on Transforming Engineering Education Through Virtual Reality*. Paper presented at the Virtual Worlds. DOI: 10.3390/virtualworlds3040026

Mystakidis, S. (2022). Metaverse. *Encyclopedia*, *2*(1), 486–497. DOI: 10.3390/encyclopedia2010031

Nafus, D., Schooler, E. M., & Burch, K. A. (2021). Carbon-responsive computing: Changing the nexus between energy and computing. *Energies*, *14*(21), 6917. DOI: 10.3390/en14216917

Nair, A. J., Manohar, S., Mittal, A., & Chaudhry, R. (2024). Unleashing digital frontiers: Bridging realities of augmented reality, virtual reality, and the metaverse. In *The metaverse dilemma: Challenges and opportunities for business and society* (pp. 85–112). Emerald Publishing Limited. DOI: 10.1108/978-1-83797-524-220241006

Nakandala, S., Ciampaglia, G., Su, N., & Ahn, Y. (2017). Gendered conversation in a social game-streaming platform. *Proceedings of the International AAAI Conference on Web and Social Media*. DOI: 10.1609/icwsm.v11i1.14885

Namukasa, S. (2025). The Role of Technology in Shaping Future Generations' Values. Researchgate, Available online at https://www.researchgate.net/profile/Kampala-International-University-Vi/publication/390398719_The_Role_of_Technology_in_Shaping_Future_Generations'_Values/links/67ec38df95231d5ba5a9b443/The-Role-of-Technology-in-Shaping-Future-Generations-Values.pdf

Nashid, S. M. (2024). Circular economy in IT device lifecycle: analysing European Union market practices and policy alignment. Academic Press.

Nasir, S. M., Hashim, M. E. A. H., Chee, K. N., Kamaruddin, N. H., Wibawanto, W., & Hanapiah, M. M. (2024). Enhancing student engagement in learning management systems through exploration of avatars in virtual classrooms: A systematic review. *Journal of Advanced Research in Applied Sciences and Engineering Technology*, 187–200.

Navarro-Parra, S. L., & Chiappe, A. (2024). Simulated Learning Environments as an Interdisciplinary Option for Vocational Training: A Systematic Review. *Simulation & Gaming*, *55*(2), 135–158. DOI: 10.1177/10468781231221904

Ndunagu, J. N., Ukhurebor, K. E., & Adesina, A. (2023). *Virtual Laboratories for STEM in Nigerian Higher Education: The National Open University of Nigeria Learners' Perspective*. Paper presented at the TELL.

Neher, A. N., Bühlmann, F., Müller, M., Berendonk, C., Sauter, T. C., & Birrenbach, T. (2025). Virtual reality for assessment in undergraduate nursing and medical education – a systematic review. *BMC Medical Education, 25*(1), 1–11. DOI: 10.1186/s12909-025-06867-8 PMID: 39743510

Neuendorf, K., & Kumar, A. (2015). Content analysis. In, G. Mazzoleni, *The International Encyclopedia of Political Communication, First Edition.* John Wiley & Sons.

Neuendorf, K. (2002). *The content analysis guidebook.* CA. *Sage.*

NguyenDuc, H., VuThi, K., NguyenDinhVi, D., Emara, T. Z., & Trinh, T. (2025). A Hybrid Feature Selection Paradigm for High-Dimensional Data. In H. A. Le Thi, H. M. Le, & Q. T. Nguyen (Eds.), Advances in Data Science and Optimization of Complex Systems (pp. 239–250). Springer Nature Switzerland. DOI: 10.1007/978-3-032-00267-9_22

NguyenDuc, T., VuThi, T., & Emara, A. (2025). Hybrid feature selection for robust predictive models. *Expert Systems with Applications, 250*, 123512.

Nic Giolla Easpaig, C. (2018). An exploratory study of sexism in online gaming communities: mapping contested digital terrain. *An exploratory study of sexism in online gaming communities: mapping contested digital terrain, 4*(2), 119-135. DOI: 10.1285/i24212113v4i2p119

Nieborg, D. B., & Poell, T. (2023). Platformization of cultural production: The case of the video game industry. *Social Media + Society, 9*(1), 1–12.

Nieborg, D., & Foxman, M. (2023). *Mainstreaming and game journalism.* MIT Press. DOI: 10.7551/mitpress/13837.001.0001

Noble, S. U. (2018). *Algorithms of oppression: How search engines reinforce racism.* NYU Press. DOI: 10.18574/nyu/9781479833641.001.0001

Noomene, W., & Abed, M. (2025). Adaptive educational avatars: A systematic review of generative AI and metaverse integration for personalized learning. *SSRN.* DOI: 10.2139/ssrn.5276474

Norman, D. A. (1999). Affordance, conventions, and design. interactions, 6(3), 38-43.

NVIDIA. (2023). *Industrial metaverse: Building photorealistic digital twins with Siemens.* NVIDIA Corporation.

O'Connor, C., & Weatherall, J. O. (2019). *The misinformation age: How false beliefs spread.* Yale University Press.

O'Donovan, J. (2022). Algorithmic fairness in social systems. *AI & Society, 37*(3), 1125–1137.

Ogasawara, M. (2025). In the Heart of Liberal Democracy: Whitewashing Authoritarian Surveillance a Decade After the Snowden Revelations. *Surveillance & Society, 23*(1), 133–139. DOI: 10.24908/ss.v23i1.18894

Okwudili, U. M., & Kazaure, J. S. (2020). Digital activism and digital revolution in objective journalism. *International Journal of Interactive Communication Systems and Technologies, 10*(2), 39–56. DOI: 10.4018/IJICST.2020070104

Ong, C. W., Tan, M. C. J., Lam, M., & Koh, V. T. C. (2021). Applications of extended reality in ophthalmology: Systematic review. *Journal of Medical Internet Research, 23*(8), e24152. DOI: 10.2196/24152 PMID: 34420929

Ortega-Gras, J. J., Gómez-Gómez, M. V., Bueno-Delgado, M. V., Garrido-Lova, J., & Cañavate-Cruzado, G. (2023). Designing a Technological Pathway to Empower Vocational Education and Training in the Circular Wood and Furniture Sector through Extended Reality. *Electronics (Basel), 12*(10), 2328. Advance online publication. DOI: 10.3390/electronics12102328

Oyekunle, D., Claude, B. E. A., Waliu, A. O., Adekunle, T. S., & Matthew, U. O. (2024). Cloud based adaptive learning system: virtual reality and augmented reality assisted educational pedagogy development on clinical simulation. *Journal of Digital Health*, 49-62.

Oyekunle, D., Ugochukwu, O. M., Rosa, R. L., Rodriguez, D. Z., & Fatai, L. O. (2024). Novel Approaches in Clinical Simulation: Immersive Educational Technology to Enhance Nursing Education. *INFOCOMP Journal of Computer Science, 23*(1).

Oyekunle, D. O., Esseme, A. C. B., Oladipupo, M. A., Oseni, V. E., Adebola, N. T., Nwaiku, M., & Matthew, U. O. (2025). *Artificial Neural Network Algorithm in Nutritional Assessment: Implication for Machine Learning Prediction in Nutritional Assessments Precision Health in the Digital Age: Harnessing AI for Personalized Care.* IGI Global Scientific Publishing.

Oyekunle, D. O., Nwaiku, M., Matthew, U. O., Ogechukwu, O. N., Nwanakwaugwu, A. C., Adebola, N. T., & Olawoyin, O. O. (2025). *Transition to Sustainable Human-Centric Education in Emerging Artificial Intelligence Industry 5.0: Conversational AI With User-Centric ChatGPT-5 Higher Education and Quality Assurance Practices.* IGI Global Scientific Publishing.

Oyekunle, D., Matthew, U. O., Waliu, A. O., & Fatai, L. O. (2024). Healthcare applications of Augmented Reality (AR) and Virtual Real-ity (VR) simulation in clinical ceducation. *Journal of Clinical Images and Medical Case Reports, 5*(6), 3141.

Oyewole, A. T., Ogusfolor, B. B., Enoh, N. C., Akpobure, C. U., & Ereforo, S. E. (2024). DATA PRIVACY LAWS AND THEIR IMPACT ON FINANCIAL TECHNOLOGY COMPANIES [Review of *DATA PRIVACY LAWS AND THEIR IMPACT ON FINANCIAL TECHNOLOGY COMPANIES: A REVIEW*]. *RE:view.*

Paniagua-Gómez, M., & Fernandez-Carmona, M. (2025). Trends and challenges in real-time stress detection and modulation: The role of the IoT and artificial intelligence. *Electronics (Basel), 14*(13), 2581. DOI: 10.3390/electronics14132581

Pan, J., & McElhannon, J. (2017). Future edge cloud and edge computing for internet of things applications. *IEEE Internet of Things Journal, 5*(1), 439–449. DOI: 10.1109/JIOT.2017.2767608

Papanastasiou, G., Drigas, A., Skianis, C., Lytras, M., & Papanastasiou, E. (2019). Virtual and augmented reality effects on K-12, higher and tertiary education students' twenty-first century skills. *Virtual Reality (Waltham Cross), 23*(4), 425–436. DOI: 10.1007/s10055-018-0363-2

Park, S., & Humphry, J. (2024). Educating users in decentralized virtual environments. *New Media & Society, 26*(7), 1531–1549.

Park, S., & Kim, S. (2022). Avatars with agency: Ethical dilemmas in AI-driven virtual interactions. *Computers in Human Behavior, 128*, 107084.

Park, S.-M., & Kim, Y.-G. (2022). A metaverse: Taxonomy, components, applications, and open challenges. *IEEE Access : Practical Innovations, Open Solutions, 10*, 4209–4251. DOI: 10.1109/ACCESS.2021.3140175

Partarakis, N., & Zabulis, X. (2024). A Review of Immersive Technologies, Knowledge Representation, and AI for Human-Centered Digital Experiences. *Electronics, 13*(2), 269. DOI: 10.3390/electronics13020269

Pennino, D., Pizzonia, M., Vitaletti, A., & Zecchini, M. (2022). Blockchain as IoT Economy enabler: A review of architectural aspects. *Journal of Sensor and Actuator Networks, 11*(2), 20. DOI: 10.3390/jsan11020020

Peredy, Z., Vigh, L., Wei, Q., & Jiang, M. (2024). Analysing generation Z communication attitudes, values and norms. *Acta Periodica (Edutus), 30*, 4–19.

Perez, C. (2022). Emergent behavior in AI-driven games: Lessons from adaptive NPC design. *Games and Culture, 17*(5), 653–671.

Perreault, G., & Vos, T. (2018). The GamerGate controversy and journalistic paradigm maintenance. *Journalism, 19*(4), 553–569. DOI: 10.1177/1464884916670932

Pervez, F., Shoukat, M., Usama, M., Sandhu, M., Latif, S., & Qadir, J. (2024). Affective computing and the road to an emotionally intelligent metaverse. *IEEE Open Journal of the Computer Society, 5*, 195–214. DOI: 10.1109/OJCS.2024.3389462

Peterson, A. (2024). Jarvis: A Cognitive Memory Architecture for AI-Augmented Learning Reimagining Persistence, Reflection, and Personalization in Human-AI Educational Partnerships. *Reflection, and Personalization in Human-AI Educational Partnerships.*

PMC. (2025). Digital twins for building industrial metaverse: Status quo, challenges, and opportunities. *Progress in Materials Science, 145*, 100954.

Poggianti, C., Chessa, S., Pelagatti, S., & Kocian, A. (2025). Immersive technologies for inclusive digital education: A systematic survey. *Human Behavior and Emerging Technologies, 2025*(1), 8888303. DOI: 10.1155/hbe2/8888303

Poland, B. (2016). *Haters: Harassment, abuse and violence online*. Potomac Books., DOI: 10.2307/j.ctt1fq9wdp

POLYDOROU. I. (2025). Youth's Role in Sustainability: Exploring the Interplay of Generation Z, Technology, and Sustainable Development Goals. Available at https://thesis.unipd.it/handle/20.500.12608/56314

Poolsawas, B., & Chotikakamthorn, N. (2023). Using Mozilla Hubs for online teaching: A case study of an innovation design method course. In *Proceedings of the 17th International Multi-Conference on Society, Cybernetics and Informatics (IMSCI 2023)* (pp. 7–12). DOI: 10.54808/IMSCI2023.01.7

Prax, P., & Soler, A. (2016). Critical alternative journalism from the perspective of game journalists. *Proceedings of 1 st International Joint Conference of DiGRA and FDG.* DiGRA/FDG. DOI: 10.26503/dl.v2016i1.754

Prestigiacomo, R., Chan, C. C., & Kark, L. (2024). A biomedical engineering curriculum development: A qualitative study engaging four stakeholders. *European Journal of Education, 59*(2), 12632. DOI: 10.1111/ejed.12632

Puchkova, E. B., YuV, S., & Temnova, L. V. (2017). A study of Generation Z's involvement in virtual reality. *Psychology in Russia : State of the Art, 10*(4), 46.

Putawa, R. A., & Sugianto, D. (2024). Exploring User Experience and Immersion Levels in Virtual Reality: A Comprehensive Analysis of Factors and Trends. *International Journal Research on Metaverse, 1*(1), 20–39. DOI: 10.47738/ijrm.v1i1.3

Putnam, R. D. (2000). *Bowling alone: The collapse and revival of American community*. Simon and schuster.

PwC UK. (2023). *How virtual reality is redefining soft skills training: VR training evaluation report.* PricewaterhouseCoopers UK.

Raad, H., & Rashid, F. K. M. (2023). The metaverse: Applications, concerns, technical challenges, future directions and recommendations. *IEEE Access : Practical Innovations, Open Solutions, 11*, 110850–110861. DOI: 10.1109/ACCESS.2023.3321650

Radianti, J., Majchrzak, T. A., Fromm, J., & Wohlgenannt, I. (2020). A systematic review of immersive virtual reality applications for higher education: Design elements, lessons learned, and research agenda. *Computers & Education, 147*, 103778. DOI: 10.1016/j.compedu.2019.103778

Rane, N., Choudhary, S., & Rane, J. (2023). Enhanced product design and development using Artificial Intelligence (AI), Virtual Reality (VR), Augmented Reality (AR), 4D/5D/6D Printing, Internet of Things (IoT), and blockchain: A review. *Virtual Reality (VR), Augmented Reality (AR) D, 4.*

Rankin, Y. (2021). Representation and inclusion in game development. *Communications of the ACM, 64*(9), 28–31.

Rao, S. P., Sekhar, S. C., Yadav, T. C., Kumar, V. P., & Haran, B. H. (2024). Implementing experiential learning strategies for enhanced business education in India: Challenges and opportunities. *Journal of Informatics Education and Research, 4*(3), 20–33.

Rashid, M. A. A., Rafi, A. A., Islam, Md. A., Shorkar, S. U., Kuri, E. H., Islam, M. H., & Khan, M. H. H. (2024). *Enhancing land management policy in Bangladesh: A blockchain-based framework for transparent and efficient land management.*

Rawat, D. B., & Hagos, D. H. (2024). Metaverse survey & tutorial: Exploring key requirements, technologies, standards, applications, challenges, and perspectives. *arXiv preprint arXiv:2405.04718.*

Redford, A. C. (2021). Perceptions of the use of augmented and virtual reality supporting emergency response education and training [Doctoral dissertation, Capella University]. *ProQuest Dissertations Publishing.*

Reuters. (2025, January 12). EU fines AI companion app provider over privacy violations. *Reuters Technology.*

Reynolds, J., & de Zwart, M. (2020). Data protection in virtual worlds: Emerging regulatory trends. *Computer Law & Security Review, 36*(5), 105396.

Richard, G., & Couchot-Schiex, S. (2020). Cybersexism: How gender and sexuality are at play in cyberspace. In, D. Farris, D. Compton, & A. Herrera, *Gender, Sexuality and Race in the Digital Age* (s. 17-30). Springer.

Riot Games. (2023). *Behavioral systems update: Transparency and fairness in League of Legends moderation*. Riot Games Official Blog.

Ritsos, P. D. (2006). *Architectures for untethered augmented reality using wearable computers* (Doctoral dissertation, University of Essex). University of Essex Repository.

Roblox Education. (2022). *Learning and teaching on Roblox: Education in the metaverse case study*. Roblox Corporation.

Rogstad, E. (2022). Gender in eSports research: A literature review. *EJSS European Journal for Sport and Society, 19*(3), 195–213. DOI: 10.1080/16138171.2021.1930941

Rospigliosi, A. (2022). Metaverse or Simulacra? Business education and the challenge of teaching in virtual worlds. *International Journal of Management Education, 20*(3), 100688.

Rubio-Tamayo, J. L., Gertrudix Barrio, M., & García García, F. (2017). Immersive environments and virtual reality: Systematic review and advances in communication, interaction and simulation. *Multimodal Technologies and Interaction, 1*(4), 21. DOI: 10.3390/mti1040021

Ruth, J., Willwacher, S., & Korn, O. (2022). Acceptance of Digital Sports: A Study Showing the Rising Acceptance of Digital Health Activities Due to the SARS-CoV-19 Pandemic. *International Journal of Environmental Research and Public Health, 19*(1), 1–16. DOI: 10.3390/ijerph19010596 PMID: 35010849

Ruttkamp, E. (2025). *Relationality and Data Justice for Trustworthy AI Practices in Africa*.

Ruvalcaba, O., Shulze, J., Kim, A., Berzenski, S., & Otten, M. (2018). Women's experiences in eSports: Gendered differences in peer and spectator feedback during competitive video game play. *Journal of Sport and Social Issues, 42*(4), 295–311. DOI: 10.1177/0193723518773287

Saarinen, S. (2025). Technology Convergence and the Metaverse. In Martins, L. B., & Moutinho, L. A. M. (Eds.), *Impacts of Sensetech on Society* (pp. 1–20). IGI Global., DOI: 10.4018/979-8-3693-7147-3.ch001

Sabater, A., López, B., Campdepadrós, R., & Sánchez, C. (2025). *Participatory Action Research for AI in Social Services: An Example of Local Practices From Catalonia*.

Saber, A., Sakr, M., Abo-Seida, O. M., & Keshk, A. (2021, May). Automated breast cancer detection and classification techniques–a survey. In *2021 International Mobile, Intelligent, and Ubiquitous Computing Conference (MIUCC)* (pp. 200–207). IEEE. DOI: 10.1109/MIUCC52538.2021.9447655

Saber, A., Al-Zoghby, A. M., & Elmougy, S. (2018, January). Big-data aggregating, linking, integrating and representing using semantic web technologies. In *International Conference on Advanced Machine Learning Technologies and Applications* (pp. 331-342). Cham: Springer International Publishing. DOI: 10.1007/978-3-319-74690-6_33

Saber, A., Hassan, E., Elbedwehy, S., Awad, W. A., & Emara, T. Z. (2025). Leveraging ensemble convolutional neural networks and metaheuristic strategies for advanced kidney disease screening and classification. *Scientific Reports*, *15*(1), 12487. DOI: 10.1038/s41598-025-93950-1 PMID: 40216822

Saber, A., Hussien, A. G., Awad, W. A., Mahmoud, A., & Allakany, A. (2023). Adapting the pre-trained convolutional neural networks to improve the anomaly detection and classification in mammographic images. *Scientific Reports*, *13*(1), 14877. DOI: 10.1038/s41598-023-41633-0 PMID: 37689757

Saber, T., Emara, A., & Huang, C. (2018). Semantic web integration for big data aggregation. *Journal of Network and Computer Applications*, *105*, 123–138.

Saber, T., Emara, A., & Huang, C. (2025a). Deep learning-based breast cancer detection using optimized models. *Biomedical Signal Processing and Control*, *94*, 105676.

Sadeghi-Niaraki, A., Rahimi, F., Azlan, N. A. E. B., Song, H., Ali, F., & Choi, S.-M. (2025). Groundbreaking taxonomy of metaverse characteristics. *Artificial Intelligence Review*, *58*(8), 244. DOI: 10.1007/s10462-025-11243-5

Sağlam, S. (2021, April 23). *E-Sporlar artık olimpiyatlarda*. GQ: https://gq.com.tr/gq-sports/e-sporlar-artik-olimpiyatlarda retrieved from.

Sakr, M., Saber, A., Abo-Seida, O. M., & Keshk, A. (2020). Machine learning for breast cancer classification using K-star algorithm. *Applied Mathematics & Information Sciences*, *14*(5), 855–863. DOI: 10.18576/amis/140513

Sales, N. (2024, January 5). *A girl was allegedly raped in the metaverse. Is this the beginning of a dark new future?* Theguardian.com: https://www.theguardian.com/commentisfree/2024/jan/05/metaverse-sexual-assault-vr-game-online-safety-meta retrieved from.

Salt, B., Atkins, C., & Blackall, L. (2008). Engaging with Second Life: Real education in a virtual world. Academic Press.

Samek, W., Montavon, G., Lapuschkin, S., Anders, C. J., & Müller, K. R. (2021). Explaining deep neural networks and beyond: A review of methods and applications. *Proceedings of the IEEE, 109*(3), 247–278. DOI: 10.1109/JPROC.2021.3060483

Santer, N., Manago, A., & Bleisch, R. (2023). Narratives of the self in polymedia contexts: Authenticity and branding in Generation Z. *Qualitative Psychology, 10*(1), 79.

Santoro, F., Scarpini, C., & Okiya, S. (2025). *The Potential of Digital ID Systems for Tax Administration: the Case of Ghana.*

Saudagar, A. K. J., Kumar, A., & Khan, M. B. (2024). Mediverse Beyond Boundaries: A Comprehensive Analysis of AR and VR Integration in Medical Education for Diverse Abilities. *Journal of Disability Research, 3*(1), 20230066. DOI: 10.57197/JDR-2023-0066

Savaglio, C., Ganzha, M., Paprzycki, M., Bădică, C., Ivanović, M., & Fortino, G. (2020). Agent-based Internet of Things: State-of-the-art and research challenges. *Future Generation Computer Systems, 102*, 1038–1053. DOI: 10.1016/j.future.2019.09.016

Schick, N. (2022). The art of immersion: How AI reshapes virtual storytelling. *Game Studies Journal, 22*(1), 1–19.

Schreier, M. (2012). *Qualitative content analysis in practice.* CA. *Sage (Atlanta, Ga.).*

Schubert, T., Stenslie, S., & Nordahl, R. (2022). Representation in AI-generated characters: Cultural implications and design ethics. *AI & Society, 37*(4), 1745–1759.

Seiner, J. (2019, January 3). *"You're a girl, you're being targeted": Women in esports navigate toxicity, other barriers.* The Denver Post: https://www.denverpost.com/2019/01/03/esports-women-navigate-toxicity-barriers/ retrieved from.

Sestino, A., Guido, G., & Peluso, A. M. (2022). *Non-fungible tokens (NFTs). Examining the Impact on Consumers and Marketing Strategies, 1–15.* IGI Global. DOI: 10.1007/978-3-031-07203-1

Shaikh, S., & Jammal, M. (2024). Survey of fault management techniques for edge-enabled distributed metaverse applications. *Computer Networks, 254*, 110803. DOI: 10.1016/j.comnet.2024.110803

Sharma, M., Mahajan, Y., & Saber, A. (2024). Using augmented reality (AR) and the Internet of Things (IoT) to improve water management maintenance and training. In *Innovations in machine learning and IoT for water management* (pp. 252–270). IGI Global Scientific Publishing.

Sharma, M., Mahajan, Y., & Saber, A. (2024). Using augmented reality (AR) and the Internet of Things (IoT) to improve water management maintenance and training. In *Innovations in Machine Learning and IoT for Water Management* (pp. 252–270). IGI Global Scientific Publishing.

Sharma, M., Mahajan, Y., & Saber, A. (2024). Using Augmented Reality (AR) and the Internet of Things (IoT) to improve water management maintenance and training. In *Innovations in Machine Learning and IoT for Water Management* (pp. 252-270). IGI Global Scientific Publishing.

Shen, C., Ratan, R., Dora Cai, Y., & Leavit, A. (2016). Do men advance faster than women? Debunking the gender performance gap in two massively multiplayer online games. *Journal of Computer-Mediated Communication, 21*(4), 312–329. DOI: 10.1111/jcc4.12159

Shen, L.-H., Feng, K.-T., & Hanzo, L. (2023). Five facets of 6G: Research challenges and opportunities. *ACM Computing Surveys, 55*(11), 1–39. DOI: 10.1145/3571072

Shneiderman, B. (2022). *Human-centered AI*. Oxford University Press. DOI: 10.1093/oso/9780192845290.001.0001

Shojaei, P., & Moieni, R. (2025). *Empirical Analysis of Data Privacy Concerns in DLT*.

Short, J., Williams, E., & Christie, B. (1976). *The social psychology of telecommunications*. John Wiley & Sons.

Silverman, J., Smith, T., & Lee, K. (2021). Adaptive NPC behavior through reinforcement learning. *Entertainment Computing, 39*, 100443.

Singh, B., Singh, G., & Ravesangar, K. (2025). *Teacher-Focused Approach to Merging Intelligent Tutoring Systems With Adaptive Learning Environments in AI-Driven Classrooms: Empowering Educators Higher Education and Quality Assurance Practices*. IGI Global Scientific Publishing.

Singh, B., Wongmahesak, K., & Chandra, S. (2025). Transforming digital ownership and assessing role of blockchain technology and NFTs in future economy. In *Practical Strategies and Case Studies for Online Marketing 6.0* (pp. 343–368). IGI Global Scientific Publishing. DOI: 10.4018/979-8-3373-2058-8.ch015

Skinner, H., Sarpong, D., & White, G. R. (2018). Meeting the needs of the Millennials and Generation Z: gamification in tourism through geocaching. Journal of tourism futures, 4(1), 93-104.

Smith, G. (2025). *Mindsets and Management: AI and Gender (*. Equitable Access to Financial Services.

Smutny, P., Babiuch, M., & Foltynek, P. (2019). A review of the virtual reality applications in education and training. *Proceedings of the 2019 20th International Carpathian Control Conference, ICCC 2019*. DOI: 10.1109/CarpathianCC.2019.8765930

Soliman, M., Ismail, D. S., Ahmed, S., Ali, S., Salama, S., Khalil, I., Nassar, M., Zaki, M., & Rizk, M. (2025). Are we ready for the metaverse? Implications, legal landscape, and recommendations for responsible development. *Digital Society : Ethics, Socio-Legal and Governance of Digital Technology*, *4*(1), 9. Advance online publication. DOI: 10.1007/s44206-025-00163-0

Spaticchia, U. (2024). Generational Transformations and Digital Media: continuity and change. Addiction & Social Media Communication, 1(2).

Spears, L. I., Seyal, A. H., & Khan, A. R. (2015). Learning communities: Exploring hybrid social interactions with Generation Z. *American Journal of Educational Research*, *3*(10), 1308–1314. https://files.eric.ed.gov/fulltext/EJ1112534.pdf

Spitzer, M. (2019). E-Sport lobbyismus versus gemeinnützigkeit und gesundheit. *Nervenheilkunde: Zeitschrift für Interdisziplinaere Fortbildung*, *38*(4), 157–168. DOI: 10.1055/a-0817-7741

Sugiarto, E., & Arif, M. F. (2024). Digital footprints: Unpacking cultural identity through english-language practices on social media. English Review. *Journal of English Education*, *12*(3), 983–992.

Sümer, M., & Vaněček, D. (2025). A systematic review of virtual and augmented realities in higher education: Trends and issues. *Innovations in Education and Teaching International*, *62*(3), 811–822. DOI: 10.1080/14703297.2024.2382854

Supriya, Y., Bhulakshmi, D., Bhattacharya, S., Gadekallu, T. R., Vyas, P., Kaluri, R., Sumathy, S., Koppu, S., Brown, D. J., & Mahmud, M. (2024). Industry 5.0 in Smart Education: Concepts, Applications, Challenges, Opportunities, and Future Directions. *IEEE Access : Practical Innovations, Open Solutions*, *12*, 81938–81967. DOI: 10.1109/ACCESS.2024.3401473

Swenson, A. (2023). Teaching digital identity: Opportunities, challenges, and ethical considerations for avatar creation in educational settings. *Brazilian Creative Industries Journal*, *3*(2), 41–58. DOI: 10.25112/bcij.v3i2.3538

Taghian, A., Abo-Zahhad, M., Sayed, M. S., & Abd El-Malek, A. H. (2023). Virtual and augmented reality in biomedical engineering. *Biomedical Engineering Online*, *22*(1), 76. DOI: 10.1186/s12938-023-01138-3 PMID: 37525193

Tang, Y. M., Chau, K. Y., Kwok, A. P. K., Zhu, T., & Ma, X. (2022). A systematic review of immersive technology applications for medical practice and education-trends, application areas, recipients, teaching contents, evaluation methods, and performance. *Educational Research Review*, *35*, 100429. DOI: 10.1016/j.edurev.2021.100429

Tene, T., Marcatoma Tixi, J. A., Palacios Robalino, M. L., Mendoza Salazar, M. J., Vacacela Gomez, C., & Bellucci, S. (2024). *Integrating immersive technologies with STEM education: a systematic review.* Paper presented at the Frontiers in Education. DOI: 10.3389/feduc.2024.1410163

Thacharodi, A., Singh, P., Meenatchi, R., Tawfeeq Ahmed, Z., Kumar, R. R., v, N., Kavish, S., Maqbool, M., & Hassan, S. (2024). Revolutionizing healthcare and medicine: The impact of modern technologies for a healthier future—A comprehensive review. *Health Care Science*, *3*(5), 329–349. DOI: 10.1002/hcs2.115 PMID: 39479277

The Guardian. (2025, June 10). The misogyny of the metaverse: Is Mark Zuckerberg's dream world a no-go area for women? Retrieved from https://www.theguardian.com/society/2025/jun/10/the-misogyny-of-the-metaverse-is-mark-zuckerbergs-dream-world-a-no-go-area-for-women

Theatre, W. L., & Wright, J. (2023). Labs and learning technologies. In *Variety in Chemistry Education/Physics Higher Education Conference (ViCE/PHEC) 2023.*

Theodorakopoulos, L., Theodoropoulou, A., & Klavdianos, C. (2025). Interactive Viral Marketing Through Big Data Analytics, Influencer Networks, AI Integration, and Ethical Dimensions. *Journal of Theoretical and Applied Electronic Commerce Research*, *20*(2), 115.

Thomas, R. (2025). Exploring Tomorrow: Evolution of Virtual Communities and Social Media. In Building Power, Safety, and Trust in Virtual Communities (pp. 333-358). IGI Global.

Time. (2025, February 14). AI companions and the blurred line between empathy and manipulation. *Time Magazine*.

Tinsley, H., & Weiss, D. (2000). Interrater reliability and agreement. In Tinsley, H. E. A., & Brown, S. D. (Eds.), *Handbook of applied multivariate statistics and mathematical modeling* (pp. 95–124). Academic Press. DOI: 10.1016/B978-012691360-6/50005-7

Tiwari, M., Zhou, Y., Childs, A., Chang, L. Y., & Ferrill, J. (2025). Metaverse policing: A systematic literature review of challenges and recommendations. *Computers in Human Behavior, 166*, 108591. DOI: 10.1016/j.chb.2025.108591

TrinhHuy, T., Trinh, T., NguyenViet, H., Emara, T. Z., & VuongThi, N. (2025). Event scale prediction in event-based social networks. 11th EAI International Conference on Industrial Networks and Intelligent Systems, Da Nang, Vietnam. https://doi.org/10.1007/978-3-032-02362-9_3

TrinhHuy, T., VuThi, T., & Emara, A. (2025). Predicting social event scales using location-based topic models. *IEEE Access : Practical Innovations, Open Solutions, 13*, 12410–12425.

Trinh, T. H., Vu, T., & Emara, A. (2019). Topic models for event prediction in social networks. *IEEE Transactions on Knowledge and Data Engineering, 31*(12), 2275–2289.

Trinh, T. H., Vu, T., & Emara, A. (2022). Efficient small-cluster processing for high-dimensional data. *Future Generation Computer Systems, 128*, 327–339.

Trinh, T., Duc, L. P., Tran, C. T., Duy, T. T., & Emara, T. Z. (2022). A New Stratified Block Model to Process Large-Scale Data for a Small Cluster. In *Lecture Notes on Data Engineering and Communications Technologies* (Vol. 124, pp. 253–263). Springer Science and Business Media Deutschland GmbH. DOI: 10.1007/978-3-030-97610-1_21

Trinh, T., Nguyen, N., Wu, D., Huang, J. Z., & Emara, T. Z. (2019). A New Location-Based Topic Model for Event Attendees Recommendation. In *2019 IEEE-RIVF International Conference on Computing and Communication Technologies (RIVF)* (pp. 106–111). DOI: 10.1109/RIVF.2019.8713716

Tripathi, D., Hajra, K., Mulukutla, A., Shreshtha, R., & Maity, D. (2025). Artificial Intelligence in Biomedical Engineering and Its Influence on Healthcare Structure: Current and Future Prospects. *Bioengineering (Basel, Switzerland), 12*(2), 163. DOI: 10.3390/bioengineering12020163 PMID: 40001682

Tudor, E. (2020). The emergence of eSport during Covid-19: How sim racing replaced live motorsport in 2020. *Journal of Motorsport Culture & History, 1*(1).

Tugtekin, U., & Odabasi, H. F. (2022). Do interactive learning environments have an effect on learning outcomes, cognitive load and metacognitive judgments? *Education and Information Technologies, 27*(5), 7019–7058. DOI: 10.1007/s10639-022-10912-0

Tyagi, A. K., & Nair, M. M. (2024). *Future of Industry 5.0 in Society 5.0 Industry 4.0, Smart Manufacturing, and Industrial Engineering*. CRC Press.

U.S. Congress. (2023). *Augmented Reality and Virtual Reality Privacy Act* (H.R. 5498). 118th Congress.

UK Information Commissioner's Office. (2024). *Age appropriate design: A code of practice for online services* (Updated ed.). ICO.

UNESCO. (2021). *Recommendation on the ethics of artificial intelligence*. Retrieved from https://unesdoc.unesco.org/ark:/48223/pf0000380455

UNESCO. (2021). *Recommendation on the ethics of artificial intelligence*. United Nations Educational, Scientific and Cultural Organization.

UNESCO. (2022). *Digital equity in global education: Bridging the digital divide*. United Nations Educational, Scientific and Cultural Organization.

UNESCO. (2023). *Guidance for generative AI in education and research*. Retrieved from https://www.unesco.org/en/articles/guidance-generative-ai-education-and-research

van As, J., & Cooke, R. (2024). *Immersive Virtual Community Engagement: Unleashing the Potential of AI Avatars and Virtual Reality in Education to Enhance Learning Excellence Integrating Cutting-Edge Technology Into the Classroom*. IGI Global. DOI: 10.4018/979-8-3693-3124-8.ch009

van den Hoven, J., Miller, S., & Pogge, T. (2021). *Designing in ethics*. Cambridge University Press.

Vasarainen, M., Paavola, S., & Vetoshkina, L. (2021). A Systematic Literature Review on Extended Reality: Virtual, Augmented and Mixed Reality in Working Life. *Internationa Journal of Virtual Reality*, *21*(2), 1–28. DOI: 10.20870/IJVR.2021.21.2.4620

Venkatakrishnan, R. (2023). *All Hands on Deck: Choosing Virtual End Effector Representations to Improve Near Field Object Manipulation Interactions in Extended Reality* (Doctoral dissertation, Clemson University).

Vergel, P., La Parra-Casado, D., & Vives-Cases, C. (2024). Examining cybersexism in online gaming communities: A scoping review. *Trauma, Violence & Abuse*, *25*(1), 1201–1218. DOI: 10.1177/15248380231176059 PMID: 37243440

Vincent, J. (2022, December 5). Meta's metaverse under scrutiny for privacy lapses. *The Verge*.

Vogue Business. (2022). *Luxury fashion's next frontier: The metaverse and NFT strategies*. Vogue Business.

VuThi, K., VuongThi, N., NguyenXuan, H., Emara, T. Z., & Trinh, T. (2024). Feature Selection Based on Top Frequency. In M. and N. L. A. and L. K. Y. Nguyen Thi Dieu Linh and Dawson (Eds.), Proceedings of the International Conference on Intelligent Systems and Networks (pp. 58–65). Springer Nature Singapore. DOI: 10.1007/978-981-97-5504-2_7

VuThi, T., NguyenDuc, T., & Emara, A. (2024). Hybrid paradigms for high-dimensional data analysis. *Applied Soft Computing*, *156*, 110216.

W3C. (2023). *XR accessibility user requirements*. World Wide Web Consortium.

Waliu, A. O., Matthew, U. O., Oseni, V. E., Oyekunle, D. O., Oladipupo, M. A., Adekunle, T. S., & Esseme, A. C. B. (2025). *Immersive Educational Pedagogy Development: Cloud-Based Adaptive System for Higher Education Generative AI Approaches to Sustainable Development in Higher Education*. IGI Global Scientific Publishing. DOI: 10.4018/979-8-3693-5623-4.ch008

Waliu, A. O., Muojekwu, E. E., Matthew, U. O., Kazaure, J. S., Oseni, V. E., Ononiwu, C. C., & Haruna, K. (2025). *Clinical Simulation in nursing education: Immersive Educational Tech for nurses and midwives Creating Immersive Learning Experiences Through Virtual Reality (VR)*. IGI Global.

Wallin, S. (2025). From Traits To Leadership: Understanding Gen YZ In The Digital Commerce Sector. Accesible at https://www.doria.fi/handle/10024/192558

Wang, Y., Ravanelli, M., & Yacoubi, A. (2023). Metaverse Virtual Interview Platform Leveraging Generative AI and Speech Recognition. *ResearchGate*. https://www.researchgate.net/publication/382070538_Metaverse_Virtual_Interview_Platform_Leveraging_Generative_AI_and_Speech_Recognition

Wang, R. (2022). Algorithmic fairness in gaming: Emerging metrics and measurement challenges. *Journal of AI Ethics*, *2*(4), 567–581.

Wang, Y., Wang, L., & Siau, K. L. (2025). Human-centered interaction in virtual worlds: A new era of generative artificial intelligence and metaverse. *International Journal of Human-Computer Interaction*, *41*(2), 1459–1501. DOI: 10.1080/10447318.2024.2316376

Weber, R. (1990). *Basic content analysis*. Sage Publications. DOI: 10.4135/9781412983488

Webster, A. (2018, February 14). *The Overwatch League signs its first female player*. Theverge.com: https://www.theverge.com/2018/2/14/17011504/overwatch-league-first-woman-player-geguri-shanghai-dragons retrieved from.

West, S. M., Whittaker, M., & Crawford, K. (2019). Discriminating systems: Gender, race, and power in AI. *AI Now Institute Report.*

West, S. M., Whittaker, M., & Crawford, K. (2023). Inclusive AI design for the metaverse: Ethical challenges and opportunities. *Journal of Responsible Technology, 13*, 100084.

Whittington, R. (2022). Algorithmic governance in virtual economies. *Technology in Society, 70*, 102005.

Williams, I. (2014, September). *Death to the gamer.* Jacobin.com/: https://jacobin.com/2014/09/death-to-the-gamer/ retrieved from.

Williams, S. (2025). Decentralized identity management for academic credentials using blockchain technology. *SSRN.*

Wohlgenannt, I., Simons, A., & Stieglitz, S. (2020). Virtual reality. *Business & Information Systems Engineering, 62*(5), 455–461. DOI: 10.1007/s12599-020-00658-9

World Bank. (2023). *Closing the digital divide: Global infrastructure and connectivity report.* The World Bank Group.

World Economic Forum. (2023). *Digital twins for smart cities: Urban transformation case studies.* WEF Reports.

World Economic Forum. (2023a). *Defining and building the metaverse: An action plan for responsible innovation.* Retrieved from_https://initiatives.weforum.org/defining-and-building-the-metaverse/home

World Economic Forum. (2023b). Interoperability in the metaverse. Governance briefing paper. Retrieved from https://www.weforum.org/press/2023/01/landmark-reports-on-future-of-metaverse-focus-on-interoperability-and-value-creation/

World Economic Forum. (2023c). *Social implications of the metaverse.* Retrieved from https://www.weforum.org/reports/social-implications-of-the-metaverse/

Wright, A. (2020). The rise of decentralized autonomous organizations: Opportunities and challenges. *Stanford Journal of Blockchain Law & Policy, 4*, 1.

Wu, S., Stendal, K., & Thapa, D. (2024a). *Emerging Trends in XR-mediated Virtual Team Collaboration in Digital Workspaces: A Systematic Literature Review.* DOI: 10.1007/978-3-031-57189-3_5

Wu, S., Stendal, K., & Thapa, D. (2024b). Emerging trends in XR-mediated virtual team collaboration in digital workspaces: A systematic literature review. *Advances in Information Systems Development: Information Systems Development, Organizational Aspects, and Societal Trends*, 85–108.

Wu, Q., He, K., & Chen, X. (2020). Personalized federated learning for intelligent IoT applications: A cloud-edge based framework. *IEEE Open Journal of the Computer Society*, *1*, 35–44. DOI: 10.1109/OJCS.2020.2993259 PMID: 32396074

Xu, W., Yang, Z., Ng, D. W. K., Levorato, M., Eldar, Y. C., & Debbah, M. (2023). Edge learning for B5G networks with distributed signal processing: Semantic communication, edge computing, and wireless sensing. *IEEE Journal of Selected Topics in Signal Processing*, *17*(1), 9–39. DOI: 10.1109/JSTSP.2023.3239189

Xu, Z., Li, H., & Zhao, Y. (2022). Scaling AI for large-scale virtual environments. *Computers & Graphics*, *107*, 55–64.

Yadav, S. (2025). Navigating the Virtual Classroom With Virtual Reality: Revolutionizing Education Through Immersive Experiences *Virtual Technology* [IGI Global Scientific Publishing.]. *Innovación Educativa (México, D.F.)*, 29–54.

Yang, J. (2023). *Technology-Enhanced Preclinical Medical Education (Anatomy, Histology and Occasionally, Biochemistry): A Practical Guide Biomedical Visualisation: Volume 17–Advancements in Technologies and Methodologies for Anatomical and Medical Education*. Springer.

Yang, K., Markovic, D., Krenn, S., Agrawal, V., & Richard, A. (2022). Audio-Visual Speech Codecs: Rethinking Audio-Visual Speech Enhancement by Re-Synthesis. *arXiv*. DOI: 10.1109/CVPR52688.2022.00805

Yang, L. (2023). Recommendations for metaverse governance based on technical standards. *Humanities & Social Sciences Communications*, *10*(1), 253. DOI: 10.1057/s41599-023-01750-7

Yang, L., Ni, S.-T., Wang, Y., Yu, A., Lee, J.-A., & Hui, P. (2025). Interoperability of the metaverse: A digital ecosystem perspective review. *IEEE Engineering Management Review*, *53*(3), 29–54. Advance online publication. DOI: 10.1109/EMR.2025.3564923

Yang, S., Tian, H., Sun, L., & Yu, X. (2019). From one-size-fits-all teaching to adaptive learning: The crisis and solution of education in the era of AI. *Journal of Physics: Conference Series*, *1237*(4), 042039. DOI: 10.1088/1742-6596/1237/4/042039

Yang, W., Fang, M., Xu, J., Zhang, X., & Pan, Y. (2024). Exploring the mediating role of different aspects of learning motivation between metaverse learning experiences and gamification. *Electronics (Basel), 13*(7), 1297. DOI: 10.3390/electronics13071297

Yee, N., & Bailenson, J. (2007). The Proteus effect: The effect of transformed self-representation on behavior. *Human Communication Research, 33*(3), 271–290. DOI: 10.1111/j.1468-2958.2007.00299.x

Yeganeh, L. N., Fenty, N. S., Chen, Y., Simpson, A., & Hatami, M. (2025). The future of education: A multi-layered metaverse classroom model for immersive and inclusive learning. *Future Internet, 17*(2), 63. DOI: 10.3390/fi17020063

Yfantidou, I., Hatzigianni, M., & Dardas, D. (2023). Fairness and ethics in gaming AI: A systematic review. *Games and Culture, 18*(2), 135–156.

Zafar, M. H., Langås, E. F., & Sanfilippo, F. (2024). Exploring the synergies between collaborative robotics, digital twins, augmentation, and industry 5.0 for smart manufacturing: A state-of-the-art review. *Robotics and Computer-integrated Manufacturing, 89*, 102769. DOI: 10.1016/j.rcim.2024.102769

Zagalo, N., Morgado, L., & Boa-Ventura, A. (Eds.). (2012). *Virtual Worlds and Metaverse Platforms: New Communication and Identity Paradigms*. IGI Global. DOI: 10.4018/978-1-60960-854-5

Zawish, M., Dharejo, F. A., Khowaja, S. A., Raza, S., Davy, S., Dev, K., & Bellavista, P. (2024). AI and 6G into the metaverse: Fundamentals, challenges and future research trends. *IEEE Open Journal of the Communications Society, 5*, 730–778. DOI: 10.1109/OJCOMS.2024.3349465

Zechner, O., Schrom-Feiertag, H., Wespi, R., Pretolesi, D., Nguyen, Q., & Tscheligi, M. (2024). Enhancing mixed reality simulation training technology with real-time performance visualization: Mixed methods study with medical first responders. *JMIR XR and Spatial Computing, 1*(1), e57655. DOI: 10.2196/57655

Zhang, Y., Feijoo-Garcia, M. A., Gu, Y., Popescu, V., Benes, B., & Magana, A. J. (2024). Virtual and Augmented Reality in Science, Technology, Engineering, and Mathematics (STEM) Education: An Umbrella Review. *Information, 15*(9), 515. DOI: 10.3390/info15090515

Zhang, L., & Lee, J. (2024). Emotion-adaptive soundscapes in interactive digital art. *ACM Transactions on Multimedia Computing Communications and Applications, 20*(1), 1–16.

Zhang, S., & Yao, Z. (2025). The challenge of the application of augmented reality in science education in China: A systematic review. *Disciplinary and Interdisciplinary Science Education Research*, *7*(1), 1–13. DOI: 10.1186/s43031-025-00123-1

Zhang, X., Yu, Z., & Zhao, Y. (2023). Metaverse in education: A systematic literature review. *Computers & Education. Artificial Intelligence*, *4*, 100089.

Zhao, Y., Jiang, J., Chen, Y., Liu, R., Yang, Y., Xue, X., & Chen, S. (2022). AI-based Visual Speech Recognition Towards Realistic Avatars and Lip-Reading Applications in the Metaverse. *Applied Soft Computing*. https://dl.acm.org/doi/10.1016/j.asoc.2024.111906

Zhu, H., Sun, Y., & Tang, J. (2025). Towards responsible artificial intelligence in education: A systematic review on identifying and mitigating ethical risks [Review of Towards responsible artificial intelligence in education: a systematic review on identifying and mitigating ethical risks]. *Humanities & Social Sciences Communications*, *8*(1), 100231. DOI: 10.1057/s41599-025-05252-6

Zimba, M., Jouini, M., & Nsaka, A. (2025). *Comfort-ware Africa: Led Designing of Responsible Artificial Intelligence Technologies* (p. 145).

Zuboff, S. (2019). *The age of surveillance capitalism: The fight for a human future at the new frontier of power*. PublicAffairs.

Zuñiga-Aviles, L. A., & Cruz-Martinez, G. M. (2024). *Designing Exoskeletons*. CRC Press. DOI: 10.1201/9781003261995

Zwitter, A. J., Gstrein, O. J., & Yap, E. (2020). Digital identity and the blockchain: Universal identity management and the concept of the "self-sovereign" individual. *Frontiers in Blockchain*, *3*, 26. DOI: 10.3389/fbloc.2020.00026

About the Contributors

Esraa Hassan was born in Kafrelsheikh, Kafrelsheikh, Egypt, in 1992. She received a B.Sc. Degree in Computer Science and a M.Sc. Degree in Computer Science from Mansoura University, Egypt, in 2013 and 2018, respectively. She received her Ph.D. in computer science from Mansoura University, Egypt, in 2022. She is currently a lecturer at the Faculty of Artificial Intelligence, Kafrelsheikh University, Egypt. She has published many research articles in prestigious international conferences and reputable journals. She is also a reviewer for many journals. Her research interests include machine learning, deep learning, optimization, and bioinformatics

Abeer Saber was born in Damietta, Dumyat, Egypt, in 1992. She received the B.Sc. Degree in Computer Science and the M.Sc. Degree in Computer Science from Mansoura University, Egypt, in 2013 and 2018, respectively. She received her Ph.D. in computer science from Menoufia University, Egypt, in 2022. She is currently a Lecturer in information technology with the Faculty of Computers and Artificial Intelligence at Damietta University, Egypt. She published many research articles in prestigious international conferences and reputable journals. She is also a reviewer for many journals. Her current research interests include big data analysis, semantic web, linked open data, Optimization, machine learning, Deep learning, bioinformatics, and IoT.

Deepak Gupta is an eminent academician; plays versatile roles and responsibilities juggling between lectures, research, publications, consultancy, community service, PhD and post-doctorate supervision etc. With 16 years of rich expertise in teaching and two years in industry; he focuses on rational and practical learning. He has contributed massive literature in the fields of Human-Computer Interaction, Intelligent Data Analysis, Nature-Inspired Computing, Machine Learning and Soft Computing. He is working as Assistant Professor at Maharaja Agrasen Institute of Technology (GGSIPU), Delhi, India. He has served as

Editor-in-Chief, Guest Editor, Associate Editor in SCI and various other reputed journals (IEEE, Elsevier, Springer, Wiley & MDPI). He has actively been an organizing end of various reputed international conferences. He is not only backed with a strong profile but his innovative ideas, research's end-results and notion of implementation of technology in the medical field is by and large contributing to the society significantly. He has completed his Post-Doc from Internet of Things research group, National Institute of Telecommunications (Inatel), Brazil in 2018 and eHealth and Telemedicine Group (GTe), University of Valladolid (UVA), Spain in 2019, Federal University of Piauí (UFPI), Teresina - Pi, Brazil in 2021 and Ph.D. from Dr. APJ Abdul Kalam Technical University, India in 2017. He has authored/Edited 70 books with National/International level publisher (IEEE Press, Elsevier, Springer, Wiley, CRC, DeGruyter). He has published 330 scientific research publications in reputed International Journals and Conferences including 213 SCI Indexed Journals of IEEE, Elsevier, Springer, Wiley and many more. He has also granted/published 8 patents. He is the recipient of 2021 IEEE System Council Best Paper Award and Highly Cited Paper Award in Applied Sciences Journal. He has been featured in the list of top 2% scientist/researcher database in the world in 2019, 2020, 2022 with Rank 51 in AI & Image Processing, Rank 423 in India overall and Rank 80604 in World overall. He has got a grant of Rs 1.31 CR from Department of Science and Technology against the Indo-Russian Joint call for project proposal on Multiscale modeling of deformation behavior of carbon fiber reinforced high-end thermoplastics as CO-PI. He is Associate Editor of Alexandria Engineering Journal (Elsevier), Computer & Electrical Engineering Journal (Elsevier), Expert Systems (Wiley), Intelligent Decision Technologies (IOS Press), Journal of Computational and Theoretical Nanoscience, Honorary Editor of ICSES Transactions on Image Processing and Pattern Recognition. He is also a series editor of "Biomedical Engineering" and "Computational Modeling for Existential Risks" at Academic Press, Elsevier, "Intelligent Biomedical Data Analysis" at De Gruyter, Germany, "Explainable AI (XAI) for Engineering Applications" and "Artificial Intelligence for Sustainable Engineering and Management" at CRC Press and "Computational Intelligence for Data Analysis" at Bentham Science. He is appointed as Consulting Editor at Elsevier. He is also associated with various professional bodies like IEEE, ACM, ISTE, IAENG, IACSIT, SCIEI, ICSES, UACEE, Internet Society, SMEI, IAOP, and IAOIP. Invited as a Faculty Resource Person/Session Chair/Reviewer/TPC member in different FDP, conferences and journals. He is the convener and organizer of 'DoSCI' and "ICCCNet" springer conference series. He has also associated with a research based startup "Adroid Connectz".

Tamer Emara holds a Ph.D. in Information and Communication Engineering from Shenzhen University, China, and is an Assistant Professor at the Faculty of

Computers and Artificial Intelligence, Damietta University, Egypt. He earned his M.Sc. and B.Sc. degrees from Mansoura and Tanta Universities, respectively. Dr. Emara has received numerous awards, including the Excellent Paper Award from the Big Data Mining and Analytics journal in 2021, the Outstanding Scientific Award from the Higher Institute of Engineering and Technology Kafrelsheikh, the Shenzhen Universiade International Scholarship, and recognition as the Outstanding Doctoral Student of Shenzhen University in 2016. Dr. Emara is actively engaged in the academic community, serving as Program Committee Chair for the 2025 IEEE International Conference on Computer Science, Technology, and Engineering (ICCSTE2025) in Wuhan, China, and as General Chair for the 2024 International Conference on Artificial Intelligence and Mechanical Engineering (ICAIME2024) in Nanjing, China. He also contributes as a member of the Technical Program Committee (TPC) and Organization Committees for various conferences and serves as a reviewer for multiple journals. Dr. Emara is a senior member of the IEEE and a member of the ACM. His research interests span big data management and applications, machine learning, distributed and parallel computing, bioinformatics, and IoT.

***

A.Ananthakumari is currently working as a Assistant Professor in the Department of Computer Science and Engineering, Dr.G.U Pope College of Engineering, Thoothukudi, Tamilnadu,India. At present, She is pursuing her PhD in Anna University Chennai. She completed her MTech degree in 2011 from Manonmaniam Sundaranar University, Thirunelveli and did her BE in Computer Science and Engineering in 2007 from Anna University. She has more than 9+ years of experience in teaching. She has participated in various Workshops, Seminars and Faculty development programmes to boost up the knowledge of students' community. She published a patent in 2022 under the title of "Smart Non-Invasive Blood Glucose Monitoring Device For Diabetes Patient" as IPR application Number 202241044319.She has published a paper in UGC care Group-I journal. She has presented papers in various National and International conferences. She has published papers in International journal of Multidisciplinary Research Academy (IJMRA). She participated in research oriented Faculty development programme. She has organized Hands-on- Training and webinars. Her research area includes Machine Learning and Deep Learning.

Munir Ahmad is a seasoned professional in the realm of Spatial Data Infrastructure (SDI), Geo-Information Productions, Information Systems, and Information Governance, boasting over 25 years of dedicated experience in the field. With a PhD in Computer Science, Dr. Ahmad's expertise spans Spatial Data Production, Management, Processing, Analysis, Visualization, and Quality Control. Throughout his career, Dr. Ahmad has been deeply involved in the development and deployment of SDI systems specially in the context of Pakistan, leveraging his proficiency in Spatial Database Design, Web, Mobile & Desktop GIS, and Geo Web Services Architecture. His contributions to Volunteered Geographic Information (VGI) and Open Source Geoportal & Metadata Portal have significantly enriched the geospatial community. As a trainer and researcher, Dr. Ahmad has authored over 50 publications, advancing the industry's knowledge base and fostering innovation in Geo-Tech, Data Governance, and Information Infrastructure, and Emerging Technologies. His commitment to Research and Development (R&D) is evident in his role as a dedicated educator and mentor in the field.

Aishwarya Arya Pursuing Ph.D. in Management, Accomplished her Bachelor's and Master's from Institute of Hotel Management and Catering Technology, Lucknow in Hospitality Administration thereafter another Master's in Travel & Tourism Management. She started her academic career in the year 2019 from IHM Lucknow, previously worked with Babu Banarsi Das University, Lucknow as Assistant Professor. She presented and attended many National and International Conferences, seminars and webinars. Her area of specialization includes Room Division, Hospitality Management & Sales and Marketing. She has patents published in Under the office of the controller General of Patents, Designs and Trademarks Department of Industrial Policy and Promotions, Ministry of Commerce and Industry, Government of India.

Anorgul Atajanova is working as Department Head, Department of Primary Education Methodology, Urgench State Pedagogical Institute, Urgench, Uzbekistan

Bünyamin Ayhan completed his undergraduate and graduate studies in sociology and his PhD in research methods. Ayhan's associate professorship is on communication research. Currently working at Selçuk University Faculty of Communication, Prof. Dr. Bünyamin Ayhan continues his studies on sociology of communication, social media research and digitalisation.

Mgbike Francisca Chinenye is a renowned academic doctor in Counselling Psychology, dedicated to shaping the minds of future generations as a lecturer at Federal College of Education (Technical) Umunze. With a passion for research, psychology, and mentorship, she has established herself as a respected authority in her field. Through her work as a counsellor, researcher, and educator, Dr. Mgbike empowers students, colleagues, and individuals to reach their full potential, fostering a culture of growth, well-being, and academic excellence.

Jayanth DV is a researcher from department of management studies Dayanand Sagar college of engineering.

Lucky Oghenechodja Daniel is a dedicated Artificial Intelligence and Machine Learning enthusiast with a strong academic background in Data Science, Statistics, and Electrical and Electronic Engineering. With a PhD at the University of Johannesburg, his research focuses on Distributed Artificial Intelligence for 5G/6G communication systems, particularly Federated Learning for Interference Management in Ultra-Dense Networks (UDNs). His work bridges cutting-edge AI methodologies with real-world telecommunication challenges, aiming to enhance network efficiency and security. Lucky holds an M.Sc in Statistics from the University of Venda, where he explored machine learning applications in wind speed forecasting, and completed coursework in Data Science (e-Science) at the University of Witwatersrand. His academic journey also includes a B.Tech in Computer Science from Ladoke Akintola University of Technology, Nigeria, where he graduated with Second Class Upper Division honors. With a robust publication record, Lucky has contributed to peer-reviewed journals and conferences, including MDPI Algorithms and IEEE Xplore. His research spans topics such as privacy-preserving AI, network slicing, and intrusion detection systems, with several manuscripts under review or in development for prestigious venues like IEEE Access and Wiley journals. Professionally, Lucky has gained diverse experience as an IT Lecturer at Eduvos College, where he teaches courses on Python, cybersecurity, and IoT, and mentors students in research projects. His industry roles include internships at Eden AI (developing AI chatbots) and Altron Karabina (specializing in Azure data engineering and Power BI). He is certified in Microsoft Azure (DP-900, AI-900, DP-203) and actively engages with professional bodies like the Nigeria Computer Society and IITPSA. A skilled communicator and collaborator, Lucky combines technical expertise in Python, R, MATLAB, and SQL with a passion for mentoring and knowledge sharing. His interdisciplinary approach—rooted in statistics, computer science, and engineering—positions him as a forward-thinking researcher and educator in the evolving fields of AI and telecommunications. Key Highlights: Research: Federated Learning, 5G/6G networks, privacy-preserving AI. Technical Skills: Python, Azure, Data Engineering, Machine Learning. Teaching: IT courses, cybersecurity, and student research supervision. Certifications: Microsoft Azure Data/AI Fundamentals, Data Engineering. For collaboration or inquiries, connect via email: luckydaniel85@gmail.com.

Ponseka G is an experienced Assistant Professor with over 17 years of academic expertise at Dr. G.U. Pope College of Engineering. Having worked in both the Electronics and Communication Engineering (ECE) and Computer Science

Engineering (CSE) departments, Ponseka brings a multidisciplinary approach to teaching and research. Currently pursuing a Ph.D., Ponseka specializes in Image Processing, Machine Learning Approaches, and Microprocessors & Microcontrollers (MPMC). As a member of ISTE (Indian Society for Technical Education), Ponseka actively engages in professional development and knowledge-sharing within the academic community. Passionate about innovation, Ponseka has guided numerous students in research projects, contributing to advancements in technology. Dedicated to academic excellence, Ponseka continues to inspire and mentor the next generation of engineers.

Erkin Iskandarov is working in the Department of Pedagogy and Psychology, Urgench State University, Uzbekistan

M. Robinson Joel received the Doctorate Ph.D degree in Computer and Information Technology from the Manonmaniam Sundaranar University, Tirunelveli in March 2019. He completed his M.Tech and MCA from the same university year 2008 and 2002 respectively. He is currently working as an Associate Professor in the Department of Computer Science and Engineering at KCG College of Technology, Chennai. He has 16 years of teaching experience.

Benitlin Subha K is an Assistant Professor at Kings Engineering College, specializing in Artificial Intelligence applications in agriculture. Her research focuses on precision agriculture, aiming to develop AI-driven solutions that enhance agricultural productivity, sustainability, and efficiency. Beyond her research, she is deeply passionate about teaching and mentoring students. She strives to create an engaging and interactive learning environment, encouraging students to think critically, innovate, and apply their knowledge to real-world challenges. With a commitment to bridging the gap between technology and agriculture, she continues to inspire the next generation of engineers and researchers in the field of AI.

DanielRaj K is a passionate postgraduate scholar at Dr. G.U. Pope College of Engineering, currently pursuing a Master of Engineering degree. With a strong academic foundation built during his undergraduate studies at Kings Engineering College (CGPA 8.1), Daniel continues to excel in both academics and extracurriculars. Driven by a deep love for teaching and mentoring, he has served in multiple leadership roles such as School People Leader, Class Representative, and Bible School Teacher, and remains actively involved in his church ministries. His dedication extends into the technical domain as well, having worked as a System Administrator, Teaching Assistant, and Media Archiver at St. Joseph's College of Engineering in Chennai.Known among peers as Jojo, Daniel is also a talented violinist, a YouTuber sharing insights with his community, and someone who treasures meaningful relationships—especially with elders. He aspires to earn a Ph.D. and dreams of becoming an educator who not only teaches but transforms lives, just like his mentors Mrs. Yasotha and Mrs. Benitlin Subha.

Ganesha K S is an Assistant Professor in the Department of Management Studies, at Dayananda Sagar College of Engineering, Bangalore, India. He has 15 years of experience in Corporate, Teaching and Research. He is a Member of the International Safety Quality Environment Management Association (ISQEM), UK. His primary research interests are tourist behavior, social media, sentiment analysis, human resource management, and labor studies. He has presented at multiple conferences and published articles in Scopus and other International Indexed journals. He has conducted FDP, workshops, and training in the areas of Digital Marketing, Statistical Analysis using SPSS, Project Management, Research Methodology, Entrepreneurship etc.

Jazuli Sanusi Kazaure is a 45 years old Nigerian, an Electrical Engineer and IT Professional. He is a registered Engineer with all engineering professional bodies in Nigeria. He is an expert on electrical circuit and project designs. He is a consultant who designs and supervises projects in Nigerian. Jazuli is an academician, who teaches in Polytechnics and Universities in Nigeria as well as other Universities in West Africa. Jazuli attended technical school and read electrical installation as a trade, he continue to obtained a National Diploma, Higher National Diploma and a Post Graduate Diploma all in electrical engineering. He obtained his Masters Degree on Software Engineering and Computer applications. In 2005, Jazuli was certified as a network cabling specialist in copper and fiber optic based systems, he was also certified as an instructor in Integrated System Voice and Messaging by C-Tech in Sparta, New Jersey, USA. In 2011, Jazuli was awarded with a degree of Doctor of Philosophy in Management Information Technology specialized on ICT Management Frameworks. Dr. Jazuli is discharging his lecturing job with passion. He started his job carrier from the lowest rank of Assistant Lecturer and grew to the highest rank of Chief lecturer in Nigerian Polytechnic. He is a visiting Senior Lecturer in his state own University from 2013 to date, also a visiting Senior Lecturer in a University in Niger republic from 2016 to date. Dr. Jazuli is an external examiner for Open University and Digital Bridge Institute in Nigeria. Dr. Jazuli held many academic positions in the Polytechnic, among other are Head of Academic Department, Director Center for Information Technology, Director College of Engineering and Deputy Dean Student Affairs. Currently, Dr. Jazuli is the Director Academic Planning and Research Development in a Polytechnic in Nigeria. Dr. Jazuli published 17 journal articles, presented 16 conference papers and a Co-authored in 5 different books.

Zokir Mamadiyarov is a Professor of Economics at Mamun University, Khiva, Uzbekistan, and also serves as Professor at the Department of Finance and Tourism at Termez University of Economics and Service, Termez, Uzbekistan. He earned his academic qualifications in economics and finance and has over two decades of teaching and research experience in higher education. Prof. Mamadiyarov is a member of several national and regional academic initiatives and actively participates in conferences and journal publications. His primary research interests cover economic policy, financial systems, tourism management, and sustainable regional development.

Ugochukwu O. Matthew, presently is an Academic scholar with Hussaini Adamu Federal Polytechnic, Nigeria, in the Department of Computer Science with specialty in AI, Big Data Science, Cloud Computing, Internet of Things, Data Mining, Multimedia and E-Learning Education. A Member of Nigeria Computer Society (NCS), Nigeria Institute of Management (NIM), International Association of Computer Science & Information Technology (IACSIT), European Alliance for Innovation(EAI) and also a member of Teaching & Education Research Association (TERA). Ugochukwu O. Matthew hold Masters in Computer Applications from Bayero University Kano, Nigeria. Ugochukwu O. Matthew had reviewed several Journals and a member of Review Board Committee of Journals Indexed by Scopus and Web of Science including IEEE Access, SN Computer Science (Springer), International Journal of Information Communication Technologies & Human Development(IJICTHD), International Journal of Business Data Communications and Networking (IJBDCN), International Journal of Cloud Applications and Computing (IJCAC). Ugochukwu O. Matthew is a cofounder of U&J Digital Consult Limited, an IT and Educational Consulting Firm in Nigeria.

Nwosu Obinnaya Chikezie Victor is a multidisciplinary professional with expertise spanning Geophysics, Environmental Technology, Artificial Intelligence, and Computer Networking. Currently pursuing a PhD in Environmental Sciences at the University of South Africa, his research bridges environmental science with cutting-edge technologies like AI and machine learning to address sustainability challenges. With an M.Sc in Environmental Technology from Teesside University (UK) and a B.Sc in Geophysics from the Federal University of Technology Owerri (Nigeria), Victor has a strong foundation in both earth sciences and engineering. His technical skills are further enhanced by certifications in AI (University of Johannesburg), Cisco Networking (CCNA), and Blockchain, reflecting his adaptability to the Fourth Industrial Revolution (4IR). Victor's career blends academia, industry, and freelance work. As an Online Tutor at Kalvie, he teaches Mathematics, Computer Science, and Environmental Sciences, mentoring students for exams like WAEC and IELTS. His role as a Freelance Journal Reviewer for IGI Global and Science Publishing Group underscores his commitment to scholarly rigour, peer review, and research dissemination. His industry experience includes: Machine Learning Projects: Collaborated with the University of Johannesburg and Accenture on AI/4IR initiatives, developing data-driven solutions. Construction & Renewable Energy: Worked as a labourer and solar technician, gaining hands-on experience in sustainable technologies. Freelance Content Writing: Creates tech and AI-focused content for platforms like Smashoid, translating complex topics for diverse audiences. Victor is an active researcher with publications in AI applications for construction, sustainable sourcing, and seismic interpretation. His leadership roles—such as Provost Marshall for geosciences students and Chairman of electoral committees—highlight his ability to organise and inspire teams. Key Strengths: Technical Skills: Python, Machine Learning, Data Analysis, SPSS, MATLAB, Cisco Packet Tracer. Certifications: Microsoft Office, Agile Practices, Cybersecurity, Solar PV Systems. Interests: AI in environmental engineering, blockchain, and geophysical data analysis. A lifelong learner, Victor holds over 20 Coursera certifications in palaeontology, software management, and Arctic climate studies, demonstrating his intellectual curiosity. He is fluent in leveraging technology for environmental and industrial innovation. For collaborations or inquiries, contact: | ORCID: 0000-0003-3974-4755

David Oyekunle is a highly esteemed expert with extensive education and experience in the fields of information technology research, project management, business analysis and artificial intelligence. He earned his Bachelor of Science degree in Statistics from the University of Ilorin in Nigeria. Furthering his education, he obtained a Postgraduate Diploma in International Business Administration and Management from the National Open University in Nigeria, and a (Summer online) Master of Business Administration in Leadership and Team Building from the University of New Haven in the United States of America. He excelled as a postgraduate research scholar at the University of Salford, graduating with a Master of Science degree in project management with distinctions. David significant organizational experience includes leading cross-functional teams, crafting strategic project policies, implementing logistics, ensuring adherence to risk standards and compliance, and analyzing vast datasets to uncover trends and patterns. Among his accomplishments are the successful implementation of intelligent lean management and Six Sigma with data analysis, the delivery of comprehensive business reports, and the utilization of technological innovation for more effective customer service improvements. Currently serving as an educational consultant at U& J Digital Consult Limited in Nigeria, David continues to contribute significantly to the fields of information technology and educational consulting. His research, published in global journals, spans various subjects, including strategic management, project management, international business, business informatics, and ethics in project management. Demonstrating his commitment to academic collaboration and human capital development, David actively participates in volunteer positions and committee memberships at conferences both locally and internationally. David aims to continue leveraging his expertise to drive innovation and excellence in the field of research, education, project management and information technology.

Fatma Öztat completed her undergraduate studies at the Faculty of Communication, studied face-to-face communication and social media use within the family for her master's degree, and studied online social capital for her doctorate. Currently an assistant professor at the Faculty of Communication at Selçuk University, Fatma Öztat continues her work on communication research, social media, and social transformation.

S Sumathi received her Bachelor's in Computer Science and Engineering, a Master's in Computer Science and Engineering, and a Ph.D. in Computer Science and Engineering from Anna University, Chennai, India. She is an Assistant Professor (Senior Grade) at the University VOC College of Engineering, Thoothukudi, Tamil Nadu, India. Professor Sumathi has over a decade of experience teaching and conducting research at both the undergraduate and postgraduate levels. She did extensive research work in the field of cyber security attack detection using machine learning. Her research areas include machine learning, deep learning, cyber security, and biomedical data analysis.

Index

Symbols

A

B

C

D

E

F

G

H

I

L

M

N

O

www.ingramcontent.com/pod-product-compliance
Lightning Source LLC
LaVergne TN
LVHW080909300926
849162LV00003B/620